D0907533

The Trees of Florida

A Reference and Field Guide

The Trees of Florida

A Reference and Field Guide

Gil Nelson

Drawings by R. Marvin Cook, Jr.
Photographs by the Author

Pineapple Press, Inc.
Sarasota, Florida

To
Brenda Nelson and Hope Nelson
for their love, encouragement, and patience

Inquiries should be addressed to:
Pineapple Press, Inc.
P.O. Box 3899
Sarasota, Florida 34230-3899

Library of Congress Cataloging-in-Publication Data

Nelson, Gil, 1949–
    The trees of Florida : a reference and field guide / Gil Nelson: with line illustrations, R. Marvin Cook, Jr.—1st ed.
        p.   cm.
    Includes bibliographical references and index.
    ISBN 1-56164-053-0 : Hb. ISBN 1-56164-055-7 : Pb
    1. Trees—Florida. 2. Trees—Florida—Identification. 3. Trees—Florida—Pictorial works. I. Title.
QK154.N44   1994
582.1609759—dc20   93-41607
                                                                                                          CIP

First Edition
10 9 8 7 6 5 4 3 2

Design by R. Marvin Cook, Jr.
Composition by E.T. Lowe, Nashville, Tennessee
Printed and bound by Edwards Brothers, Ann Arbor, Michigan

TABLE OF CONTENTS

Introduction   xi
How to Use This Book   xii
Glossary   xiii

PART I—AN INTRODUCTION TO FLORIDA'S TREE FAMILIES

1 — Cedars, Yews, and Cypress Trees   3
        Cupressaceae
        Taxaceae
        Taxodiaceae

2 — The Pines and Pinelike Trees   7
        Pinaceae
        Casuarinaceae

3 — The Palms   13
        Palmae (Arecaceae)

4 — Magnolias, Custard Apples, and Anise Trees   17
        Annonaceae
        Illiciaeae
        Magnoliaceae

5 — Laurels and Wild Cinnamon   22
        Canellaceae
        Lauraceae

6 — Hollies, Teas, and Titi Trees   25
        Aquifoliaceae
        Cyrillaceae
        Theaceae

7 — The Heath Family   30
        Ericaceae

8 — Sapodillas, Ebony, Horse Sugar, and Silverbells   34
        Ebenaceae
        Sapotaceae
        Styracaceae
        Symplocaceae

9 — Myrsines, Garcinias, and Joewood   38
        Clusiaceae (including the Guttiferae)
        Myrsinaceae
        Theophrastaceae

10 — Tamarisks, Papaya, and Caper Trees   40
        Capparaceae
        Caricaceae
        Tamaricaceae

11 — Willows and Cottonwoods   42
    Salicaceae

12 — Mallows, Basswood, and the Parasol Tree   45
    Malvaceae
    Sterculiaceae
    Tiliaceae

13 — Elms and Mulberries   48
    Moraceae
    Ulmaceae

14 — Buckthorns, Nightshades, and Spurge   53
    Euphorbiaceae
    Rhamnaceae
    Solanaceae

15 — Olives, Tallowwood, and Spindle Trees   57
    Celastraceae
    Olacaceae
    Oleaceae

16 — Byrsonima, Rues, and Lignum Vitae   61
    Malpighiaceae
    Rutaceae
    Zygophyllaceae

17 — Gumbo Limbo, Mahogany, Quassias, and Bay Cedar   65
    Burseraceae
    Meliaceae
    Simaroubaceae
    Surianaceae

18 — Bayberries, Cashews, and Corkwood   69
    Anacardiaceae
    Leitneriaceae
    Myricaceae

19 — Walnuts and Hickories   73
    Juglandaceae

20 — Maples, Buckeyes, Soapberries, and Bladdernut   76
    Aceraceae
    Hippocastanaceae
    Sapindaceae
    Staphyleaceae

21 — Blolly, Cockspur, Sea Grapes, and Cacti   80
    Nyctaginaceae
    Polygonaceae
    Cactaceae

22 — Beech, Oaks, and Chinquapin   83
        Fagaceae

23 — Witch Hazel, Sycamore, and Birches   87
        Betulaceae
        Hamamelidaceae
        Platanaceae

24 — Roses and Coco-plum   90
        Chrysobalanaceae
        Rosaceae

25 — Legumes   93
        Leguminosae (Fabaceae)

26 — Mangroves, Baccharis and Buttonwood   99
        Avicenniaceae
        Combretaceae
        Compositae (Asteraceae)
        Rhizophoraceae

27 — Crape Myrtle, Stoppers, Guava, Melaleuca, and Tetrazygia   103
        Lythraceae
        Melastomataceae
        Myrtaceae

28 — Madders, Bignonias, and Oleanders   107
        Bignoniaceae
        Rubiaceae
        Apocynaceae

29 — Aralia, Dogwoods, Honeysuckles, and Tupelos   111
        Araliaceae
        Caprifoliaceae
        Cornaceae
        Nyssaceae

30 — Geiger Tree, Strongbarks, and Fiddlewood   115
        Boraginaceae
        Verbenaceae

PART II—FIELD GUIDE TO FLORIDA'S TREES

        Gymnosperms   120

        Angiosperms   127
            Monocots
            Dicots

COLOR PHOTO SECTION BETWEEN PAGES 150 AND 151

APPENDIX: WHERE TO FIND TREES

REFERENCES

INDEX TO COMMON NAMES

INDEX TO SCIENTIFIC NAMES

ACKNOWLEDGMENTS

A number of people have provided significant assistance to me throughout the writing of this book. Many have offered direct help in the form of critical readings and reviews, suggestions about content, assistance with fieldwork, or by serving as a sounding board for ideas. However, I would be remiss in my responsibility as a writer if I did not first acknowledge at least two people who have indirectly but profoundly influenced this work.

The first of these is the late Reverend Canon James A. Hardison, Jr. Jim and I were regular field companions for nearly two decades, spending countless hours exploring Florida's swamps, uplands, marshes, and magnificent natural places. During our time afield, he stimulated and joined in my learning about Florida's native plant communities. Our combined explorations allowed me to test ideas and conclusions about what I was learning, and encouraged my continued interest. It was largely through these many excursions that I acquired the foundation upon which this book was written. Although Jim's death came before I began work on this volume, his spirit pervades every page.

The second individual is Dr. Robert K. Godfrey, Professor Emeritus at Florida State University, and one of the southeastern United States' respected botanists. His several outstanding works on Florida's trees, shrubs, and herbaceous flora have contributed significantly to my understanding of our native plants. In addition, Dr. Godfrey graciously consented to review the list of trees to be included in the present work. He also read and offered suggestions on an earlier manuscript, much of which eventually served as the springboard from which this book was launched. I am indebted to him and his work for much of what I have learned.

Of those who directly impacted this book, none are more important than my illustrator, working partner, creative consultant, and good friend, R. Marvin Cook, Jr. Marvin's easy manner, immense knowledge, and tremendous talent has made my association with him both pleasurable and stimulating. His willingness to take on this project relieved one of my earliest and most pressing anxieties, and his willingness to do much more than he originally agreed to is much appreciated. His drawings are one of the best parts of this volume and I am greatly indebted to him for his outstanding contribution.

I also owe a great debt to Mr. Joseph Nemec, a ranger with the Florida Park Service who is stationed at John Pennekamp Coral Reef State Park, and to his wife and field companion, Marcella. The Nemecs' extensive knowledge of the trees and shrubs of the Florida Keys, their expertise in the field, their willingness to accompany me on field excursions and to show me things I otherwise would not have found, and their review of the manuscript, illustrations, and photogaphs have all proved invaluable in the preparation of this work.

Three other individuals also provided significant assistance. These include Dr. Loran C. Anderson, professor of biological sciences at Florida State University, Curator of the FSU Herbarium, and expert on the flora of the panhandle; Dr. Daniel F. Austin, professor of biological sciences at Florida Atlantic University and expert on Florida's subtropical flora; and Angus Gholson, accomplished naturalist and expert on the flora of northern Florida and the panhandle. All of these individuals reviewed and commented on the finished manuscript which led to a number of refinements and revisions. Several also suggested important sites to include in my fieldwork.

I also owe a debt to Wilson Baker for reviewing the final photographs and artwork and for making several valuable suggestions which led to important revisions. His time and assistance are much appreciated.

As with any work such as this, a number of other individuals also assisted with specific tasks ranging from hands-on fieldwork to suggestions about my treatments of particular species. Barbara Cook assisted me in the field on a number of occasions, helped me find several field sites, and helped me locate and procure a number of important publications. Culver S. "Red" Gidden helped me find some particularly large and impressive specimens of *Leitneria* as well as adding much to my understanding of coastal plant communities. Roger Hammer directed me to several south Florida locations and reviewed and commented on my treatment of several species. Stephen Lenberger helped me find several specimens at Highlands Hammock State Park and in the nearby scrub. Dr. Gayle Muenchow, a Tallahassee-based botanist with field experience in many parts of the United States, read an early version of the manuscript, offered encouragement throughout the project, and accompanied me on a number of field trips. Al Thompson accompanied me on many outings in both the northern and southern parts of the state, and Dr. Richard Wunderlin graciously responded to my query about nomenclature. In addition, Dana Bryan, Gene Cleversey, Bob Ehrig, Gail Fishman, Carol Lippincot, Tom Markey, Frank Strickland, and Robin Will helped direct me to important resource people or appropriate field sites.

The above assistance notwithstanding, I must take full responsibility for the content that follows. Any mistakes or inaccuracies that might appear in these pages should be credited to me alone. I only hope that the readers of this guide will have as much fun using it as I did writing it.

INTRODUCTION

This book is about Florida's trees. It is directed to the general reader as well as the accomplished naturalist and is designed to serve as both a field guide and a ready reference. All of Florida's native and naturalized tree species are included, as well many of the state's more common exotics. The book describes or discusses over 350 trees and related plants that inhabit the mosaic of vegetative communities that dot the Florida landscape.

Florida's Tree Diversity

Florida supports more tree species than any other state in the continental United States. Of the approximately 625 trees native to North America, at least 275 are found within the confines of Florida. Add to this an extensive list of introduced and naturalized species and Florida's tree flora becomes expansive indeed.

The reason for Florida's dominance in sheer numbers of trees is not difficult to discern. Located along the southeastern perimeter of the North American continent and surrounded by vast expanses of ocean water, the state is strategically positioned to share in the flora of both the temperate and the tropical climatic zones. Many of the plants of the northernmost part of Florida find the southern extremity of their ranges in the rolling uplands that characterize the state's Northern Highlands geologic province. A number of these plants were pushed southward by ancient ice age glaciers and remain today only as disjunctive outliers of a more generally northern distribution. Many plants of the southern peninsula and Florida Keys, on the other hand, are the northernmost representatives of a typically tropical flora that extends throughout the Virgin Islands and South America. Add to these a handful of central and north Florida specialties, some of which are found nowhere else in the country, and the uniqueness of the state's tree flora becomes even more obvious.

What is a Tree?

There is no generally accepted and botanically precise definition of the constellation of characters that constitutes a tree. This is not to say that definitions have never been advanced nor general rules of thumb adopted. A number of botanists and other authors have attempted to delimit the meaning of the term for an assortment of purposes. Those who desire to exclude questionable species from a particular list of our tree flora tend toward a more restrictive definition that effectively reduces the number of plants that meet the definition. Others present definitions that are more inclusive in nature.

It is the distinction between what constitutes a shrub and what constitutes a tree that is at the heart of this definitional dilemma. While many plants, such as the pines, for example, generally express themselves only in treelike stature, appearing single-trunked and arborescent even from their earliest life stages, others are not so easily classified. There are a vast number of plants that express themselves sometimes as trees and other times as shrubs, depending upon habitat, climate, or other, often much less obvious, factors.

The rough velvetseed (*Guettarda scabra*) is a good case in point. In the south Florida pinelands, the rough velvetseed is generally a single-stemmed shrub, usually not exceeding 1.5 m in height. In nearby hammock locations, however, it may become a small tree that reaches a height of nearly 5 m. The long-stalked stopper (*Mosiera longipes*), another south Florida species, offers an even more dramatic example. It seldom exceeds a height of even 30 cm in the pinelands. Yet, it, too, becomes a tree where it invades the hammocks.

I have chosen to use a somewhat inclusive definition of a tree for the purposes of this book. As a student of our flora and one who has had the opportunity to use a wide assortment of field guides, I have always found myself more appreciative of those volumes that seem complete than those with a more limited coverage. As a result, in this book I have attempted to include all of those species which are regularly classed as trees as well as those plants that may be more generally known as shrubs but that sometimes, even if rarely, take on tree stature. In addition, I have attempted to point out those instances where a plant more typically thought of as a tree might be easily confused in its shrubby form with one or more of the common shrubs. In such cases, I have tried to assist the reader in distinguishing between the two by describing the shrub also.

For the purposes of this volume, therefore, a tree is any plant that, even if in only a few instances, exhibits a single, well-defined trunk of approximately 5 cm in diameter, reaches a height approaching 4 m, and, at least to the casual observer, sometimes exhibits the gestalt of a tree.

It is possible that some readers will not agree with some of the species that I have chosen to include. Again, however, my guiding assumption has been that any errors should be made on the side of completeness rather than on the side of deficiency.

How To Use This Book

Learning to identify trees is an exciting activity. Whether one is simply a casual enthusiast, interested in knowing only the common species that are most often associated with our parks and roadsides, or a passionate naturalist intent on developing an intimate understanding of those species that are rare or well hidden, the accomplishment that is derived from learning a tree's name is a rich reward.

One of the best ways to learn tree identification is through frequent visits to the natural areas in which they occur. There is simply no substitute for firsthand observation of a tree in its native habitat. When coupled with armchair reading and continued study of the chief characteristics of our tree flora, regular field trips become the most important method for learning the identity of any of our native plants. It is recommended, therefore, that this book be carried into the field as often as possible; that it be studied diligently in the quietness of one's home or office; and that it be annotated with one's own firsthand observations and illustrations.

Several features make this book useful as a field guide. Part I includes 30 chapters that offer interesting and valuable information about the families of Florida trees as well as about the genera and species of which these families are composed. These chapters offer much more about our tree flora than can be provided in a simple field description, including additional tips for distinguishing between similar species. These chapters are designed to add significant detail to the reader's knowledge about a particular species and to engender a broader and more systematic understanding of the state's tree flora.

Part II contains descriptions of the key field characteristics and statewide distribution data for each of 342 species. Most of the species are illustrated by line drawings and/or color photographs. The locations of all illustrations for a particular species are noted adjacent to the field description for that species.

The Language of Botany

Mastering the language of botany can seem an overwhelming task for the beginning student of our native flora. There often appears to be no end to the complex technical vocabulary that is commonly used in describing the various characteristics of a plant's morphology. Unfortunately, acquiring a command of such language is a necessary prerequisite for learning the identity of many plant species. While space does not permit a complete treatment of this important vocabulary, the glossary and descriptive drawings that follow should assist the reader in mastering the majority of terms used in this book.

Glossary of Common Botanical Terms

Actinomorphic. Said of a flower that is radially symmetrical, or having the symmetry of a wheel with spokes.

Acuminate. Tapering to a pointed apex, the sides of the taper concave in shape.

Alternate leaves. Leaves that arise singly from the stem rather than in pairs or whorls.

Anaerobic. Generally used to refer to soils that lack free oxygen.

Anther. The pollen-bearing portion of a stamen.

Anthesis. The time at which a flower is open and in full bloom.

Apex. Used to refer to the distal tip of a leaf.

Apices. Plural of apex.

Appressed. Pressed flat, or nearly so, against another structure.

Aril. Pulpy appendage to a seed.

Ascending. Said of a plant or appendage that is curving or pointing upwards at an angle of less than 90 degrees.

Axil. The angle formed where two plant parts are joined; commonly used in reference to the angle between leaf and stem.

Axillary. In or arising from an axil.

Biennial. A plant whose life cycle is completed in two years.

Bipinnate. Doubly pinnate.

Bloom. A waxy, whitish covering sometimes found on leaves, stems, or other plant parts, i.e., glaucous.

Bract. A typically (but not always) reduced, leaflike structure that is normally situated at the base of a flower.

Calyx. The sepals of a flower when referred to collectively.

Cambium. Layer of soft tissue between the bark and the wood which adds width to a trunk or branch.

Campanulate. Said of a flower that has joined petals and is bell-like in shape.

Catkin. A spikelike inflorescence bearing small unisexual flowers; often hangs pendantlike from a branch.

Cauline. Said of leaves that occur along a stem rather than basally.

Ciliate. Having hairs along the margins of a leaf or other structure.

Clasping. Said of a leaf whose base partially encircles the stem.

Complete. A flower that contains all basic parts including sepals, petals, stamens, and pistil.

Compound leaf. A leaf divided into smaller leaflets along a common axis.

Conspecific. Said of two plants belonging to the same species.

Cordate. Said of a structure (usually a leaf) that is heart shaped at the base.

Corolla. The petals of a flower when referred to collectively.

Crenate. Said of leaf margins with rounded teeth.

Cuneate. Wedge-shaped.

Cuspidate. With a short, sharp apex.

Cyme. A flower structure in which the distal or apical flowers bloom first.

Cymose. Arranged in a cyme.

Deciduous. Trees or shrubs that shed their leaves each year; opposite of evergreen.

Dentate. Having teeth that are perpendicular to rather than angled from the supporting margin.

Dioecious. Said of plants that have unisexual male and female flowers on separate plants.

Distal. Generally used to denote the point that is farthest from the point of attachment, as in the distal end (apex) of a leaf.

Drupe. Fleshy fruit in which the inner wall is hardened into a pit and surrounds the seed or seeds.

Ecotone. The transition zone between two different plant communities.

Endemic. Peculiar to a particular locality.

Entire. Said of a margin which is smooth rather than toothed.

Epiphytic. Said of a plant that grows on the bark of another plant but does not obtain food from and, therefore, is not parasitic on its host; such plants are called epiphytes.

Equisetum-leaved. Having leaves reduced in size and reminiscent of members of the genus *Equisetum*.

Evergreen. Trees and shrubs that remain green in winter; opposite of deciduous.

Fascicle. Bundle or tightly bound cluster, such as a fascicle of pine needles.

Filiform. Threadlike and slender; usually rounded in cross-section.

Foliaceous. Having leaflike foliage.

Glaucous. Covered with a whitish bloom that can be removed by rubbing.

Glabrous. Lacking pubescence.

Globose. Rounded.

Habit. Overall appearance or growth form of a plant.

Halophyte. A plant which grows in salty or alkaline conditions, such as plants of the saltmarsh.

Head. A crowded cluster of flowers at the tip of a single flower stalk, as in a sunflower.

Herbaceous. Not woody and dying to the ground each year (or annual).

Inflorescence. Used variously to refer to the flowering portion of a plant; to the type of flower arrangement; or to a flower cluster.

Irregular. Said of a flower with bilateral symmetry, meaning that it can be cut through the center in only one way to form equal halves; like the flower of a violet.

Lanceolate. Lance shaped, wider at the base and tapering toward the apex, entire structure appearing narrow.

Leaflet. An individual blade on a compound leaf.

Lepidote. Covered with small scales; often used to describe a leaf surface.

Locular. Said of an ovary or fruit which has compartments or cavities (locules).

Monoecious. Said of plants having unisexual flowers with both male and female flowers borne on the same individual.

Oblanceolate. Reverse of lanceolate; widest portion near the apex rather than the base.

Obovate. Opposite of ovate; shaped like an egg but widest toward the apex.

Opposite leaves. With leaves arising from the stem in pairs opposite one another.

Orbicular. Circular in outline.

Ovate. Shaped like an egg; widest toward the base.

Palmate. Radiating from a single point like the fingers of a hand, as in palmately compound leaves or palmate venation.

Panicle. A loosely branched, compound inflorescence with stalked flowers.

Pedicel. The stalk of a flower.

Peduncle. Stalk of an inflorescence or flower.

Peltate. Stalked from the center rather than the edge like an umbrella.

Perennial. Plants that persist through the winter or dormant season.

Perfect. Said of a flower with both stamens and pistils.

Petal. A whorl of flower parts separating the sepals from the stamens in a perfect flower; usually but not always showy.

Petiole. The stalk of a leaf.

Pinna. A leaflet or other major division of a pinnately compound leaf.

Pinnae. Plural of pinna.

Pinnate leaf. A compound leaf with leaflets along opposite sides of a central stalk.

Pistil. The ovary, style, and stigma collectively; female portion of a flower.

Pome. A fleshy fruit in which the ovarial portion of the flower becomes surrounded by an enlarged floral tube, such an apple or pear.

Prop root. Said of the aerial roots of a red mangrove that extend to the ground from the lower trunk and branches and provide stability to the tree.

Pubescent. Covered with soft hairs.

Raceme. An inflorescence with a single axis in which the basal flowers open first.

Rachis. The main axis of a compound leaf.

Revolute. With rolled-under margins; usually said of a leaf.

Rhombic. Having the outline of a rhombus; diamond shaped.

Riparian. Said of a plant that is typically situated along the banks of a river or other body of water.

Rosette. A radiating cluster; often refers to leaves radiating from the base of a plant.

Rotate. Said of a flower that spreads radially and in one plane.

Ruderal. Said of highly disturbed habitats such as roadsides, vacant lots, and fields.

Rugose-veiny. With a roughened, veiny surface; usually refers to the surface of a leaf.

Samara. Winged fruit.

Scabrid. Said of a structure that is rough to the touch due to stiff hairs.

Scandent. Climbing or vinelike.

Sepal. Member of the outermost whorl of flower parts (calyx).

Serrate. Said of a margin that is toothed rather than smooth or lobed.

Sessile. Without a stalk.

Spatulate. Having the shape of a spatula.

Specific epithet. The species designation, or second word, in a binomial scientific name.

Stamen. The anther and filament collectively; the male portion of a flower.

Steephead. A steep-sided ravine located along a natural gradient created by the seepage of ground water near the base of the ravine.

Stellate. Star shaped; often refers to leaf hairs that radiate in a starlike pattern.

Stilt root. Same as prop root.

Stipe. The stalk that supports a fruit or pistil.

Stipule. A leaflike appendage at the base of a leaf or petiole.

Tepal. Said of petals and sepals when not easily distinguishable from one another.

Terete. Rounded in cross-section.

Terminal. Referring to an appendage that is situated at the apex of a structure.

Tomentose. Densely covered with short, matted, or wooly hairs.

Trifoliolate. A compound leaf with three leaflets.

Tripinnate. A compound leaf with a central axis, one to several secondary axes, with the leaflets attached to the secondary axes.

Truncate. Having a flat or squared-off apex or base.

Zygomorphic. Bilaterally symmetrical or asymmetrical (see irregular flower above).

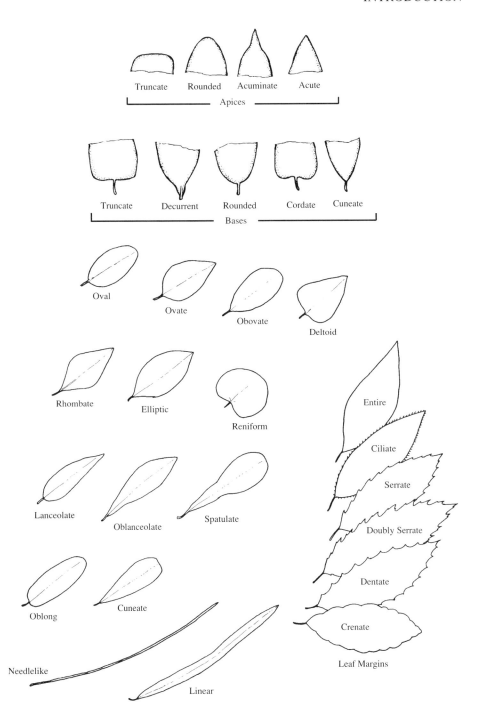

Truncate Rounded Acuminate Acute

Apices

Truncate Decurrent Rounded Cordate Cuneate

Bases

Oval

Ovate

Obovate

Deltoid

Rhombate

Elliptic

Reniform

Entire

Ciliate

Serrate

Lanceolate

Oblanceolate

Spatulate

Doubly Serrate

Dentate

Oblong

Cuneate

Crenate

Needlelike

Linear

Leaf Margins

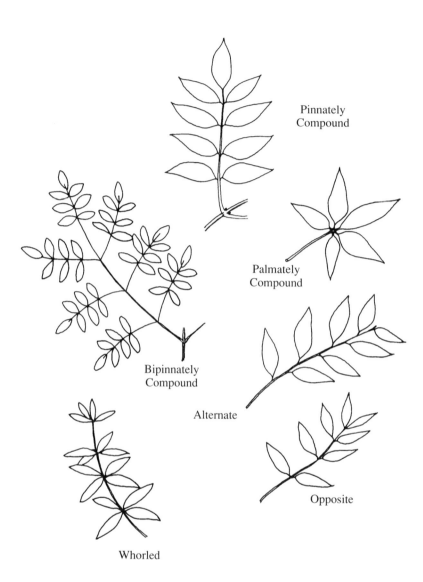

Pinnately
Compound

Palmately
Compound

Bipinnately
Compound

Alternate

Opposite

Whorled

PART I

AN INTRODUCTION TO FLORIDA'S
TREE FAMILIES

CHAPTER 1

CEDARS, YEWS, AND CYPRESS TREES

The cedars, yews, and cypress trees are among Florida's most primitive arborescent plants. All are classified as gymnosperms, a group of about 675 seed-bearing, woody plants that are distinguished from the more highly evolved angiosperms by having their seeds borne naked (often but not always in a protective cone) rather than enclosed in a fleshy ovary. All are also characterized by relatively short to diminutive needle- or scalelike, dark green leaves that do not resemble the leaves of any other of Florida's trees except, perhaps, the tamarisk (*Tamarix gallica*).

The Yew Family

Northernmost Florida has two members of the yew family, both exceedingly rare and both occurring almost solely within two counties of the central panhandle. In earlier years, the least abundant of the two was probably the Florida yew (*Taxus floridana*), a small tree with short, dark green leaves that are typically less than 2.5 cm long. However, in the last several decades it is the yew's cousin, the torreya tree (*Torreya taxifolia*), that seems to be in the most distress.

The Florida yew is a bushy, evergreen relic of preglacial times. Its nearest relative in North America is the American yew (*Taxus canadensis*), which ranges from Newfoundland and Manitoba to Indiana, Kentucky, and western Virginia. In contrast, the Florida species is narrowly endemic to the bluffs, ravines, and slopes associated with the northern drainage area of the Apalachicola River. The main part of its range extends from just north of Bristol to just north of Torreya State Park.

The torreya tree is the species from which Torreya State Park takes its name and is a species closely related to the yew. A disease that probably first attacked the tree in the 1950s has since reduced its population dramatically, and today its continuing existence appears to be in grave danger. The current population is composed almost entirely of saplings, most of which appear to be sprouts from the root crowns of previously killed trees. Also called gopher-wood or stinking cedar, the torreya is similar to the yew in form and leaf shape.

The easiest method for distinguishing between these species is to touch the tips of the leaves. Those of the Florida yew are soft and pliable; those of the torreya, quite sharp and piercing to the finger. Previously, it was useful to crush the leaves of a specimen to assure its identify because the leaves of the torreya are strongly aromatic. Given their limited numbers, however, such disturbance to these two species today is neither wise nor recommended.

Both the Florida yew and the torreya tree can be seen at Torreya State Park, north of Bristol. A labeled specimen of the former species once stood on the edge of the bluff behind the Gregory House but has now succumbed to disease. Unlabeled specimens of both can be found along or just off the trail at various points throughout the park. A transplanted specimen of the torreya tree can be seen at Maclay State Gardens on North Highway 319 in Tallahassee or at Florida Caverns State Park near Marianna. These latter trees were taken from Torreya State Park.

The Cypress Trees

The cypress trees are counted among Florida's most impressive plants. Their tall, straight, limbless boles reach skyward for more than 40 m and their thin, grayish brown bark rises up the main stem in a close-knit pattern of ridges and furrows that sometimes spirals the trunk. Found in all parts of Florida except the Keys, they are among our easier trees to recognize and have long been revered for the beauty they add to the landscape.

Taxonomically, the cypresses are members of the family *Taxodiaceae*. This is the same family that includes the famed redwoods and giant sequoias of California's northwestern coast and Sierra Nevada mountains. Although our trees are not nearly so large, they still exhibit a grandeur befitting their noble lineage.

Unlike the state's other conifer species, the cypresses are deciduous rather than evergreen. In early fall their leaves turn a beautiful reddish brown and fall to the water below, sometimes leaving the shallow edges of cypress-ringed ponds literally covered with floating foliage.

At first glance, the leaves of the cypress trees look compound in structure. Fallen foliage appears to consist of a rachis with small, needle-shaped leaflets. These alleged leaflets, however, are actually leaves, and the supposed rachis is a small branchlet on which the leaves grow. Unlike most trees, these branchlets are deciduous along with the leaves and are often found on the ground with the tiny leaves still attached.

There are two mysteries about the cypress trees. The first is the function of their "knees," the odd-looking structures that arise from the root system and protrude above the water or ground. Some stand only a few inches high; others may be several feet tall. It was once believed that the knees help aerate the tree's root system. However, this is no longer thought to be the case since removal of the knees seems to have no apparent impact on the vitality of the tree.

The second mystery is the purpose of the large buttressed base characteristic of the bald-cypress. One would think that these oversized bases play a role in supporting the tree. However, such bases are often completely hollow and in some instances actually terminate just below the surface of the water and do not even come into contact with the earth. All that can be said with certainty is that these expanded bases seem to be associated with water level. The height of the swollen base seems to be directly correlated with the average level of the water in which the tree stands.

Our two cypresses are the pond-cypress (*Taxodium ascendens*) and the bald-cypress (*T. distichum*). Both are wet-foot species that prefer to stand in water most of the time. The pond-cypress is more common on the edges of sandy lakes and in flatwoods swamps and ponds. The bald-cypress is commonly associated with rivers. At maturity the two trees can be most easily distinguished by their leaves. Pond-cypress leaves are commonly closely appressed to the branchlets on which they grow. Bald-cypress leaves, on the other hand, stand on either side of, and at an angle slightly less than perpendicular to, the branchlets, making the entire appendage take on the appearance of a feather. On older bald-cypress, however, many of the leaves, particularly those higher up on the tree, become reduced in size and look more like pond-cypress leaves, making identification slightly more difficult.

Pond-cypress trees often grow in characteristic stands called domes, stringers, and strands. Domes are circular stands with taller trees growing in the center and progressively shorter trees growing toward the edges. This growth pattern gives the combined crowns a characteristic dome-shaped appearance. Cypress strands and stringers, on the other hand, are linear stands that occur in those areas where cypresses line small streams or intermittent drainage areas. It is often easy to recognize these characteristic stands in the field.

The Cedar Trees

The eastern red cedar (*Juniperus virginiana*) is Florida's most common cedar tree and is found in all but the state's most southern counties. It is a sun-loving tree, often growing best on its most sun-exposed side. Female red cedars produce bluish, berry-like cones that are most apparent on the tree throughout the winter. The berries are a favorite food of birds, which partly explains why lines of cedar trees are common along old fencerows. Birds eat the berries, perch on the fence, and then sow the seeds with their droppings.

Although similar in appearance to the red cedar, the Atlantic white cedar (*Chamaecyparis thyoides*) is of more limited distribution. It is most commonly found west of the New River, a swampy creek coursing through the swamplands of south-central Liberty County, in the heart of north Florida's Apalachicola National Forest. However, the species is also reported in swamps and along streams in Marion and Putnam counties. Three of the best places to see this tree in abundance are near the floodplain of the middle reaches of the Apalachicola River, along the banks of the Blackwater River in the western panhandle, and in the Morman Branch scenic area of the Ocala National Forest. In the latter two sites, especially, the trees are tall and straight, and tower over the understory in beautiful stands.

One of the most interesting features of the white cedar in its Morman Branch location is its close association with climbing pieris (*Pieris phillyreifolius*). Pieris is a woody heath that sometimes appears as a weakly erect shrub that is often associated with cypress trees. In the Morman Branch area, however, it is more commonly observed ascending the inner bark of white cedar trees. The plant is not parasitic and apparently does no harm to its host. Its leafy branches emerge from under the white cedar's bark at various places along the cedar's trunk, often as much as 3 m or more above the ground.

Atlantic white cedar expresses a somewhat unusual distribution. It is common and distinctive along the coastal portions of much of the eastern and northeastern seaboard from about North Carolina to Maine, but occurs in the southeast only in widely disjunct communities. The populations that appear sporadically across northern Florida, southern Alabama, and Mississippi are, in many ways, geographic isolates, well separated from each other as well as from the main part of the tree's generally northern range. Although adequate explanations for this phenomenon are conjectural, Daniel Ward and Andy Clewell, writing for *Florida Scientist,* suggest that this odd distribution dates back to the close of the ice ages when water tables were higher and greater expanses of swamps and wetlands probably dotted the landscape. Today's communities, they argue, are likely only localized remnants of what may have once been extensive white cedar wetlands that stretched across much of northern Florida and the central peninsula.

The red cedar and the white cedar look similar, differing mainly in the shape of their twigs and the appearance of their fruits. The twigs of the former are squarish or angled when viewed in cross-section; those of the latter are more flattened. The white cedar also lacks the red cedar's bluish, berrylike cones.

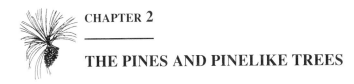

CHAPTER 2

THE PINES AND PINELIKE TREES

Florida supports two kinds of trees that are typically referred to as pines. The true pines of the family Pinaceae and genus *Pinus* are native to the state and are the more widespread of the two. The Australian pines are nonnative plants that were introduced to Florida around the turn of the century and have now become naturalized in southern Florida. The latter trees, which are classified in the family Casuarinaceae and the genus *Casuarina*, are tropical species and are, as their name suggests, native mostly to Australia.

It is unfortunate that these two families are associated with the same common name. They are not closely related and are actually quite different in structure and overall biology. They are presented together in this chapter only because of their common appellation.

The True Pines

Seven species of true pine trees inhabit various parts of the Florida landscape. Stretching across much of the state and existing in a variety of situations, they are part of a worldwide genus of nearly 100 species, at least 35 of which are native to north America. They are also some of Florida's best known and most often seen plants.

Pine trees are members of the order Coniferales, or conifers. The name is derived from the general shape of the order's distinctive fruit, or cone, though in some instances it may also refer to the overall shape of younger specimens of the trees themselves.

The typical cone of all of Florida's pines is somewhat oval in general outline and is composed of brownish, protective scales that have variously sharp prickles on their outer tips. The cones are actually protective cases for a pine tree's delicate seeds and insure that as many of the seeds as possible develop properly and with little interference. When unopened, the cone scales are held tightly appressed with the seeds tucked away safely inside. As the cone expands and drops its seeds, a tiny winged appendage that is attached to each seed acts as a sail in the breeze and effectively carries the entire structure far distant from its parent tree. In summer, it is not uncommon to see these seeds spinning and floating as they flutter to the ground in a dispersal strategy that maximizes genetic mixing and guarantees the vitality of future generations of the species.

The pines are also noted for their generally sharp-pointed, needlelike, evergreen leaves, the biology of which constitutes an interesting story of adaptation and design. That these leaves appear as they do is certainly not a chance occurrence. In fact, in the absence of such leaves, the pines might find it difficult to survive as evergreen species.

Like all living things, trees have evolved strategies for maintaining their internal temperatures in compensation for the annual cycle of hot and cold. Cool climate, broad-leaved trees, for example, deal with winter chill by dropping their leaves and reducing the amount of exposed surface area from which heat can escape. Desert plants such as cacti, on the other hand, have the opposite problem; they must avoid absorbing rather than losing heat. As a result, they have evolved a relatively narrow, elongated form that mitigates the tendency to overheat. The pine needle seems to use a strategy similar to that of the cactus, but in a way that solves both the heating and cooling problems simultaneously. A pine needle's high volume-to-surface ratio insures against losing too much heat during north Florida's cooler winters, much the same way as many conifers do in the far north. But, it also insures against absorbing too much of the state's intense summer sun by presenting less surface area for the sun's rays to strike. In addition, the surfaces of pine needles are thick and waxy, thus preventing the loss of too much water. As a result, pine needles can remain on the tree year-round, without the risk of taxing the tree's essential heat balance.

Learning to differentiate the pines is not a particularly difficult task and can usually be accomplished with a little fieldwork and some corresponding attention to detail. This does not mean that you will learn to differentiate each individual pine tree immediately upon sight, or that you will be able to specifically identify every pine tree that you find. There are always those particular trees whose characteristics do not match the rule or seem to have a combination of features that suggest their membership in more than one species. Some pine trees can be quite challenging to classify, even for the experts.

Nevertheless, several physical characteristics help in identifying most of the individual pine trees that one is likely to encounter. Chief among these distinguishing attributes include the bark, the cones, and the length of the needles. Many authors also suggest differentiating the pines by the number of needles bound together in each fascicle or cluster. This is sometimes a useful method if the needles are accessible, either on low branches or on the ground. In mixed stands, however, it may be difficult to determine which tree produced which fallen cluster. In addition, fascicles of needles from the same tree do not always conform in number to the norm for the species. It is important to note that in most cases no single characteristic is sufficient to make a positive identification of a pine tree. All of the tree's features must be taken into consideration when making the determination.

As with many of our trees, the habitat in which a pine grows is also a helpful identifying mark. Some, for example, are restricted to very specific habitats and are seldom or never found anywhere else, while others occur widely across the state. Reference to habitat is made often in the following discussion. Particular attention is given to noting those trees whose habitat preferences help in their identification.

Our two most common pines, and the two most easily confused, are the longleaf (*Pinus palustris*) and the slash (*P. elliottii*). These two trees typically have longer needles than our other pines, although the range of individual needle length in both species can be quite variable. For example, most of the needles on the slash average 20 - 25 cm in length, but some may be as short as 8 or 10 cm or as long as 28 cm. Longleaf needles, on the other hand, are usually not shorter than 15 cm, and may be as long as

30 cm or even longer. Longleaf pines with particularly long needles are easy to recognize. In addition, longleaf pines typically have three needles to a fascicle, whereas slash pines predominately have only two.

Three primary features help differentiate the slash from the longleaf. The first is the way in which the leaves extend from the end of the branches. Longleaf needles all seem to originate from one point, resulting in large globular clusters of needles; slash pine branches appear more brushlike. The second distinguishing feature is the size of the fully mature cones. Although both cones are similar in appearance, longleaf cones are usually longer than 15 cm, whereas slash pine cones are usually shorter than 15 cm. The third feature is the color of the terminal buds that can be seen among the leaf clusters in early spring. On the longleaf these buds are silvery white; on the slash they are brownish.

The slash is our most widespread pine tree. Stretching from the westernmost panhandle to the tip of the peninsula and even into the lower keys, it is the quintessential Florida pine and is challenged in distribution only by the somewhat less widespread longleaf. South Florida slash pine is more appropriately termed *P. elliottii* var. *densa*. It is often referred to by the common name Dade County or South Florida pine because of its wide use as an important building material during the early development of the Miami and Homestead areas.

Both slash and longleaf pines are commonly associated with the state's flatwoods ecosystem. Characterized by an overstory of pines and an understory of saw palmetto (*Serenoa repens*), wire grass (*Aristida stricta*), and perhaps as many as 200 other terrestrial herbs, these typically wetland communities provide ideal growth circumstances for both of these trees.

The longleaf, which is also found in dry sandhill uplands, is the original Florida pine and is indigenous to much of the state. Its success in earlier times was due primarily to its adaptation to frequent fire. Before the days of fire suppression and controlled burning, Florida's pinelands ignited naturally, being set to blaze often by the lightning from numerous thunderstorms. While wildfire is destructive to many species of trees and shrubs, it has actually contributed to the longleaf's dominance in the landscape. The longleaf is one of the most fire-resistant trees in eastern North America, protecting itself by remaining in a grasslike stage until the subterranean trunk reaches such proportions as to withstand the flames. Depending on soil, moisture, and competition, this grass stage may last as few as three or, allegedly, as many as 20 years. Once the underground trunk has reached sufficient size, the tree grows upward rapidly, as much as 1 m or more in only 12 months. Such growth elevates the growing tip of the longleaf above the potential flames, thus insuring its protection. Other trees, not so adapted, cannot survive these natural fires, resulting in nearly pure, parklike stands of longleaf pine with no understory.

The slash pine, too, is partial to environments that support regularly occurring natural fires. Unlike the longleaf, however, the slash is more appropriately considered fire dependent than fire resistant. Its cones open best when subjected to heat, and the frequent fires of the flatwoods ecosystem insure this advantage.

The pond pine (*Pinus serotina*) is the third of Florida's fire-associated pine species. Often occurring on the edges of the flatwoods in somewhat wetter conditions than either the slash or the longleaf, the pond pine is widespread only in northern Florida and is a relatively easy tree to recognize. The pond pine often, but by no means always, appears twisted and deformed, and is usually characterized by numerous short branches and scraggly twigs that sprout from many points along its trunk. Its leaves average about 8 to 20 cm long, sometimes slightly shorter, and are commonly bound together in fascicles of three. Its cones are smaller than the longer leaved pines, are somewhat squatty in appearance, and on many trees are held tightly closed until the heat of a forest fire causes them to open and shed their seeds. (It should be noted, however, that the cones will also open under artificial circumstances, such as when they are left on the dashboard of an automobile in the heat of a midsummer's day.) The pond pine's specific epithet, *serotina*, literally means "late" and apparently refers both to the tree's tardiness in dropping its newly formed seeds and to its habit of retaining its cones on the branches for several years. However, the term is also often associated with fire-dependent species. For those who want an opportunity to see this tree, there are a number of nearly pure stands along forest road 295 in the Osceola National Forest, just south of Highway 2, or in several locations in the Apalachicola National Forest southwest of Tallahassee.

Three of our pines can be distinguished by a combination of their extremely short needles (ranging 4 - 11 cm in length) and the habitats in which they grow. The sand pine (*P. clausa*) is most common on inland white sand ridges in the central part of the state but is also known along the coastal strand of the northwest Florida panhandle. In appearance, the sand pine is most like the spruce pine (*P. glabra*). Both have smooth instead of scaly branchlets, and young trees of both species even have smooth grayish bark. The bark of older spruce pines is quite hard, closely furrowed, and looks quite unlike our other pines. At first glance, the lower trunk of *Pinus glabra* might even be mistaken for one of Florida's many hardwoods.

The easiest characteristic to use for separating the spruce and sand pines is their habitat. The most magnificent stands of sand pine are found in the ancient relict dune fields that are now incorporated as part of the sprawling Ocala National Forest. The spruce pine, on the other hand, occupies rich woods and calcareous bottomlands in association with mixed hardwood forests. It is never found on coastal or inland white sand ridges. Conversely, the sand pine is never found growing naturally on sites conducive to the spruce pine. Possibly the closest spruce pines to the coast are those found along North Line Road in the Wakulla Unit of the St. Marks National Wildlife Refuge. Even these latter trees, however, are situated on the edge of a swampy, hardwood hammock that is closely underlain by the top of the limestone subsurface.

The other pine with short needles, and the pine with the most restricted distribution in the state, is the shortleaf (*P. echinata*). It is found in the fertile uplands of northwest Florida's hill country, and sometimes occupies mixed hardwood stands in conjunction with the spruce pine. Although both the shortleaf and spruce have relatively short needles, their barks are quite different. Whereas spruce pine bark is closely ridged and looks somewhat like an oak, the bark of a mature shortleaf pine usually consists of large, flat, reddish to reddish brown plates with only shallow furrows between them. The bark of young shortleaf pines is more tightly furrowed than that of mature specimens, but even it is characteristically pinelike and quite distinguishable from the bark of a spruce pine.

The loblolly pine (*P. taeda*) is also an upland tree and often occupies sites together with the shortleaf. However, it is not uncommon in lower sites. Loblolly needles are typically longer than those of the shortleaf, averaging 8 - 22 cm in length. It is most easily confused with the other three longer-leaved pines.

The bark of a loblolly can be a conspicuous field mark. On older trees the bark is deeply furrowed, the furrows appearing to extend in single vertical lines for long distances up the trunk. The ridges between these furrows are broken up into vertically elongated plates in a more or less regular pattern. This bark pattern is particularly evident on older or slow-growing trees and is often helpful in distinguishing the species.

The Australian Pines

As indicated above, it is probably misleading to incorporate the Australian pines into this chapter on pine trees. They are not conifers. In fact, they are not even gymnosperms. However, their pinelike appearance and the fact that they are commonly referred to as pines seems to justify the inclusion.

Australian pines are members of the Casuarinaceae, or beefwood, family. The family contains only one genus with about 45 species, most of which are native to Australia. However, three species have been introduced into southern Florida. The genus name *Casuarina* reportedly comes from the supposed resemblance of the tree's branchlets to the drooping feathers of the Australian cassowary bird. Originally used as windbreaks and as beauty strips along roadways, the Australian pines have become well-established members of tropical Florida's naturalized tree flora.

Florida's three species of Australian pines are so nearly similar in appearance that the casual observer would probably assume they are one and the same. All are characterized by tall, straight trunks and long, needlelike branchlets that often hang shaggily from the ends of the branches. Many stand as much as 30 m tall and take on the appearance of a large, bushy Christmas tree. Once learned, their form is unmistakable.

Australian pines are equipped with tiny, scalelike leaves that constitute this family's most distinctive feature. What appear to be needles are actually jointed branchlets that represent the current year's growth. The real leaves are borne in minute whorls that encircle each joint and are so small that they are difficult to see with the naked eye. They usually require a hand-held magnifier for close inspection. The reduced size of the leaves and needlelike branchlets help the Australian pines conserve heat and water in much the same way as described above for the pine trees.

The number of leaves at each joint is the key characteristic that separates one species of Australian pine from another. The horsetail or equisetum-leaved casuarina (*Casuarina equisetifolia*), probably the most common member of the genus, is characterized by 6 - 8 leaves in each whorl. Cunningham's beefwood (*C. cunninghamiana*), the most cold tolerant of the three, has 8 - 10 scales per whorl, and Brazilian beefwood (*C. glauca,* also sometimes referred to as *C. cristata* and *C. lepidophloia*) has 10 - 16.

The Australian pines are not welcomed additions to south Florida's flora. Although sometimes enjoyed for their shade, they are extremely destructive to the natural vegetation and tend to take over the areas they invade. *C. equisetifolia,* in particular, is well known along the coastal strand from about St. Lucie and Lee counties southward, where it rapidly invades newly formed beaches and carpets the ground with its fallen branchlets. Its dense foliage shades out and displaces an array of native trees and shrubs including the sea grape, coco-plum, and bay cedar, and its fallen branchlets release chemicals that suppress the growth of surrounding vegetation. Even knowing its pestiferous nature, however, it is still difficult not to enjoy the soothing sound of coastal winds blowing through this tree's shaggy crown.

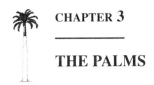

CHAPTER 3

THE PALMS

Palm trees have long been associated with Florida's balmy, tropical weather. Vacationers new to the state often arrive with mental images of wide sandy beaches bordered on their landward edges by picturesque lines of curving trunks and gently swaying fronds. Whether or not these romantic visions are founded in truth, the fact remains that the palm tree is one of the Sunshine State's most common and persistent symbols.

Florida's formal relationship with the palm dates to 1953, the year the legislature voted to designate the sabal palm (*Sabal palmetto*) as Florida's official state tree. The 1949 House of Representatives had initially selected the royal palm (*Roystonea elata*) for this distinction, presumably for its huge stature and regal appearance, but the Senate rejected the idea in favor of several other species. Four years later, however, at the encouragement of the Florida Federation of Garden Clubs, the *Sabal palmetto* edged out the competition to be named the state's most representative tree species.

Worldwide, the family Palmae (also sometimes called the Arecaceae or, erroneously, Palmaceae) is composed of over 230 genera and perhaps as many as 3,000 species. Only a few of these are indigenous to the continental United States, and most are restricted to the warmer regions of southern Florida and southern California. However, a large number of exotic species have been imported for ornamental purposes, and at least a few of these have become widely naturalized.

Eight tree-sized palms in seven genera are native to Florida. All are of tropical origins and, with only two exceptions, are found mostly in the state's southern counties where they are better protected from the killing effects of north Florida's occasionally freezing temperatures. In addition, three other species have found wide popularity as ornamental plants in the state and have now become established components of our naturalized flora. All 11 of these trees are described and differentiated in Part II.

It should be emphasized that these 11 species are not the only palms to be found in the state. A large number of nonnative species are available from commercial nurseries and are regularly cultivated for resale. One common handbook lists more than 25 species of introduced palms in Florida, all of which are recommended for use as ornamental landscape plants. At least a few of these are similar to some of our native species, which sometimes makes identification of these latter plants difficult.

The palms are distinguished as Florida's only monocotyledonous trees. As such, they differ from all of the other trees treated in this book. They are phylogenetically more advanced than the gymnosperms presented in Chapters 1 and 2, but exhibit a very different appearance than the numerous dicotyledonous species treated in the chapters that follow.

Monocotyledons and dicotyledons take their names from the number of seed leaves, or cotyledons, contained in their embryos; monocots have one, dicots two. For practical purposes, whether an individual plant is a monocot or dicot can be most easily determined by the number of its flower parts. Monocots typically (though not always) have flower parts in threes or multiples of three, whereas the flower parts of the dicots are usually (but, again, not always) in fours or fives. More important for identification purposes, monocots usually have parallel rather than netted leaf venation, a characteristic that can easily be seen in most palm leaves.

As a result of their monocotyledonous heritage, palm trees are quite different from other tree species in a number of important ways. Unlike dicotyledonous trees, for example, the trunks of palm trees are not divided into bark and wood. Instead, there is only an outer shell and inner cylinder, both of which are composed of living tissue. Palms are also typically unbranched and their primary growth is upward from a single terminal bud. Although they grow in girth, they do so only through enlargement of the living tissue held in the center of the trunk. Hence, they never shed or replace their outer layer, as do most other trees.

The palm trees also have the distinction of being one of the few collections of Florida trees that can be easily recognized by their overall shape in the landscape. Whereas the accurate identification of many tree species requires closeup inspection of an individual specimen's leaves or flowers, the palms are more forgiving to the casual observer. Even at a distance, many of our palms are relatively easy trees to identify.

For identification purposes, the palm trees can be divided into two major groupings: those that have palmate, or fan-shaped, leaves; and those that have pinnate, or feather-shaped, leaves. The palmate-leaved species are characterized by a leaf structure in which all leaf segments arise from a single point, similar to the structure of the human hand. Pinnate leaves, on the other hand, are characterized by leaves with rows of leaflets along each side of a central axis, similar in design to that of a feather.

Florida's palmate-leaved palms include the paurotis palm (*Acoelorrhaphe wrightii*), silver palm (*Coccothrinax argentata*), sabal palm (*Sabal palmetto*), saw palmetto (*Serenoa repens*), Key thatch palm (*Thrinax morrisii*), Florida thatch palm (*Thrinax radiata*), and Washington palm (*Washingtonia robusta*). With the exception of the Washington palm, which has escaped from cultivation, all of these are native to the state.

The sabal palm and saw palmetto are the most widely distributed members of the palm family and are found in a variety of habitats throughout the state. The others are restricted primarily to the southern counties. The sabal palm and saw palmetto are interesting and important Florida trees. The fruits of the sabal palm, in particular, were once eaten by Florida's Indians, and it is well known today that the tree provides homes to a number of cavity-nesting birds and food for a variety of wildlife.

The silver palm and both thatch palms are commercially exploited species and are included on the state's list of protected flora. They are most common in Dade County and the Keys. A trail named for the silver palm has been established at Bahia Honda State Recreation Area and offers an outstanding opportunity for close observation of this diminutive and attractive species.

The nature trail at Key Deer National Wildlife Refuge is an excellent place to study the differences between the silver and Key thatch palms. There is a marked specimen of each along the path. However, it should be noted that the sign marking the thatch palm is actually located directly in front of a silver palm that obstructs the view of the thatch palm; the latter is the second tree from the sign.

Only four species of Florida's native or naturalized palms have pinnate leaves. Of these, the royal palm is by far the most majestic and easily identified. It is a tall, stately tree that is characterized by a smooth, bright green shaft separating the top of its light gray trunk from the bottom of the spreading leaf crown. This shaft completely encircles the trunk and is actually the single sheath of the oldest leaf in the crown. It often extends down the trunk for more than 1 m and is a distinctive and easily recognizable field mark.

The other three species with pinnate leaves include the coconut palm (*Cocos nucifera*), the date palm (*Phoenix dactylifera*), and the Sargent's cherry or buccaneer palm (*Pseudophoenix sargentii*).

Sargent's cherry palm is native to the state and is an often-used ornamental. However, it is very rare in the wild and is known in quantity only from Elliott Key in Biscayne National Park. In appearance it has several characters of the royal palm, but is generally smaller in stature. Joseph and Marcella Nemec, who thoroughly surveyed the Elliott Key population for the National Park Service, found 39 specimens that survived the winds and waves of Hurricane Andrew. Twelve of these were naturally occurring mature trees, 14 were seedlings, and 13 were from a recent reintroduction effort. Prior to the storm there were 32 mature trees and 15 seedlings.

J. K. Small, one of the southeastern United State's most celebrated botanists, reported the cherry palm from both Elliott and Long Keys in the 1913 edition of his *Flora of the Southeastern United States* and in 1922 discovered at least one plant on Sands Key. According to Charles S. Sargent, the Harvard botanist for whom the tree is named, the Long Key population included about 200 trees in the late 1800s. However, a variety of observers reported a steadily decreasing number throughout the early 1900s, and by the mid-1960s the naturally occurring population on Long Key had completely disappeared due primarily to the large-scale transplantation of wild specimens for ornamental use.

In 1991 several specimens were planted on Long Key in an attempt to reestablish the population. In addition, 16 were also planted on Elliott Key and three on adjacent Sands Key. Of these 19 specimens, 13 have survived. Fairchild Tropical Garden, together with the National Park Service and the Florida Department of Natural Resources, plans to continue to pursue these reintroduction efforts.

The coconut and date palms are both introduced species that are best known for, and most easily recognized by, their fruits. The former species produces conspicuous clusters of its large, three-sided fruit, making it an easy palm to identify. It is also widely used along streets and roadways throughout southern Florida and the Keys and is one of the easiest of the palms to find. The coconut palm has been said to rank among the 10 most useful trees in the world. The fruits are eaten raw or fashioned into candies, and their inner liquid makes a cool, refreshing drink. The dried, whitish, oily parts of the fruit are also sold in large quantities for the manufacture of soaps and coconut oil. The leaves serve as thatch for roofs of tropical dwellings and the trunks are used for posts. Coconut shells have been used as bowls and cups and the tree's fibers have been fashioned into ropes, mats, and brushes. In addition, the tree is often planted for its beauty and grace throughout southern Florida and the West Indies and, in many ways, has come to serve as a symbol of the tropics.

The date palm is one of two species that comprise the source of commercially produced dates. It is a handsome tree that is sometimes grown as far north as the Tampa area. It resembles the royal palm in general shape but lacks the latter's shiny green crown-shaft. The date palm is easy to cultivate but requires warmth and humidity at the roots as well as high temperatures and full sun. It is very similar in appearance to the Canary Island date palm (*P. canariensis*); the two plants are sometimes difficult to distinguish.

CHAPTER 4

MAGNOLIAS, CUSTARD APPLES, AND ANISE TREES

As a group, the magnolias, custard apples, and anise trees constitute some of the oldest of our dicotyledonous tree species. All are members of the botanical order Magnoliales or Annonales, and all have simple leaves, eye-catching flowers, and uniquely interesting fruits.

The Magnolias

The large, showy flowers of the Magnoliaceae are this family's link with a long history and a remote origin. The original magnolias, of which only a few species are left, were among the first trees to develop flowers and at one point ranged nearly worldwide. Fossil evidence indicates that they, along with ancient gymnosperms, were once distributed widely throughout Europe, western North America, Canada, and even Greenland before being pushed southward by the advancing glaciers of the ice ages. Today's members of this family are the descendants of what may be the world's most ancient family of trees and are well represented in both the southeastern United States and eastern Asia. At least two species are also known from the tropics, including one that is native only to the Luquillo Mountains of eastern Puerto Rico.

Our most commonly recognized member of this family is the southern magnolia (*Magnolia grandiflora*). The large, beautiful, fragrant, creamy white flowers that appear on this tree in late spring and early summer certainly justify its specific name. Probably no other common southern tree, including the flowering dogwood, has such arresting blossoms.

The southern magnolia occurs in a wide variety of habitats. It is most often associated with shady, well-drained sites, but is also found in hammocks, on slopes and ravines, in floodplain woods, and on coastal dunes. Its large, thick, evergreen leaves are dark shiny green above and rusty-orange below, and are easily distinguishable from any of our other native trees.

Although less often seen by the general populace, the sweetbay (*M. virginiana*) is probably even more abundant than the southern magnolia. It is predominantly a tree of the swamps, bays and branches of northern Florida, but is a component of flatwoods depressions throughout the state as far south as Dade and Monroe counties. As a result of its out-of-the-way habitat, it is less apt to be noticed than its more obvious cousin. It, too, has fragrant, creamy white flowers that appear in spring, though the flowers are much smaller in size than those of the southern magnolia.

The most distinguishing characteristic of the sweetbay is its leaf. Considerably more narrow than those of *M. grandiflora*, sweetbay leaves are mostly elliptic in shape, dull green above and silvery below. Even in the slightest breeze the foliage of this tree twists and turns, exposing this silvery undersurface to view. In its habitat, the sweetbay is likely to be confused only with the swamp bay (*Persea palustris*) or loblolly bay (*Gordonia lasianthus*). However, even though the leaves of the three species are generally similar in shape, the undersurfaces of the leaves of the latter two never display the silvery sheen of the sweetbay.

Four other species of magnolia are reported from the Florida panhandle, west of the Suwannee River. All four are of limited distribution, all are deciduous, and two are quite rare in the state. The cucumber tree (*M. acuminata*) occurs in Florida only in Walton and Holmes counties. The Ashe magnolia (*M. macrophylla* subsp. *ashei*), although endemic to northern Florida, is a threatened species found only sporadically along bluffs and steepheads from Santa Rosa to Leon and Wakulla counties. It may be easily found along the hiking trail through Torreya State Park. The pyramid magnolia (*M. pyramidata*) is an uncommon component of bluffs and ravines along the Escambia, Apalachicola, and Ochlockonee rivers. The umbrella magnolia (*M. tripetala*) is actually a northern tree found from Pennsylvania to northern Georgia and Alabama. It is reported in Florida from only a single location in Okaloosa County.

The tuliptree or yellow poplar (*Liriodendron tulipifera*) is also a member of the magnolia family. Although the common name associating this tree with the poplars is misleading, its correct botanical name is quite descriptive. The name *Liriodendron* is actually composed of two Greek words meaning lily and tree. *Tulipifera* literally means tulip-bearing and refers to the tree's greenish yellow and orange tuliplike flowers. In early spring when this magnificent tree is in bloom, the name lily tree certainly seems to fit its character.

In addition to its distinctive flowers, the leaf of the tulip tree is also unlike any other. Glossy green above, it is truncate, or cut off, at both its base and apex and appears somewhat squarish, and its central vein often terminates at a notch in the squared-off apex.

The yellow poplar is one of the most important and commercially valuable trees of the entire eastern United States. Ranging from upstate New York to the Ohio Valley, it finds its southern limits in the central Florida peninsula. Although most Florida specimens are somewhat modest in size, the tree has the potential to grow as tall as 50 m with a trunk diameter of between 3 and 4 m. Such trees provide many board feet of commercial lumber.

Pawpaws and Custard Apples

The pawpaws and custard apples are members of the Annonaceae or custard apple family. Most members of this large family are found in the tropical regions of the world, but a few are found in more temperate climes. They are sometimes confused with the monocots because their flower parts are in threes rather than fours or fives. Only two genera are native to the United States, both of which are found in Florida. All of Florida's species are characterized by relatively large, yellow to yellowish green fruits that are quite distinctive.

Only three of Florida's pawpaws become large enough to be called trees. All of these are found solely in the northern or north-central parts of the state. However, at least six other shrubby species are also found in a variety of habitats.

The dog banana, or Indian banana (*Asimina triloba*), is the species that most commonly attains tree stature. It is also the pawpaw that expresses the most restricted distribution in Florida. It is most common from about northern Alabama, Georgia, and Mississippi to the southern edge of the Great Lakes. The Florida population is at the southernmost boundary of the tree's range. Limited to the central panhandle from about Okaloosa to Liberty counties, it is found in rich bottomlands, mesic woods, and upland slopes in several locations. It is a small understory tree that usually stands between 5 and 10 m in height. Its leaves are deciduous and rather large, usually measuring between 15 and 30 cm in length. They are widest near their usually sharp-pointed tip, and taper gradually to a somewhat narrowed base. The shape of the larger leaves is a distinctive field mark. Once learned, it provides a quick cue to the tree's identification.

Even more conspicuous, however, are the oblong, yellowish green fruits that appear on the tree in early summer. Ripening into a soft, fleshy berry up to 15 cm long, they are a favorite food for a wide variety of animals from raccoons to bears. They are also quite tasty to humans and were relished by both the American Indians and the early settlers of eastern North America.

The other two tree-sized pawpaws are more often found as shrubby rather than arborescent species. The small-flowered or dwarf pawpaw (*A. parviflora*) is more widespread and common than the previous species and thrives in a greater number of habitats. It is found in rich woods and coastal hammocks, as well as along the borders of sinkholes across much of the northern part of the state. It differs from the dog banana mainly by having shorter leaves, smaller fruits, and a generally smaller stature. Otherwise, the two plants are quite similar. Distinguishing between them in the field is particularly difficult when their flowers or fruits are not present.

The flag pawpaw (*A. obovata*) is an arborescent shrub inhabiting the pine flatwoods, sand pine scrub, and coastal dunes of the eastern peninsula to about the central part of the state. It, too, produces large, fleshy, berrylike fruit. Its leaves are oblong to oval, and more rounded than either of the other two species. It may be separated from the previous two species by its habitat.

Pawpaw species can be divided into two groups based upon the color and aroma of their flowers. Those with maroon flowers, like the dog banana and small-flowered pawpaw, exhibit a fetid odor somewhat like the scent of rotting meat. Those with white flowers, like the flag pawpaw, exhibit a pleasant fragrance. The reason for the association between the color and aroma of pawpaw flowers is not well understood, but may have to do with the varying preferences of the several beetle species that pollinate the plants.

Only two members of the custard apples inhabit the United States, both of which are found only in southern Florida. The pond apple (*Annona glabra*) is the more common and more widely known of the two. It is also the northernmost-ranging member of this relatively large, mostly tropical genus and extends up the southeastern Florida peninsula to about Brevard County. It is common along the margins of freshwater streams and lakes, on the edges of sinkholes, and in swampy places, and is an easy tree to find and to identify. Its leaves often tend to fold upward from the central axis in a dihedral, or V-shaped, pattern, a characteristic which helps separate the pond apple from several closely similar members of the genus *Ficus*. Its flowers, which appear in the spring and open at night, have creamy yellow petals with purple bases and hang pendently from the branches. Its fruit is large, apple-shaped, fleshy, matures in the fall, and is an important wildlife food. No other native south Florida tree has such large or distinctive fruit.

The sugar apple (*A. squamosa*) is not native to Florida. It was originally introduced for its sweet-tasting fruit and persists in the Keys only from cultivation. Its leaves are quite similar to the pond apple, but its fruit is characterized by a conspicuous covering of small, knobby protrusions which makes the tree easy to identify. The pulp of ripe fruits may be eaten raw and has been used in the preparation of beverages and sherbets.

Anise Trees

The Illiciaceae, or star anise family, is composed of a single genus with approximately 35 to 40 species worldwide, most of which are native to southeastern Asia. Only two species occur in the United States; both are found in Florida.

The Florida anise (*Illicium floridanum*) is a small understory tree of rich wooded areas in ravines and steepheads and alongside streams in the northern and western panhandle as well as in portions of Alabama, Mississippi, and Louisiana. Often appearing as a large, multistemmed shrub with dense, dark green foliage, a population of anise trees is somewhat reminiscent of the heavily vegetated rhododendron thickets that characterize many of the hillsides in the southern Appalachian mountains. Their sprawling stature and mass of leaning branches often make walking among them a difficult task.

The leaves of the Florida anise bear few visibly distinguishing characteristics. Their most obvious trait is the pungent odor that arises when they are crushed. Reminiscent of licorice to some, many consider the aroma an agreeable fragrance. Prolonged exposure to its bouquet, however, tends to detract from its pleasantness.

Perhaps the most interesting feature of the Florida anise is the odd structure of its rather complicated flowers. Unlike many so-called perfect flowers, which generally contain numerous stamens but only one pistil, the flower of the Florida anise commonly includes as many as 15 pistils and up to 30 stamens. In fact, everything about its flower seems to be in quantity. Even the flower's long, narrow, deep red petals (which are rarely pink or whitish) usually number near 30. The flowers make a beautiful show in the dim light that is characteristic of the habitat in which they are found. The family takes its common name from the star-shaped fruits that appear after flowering.

Our other *Illicium,* the yellow anise (*I. parviflorum*), is a strictly Florida species and is found nowhere else in the world. Although it has been somewhat broadly distributed for ornamental purposes, it occurs naturally only in low, wet sites of several of the state's north-central counties, including Marion, Lake, and Volusia. Its leaves are similar to the Florida anise in shape, size, and general appearance, except that they lack the latter's sharp-pointed tips. The flowers of the two species, however, are quite different from one another. The petals of the yellow anise are fewer in number, relatively wider and shorter than those of the star anise, and yellow in color. They are also much smaller than the flowers of the Florida anise, and much less conspicuous.

It is possible to see the anise trees in several places in Florida. One of the best locations for the Florida anise is along the wetter portions of the foot trail that leads across Sweetwater Creek just east of the Krul Recreation Area campground in the Blackwater River State Forest northeast of Pensacola. The yellow anise can be found in the Morman Branch Scenic area, just south of the Juniper Creek Bridge and east of Highway 19, in the Ocala National Forest. However, no marked trails lead into the Morman Branch area, and the vegetation there is often quite dense.

CHAPTER 5

LAURELS AND WILD CINNAMON

The laurel and wild cinnamon families are represented by only ten tree species in Florida. Like their close relatives presented in Chapter 4, they are grouped together here because they, too, belong to one of the oldest orders of flowering plants. The members of both of these families contain ethereal oil cells in their tissues, a somewhat primitive characteristic that imparts a distinctive aroma when disturbed. As a result, nearly all members of these two families are noted for the highly volatile fragrances of their leaves, roots, fruits, and bark.

The Laurel Family

The laurels, or Lauraceae, compose a large family of nearly 2500 species in over 35 genera, most of which are found in the tropical or warm-temperate zones of both hemispheres. Nine tree species in six genera are found in Florida. These include the camphor-tree (*Cinnamomum camphora*), the bays and avocado (*Persea* spp.), the sassafras (*Sassafras albidum*), the gulf licaria (*Licaria triandra*), the spicebush (*Lindera benzoin*), and the lancewood (*Ocotea coriacea,* also often referred to as *Nectandra coriacea*).

The camphor-tree is part of a large genus found exclusively in Asia and Australia and is not indigenous to Florida. It is one of more than 200 species in its genus, most of which are found in India, China, and Japan. The camphor was introduced as a shade tree in Florida at least as early as 1875 and was once used widely as an ornamental. As a result, it has now become a naturalized and common component of our flora. The camphor has shiny, evergreen leaves which give off a strong odor of camphor when crushed.

The camphor's wood is the source of the same camphor oil that is used in the production of medicine. The tree's rapid expansion in the southeastern United States probably resulted from an early, and not very successful, attempt to compete with Japan and Formosa's camphor industry.

Florida's flora includes four members of the genus Persea: the red bay (*P. borbonia*), the swamp bay (*P. palustris*), the silk bay (*P. humilis*), and the avocado (*P. americana*). All have alternate, evergreen leaves and small yellowish flowers that are produced in clusters in those leaf axils that are nearest the ends of the branchlets.

The red bay and swamp bay are quite similar in appearance. The major difference between the two is the color of the undersurface of their leaves. The leaves of the red bay are whitish, or glaucous, below, while those of the swamp bay are more brownish and are characterized by shaggy pubescence along the central axis as well as the major veins.

The red bay is a tree of moist woodlands, hammocks, bluffs, and coastal dunes, whereas the swamp bay is a wetland species, inhabiting swamps, wet pine flatwoods, and the edges of marshes. Although more variable in its habitat preference than the swamp bay, the red bay is seldom found in the intensely wet habitats in which the swamp bay seems to thrive.

There has been some disagreement among taxonomic botanists about whether the swamp bay and red bay actually constitute separate species. Some believe that eventually both of these trees, as well as the silk bay, will be considered conspecific. They are considered as distinct species here, and all can be readily separated in the field.

Unlike either the red or swamp bay, the silk bay is a tree of the white sand scrub of the central peninsula. It may be distinguished from the previous two species by its blackish stems and branches and by the uniform covering of smooth, golden-colored, silky pubescence on the lower surfaces of its leaves, although the latter characteristic is certainly not stable throughout its range.

The avocado (*Persea americana*) is a well-known member of this otherwise easily overlooked genus. Noted particularly for its shiny, rounded to pear-shaped, yellow-green fruit, it is widely grown in the lower peninsula, where it sometimes persists from cultivation. The avocado has long been used as a food source and was probably an important fruit to both the Incas and the Aztecs. It was first introduced into Florida by the Spaniards, probably during their earliest explorations of the New World. It wasn't until the 20th century, however, that the plant found its way into the New World marketplace as an increasingly important fruit crop.

The avocado fruit is very nutritious and quite palatable. It is eaten as a raw vegetable, used in salads, or added to soups for flavoring. In addition to its importance as a food product, it is also used in the production of commercial vegetable oils and has a long history among south American natives in the concoction of folk medicines.

Lancewood is closely related to our three native members of the *Persea* genus and is quite similar in appearance. It is common in the United States only in the hammocks and associated pinelands of the south Florida coastal strand, the Miami Rock Ridge, the Everglades, and the Florida Keys. However, it is found as far north as Cape Canaveral along the east coast but probably not further north than Lee County on the west coast.

Lancewood has alternate, lanceolate leaves that are usually pointed at the tips. Like the other bays, its leaves are aromatic when rubbed or crushed. Its heartwood is dark brown and has been used for carpentry and cabinetwork in some parts of the tropics, but the tree has no commercial value in Florida. It is most easily separated from the red bay, the only other bay with which it regularly associates, by the color of its lower leaf surfaces. Lancewood leaves are green below, whereas those of red bay are grayish white. The Gumbo Limbo Nature Center in Boca Raton has marked specimens of lancewood along its boardwalk and is an excellent place to study this plant in detail.

The sassafras is a common tree of well-drained upland woods and bluffs as well as roadsides across northern Florida. Unlike the bays, the form of its leaves is quite distinctive. Commonly 5 - 10 cm long, sassafras leaves often contain two or three terminal lobes, which give them the appearance of a mitten or three-fingered glove.

The sassafras is rich in history. Its spicy, aromatic roots and bark once formed the basis of sassafras tea, and its leaves were used by Indians and early southerners to add flavor to their food. Many parts of the tree were reputed to have great medicinal value and the ability to prolong life. Early colonists grubbed roots and stripped bark by the ton to ship back to the motherland for use as a tonic and in the manufacture of perfumes and soaps. Children even benefitted from the tree; their parents used its candy-like flavor to disguise the bad taste of necessary medicine. We now know, however, that this last practice is actually detrimental since the plant contains toxic compounds that are stored in the body. As a result, the historical romance with the sassafras has given way to a calmer recognition of this species as just a pretty little tree that grows in rich woodlands or occasionally springs up in backyard flower beds.

The Gulf licaria (*Licaria triandra*) is one of the rarest members of Florida's flora, and is the rarest of our native Lauraceae. First recorded in 1910 from Brickell Hammock in Miami, it was never known in abundance and is nearly extirpated in its native habitat due to the development and expansion of Miami's suburban areas. Like many members of its family, it has elliptic, aromatic leaves. Its distinctive fruit is deep blue, about 2 cm long, and rests in a thick, red, double-rimmed cup that is a little over 1 cm in length. The Gulf licaria is also reported from other tropical locations outside of Florida.

The spicebush (*Lindera benzoin*) is a dioecious, alternate-leaved, aromatic shrub of northeast Florida and the central panhandle. It is a member of a rather large genus of about 100 species, most of which are confined to eastern Asia. *Lindera benzoin* is one of only three species of this genus found in North America. Spicebush is a handsome shrub or, infrequently, a small tree which inhabits alluvial woodlands as well as the banks of streams from about Maine, Ontario, and Michigan southward. Its yellow male blossoms are among the earliest spring flowers and are a noticeable addition to the otherwise dim understory.

The Wild Cinnamon Family

The Canellaceae, or wild cinnamon family, is a small family with only a few genera. Found intermittently throughout the West Indies, Brazil, and Venezuela as well as East Africa, Madagascar, and southern Florida, its rather spotty distribution and limited number of species are probably indicative of the family's ancient origin.

The cinnamon bark (*Canella winterana*) is Florida's only member of the Canellaceae. It is found in tropical hammocks of the Keys as well as in the Cape Sable area. The plant's scientific name is derived from the root word *canella,* which is the Latin term for cinnamon. Both its common and scientific names refer to the cinnamonlike aroma of its inner bark. The plant is widely distributed in the West Indies and has been used throughout history variously as a spice, aromatic stimulant, and tonic. The spicy, fiery taste of the leaves provides a good trait for identifying the plant.

CHAPTER 6

HOLLIES, TEAS, AND TITI TREES

The hollies, teas, and titis are part of a loosely related group of tree families that are widely represented in Florida. All have simple, alternate leaves with margins that are variously serrate, crenate, or entire.

The Hollies

Florida's hollies comprise an ecologically diverse group of trees and shrubs. From the American holly (*Ilex opaca*) of rich, well-drained woods to the myrtle-leaved holly (*I. myrtifolia*) of bogs and wetlands; from the predominately coastal dahoon (*I. cassine*) to the relatively rare tawnyberry holly (*I. krugiana*) found only in hammocks and pinelands of Dade County, holly species appear in a varied assortment of our native floral communities.

The hollies are part of the family Aquifoliaceae. The family consists of three genera and about 400 species, at least 350 of which are classified in the genus *Ilex*. The family name literally means "trees with needles on their leaves," which is an apt description for a number of holly species. The family is characterized by having simple, alternate, petiolate leaves with minute stipules at the point at which the petiole joins the branch.

The hollies are dioecious plants, meaning that most male and female flowers are borne on separate trees. The flowers are typically quite small and usually arise in small clusters at the leaf axils. They are white to green in color and appear in profusion in early spring. The individual flowers are not particularly showy and might even go unnoticed if they appeared as solitary blossoms. Blooming in abundance as they do, however, they are an obvious part of the springtime landscape.

Hollies bear berrylike fruits that are not unlike those of the flowering dogwood. With the exception of the sometimes purplish drupes of the tawnyberry holly (*I. krugiana*) or the shiny black fruits of the large sweet gallberry (*I. coriacea*), the fruits of all our tree-sized holly species are typically either red or reddish orange. Even the drupes of the tawnyberry are red to dusky orange most of the time, turning dark only at maturity. Holly berries appear late in the season and are a favorite and important fall forage for a variety of animals and songbirds.

The fruits are also useful to humans when attempting to identify the plants. Several of the more similar species may be separated, at least partly, on the basis of the size and color of their berries. Even without the fruits present, however, learning to distinguish between the several species of hollies does not pose an overwhelming challenge.

Even the most casual observer will notice that only some holly trees seem to bear fruit in a given year. At first, it might be suspected that the fruitless trees are merely late in flowering, or that perhaps holly trees bear fruit only in alternating years. Neither of these assumptions is correct. The real answer lies in the sex of the tree. Only the pistillate, or female, flowers develop into the bright berries that are so often associated with the holly genus. Since holly trees are either one sex or the other, only a limited number of individuals can be expected to bear the holly's distinctive trademark.

Florida has a total of 11 holly species, only ten of which attain tree stature. Of these ten, however, at least six are more commonly seen as shrubs and only occasionally reach treelike proportions. The four most likely to be seen as full-grown trees include the American holly, dahoon, myrtle-leaved holly, and possum-haw (*I. decidua*).

Of the more shrubby hollies, the yaupon (*I. vomitoria*) is our commonest and most extensively distributed species. It has also had a long and colorful history in the eastern United States. Although known today as one of the many native plants that have been successfully adapted for ornamental purposes, its usefulness to Florida residents is certainly not a recent phenomenon. Nor has this usefulness been limited only to horticultural utility.

The early Indians used the plant to produce the ceremonial "black drink" made famous by the writings of the early Spanish explorers and other New World travelers. Concocted by first drying, then boiling the yaupon's caffeine-rich leaves, the tealike liquid became a popular beverage for early pioneers along much of the eastern seaboard. Many of the early settlers became so accustomed to the brew that they came to prefer it over the more costly and socially acceptable teas imported from their European homelands.

The stories of the black drink's use as a purgative are probably the plant's best known legacy. Indeed, ingesting large quantities of the potent drink is sure to induce vomiting in those who choose to imbibe, and there is significant historical evidence that the Indians used the drink regularly in religious rituals designed to purify and cleanse the body. Its widespread acceptance as an agreeable beverage by the white European colonists, however, suggests that its emetic value was probably much less important to this latter population than was its taste.

The large sweet gallberry (*I. coriacea*) is another of our holly species that is more often seen as a shrub. In rare instances, it may take on the proportions of a small tree and will sometimes reach a height of 5 m. It is probably most easily confused with the gallberry or inkberry (*I. glabra*) with which it commonly associates. The latter plant is strictly a shrub and is a common component of the pine flatwoods ecosystem. It may be separated from the former species by its leaves. The leaf of the large sweet gallberry typically has small teeth scattered all along its leaf edge, from the apex to the base. Similar teeth on the inkberry, however, normally occur only toward the tip of the leaf, generally only above the leaf's middle. In addition, the fruit of the inkberry is noticeably smaller than that of the large sweet gallberry.

The American holly (*I. opaca*) is probably our best known tree-sized *Ilex* and is normally a medium-sized tree averaging between 5 and 15 m in height. It is also quite attractive, with dark, evergreen, spiny-tipped leaves and smooth, light gray bark. When conditions allow, it grows into a beautifully shaped plant with well-spaced branches that extend perpendicular to the trunk. It is prized for its bright red berries which occur in late fall just in time for Christmas.

The American holly has long been associated with festive decorations and a cheerful spirit. Its lustrous green leaves and shiny red berries have been used extensively to add accent to a room in preparation for the holiday season. Long before the early explorers began to settle the New World, branches from the American holly's English cousin (*I. aquifolia*) were used widely in the British Isles. It is little wonder, then, that the early pioneers would make use of the New World's holly in much the same way.

Our other common tree-sized hollies include the dahoon and the myrtle-leaved holly, both of which prefer wet, but slightly different, habitats. The dahoon is most often associated with the coastal strand and occurs in coastal hammocks and flatwoods depressions across much of the state. Only the extreme lower tip of the Florida peninsula is devoid of the species, which is an interesting phenomenon since the plant has been reported from the West Indies, including Puerto Rico. It has medium-sized entire leaves that are similar in size to the American holly but lack the sharp-pointed lobes. It is not a large tree, perhaps not even exceeding 10 m in height. Its light grey bark and bright red berries make it an unmistakable element of its coastal wetland environment.

Ilex myrtifolia, on the other hand, has narrowly linear leaves. Although closely related to the dahoon, and often overlapping in habitat, it is quite different in appearance from the other holly species and is easily distinguishable. Myrtle-leaved holly occurs in coastal swales, near flatwoods depressions, and in sandy pinelands across much of the northernmost part of the state from the Atlantic coast on the east into southern Alabama on the west.

The tawnyberry or Krug's holly (*I. krugiana*) is one of Florida's least known holly species. A tree of southern hammocks and pinelands, it is found in Florida only in Dade County, and outside of the state sparingly on a few of the Bahama Islands. The tawnyberry is considered a threatened species in Florida due to its limited abundance and because of its association with the endangered south Florida hammock ecosystem.

Four of Florida's hollies are deciduous. The aptly named *Ilex decidua* or possum-haw, the Carolina or sand holly (*I. ambigua*), the sarvis holly (*I. amelanchier*), and the winterberry (*I. verticillata*) all lose their leaves with the onset of cooler weather. With the exception of the possum-haw, the other deciduous hollies are typically shrubs, reaching tree stature only occasionally. In addition, the sarvis holly and winterberry are confined to a relatively small distribution in the northern panhandle. All four of the deciduous hollies can be separated from the evergreen hollies by their membranous rather than leathery leaves and by the presence of leaf scars on wood of the previous season.

The possum-haw is a tree of alluvial floodplains and low woodlands from the westernmost panhandle to just east of the Suwannee River. It is also found in upland woods and thickets within a narrow band that stretches southeastward through parts of Pinellas, Hillsborough, Manatee, Hardee, and DeSoto counties. *Ilex decidua* is a rather common plant in the appropriate habitat and is not particularly difficult to find with a little exploration along the backwoods and drainage basins of the Chattahoochee, Choctawhatchee, Apalachicola, and Ochlockonee rivers.

The range of the Carolina holly, Florida's only other widespread deciduous holly, is somewhat more extensive than that of the possum-haw, reaching nearly as far south as Lake Okeechobee. It is a frequent constituent of sandy upland woods and dry hammocks throughout its range. Carolina holly can be distinguished from the possum-haw by its serrate rather than crenate leaf margins, and from both the winterberry and sarvis holly by its well-drained rather than generally wetland habitat.

The Titis

The titi (pronounced tie-tie) family, or Cyrillaceae, includes trees of the swamps and bays of northern and central Florida as well as the adjacent states along the southeastern coastal plain. The family contains a total of only three genera and 13 species worldwide. The two genera that occur in Florida have but one species each, both of which are common components of their primarily wetland habitats.

In early spring the swamps of the Florida panhandle turn white with the copious blooms of the black titi, or buckwheat tree (*Cliftonia monophylla*). Held erect in short racemes, these flowers give a pronounced fragrance to the bays and branches which they inhabit. The black titi is a thicket-forming tree or shrub that creates dense stands along the edges of the wetter portions of the flatwoods community from about Jefferson County westward. Although its flowers are distinctive, its buckwheatlike fruit probably provides a better means for recognizing the plant. In early summer these winged drupes are a shiny golden-amber in color and hang from the trees in beautiful clusters. More important for identification purposes, the darkened remains of spent fruit persist on the trees year-round, making them a useful distinguishing characteristic.

While the black titi is normally found on the slightly higher edges of the swamps and bays, the swamp cyrilla (*Cyrilla racemiflora*), or simply titi, inhabits the wetter portions. It, too, is a shrubby tree that sometimes forms pure stands.

The watery habitat and lack of sunlight in a titi swamp effectively reduce the ground cover in such places to near nonexistent. Even so, the short, twisted trunks and low-growing foliage of young titi communities make foot travel a challenging adventure. Older stands, however, are more accessible and certainly well worth whatever energy is required to enter them.

Some authors refer to two species of cyrilla. At one time, botanists believed that the swamp cyrilla actually comprised two distinct plants, one with long flower racemes and larger leaves, and one with shorter racemes and small leaves. The consensus today, however, is that the two trees are actually local variations of the same species.

Titi swamps are an integral part of the north Florida flatwoods community. Generally occurring in the wetter areas along the borders of the pinelands, they are an obvious part of the landscape and appear as small islands of green within the open understory of the pineland system. Unlike other members of this fire-dominated ecosystem, titis provide a poor source of fuel and generally act as deterrents to the frequent lightning fires that sweep through such areas. They encircle the edges of the more fire-susceptible bay and cypress swamp vegetation, thus protecting the swamplands from the ravages of fire and allowing the development of magnificent wetland forests dominated by black gum (*Nyssa biflora*), cypress (*Taxodium* spp.), and sweet-bay magnolia (*Magnolia virginiana*).

The titi has an interesting global distribution and growth form. More common in the United States as a wetland species from about Texas eastward and northward to Virginia, the tree is also well known from the mountainous regions of the tropics. In addition, unlike the typically shrubby specimens that are common along the coastal zones of North America, some individuals in the tropics may attain heights approaching 20 m and trunk measurements nearly 2 m in diameter.

The Teas

The Theaceae, or tea family, is composed primarily of tropical and subtropical species, only a few of which are native to North America. This is the same family that includes the horticulturally important camellias as well as the plant from which commercially made tea is produced. Members of the family are well known for their showy flowers and captivating aroma.

The loblolly bay (*Gordonia lasianthus*) is one of Florida's two members of the tea family. When in bloom in early summer it is an exceedingly beautiful tree. The pure white petals of its flowers against its leathery, dark green leaves make a striking combination. It is an evergreen tree of flatwoods depressions and bays across much of northern Florida and southward to about Highlands, Okeechobee, and Martin counties. Two particularly good locations for seeing large specimens of this tree are in the Osceola Natural Area adjacent to Forest Road 235 in the Osceola National Forest, and along the trail from the campground in Highlands Hammock State Park in Highlands County.

The silky-camellia (*Stewartia malacodendron*) is Florida's other representative of the Theaceae. Its existence in Florida is considered threatened, and its distribution is limited to slopes and wooded ravines of the central panhandle. The plant is usually a rather large shrub with several main branches. Occasionally, however, it attains the stature of a small tree.

Like the loblolly bay, it is the silky-camellia's flower that usually attracts attention. Its crinkled, creamy white petals encircle a mass of purple filaments which makes for a beautiful and stunning show during its April and May flowering period.

CHAPTER 7

THE HEATH FAMILY

The heath family (Ericaceae) is composed of over 2000 species, including a wide variety of trees, shrubs, and woody vines. Distributed worldwide in the temperate zones of both the northern and southern hemispheres, this celebrated family is probably best known for such economically valuable and sought-after ornamental species as the rhododendrons, laurels, and blueberries. Perhaps no other collection of plants has such arresting blossoms, attracts more sightseers to southern woodlands, or graces more suburban lawns.

The family Ericaceae encompasses at least ten genera in Florida, only four of which have representatives that take on distinctly treelike proportions. These include the laurels, sourwood, lyonias, and blueberries.

The Laurels

Two members of the laurel genus occur in Florida. Both are confined to the northern portions of the state, but only one reaches tree stature. The mountain laurel (*Kalmia latifolia*) is a rare member of the state's flora and is known primarily from the central panhandle westward. It is often a bushy branched shrub but sometimes expresses itself as a small tree. In the more central parts of its eastern North American range, it sometimes reaches 9 m in height. In its Florida locations, however, it usually does not exceed heights of about 4 m. It may be easily seen at Ponce DeLeon Springs State Recreation Area near Ponce DeLeon, and near the campground at Krul Recreation Area in the Blackwater State Forest.

Like the other members of its genus, the mountain laurel has uniquely structured and exquisitely beautiful flowers that are unlike the inflorescence of any other genus. The petals of the individual flowers are fused together and range in color from white to several shades of pink. The cup-shaped corolla is lined with a ring of red dots that represent ten pockets set among the petals. The anthers are lodged in these tiny depressions and are held under tension in wait for some visiting insect. When an insect trips the filament, the anther springs upward, catapulting the pollen onto its visitor's back to be carried to another flower in need of pollination.

Like all members of the genus, the leaves, flowers, and fruits of the mountain laurel are toxic to humans and domestic animals. Honey made from the plant's nectar exhibits a repulsive odor and acrid taste and has the capacity to induce cramps, vomiting, and a range of other undesirable symptoms. The andromedotoxin in the plant's foliage produces seizures and paralysis in livestock and would likely have similar results if ingested by humans. Native wildlife, however, seem to be unaffected by the plant's toxicity, and white-tailed deer are known to browse heavily on the mountain laurel's thick, evergreen leaves. Needless to say, mountain laurel is not a plant that should be identified by taste.

Sourwood

The sourwood or sorrel tree (*Oxydendrum arboreum*) is the sole representative of its genus. Native only to North America, it is a medium to large tree that is found throughout the southeastern United States generally east of the Mississippi River and south of Pennsylvania. The tree takes it generic name from combining the Greek words oxys, which means sour, and *dendron,* or tree. The name refers to the biting taste of the plant's relatively long, elliptical leaves.

Three distinctive features characterize the sourwood: its flowers, its honey, and its brilliant fall foliage. In early to midsummer, after the blossoms of most trees have all but disappeared, the sourwood sends out long racemes of small, white, urn-shaped flowers that extend well beyond the ends of its leafy branches. Each inflorescence is composed of several individual racemes emanating from a single axis, all of which are typically held in an attractive, drooping, spraylike arrangement which gives it the name lily-of-the-valley-tree, another of its common appellations. The smooth, pleasing taste of the southern Appalachian sourwood honey that is produced from the nectar of these handsome bouquets is legendary.

In addition to bearing appealing flowers, the sourwood is also one of only a handful of Florida trees that display brightly colored autumn leaves. Sparsely scattered in upland woods throughout the northern panhandle, its crimson- to scarlet-tinted foliage makes an obvious contribution to the otherwise drab October forest.

Stagger Bush

Lyonia is a moderately sized genus composed of nearly 50 species worldwide. The stagger bush or rusty lyonia (*L. ferruginea*) is one of only five members of the genus found in the United States, all of which occur in Florida. *L. ferruginea* also occurs in Mexico and the eastern Sierra Madre and is the only member of its genus in North America that regularly reaches tree stature.

Florida's *Lyonia* species are common constituents of the flatwoods, pinelands, and dryish sandhills throughout the northern two-thirds of the state. Several of the species often grow in close association and can sometimes be difficult to distinguish from one another as well as from members of the closely related fetterbushes of the genus *Leucothoe.*

The rusty lyonia is one of three evergreen members of its genus. In its shrubby form, it is most easily confused with *L. fruticosa,* another plant that bears the common name stagger bush. Both are characterized, at least in part of their life cycles, by a dense covering of rust-colored scales that appears on one or both surfaces of their leaves. As the leaves age, these scales generally disappear from the upper surfaces but remain on the lower surfaces as conspicuous rusty to gray pubescence. On *L. ferruginea* the scales are of two sizes; on *L. fruticosa,* the size is uniform for all scales. The two species may be further distinguished by their leaf edges and their methods of flowering. Most leaves of the rusty lyonia are revolute, or rolled under, along their margins, whereas those of *L. fruticosa* are rarely so. In addition, the rusty lyonia bears its flowers from the axils of the previous year's leaves, whereas the flowers of *L. fruti-*

cosa are predominately borne on newly formed twigs. Both species may be separated from *L. lucida,* the only other evergreen species, by the latter's wholly glabrous lower leaf surfaces.

The Blueberries

The blueberry genus (*Vaccinium*) is a somewhat large and taxonomically complex collection of about 150 typically shrubby species. Members of the genus are found throughout the northern hemisphere to about the Arctic Circle as well as in the higher elevations of the tropics. The genus is perhaps best known for the domesticated varieties from which commercially sold blueberries are produced. However, many people in rural areas still associate the genus with the tasty fruits of the numerous wild species that are found throughout North America.

The sparkleberry (*V. arboreum*) is the only North American blueberry that is generally agreed to reach treelike dimensions. Its specific epithet, which derives from the Latin word for tree, suggests the plant's typical form. It is an easily recognized plant that ranges widely across the southeastern United States from southern Missouri and Virginia to eastern Texas. In Florida it extends from the lower west coast northward and is common in dry woodlands throughout much of the state. The sparkleberry is most easily recognized by its twisted trunk and flaking bark that peels off in thin plates, exposing the tree's characteristic reddish color. In spring it produces a profusion of small, showy, campanulate flowers that eventually turn into shiny, black, edible berries. These berries are an important food source for a variety of wildlife from bears, opossums, and raccoons to a host of songbirds.

The deer berry (*V. stamineum*) and highbush blueberry (*V. corymbosum*) are closely related cousins of the sparkleberry. The former probably takes its common name from its attractiveness to the white-tailed deer, which browse on the plant's leaves and twigs as well as its fruits. Most authors characterize the deer berry as a large shrub rather than as a tree because it typically has multiple stems. However, some specimens reach heights approaching 5 m and sometimes display rather large main stems. Such specimens certainly seem to take on treelike proportions. Like the sparkleberry, the deer berry blooms in the spring and produces long-stalked, campanulate flowers. The small flowers are easily recognized by the mass of yellowish stamens that extend well beyond the lip of the corolla.

The highbush blueberries constitute a complex and not easily differentiated group of plants that are not clearly understood. *V. corymbosum* is a highly variable plant that most often expresses itself as a shrub. In the understory of some of northern Florida's woodlands, however, it sometimes grows to proportions that some might call a small tree. It produces edible berries that are relished by native wildlife.

As described here, the species *V. corymbosum* encompasses a rather large number of scientific synonyms. In his extensive investigation of this complex, Vander Kloet (1980) lists more than a dozen species that are included within what he considers to be a single, highly variable highbush blueberry classification. Those familiar with Godfrey's (1988) work on north Florida trees and shrubs will note that he tentatively accepts Vander Kloet's work but excludes *V. elliottii*, which he maintains is easily identifiable in the field. This objection notwithstanding, Vander Kloet is accepted for the purposes of this volume. However, in an attempt to help readers with this confusion, the drawing accompanying the description of highbush blueberry (see p. 175) is more closely representative of what Godfrey (and others) describe as *V. elliottii*, whereas photograph #52 is more representative of the typical description of *V. corymbosum*.

CHAPTER **8**

SAPODILLAS, EBONY, HORSE SUGAR, AND SILVER BELLS

The order Ebenales is a closely related group of trees and shrubs represented by four families in the United States. The order takes its name from the Ebenaceae, or ebonies, which are members of one of the order's best known families. All families in the order are characterized by united flower petals, by the number of stamens generally being two to three times that of the petals, and by minute characteristics of the ovary.

The Ebony Family

The reason for choosing the appellation Ebenaceae to denote the ebony family is somewhat atypical of the conventions normally associated with the selection of plant names. Most family names are derived from the root word of what botanists call the family's type genus. In the case of the Ebenaceae, however, the family name was chosen for the specific epithet of *Diospyros ebenum,* one of the family's more notable species. The hard, black, highly acclaimed heartwood of this important Asiatic tree is well known for its use in manufacturing piano keys.

The genus *Diospyros,* of which the Asian ebonies constitute but a few representatives, includes only one species in North America. The common persimmon (*D. virginiana*) is a predominately southern tree that is found throughout Florida but also occurs sparingly as far north as New England. It is best known in the South for its orange-colored, delicious, sweet-tasting fruit. The fruit, which is sometimes eaten raw, is at its best when fully mature and is often used in the preparation of pies and baked goods. However, unripe fruit, or the fruit of some poorly situated individuals, has an objectionable flavor and should be avoided.

The fruits generally mature near the end of the growing season and are a popular fall food source for wildlife. White-tailed deer, raccoons, rodents, opossum, and a variety of songbirds depend on them for sustenance. These animals play a significant role in distributing the plant's seeds with their droppings.

The Sapodillas

The sapodilla or sapote (pronounced sa-POTE-ee) family (Sapotaceae) encompasses six genera in Florida, most of which are confined to the state's southern counties. Worldwide, the family consists of about 600 species in more than 40 genera, all of which are woody trees or shrubs, and all of which occur primarily in the tropics. Only the genus *Bumelia* is found in the United States outside of peninsular Florida.

The family is well known for several tropical dessert fruits, some of which are cultivated in Florida. The sapodilla (*Manilkara zapota*), marmalade plum (*Pouteria mammosa*), egg fruit (*Pouteria campechiana*), and star apple (*Chrysophyllum cainito*) are all grown in the Keys or the southern peninsula. The sapodilla is the most commonly encountered of these species and is the only one from the above list that will be considered further in this guide.

The genus *Bumelia* is the most wide ranging of the Sapotaceae. Members of the genus are recognized by their relatively small, alternate, tardily deciduous leaves, thorny branches, and variously colored, berrylike fruit.

Six tree-sized bumelias are found in Florida, all of which have rather irregular distributions across the state. Several smaller, shrubby *Bumelia* also occur but are not included here. Florida's six tree-sized species include the Alachua buckthorn (*B. anomala*), saffron plum (*B. celastrina*), gum bumelia (*B. lanuginosa*), buckthorn (*B. lycioides*), smooth bumelia (*B. reclinata*), and tough bumelia (*B. tenax*). Both *B. anomala* and *B. lycioides* are considered rare in the state. The former is known primarily from a few sinkholes in the Gainesville area, although it has also been reported to occur in several other places. The latter occurs in three well-separated locations in the central panhandle. Tips for identifying all of Florida's Bumelia species are included in Part II.

The satin leaf (*Chrysophyllum oliviforme*) is the only member of its genus native to Florida. It is an attractive member of the tropical hammock community and is common only in the southern peninsula and the Keys. The satin leaf takes its common name from the dense covering of soft, brown hairs which give the undersurfaces of its leaves a distinctly satinlike feel. Its handsome foliage coupled with its small, edible, olivelike fruit have made it a popular south Florida ornamental.

At first glance the satin leaf might appear to be a diseased or dying tree. On most specimens, both upper and lower leaf surfaces can be seen simultaneously from one vantage. From a distance, the brown-colored lower surfaces contrast sharply with the shiny green upper surfaces, making the less colorful of the two appear dead. In addition, the leaves of the satin leaf often hang downward from the branch, giving the appearance that they are about ready to fall.

Willow bustic, or simply bustic (*Dipholis salicifolia*), is another south Florida hammock species with drooping, shiny green leaves. It is one of about 14 species in its genus and the only one found in Florida. The remaining species are confined to the tropics and are found predominately in the Greater Antilles. Willow bustic is most easily recognized by the clusters of numerous small, white, fragrant flowers and resulting small, black fruits that are typically borne along leafless portions of the branches. Although the willow bustic would be difficult to confuse with any of Florida's *Bumelia* species, the close relationship between these genera has led to speculation about whether the species should be placed in the same genus.

The genus *Manilkara* includes about 85 tropical trees and shrubs. The genus is probably best known for the sweet-tasting fruits produced by several of its constituent species. However, at least a few species are also exploited for their hard, strong lumber. Only two members of the genus inhabit southern Florida, one of which is native to the state, the other introduced for cultivation. Wild dilly (*M. bahamensis*), the native species, is a natural component of coastal hammocks. It occurs sparingly in the extreme southern peninsula but is far more common in the Keys. The sapodilla (*M. za-*

pota) is native to Mexico and Central America and was introduced into Florida as a fruit crop. It is quite hardy in southern Florida and is sometimes found at the edges of hammocks and in old fields of the Everglades and the Keys. The tree is famous for its chicle, or condensed latex, which is taken from trees in Guatemala, Honduras, and the Yucatan Peninsula and used in the manufacture of chewing gum. In Florida, both species are known for their large, brown, fleshy, edible fruit.

Mastic (*Mastichodendron foetidissimum*) is the only other native member of Florida's Sapotaceae. Like many of its relatives, it is a tree of the Keys and southern peninsula and is a common component of tropical hardwood hammocks. Its long-petioled, wavy-edged, yellowish leaves, and yellow, olive-shaped fruit are distinctive characteristics.

Silverbells and Snowbells

The silverbells and snowbells are diminutive, understory trees and shrubs that are confined almost exclusively to the northern part of the state. Both genera are members of the Styracaceae, or storax family, and are represented in Florida by four quite charming species. The two genera may be most easily differentiated by shaving off the outer covering of a twig to expose its pith. In *Halesia* the pith is diaphragmed and chambered; in *Styrax* it is continuous like a drinking straw.

Florida has two silverbells, both of which commonly take the form of small, attractive trees. The genus's common name comes from the characteristic shape of the handsome, bell-like flowers that adorn many of its representative species. The two-winged silverbell (*Halesia diptera*) has both the larger leaves and the larger flowers of the two and takes the first part of its common name from the flattened, two-winged fruit that hangs from the branches in drooping clusters. It is a well-defined species that ranges across much of southern Georgia, Alabama, and Louisiana as well as eastern Texas and northern Florida.

The little silverbell (*H. carolina*) is a smaller, somewhat more dainty tree than its larger cousin. It, too, has the beautiful, white flowers characteristic of the genus. Unlike the two-winged silverbell, the taxonomic placement of the little silverbell has not been precise. Some authors still refer to the species as *H. parviflora,* others as *H. tetraptera*. It is generally accepted that the former name is synonymous with *H. carolina* and should no longer be used to denote the plant. *H. tetraptera* is now recognized as a distinctly separate, though very similar, species whose native range is outside of Florida.

Two species represent the snowbells in northern Florida. The American snowbell (*Styrax americanum*) is the more wide ranging of the two, reaching at least as far south as Charlotte County along the Gulf Coast, less far in the central peninsula and along the east coast. The big-leaf snowbell (*S. grandifolia*) is found only from about the Ochlockonee River westward. Both are commonly shrub-sized species that have striking white flowers. The blossoms of the American snowbell are particularly charming. The thin, reflexed petals curve back over the flower base, leaving an attractive mass of yellowish stamens protruding from the star-shaped corolla.

The Sweetleaf Family

The common sweetleaf (*Symplocos tinctoria*) is the United States' only member of the Symplocaceae. The family has only one genus with about 300 species, most of which range in the warmer parts of America, Asia, and Australia. *S. tinctoria* is often referred to as horse sugar because its sweet-tasting leaves are a favorite food of horses, cattle, and white-tailed deer.

Horse sugar is a wide-ranging species in the eastern United States and is found from Delaware southward to Florida and westward to Texas and Oklahoma. In Florida, it occurs primarily in the sandhills, flatwoods, and hammocks of the northernmost counties. Its creamy yellow flowers appear in early spring and make it an attractive and conspicuous associate of the pines, tupelos, bays, and magnolias.

CHAPTER 9

MYRSINES, GARCINIAS, AND JOEWOOD

With one exception, the myrsines, garcinias, and joewood are south Florida species that are most commonly found in hammocks, pinelands, and coastal scrub. The myrsines and joewood are representatives of the small order Primulales, a group that includes a selection of woody tropical plants as well as a variety of temperate herbaceous species. The garcinias compose a somewhat larger family of about 50 genera and perhaps 900 species of the tropics and subtropics. None of the members of these families are particularly important economically, except a few that are occasionally used as ornamentals.

Myrsines

The Myrsinaceae are composed of more than 1000 species in over 30 genera worldwide. Only the marlberry (*Ardisia escallonioides*) and the myrsine, or rapanea (*Myrsine floridana*), occur in Florida. Both are confined predominately to the southern parts of the state and are common components of tropical hammocks and the edges of the pinelands.

The marlberry is a shrub or small tree that normally does not exceed about 3 m in height, although heights of 7 m are known. In addition to its presence in south Florida, it is abundant in Cuba and the Bahamas and is also known from Mexico and Central America. It is an attractive species that is equally showy in flower or fruit. In bloom, the marlberry exhibits a dense, conspicuous cluster of white, fragrant flowers that arise from the ends of leafy branches. In fruit, the flowers are replaced by shiny, black, globose berries that are likely to be found on some plants at almost any time of year.

The Florida myrsine, which is still referred to in some volumes as *Rapanea guianensis* or *R. punctata,* is a widespread species that is distributed throughout tropical America from the West Indies to southern Brazil and Bolivia. Although it occurs in Florida primarily in the southern part of the state, it is also known from limited portions of Levy, Citrus, and Volusia counties. In these latter locations, however, it often dies back during colder winters and is typically found only as a small, shrubby plant growing from the root crowns of diseased trees.

Myrsine most closely resembles the odorless bayberry (*Myrica inodora*), a common wetland species of the panhandle. Both have dark green leaves that are closely clustered near the ends of the branches and rounded, blue-black fruits that often arise along naked portions of the stems. However, the ranges of these two species are well separated geographically, making it impossible to confuse the two in the field.

Garcinias

The Clusiaceae family (also sometimes referred to as the Guttiferae) is represented by only two tree species in Florida, one of which is found in the United States only in northern Florida, the other only in southern Florida. The family takes its name from the characteristic, secretory cavities and canals that are present in the wood and tissues throughout the family.

The St. John's-worts of the genus *Hypericum* constitute a large and complex collection of shrubs and herbs. More than 30 species occur in Florida in a wide assortment of habitats. A number of the St. John's-worts are quite similar in appearance and may be distinguished from each other only by close and diligent observation of the small differences in their leaves, flowers, and bark. The genus is so distinctive and contains so many species that it is sometimes treated as a family.

The sponge-bark hypericum (*Hypericum chapmanii*) is the only member of its genus in Florida that reaches treelike proportions, and even it seldom does so. The plant is endemic to the central panhandle from about Santa Rosa County to the Ochlockonee River and is not found in other parts of the state. Its common name is taken from its soft, corky bark which is spongy to the touch and results from the presence of resin-filled cavities.

The balsam apple (*Clusia rosea*) is a south Florida species that is widely used as an attractive addition to yards, gardens, and roadsides. Some authors suggest that the tree is actually a native species that occurs naturally in hammocks of the Florida Keys. Others believe that its widespread success as an ornamental but relative sparsity in its supposed natural habitat suggests that it is not indigenous to the state. The plant was first reported from Big Pine Key by John Blodgett, a 19th-century botanist who lived in Key West. In the mid-20th century it was also reported from Little Torch Key. Today the plant is not known to grow wild in the Keys, which lends credence to the position that it is not part of our native flora. Whatever the case, *Clusia rosea* is a beautiful and widely planted species that adapts readily to cultivation and enjoys widespread popularity.

C. rosea is also known by the common name autograph tree. This name derives from the tendency of the plant's leaves to retain designs that are scratched into their surfaces. A signature etched in the leaf's outer tissue will hold its shape until the leaf falls with age. It has also been reported that this same character was depended upon by early Spanish visitors to the West Indies who used the leaves of this species as a substitute for playing cards, drawing the designs of the various suits on individual leaf surfaces, then shuffling and dealing them for use in their gambling games.

Joewood

The Theophrastaceae, or Joewood family, is a small family of only four genera and about 60 species. Most members of the family are found in the American tropics and Hawaii. About half of these species fall into the genus *Jacquinia*. This genus includes about 30 shrubs and small trees of which a single species, *J. keyensis,* occurs in the United States only in extreme southern Florida and the Keys. Both the scientific and common names of the genus are in honor of the Austrian botanist Nicholas Joseph Jacquin.

CHAPTER 10

TAMARISKS, PAPAYA, AND CAPER TREES

The tamarisks, papaya, and caper trees exemplify three distinct orders that are sparsely represented in Florida. Only four species are found in the state, all of which are known mostly for their flowers or fruits.

The Caper Family

The Capparaceae, or caper family (sometimes also seen spelled as Capparidaceae), is a collection of nearly 1000 species in over 45 genera that are found mostly in the tropics. The family is probably best known for *Capparis spinosa,* a species native to the Mediterranean region. The flower buds of this spiny deciduous shrub are pickled and sold as capers, a pungent condiment that is used as a garnish or seasoning.

Only two tree-sized members of the caper family occur in the United States, both of which are restricted to the coastal zone of southernmost Florida. The Jamaica caper (*Capparis cynophallophora*) and bay-leaved or limber caper (*C. flexuosa*) are evergreen shrubs that commonly reach treelike proportions only in the Keys. The latter species is often so sprawling that it sometimes appears almost vinelike.

Both of Florida's caper trees have ornate, fragrant flowers characterized by masses of long stamens that extend well beyond the flower petals. In the Jamaica caper the flower petals are white and the stamens purple; in the limber caper the petals are sometimes pinkish in the morning but are clear white by night. The capers are pollinated by night-flying moths, and their flowers open just after dark. The long stamens brush against the moth as it approaches the nectar, and the pollen is then deposited on the stigma of the next plant the moth visits. The moths are attracted to the plants by the strong fragrance of the flowers, which can be detected from a long distance.

Papaya

The papaya (*Carica papaya*) is Florida's only member of the family Caricaceae. It is a soft-wooded, palmlike, evergreen tree that is indigenous to the tropical lowlands of Central America and is thought to have originated in Mexico. Today, it is found in almost all of the world's tropical regions and has become a naturalized addition to Florida's flora. Although most commonly associated with the southern peninsula, it is also found quite far north in the state, but usually not far away from the coastline.

Some botanists do not consider the papaya to be a true tree. Its nonwoody, nearly herbaceous, mostly unbranched trunk is certainly not consistent with conventional definitions. Yet, its height, trunk diameter, and general appearance make it difficult to be judged as anything else. Nevertheless, it is still often regarded as an oversized perennial herb.

The papaya is a fast-growing, short-lived species. It produces fruit in its first year and may reach heights of up to 6 m if left standing to maturity. Under natural conditions, the plant usually doesn't live longer than about 20 years. This is a relatively short life span for a tree but quite long for an herb.

In general form the papaya is palmlike. Its leaves are large, green, deeply incised, and extend on long petioles from the top of the trunk. Its sweet, melonlike fruit is borne among the bases of the petioles, much like the fruit of several members of the palm family. Unlike the palms, the papaya's flowers are tubelike, arise from the leaf axils, and are more showy.

The papaya is best known for its fleshy, berrylike fruit which is borne on short stalks near the tip of the trunk on female trees. The pear-shaped produce is orange at maturity, nutritious, and very tasty, and its juice is used as flavoring in a variety of beverages, dairy products, sherbets, jellies, and baked goods.

All parts of the papaya, but especially the fully matured fruit, contain the enzyme papain, which has the ability to digest proteins and curdle milk. Eating the fruit raw aids in digestion, and the plant has been used medicinally for this purpose. In addition, wrapping raw meat with papaya leaves for several hours, or rubbing meat with the plant's juices, makes tough meat more tender and palatable, much the same as monosodium glutamate.

The Tamarisk Family

The Tamaricaceae is a small group of less than 100 species in four genera. Only the genus *Tamarix* is found in the United States. Most *Tamarix* species are native to Europe, Africa, and Asia, but a few species have become naturalized in North America. Members of the genus are usually used for ornamental purposes, but are sometimes planted as windbreaks in deserts or coastal regions because they are extremely tolerant of salt and drought. Most species have small, alternate, scalelike leaves and white, pink, or rose-colored flowers.

The French tamarisk, or salt-cedar (*Tamarix gallica*), is the only species likely to be found in Florida. It is a spreading shrub or small tree that is found only along coastal regions. It has been reported along beaches in Franklin County but may also extend into northeast Florida from a generally abundant southeast Georgia population. Its long racemes of tiny, pink flowers that appear in summer help in identifying the plant.

CHAPTER 11

WILLOWS AND COTTONWOODS

The willows and cottonwoods belong to the family Salicaceae, a widespread association of mostly temperate and north-temperate trees and shrubs, a few of which are found as far north as the edges of the tundra. There are between 400 and 500 willow, or *Salix,* species worldwide and nearly 50 species in the genus *Populus,* of which the cottonwoods compose only a few representatives. All are characterized by bitter and astringent bark, soft, light wood, and simple, alternate, deciduous leaves. As might be expected, Florida's members of this extensive family are relatively few in number and exist at the southern limits of the family's more generally northern distribution.

The Willows

There are five species of willows in Florida, only four of which reach tree size. Of these five, two are common, two are local in occurrence, and one is quite rare.

On a worldwide basis, the willow trees can be separated into two distinct ecological groupings: those that are considered riparian in habitat and those that are nonriparian. All of Florida's tree-sized species are riparian in nature and are usually found along rivers, in swamps, and in other generally wet places. The small pussy willow (*S. humilis*), Florida's sole shrubby species, is the only one of the state's *Salix* that is sometimes considered nonriparian. However, its preference for drier sites seems restricted to the more northern parts of its rather expansive range. In its Florida stations, it, too, is typically found only in wet places.

Florida's willows are pioneer species that invade newly formed banks along rivers and streams. Their root systems form natural mats along these waterways, helping to control soil erosion and allow other species to take hold on the newly formed ground.

Willows are well-adapted for their work as soil conservers. In addition to being prolific seed producers, whose tiny progeny are often carried great distances by the currents, free-floating willow twigs will themselves root easily in the muddy banks of silt-laden streams. Many of the willows lining our rivers may have found their start as a floating twig.

All of our willows are classed in the genus *Salix,* a term that is derived from two Celtic words meaning near water. This name is quite appropriate since many willows are extremely sensitive to the intensity of moisture in the soil. During droughts they often conserve energy by becoming dormant and may even lose some of their foliage. When rain returns, however, they recapture their normal vitality and once again put out new leaves. Because of this adaptation, they are also one of the most resilient trees after hurricane-produced defoliation.

Correctly identifying the willow trees can require a great deal of diligence. In addition to their often similar habitats, they are also well noted for their highly variable leaves and for their tendency to produce a variety of natural hybrids with a baffling range of intermediate characteristics.

The most common and most easily confused of our willow trees are the coastal plain or Carolina willow (*S. caroliniana*) and the black willow (*S. nigra*). Both of these species are found in moist areas along streams, as well as in swamps and near lakes and ponds. Although these trees are somewhat separated from each other in general geographic distribution, their ranges coincide in a considerable area of overlap in the counties of the central panhandle.

The black willow is a tree of the western panhandle that occurs eastward only to about Taylor and Jefferson counties. The coastal plain willow is more common east of the Apalachicola River and extends all the way to the Atlantic coast and throughout the central and southern peninsula. The leaves of these two trees appear similar in shape and design; both are long and narrow with finely serrated edges. On either side of their area of overlap, members of each of these species can easily be distinguished by the color of the undersurfaces of their leaves. The undersurfaces of the leaves on the coastal plain willow are whitish, whereas those of the black willow are most often green.

Distinguishing between the black and coastal plain willows in their area of overlap, however, is a more difficult task. From about Walton County in the west to Jefferson County in the east, these two species are presumed to hybridize readily and to produce at least two apparent hybrids that sometimes exist alongside trees more typical of individuals of either species. For example, certain trees in this area exhibit strongly glaucous lower leaf surfaces in conjunction with relatively short stipes, or fruit stalks, of about 1.5 mm in length, a length more typical of *S. nigra*. Other specimens, on the other hand, contain the relatively longer stipes that are characteristic of *S. caroliniana* but have leaves with nonglaucous undersurfaces. Suffice it to say that care should be taken when attempting to make a precise identification between these species in this region of the state.

The Florida willow (*S. floridana*) is much easier to identify than either of the previous two species but is much more difficult to find. First reported by A. W. Chapman, an Apalachicola physician and one of the state's earliest and most ardent botanists, the Florida willow may be North America's rarest member of the genus. Endemic to northern and central Florida as well as southern and central Georgia, it is known from only a few locations from Early and Pulaski counties in Georgia to Orange County, Florida. It is most often found as a small tree not exceeding 4 m in height and typically occupies sites in swamps, along streambanks, and on the edges of spring runs. Its leaves are quite different from the two trees discussed above. Although glaucous beneath like the coastal plain willow, the leaves of the Florida willow are broad and oblong to elliptical rather than narrowly lanceolate.

The heart-leaved willow (*S. eriocephala*) is another uncommon member of Florida's willow family. It takes its common name from the minutely cordate bases of its leaves, a characteristic that distinguishes it from all of Florida's other willow species. *S. eriocephala* is a common species in the northeastern United States from about Virginia,

Kentucky, and Missouri northward into southern Canada and throughout New England, but it is found in Florida only near the upper portions of the Apalachicola River in Gadsden and Jackson counties. In addition, its presence in Florida and south Georgia is somewhat disjunct to the rest of its range and is probably the result of the advancing and retreating glaciers of the late Pleistocene and Holocene epochs. As the huge ice sheets moved down the continent, they pushed entire plant communities ahead of them, eventually forcing whole populations far southward of their historical ranges. When the glaciers finally retreated, they left remnants of these communities behind. Those that remain today stand as important reminders of the ever-changing patterns of our native vegetation and as testimony to the geologic processes that have shaped our land.

The Cottonwoods

The cottonwoods are members of the same genus as the poplars and aspens of the far north. Like the willows, they are normally found in wet sites. Unlike the willows, however, cottonwoods become tall, straight trees with massive trunks that are sometimes clear of branches for 20 m. In dense forests the crowns of these trees remain narrow. However, less-constricting conditions allow the crown to spread out and become open.

The eastern cottonwood (*Populus deltoides*) and the swamp cottonwood (*P. heterophylla*), Florida's only two members of the genus, both occur more abundantly in the floodplain woods along the Apalachicola River, though the former can be found sparingly in the more coastal counties as far south as the Brooksville area. Both of these species are large trees with deeply ridged bark. The easiest way to tell them apart is by their leaves. The former has large deltoid-shaped leaves, somewhat truncated or flattened at the base. The leaves of the latter species have rounded or cordate bases and are more blunt tipped. The former also has flattened leafstalks whereas the leafstalks of the latter are oval in cross-section.

Cottonwoods are fast-growing, relatively short-lived trees. It is not unusual for a cottonwood to grow as much as 1 to 2 m per year and to achieve a height of 20 m in less than only two decades. A specimen 50 years old might stand 30 m tall and have a trunk 2 m in diameter. No other North American tree achieves such stature in so short a time.

The cottonwoods flower in the early spring before the leaves come out. Male and female flowers appear on separate trees as pendulous catkins that arise at points between the newly forming leaves. The fruiting capsules are generally mature by mid- to late spring when they burst open and release bounteous quantities of the downy seeds from which the trees take their common names.

In earlier days the cottonwood was well known for its soft, light, but very stiff wood. For many years it has been used in the construction of a variety of crates and boxes that are employed in the shipping industry for the transport of delicate cargo. Even today it is still one of the primary woods used in the fabrication of excelsior, a kind of fine wood shaving used for packing and stuffing.

CHAPTER 12

MALLOWS, BASSWOOD, AND THE PARASOL TREE

The Malvaceae, Tiliaceae, and Sterculiaceae constitute three families of the order Malvales. All are composed of closely related species with a variety of common characteristics. Each, however, has retained its own distinctive nature and special attributes.

Mallows

Members of the Malvaceae, or mallow family, are well known for their prominent, colorful, showy blossoms. Perhaps no other family has so many species with such ornate flowers. The family is represented in Florida by a large number of native and ornamental plants, many of which are herbaceous or woody shrubs. Probably the best known members of the family are found in the *Hibiscus* genus, though some of the family's other genera are equally beautiful when in bloom.

Only three of Florida's Malvaceae regularly reach tree stature. These include the sea hibiscus (*Hibiscus tiliaceus*), the upland cotton (*Gossypium hirsutum*), and the seaside mahoe or portia tree (*Thespesia populnea*).

The sea hibiscus is a shrub or small tree that is found widely throughout the Keys and southernmost Florida. Although there has been some disagreement about whether the sea hibiscus is a native species, it is generally agreed today that the plant originated in Asia and is actually a naturalized addition to the state's flora. The plant is easily propagated from cuttings and is often found near the coast in dense, tall thickets. Its bark is fibrous and has been peeled and used for cordage in some tropical countries, as well as for the manufacture of fish nets, mats, and a coarsely woven cloth. It is often planted as an ornamental for its large, attractive flowers.

Upland cotton is one of the state's rarest plants and is one of only a few endangered species that has become so as the result of intentional human intervention. The plant was once widespread along the hammock–mangrove ecotone of southern Florida and is an ancestor of the southern United State's commercially grown cotton crop. Its demise has resulted from fear of the pink bole worm, an invertebrate that is known to attack and destroy the plant. The insect was found on south Florida's wild cotton in the early 1930s, which led to a U. S. Department of Agriculture initiative designed to eradicate the plant and prevent the worm from spreading northward. However, there is little evidence that this eradication program has had any appreciable impact on anything but the continued existence of the plant itself.

The portia tree is a plant of coastal woods and is generally not found far away from the shore. It is another of Florida's introduced ornamentals and is frequently used as a street tree because of its attractive foliage and large, showy flowers. It originates from India but is pantropical in distribution and is now found widely in southern Florida. Its generic name, *Thespesia,* derives from the Greek word for divine, and the tree is considered sacred in Tahiti; its specific name refers to its poplarlike leaves. In its native range the portia tree has been used for cordage, coffee bags, and paper and rope making; its wood, which is resistant to attack from termites, has been used for fashioning cabinets, boats, houses, and musical instruments. The flowers are reported to be eaten and the fruit has been used medicinally to treat skin sores.

Basswood

The genus *Tilia* is composed of one highly variable species that is distributed widely across the eastern United States. Although the American basswood (*Tilia americana*) is now generally thought to be the only member of the genus in North America, the taxonomy of the complex has been subject to considerable controversy, and the precise number of species and varieties thought to compose the genus has changed often. In the early 1800s, for example, three species were thought to compose the genus. By 1918, however, C. S. Sargent, a well-known American botanist, increased the number of species to 15. By the late 1960s, the number of North American species had again been lowered to only four, including three in the United States and one in Mexico. Since that time, a number of respected botanists have agreed that there is but one species. The latter supposition has been accepted for use here.

Much of the controversy surrounding the classification of basswood stems from minute differences in the plant's leaves. Most authors who have sought to distinguish several species have based their distinctions primarily on the type and amount of pubescence found on the leaf surfaces. Indeed, there is considerable variation. Some plants exhibit copious amounts of stellate hairs on the lower surfaces of their leaves while others have almost none. Some leaves display stellate hairs only; others display predominately single hairs, or a combination of the two. The reason for this variation, however, seems to have more to do with growing conditions than species differentiation.

No matter what the eventual outcome of the taxonomic argument might be, one thing is certain: the American basswood is an extremely attractive understory tree with distinctive leaves and interesting inflorescences.

Parasol Tree

The Sterculiaceae constitutes a primarily tropical and subtropical family of about 1000 species contained within approximately 70 genera. The Chinese parasol tree (*Firmiana simplex*) is the only tree-sized member of the family found in Florida, and even it is not indigenous to the region. As its common name suggests, *F. simplex* is native to an area that encompasses eastern China, western Himalaya, and the Philippines. Its presence in Florida is the result of limited ornamental use. The plant was introduced into the United States during the mid-1700s and has since become naturalized from about South Carolina to Texas.

The Chinese parasol tree is only occasionally encountered in Florida and is limited to the northern part of the state where it is generally found only near dwellings, or closely adjacent to previous plantings. It is most easily recognized by its large, palmately lobed leaves and relatively long petioles. Its flowers appear in early summer and form long, showy clusters that extend from the tips of the branches. The flowers lack petals but have strongly reflexed, ribbonlike sepals that are yellow at first but turn red as the season progresses. The resulting fruit separates into five leaflike sections and takes on the appearance of a whorl of leaves at the tip of the flower stalk. Each of these leaflike structures supports several globular seeds along its margins. Observing an individual plant throughout a growing season can prove an interesting adventure.

CHAPTER **13**

ELMS AND MULBERRIES

The Ulmaceae and Moraceae constitute two closely related families with representatives in many parts of the world. Although probably best known for their namesake trees, the true elms and mulberries, the common names for both families are somewhat misleading because each one also contains a fairly diverse assemblage of plants that are not often associated with either of these genera.

The Elms

The Ulmaceae is a worldwide family of 15 genera and upwards to about 200 species. The family is composed mostly of temperate tree species and encompasses four genera in the United States, all of which are represented in Florida. These genera include *Ulmus*, or the true elms; *Celtis*, which is made up of the hackberries or sugarberries; *Planera*, a monotypic genus that occurs only in the southeastern United States; and *Trema*, one of the family's few tropical genera and the only U.S. member of the family confined strictly to southern Florida.

Fossil data indicate that the Ulmaceae had ancient origins and were once widespread in distribution. The remains of fossilized pollen offers strong evidence that the elms were extant at least as far back as Miocene times, or about 25 million ago. In addition, remarkably intact fossilized elm leaves have been found by researchers excavating an ancient Oregon creekbed. According to researchers Giannasi and Niklas in their 1977 article for *Science* magazine, these antediluvian leaves still retained their greenish color and showed little chemical difference from those species growing in North America today.

R. H. Richens, in his book *Elm*, suggests that the close relationship between several of the Old and New World species probably also indicates that many members of the family may have existed even prior to the continental drift that separated the Americas from the Eurasian mainland. The Wyche elm common in Europe and the British Isles, for example, is included in the same taxonomic assemblage as the slippery elm of eastern North America; and *Ulmus laevis*, a species of central and eastern Europe, is closely associated with our own American elm. All of this suggests a common ancestry that would be difficult to explain if these species had not once occupied the same land mass.

Today, the members of the genus *Ulmus* are some of the best known of American trees. Although often thought of as New England shade trees, several species also occur in the southeast.

Florida has four true elms, the largest of which is *Ulmus americana*. The American elm, as this tree is commonly known, is an associate of floodplain forests and moist woodlands across northern Florida and into the central peninsula. It is one of the last trees to shed its foliage in winter and one of the first to put out flowers in spring. Even in January or early February the beautiful golden leaves of this tree are evident in an otherwise drab winter forest.

In addition to being colorful in winter, the leaves of the American elm are unique among north Florida's deciduous trees and demonstrate the two essential characteristics that, when taken together, separate the elms from nearly all other trees. First, the American elm, like all species of *Ulmus,* has leaves with conspicuously doubly serrated edges, meaning that the larger teeth along the leaf margins each bear somewhat smaller teeth. Second, the leaf blades are always strongly asymmetrical at their bases, and often in the width of the leaf blades on either side of the rachis, or central leaf vein.

The winged or cork elm (*U. alata*) is our other widely distributed elm. This species takes both of its common names from the corky wings that are common on its branchlets. Forming on young twigs, these wings grow rapidly, reaching their full extent before the twig has achieved maturity. As the twigs enlarge, the wings cease to grow in proportion, causing them to be most evident on the younger branches. The leaves of this tree are shorter, more equilateral, and more lanceolate in shape than those of the American elm.

Two of our elms have a limited distribution in Florida. The cedar elm (*U. crassifolia*), for example, is a tree of the Ozarks and is found in Florida only along the banks of the Suwannee River. It is probably the least known elm in the state. Like *U. alata*, it has corky wings on its branchlets. Unlike our other elms, however, it has quite small leaves and distinctly cedarlike bark. The other sparsely distributed elm is the slippery elm (*U. rubra*). It is found only in the most northern portions of the state between Jackson and Jefferson counties.

The non-elm members of the Ulmaceae include the planer tree or water elm (*Planera aquatica*), the hackberries (*Celtis* spp.), and the tremas (*Trema* spp.). Named for German botanist Johann Jacob Planer, the planer tree is the only living representative of its genus. It is an inhabitant of wet riverbanks from about Union, Alachua, and Dixie counties westward and is fairly common along the sloughs and backwaters of the lower Apalachicola River. Its leaves are small, and its trunk is typically divided near the ground into several large branches that do not normally exceed 10 m in height. It typically extends out over the water and is most easily seen from a boat or canoe.

The sugarberry (*Celtis laevigata*) is unique among our Ulmaceae in having mostly entire or widely toothed rather than sharply serrated leaf margins. It is predominantly a southern tree and ranges across all parts of the state except the Keys. Although its grayish bark is smooth on young branches, many older trunks have warty outgrowths that are often aggravated by the work of the yellow-bellied sapsucker. A common misconception is that these industrious birds are searching for food from the tree's cambium. In reality, however, their work is designed to attract insects to the tree by drawing its sap. Once attracted, the hapless bugs become a meal for their avian predator.

In conjunction with the lanceolate-shaped leaves that narrow into what appear to be elongated tips, the warty outgrowths of the sugarberry help in making a positive field identification of the species.

The Georgia or dwarf hackberry (*C. tenuifolia*) is Florida's other member of the genus that reaches tree size. More typically found as a small, scraggly shrub, it seldom exceeds 10 m in height and is found chiefly along the drainage basin of the Apalachicola River and in the northern portions of Holmes and Walton counties. It may be differentiated from the sugarberry by its distinctly ovate rather than lanceolate leaves.

The berries of both the sugarberry and the dwarf hackberry are especially important to wildlife. The fruits of both are small, fleshy, brightly colored, and ripen in the fall. A wide variety of birds as well as raccoons and squirrels use them to store up energy for the winter.

Florida's two *Trema* species both inhabit the southern portions of the state and are part of a fairly small group of plants that are commonly referred to as nettle trees. The Florida trema (*T. micrantha*) is the more widespread of the two. It is found in disturbed places, waste areas, and at the edge of hammocks from about Collier and Broward counties southward and sporadically as far north as the Tampa area along the west coast. It is typically a spreading tree with a light brown trunk and long, slender, and horizontal or slightly drooping branches. The West Indian trema (*T. lamarckiana*) is a more shrubby species and is less common than the Florida trema. Restricted to the Keys and the southernmost tip of the peninsula, it also has much smaller leaves with upper surfaces that are rough to the touch.

The Mulberry Family

The Moraceae, or mulberry family, is a primarily tropical and subtropical collection of about 1000 species in approximately 75 genera worldwide. Four genera are found in Florida. These include the mulberries (*Morus* and *Broussonetia*), the figs (*Ficus*), and the osage-orange or hedge apple (*Maclura pomifera*). All are characterized by variously lobed, alternate leaves and milky sap.

The mulberries are probably the best known of the North American Moraceae. The red mulberry (*Morus rubra*), in particular, enjoys a wide distribution. Extending from New England and the Great Lakes southward, it is found in all parts of Florida with the exception of the southernmost tip of the peninsula and the Keys. It is probably best known throughout its range for the purplish black berries that appear among its branches in early summer. In the North these fruits are a favored treat of children and animals alike and provide an important food source for a variety of songbirds and mammals. In Florida, however, the red mulberry is typically a small, often unnoticed, understory tree of rich woodlands and bottomland forests.

The white mulberry (*M. alba*) is one of the red mulberry's closest relatives. Unlike *M. rubra,* the white mulberry is an introduced species and was brought to the United States long ago in an attempt to establish a North American silk industry. Cultivated in China for thousands of years, the white mulberry is a host tree for the silkmoth and its voracious caterpillar, the silkworm. The worm is highly valued for its silky cocoon and for the fabric that its work helps produce.

The paper mulberry (*Broussonetia papyrifera*) is another of Florida's naturalized species and was originally imported to the United States from Asia in the mid-1700s. The tree's common name comes from its bark, which has been used in making paper as well as tapa, an unwoven cloth of the Pacific Islands produced by first steeping and then beating the tree's inner bark. The paper mulberry is fairly frequent in the northern part of the state, chiefly in disturbed areas and around human habitations.

Two native and several nonnative figs of the genus *Ficus* inhabit the southern peninsula and the Florida Keys. The genus is comprised of about 800 species worldwide, all of which are native to the tropics and subtropics and are most abundant in Polynesia and Indonesia.

One of Florida's most interesting members of the genus is the strangler fig (*Ficus aurea*). Like many of its relatives, the strangler often begins life as an epiphyte in the bark of another tree (though it also grows directly from the ground). As it grows, it sends down roots which eventually anchor the tree to the ground. Eventually, the expanding roots kill the host and become fused into a bizarrely shaped trunk with massive aerial roots that leave the fig as a free-standing member of the forest community.

Finding specimens of the strangler fig is not difficult. Its characteristic, latticelike roots are a common sight in many of south Florida's rockland hammocks and swampy wetlands. Several easy-to-see specimens are evident along the boardwalk in the Fakahatchee Strand State Preserve. In addition to its interesting growth form, its stalkless, fleshy figs also offer a clue to the tree's identity.

The shortleaf fig (*F. citrifolia*) is the other Florida native fig. Although similar in appearance to the strangler fig, its fruits are held at the end of relatively long stalks, unlike the sessile fruits of the strangler. In addition, the shortleaf sometimes produces numerous hanging aerial roots that, when present, are unmistakable. However, the latter appendages are also well known from several of south Florida's nonnative figs and should not be used for identification of *F. citrifolia*. The shortleaf fig is not as common as the strangler but is usually found in similar habitats.

The common fig (*F. carica*) is an imported species that is grown commercially in Florida's southern counties. It sometimes persists along roadsides and in disturbed places, but is not widely distributed. This is the ancient fig mentioned often in the early chapters of The Bible. Its specific name refers to Caria, an ancient country in Asia Minor, a region of the world that is noted for its antiquity. Thought to be a native of this region, the common fig's fruits are seedless, very tasty, and probably served as a staple food for much of the ancient civilized world. Unlike the two native figs considered above, its leaves are large and deeply incised into 3 - 5 lobes, each lobe with its own central vein.

The osage-orange or hedge apple (*Maclura pomifera*) is another of Florida's members of the mulberry family. Named for American geologist William Maclure as well as for its orangelike pome, it is the only member of its genus and has been widely used for a variety of purposes.

The osage-orange's original range is subject to a bit of controversy. Some maintain that its native habitat was initially a narrow zone of open land just west of the east Texas pine–hardwood forests. Others say it originated in the Red River Valley of Oklahoma and naturally extended into Arkansas and Mississippi. Whichever is the case, today it enjoys a rather expansive geographical distribution across much of eastern North America.

Its current range is not the result of natural phenomena. Long before barbed wire and fence posts separated midwestern cattle territory or hemmed in eastern America's private lands, the osage-orange was touted as an outstanding hedgerow plant, hence the name hedge apple. A fast-growing and sun-tolerant tree, its tightly compact, orange-sized collection of fruits were highly valued for their seeds and were shipped widely for use in planting visible demarcations that helped to control the movement of cattle. Government agriculturists and foresters also encouraged the planting of osage-orange as a protection against the destructive forces of the wind-induced erosion caused by the excessive droughts of the early 1900s. According to Loran Anderson, professor of botany at Florida State University, the fruit has also been used in Kansas basements as a "bug repellent" and would presumably work in Florida as a deterrent to cockroaches and spiders.

CHAPTER **14**

BUCKTHORNS, NIGHTSHADES, AND SPURGE

The families described in this chapter represent three orders of flowering plants that encompass a large number of widely divergent genera and species. Some taxonomists consider the three orders to be at least somewhat related. Others see little relationship among them. Together, they include 15 tree species in Florida, most of which occur in the state's more tropical climes.

The Spurge Family

The Euphorbiaceae, or spurge family, is one of the world's largest and most diverse families of flowering plants. Like many primarily tropical families, the spurge family is best known to temperate plant lovers for its wide variety of herbaceous species. However, it also includes a number of trees and shrubs among its more than 300 genera and nearly 7000 species.

The spurge family takes its common name from the characteristic way in which a number of species distribute their seeds. The fruit of all members of the family is a distinctive three-lobed capsule. As the capsules dry and reach maturity they rupture, sometimes with a discernible popping sound, and hurl the enclosed seeds up to several yards. Leaving such capsules on an indoor table overnight sometimes results in the tiny seeds being scattered widely around the room by morning.

The Euphorbiaceae are also known for an incredibly diverse number of celebrated products, many of which have significant economic value. Various members of the family are noted for such important organic compounds as tung and castor oil, rubber, resins, starch, tapioca, and tannins. The well-known and sought-after Christmas poinsettia is also a member of the spurge family.

There are more than 20 genera and 75 species of Euphorbiaceae represented in Florida. Although most of these are herbaceous or shrubby plants, eight species in seven genera reach tree stature; only five species in four genera are considered native.

The native species include the crabwood (*Ateramnus lucidus*), milkbark (*Drypetes diversifolia*), guiana plum (*D. lateriflora*), manchineel (*Hippomane mancinella*), and maiden bush (*Savia bahamensis*). All are typically south Florida plants that are generally restricted to the southernmost peninsula and the Keys. While most are common and not particularly difficult to find in the appropriate habitat, at least one bears special mention.

The manchineel is now a rare tree in the wild. Once widespread and common in the coastal zone, its bright white sap, which is extremely toxic to the touch, formerly made it the target of human-engineered destruction that reduced its population dramatically. Even a tiny drop of the juicy fluid produces an intense burning sensation in some people and can result in blisterlike sores akin to those resulting from chemical burns. The foliage is also potentially toxic, and ingesting the reportedly pleasant-tasting fruit can cause intense gastric upset. Some even assert that eating the fruit can be lethal. One such account holds that in the late 1800s, 54 German seaman who landed near Curaçao ate the fruit of this tree, resulting in the death of five and severe sickness in the others. Although such claims have not always been clearly substantiated, the tree has been the target of much abuse throughout the tropics, including south Florida, and is now only sparsely scattered throughout the Keys as well as near Flamingo in Everglades National Park. Examples can be seen at John Pennekamp Coral Reef State Park, Bahia Honda State Recreation Area, and at several locations in Key Deer National Wildlife Refuge, all of which are located in the Keys. It is quite attractive and is easily recognized by its alternate, generally ovate leaves with long petioles and finely serrate margins. It is probably wise to refrain from handling specimens of this plant.

In contrast to our native species, Florida's nonnative trees of the spurge family are known primarily from the northern part of the state and include the tung oil tree (*Aleurites fordii*), popcorn tree (*Sapium sebiferum*), and manihot (*Manihot grahamii*). The tung tree is a cultivated species that was originally introduced from China. Today it has escaped and become established in a number of disturbed sites in northern Florida, particularly, but not solely, in Leon and Jefferson counties.

The popcorn or Chinese tallow tree is the other commonly seen introduced member of the family. So named for its fruit, which ruptures and turns white as the leaves fall, it is an attractive and often-used yard and street tree. However, it escapes easily and may become a serious pest. Like many members of its family, the fruit and foliage of this tree are poisonous if ingested.

By contrast, the manihot is a rarely seen tree and is used primarily for decorative landscaping. Its unique leaves, which are deeply incised into 6 to 11 narrow lobes that all emanate from a central point, are very distinctive.

The Buckthorns

The Rhamnaceae constitute a medium-sized family consisting of nearly 60 genera and about 900 species of both tropical and temperate distribution. The northernmost species in the family extend to about 55 degrees north latitude, a line that runs through northern Canada near the southern shores of Hudson Bay. Less than 20 percent of the species found in North America are trees.

The family takes both its common and scientific names from the genus *Rhamnus*, one of its most extensive genera. The buckthorn genus, of which Florida has only one member that reaches tree stature, includes about 150 species that are found on all of the world's continents except Australia and Antarctica. Most are thorny shrubs or small trees. Florida's sole member of the genus, the Carolina buckthorn (*R. caroliniana*), is somewhat atypical in this respect in that its branches are spineless.

Three other genera encompassing five additional species of the Rhamnaceae occur naturally in Florida. All are found only in the southern parts of the state and are known chiefly as part of the hammock community.

Three of these species are members of the nakedwood, or *Colubrina*, genus. The common name of this genus refers to these trees' characteristically flaking bark which leaves their trunks naked. The most common member of the genus in Florida is the soldierwood (*C. elliptica*), an orange-barked tree that takes its common name from the popping sound made by its exploding fruit, a result of the same process described above for the spurge family. The bark of the soldierwood has also been used to produce a popular Puerto Rican drink called mavi, and the leaves have been used medicinally.

The coffee colubrina (*C. arborescens*) is somewhat less common than the soldierwood but similar in appearance. It produces shiny black seeds that have been used in Jamaica to fashion attractive necklaces and other ornamental jewelry. It is most easily distinguished from the soldierwood by its lack of the two small, marginal glands that appear near the base of soldierwood leaves.

The other two species of south Florida's Rhamnaceae are typically shrubby plants, the identities of which are sometimes confused by those just learning Florida's tropical tree flora. The darling plum (*Reynosia septentrionalis*) and black ironwood (*Krugiodendron ferreum*) are tropical hammock plants, both of which have rather small leaves with notched apices. The easiest way to distinguish between the two is to touch their leaves. Those of the ironwood are pliable and soft; those of the darling plum stiff and rigid. The only other hammock species for which these plants might be mistaken are the two species of *Capparis* considered in Chapter 10. However, the leaves of *Capparis* are alternate, while those of *Reynosia* and *Krugiodendron* are opposite.

The wood of the black ironwood weighs about 89 pounds per cubic foot and is considered to be the heaviest wood in the United States. It is so heavy that it sinks in seawater, but it is very strong and is sometimes used to fashion fence posts. It is typically found only in mature hammocks.

The Nightshades

Florida has only one regularly tree-sized member of the Solanaceae, or nightshade family. The potato tree (*Solanum erianthum*) is a south Florida specialty that is known from hammock edges and disturbed sites throughout the state's tropical region. It takes its common name from its relationship to the potato, one of the family's most important and well known members. The family also includes a number of other popular foodstuffs, not least of which are the tomato, pepper, and eggplant.

Two other members of the genus *Solanum* are also found in south Florida, both of which are typically shrubs. Of these two, only the canker-berry or Bahama nightshade (*S. bahamense*) sometimes becomes large enough to approach tree stature. It may be separated from the potato tree by having blue rather than white flower petals and by lacking the woolly hairs that cover the potato tree's petiole and leaf surfaces.

The origin of the name nightshade is somewhat obscure. Some authorities presume that it arose from folk tales that portrayed members of the family as sinister and loving of the night. Others maintain that the name alludes to the narcotic or sleep-producing properties of certain of the family's berrylike fruits. The genus name *Solanum* derives from the Latin word "solamen," which translates as quieting. The family is probably best known in Florida for the several herbaceous species of ground cherry (*Physalis* spp.) and nightshades (*Solanum* spp.), many of which are low-growing plants that produce attractive and interesting inflorescences.

The family also includes one shrubby species that some might consider to be a small tree. Although it does not meet the definition of a tree proposed in this book and is not included in Part II, it would be an oversight to ignore it entirely. The Christmasberry or matrimony vine (*Lycium carolinianum*) is a narrow-leaved species that is typically found along coastal sand spits and back beaches, as well as the edges of salt and brackish marshes throughout the state including the Keys. It is best known for its delicate blue flowers and bright red berries which appear in late fall and winter and are a favorite food source for wintering birds. It is an easy plant to find in southern Florida and often grows in dense thickets, but it is less common in the northern part of the state.

CHAPTER **15**

OLIVES, TALLOWWOOD, AND SPINDLE TREES

The Celastraceae, Olacaceae, and Oleaceae constitute three natural families, each of which is composed of a number of closely related genera. Some taxonomists consider all three to be part of the same order. Others have chosen to separate them into as many as three different orders. The uncertainty of their taxonomic classification notwithstanding, they are presented together here with the recognition that future taxonomists will continue to work out their classification.

The Staff Tree Family

The family Celastraceae is a widely diverse group of plants with supposed affinities to several related families. Depending upon the taxonomic scheme chosen to represent this complex group of dicotyledons, the family may contain up to 60 genera and more than 800 species. At least five genera are represented in Florida, each of which includes only one typically tree-sized member.

The wahoo or burning bush (*Euonymus atropurpureus*) is a northern species with the main part of its range well beyond the confines of Florida. It is typically a shrub that grows in thickets, along streams, and on wooded slopes only in the northern panhandle and is an important wildlife food. Its seeds are eaten by a variety of birds, and its leaves provide browse for white-tailed deer. It is most closely related to the hearts-a-bustin'-with-love or strawberry bush (*E. americanus*), a shrub well known for its strawberrylike pods that open to expose several bright-red seeds.

The other four members of the family are all confined to the more tropical parts of the state. These include the Florida crossopetalum (*Crossopetalum rhacoma*), the false boxwood (*Gyminda latifolia*), the Florida mayten (*Maytenus phyllanthoides*), and the Florida boxwood (*Schaefferia frutescens*). All are hammock or scrub species that are more common in the Keys. However, all but the false boxwood may also be found on the mainland. With the exception of the mayten, all belong to rather small genera, and none are particularly common. In fact, the false boxwood is relatively rare and generally restricted only to the Lower Keys.

The Olax Family

Members of the Olacaceae make up a small family of less than 30 genera and not more than 200 species worldwide. The family is primarily tropical to subtropical in distribution and includes representatives in Africa, Asia, Australia, and India as well as the Americas. Two species in two genera are found in United States, both of which are restricted to southern Florida.

The hog plum or tallowwood (*Ximenia americana*) is the more widespread and common of these two species. It is typically a spreading, scraggly shrub or small tree that is normally associated with the scrub, pineland, and hammock edge communities.

It is also known to reach tree size in the heart of coastal hammocks. Its light-green leaves and sharp spines easily separate this plant from all but the several *Bumelia* species. However, the latter never exhibit the yellow, plumlike fruit of the tallowwood nor the characteristically grooved petiole.

The hog plum is known to be semiparasitic on the roots of other species, a feature common to a number of members of the olax family. Laboratory research indicates that this parasitism is neither host-specific nor a mandatory part of the plant's life cycle. The plant's haustoria (roots that have been modified for parasitism) have been found on several different associated species, and healthy plants without haustoria have also been observed. The attachment of *Ximenia* haustoria to other plants seems to cause no visible loss to the host, nor any particular increase in vigor to the parasite.

The gulf graytwig (*Schoepfia chrysophylloides*) is much less common than the hog plum. It is widely distributed in the West Indies but reaches the northern limit of its range in southernmost Florida where it is known as a tree of the hammocks. It is best known for its clusters of tiny, orange-colored flowers.

The Olive Family

The Oleaceae, or olive family, is composed of about 30 genera and more than 500 species worldwide. Six genera containing about 17 species are found in Florida, but only five of these genera are represented in our tree flora. Of the families considered in this chapter, the olives have presented the most taxonomic controversy. Although the family is generally regarded as a distinct natural grouping, its place within the orders of dicotyledonous plants is much less clear. Members of the family are characterized by opposite leaves that may be either simple or compound. For the northern part of the state, where most of these plants are found, the opposite leaf arrangement alone is enough to quickly narrow the field of possible choices about a particular plant's identity.

The genus *Fraxinus*, which includes all of the world's true ash trees, constitutes one of the olive family's best known genera. It is composed primarily of trees and shrubs and includes more than 60 species worldwide. In North America there are less than 20 members of the genus that regularly reach tree size, about 10 of which are found only in the West. All of Florida's four representatives are trees.

Distinguishing the ash genus in the field is not particularly difficult since it is among a very few genera that include trees with opposite, compound leaves. Distinguishing between individual ash species, however, can be a significant challenge. Some people confuse the ash trees with the hickories since they both have odd-pinnate leaves with relatively large leaflets. However, the leaves of our hickories are always alternate.

With one exception, our ash trees are mainly wetland plants that tend to inhabit floodplains, river swamps, and wet hardwood hammocks. Two of these wetland species are found in Florida only across the northern portion of the state from Duval and Baker counties to the Pensacola area. The other is found across much of Florida to about as far south as the Tamiami Trail.

The white ash (*F. americana*) is our only upland-dwelling member of the genus. It is confined to rich upland woods or well-drained floodplains that are never more than temporarily inundated. It is Florida's largest member of the genus. The white under-surfaces of its leaflets in conjunction with its drier habitat distinguishes this tree from all of our other ashes.

The remaining three ashes include the Carolina or pop ash (*F. caroliniana*), the green ash (*F. pennsylvanica*), and the pumpkin ash (*F. profunda*). All are very similar and extremely difficult to separate. Detailed differences in the leaf stalks and fruits are the most effective means for assigning a particular individual to species. Notes and vi-sual cues about these differences are found in the descriptions and illustrations that are provided in Part II. In addition, for those botanizing in south Florida, the pop ash is the only member of the genus likely to be encountered and should be an easy tree to iden-tify.

The other four genera in the olive family include the fringe tree (*Chionanthus*), the devilwoods (*Osmanthus*), and the privets (*Forestiera* and *Ligustrum*). Of these, the lit-tle fringe tree (*C. virginicus*) is probably the most striking and best known representa-tive, especially when in flower. In early spring this handsome tree puts out masses of fragrant, pendulous flowers, each with four linear, creamy white petals that dangle in the breeze. This striking inflorescence has earned the tree several of its common names, not the least descriptive of which include old-man's-beard and grandsie-gray-beard. The fringe tree is well known across most of the eastern United States and is often used to decorate southern lawns.

At least one, and possibly two, species of devilwood, or wild olive, occur in Florida. *Osmanthus americanus* is the more common of the two and is most notable for its dark purplish, single-stoned, olivelike drupe. It is found in a wide diversity of habitats from sandy woodlands to swamps and hammocks. In addition, some authors recognize a second plant known variously as *O. megacarpa* or *O. americana* var. *megacarpa*. As its species name suggests, this latter plant has larger fruit than the former—generally larger than 2 cm in length as opposed to generally shorter than 1.5 cm. It is frequent in its habitat but is apparently restricted solely to the sand scrub of the central peninsula, southward to about Highlands County. Although both have rather nondescript, ellipti-cal leaves, they are only two of a relatively few species with a similar range that bear such leaves in an opposite arrangement.

Florida's two tree-sized ligustrums are primarily ornamental species that have been imported from Asia. They are often used as hedges or background plants in large gar-dens, but have become sparingly naturalized. They are widely sold and are generally available in commercial nurseries. The wax-leaf ligustrum, or glossy privet (*Ligustrum lucidum*), is a fast-growing species with opposite, dark green leaves and tiny, white, fragrant flowers. It is beautiful in the fall when its hanging clusters of blue-black fruit mature. The Chinese privet (*L. sinense*), has much smaller leaves than the former species but grows to greater heights. It is generally found naturalized near abandoned homesites but may also become established along small stream courses. In these latter situations it can become quite prolific and is often considered to be an objectionable weed.

The genus *Forestiera* encompasses four species in Florida, only three of which are generally agreed to reach treelike proportions. However, the shrubby species, *F. ligustrina,* sometimes exhibits several long, curving main stems that sometimes reach up to about 4 m in length and may also be considered as treelike by at least some observers. As a result, all four species have been included in Part II. Worldwide, the genus is composed of about 20 species that range from Brazil northward through Mexico, the West Indies, and into the southern United States.

CHAPTER **16**

BYRSONIMA, RUES, AND LIGNUM VITAE

The Malpighiaceae, Rutaceae, and Zygophyllaceae encompass seven genera and nearly 20 species of Florida's trees. Only 13 are considered part of our native or naturalized flora. The others are commercially grown plants that sometimes persist in or around regions where they have been previously cultivated.

Byrsonima

The Malpighiaceae is a large, primarily tropical, family that consists of as many as 65 genera and between 700 and 1300 species. It is closely related to the rue and caltrop families, both of which are discussed below, as well as to several other important groups of south Florida plants.

Although several members of the malpighia family have been introduced in Florida and are commonly used for ornamental purposes, the locust berry, or Key byrsonima (*Byrsonima lucida*), is the only member of the family that is considered native to the state. It is part of a small genus that contains about 100 other trees and shrubs.

The locust berry occurs in the pinelands and hammocks of the Everglades and Florida Keys, where it reaches the northern limits of its range. It is another of those plants that typically takes on shrublike proportions in its pineland locations but expresses itself as a tree where it invades the hammocks. *B. lucida* is typically an evergreen shrub with showy flower clusters and globular reddish fruit. It generally blossoms in the spring, and its flowers last for several days. The blooms change from white to pink to red as they mature, making the plant quite attractive. Even so, it is seldom used for ornamental purposes.

The Rue Family

The Rutaceae, or rue family, is a rather large family of about 150 genera and perhaps as many as 1600 species. Sometimes referred to as the citrus family, it is widely distributed in the tropical and temperate regions of the world but is most abundant in tropical America, South Africa, and Australia. Members of the family are distinguished by secretory cavities in their stems, leaves, flowers, and fruits. These cavities contain volatile, aromatic oils and help in differentiating the Rutaceae from such closely related families as the Simaroubaceae, Meliaceae, Zygophyllaceae, and Burseraceae.

Five Rutaceae genera occur in Florida. While a few members of these genera are considered native species, a greater number, and perhaps the better known members of the family, are nonnative additions to the flora of the state's central and southern regions.

Florida's three native genera include *Amyris, Ptelea,* and *Zanthoxylum.* The first of these is purportedly represented by two species in the state, both of which are known by the common name torchwood. This appellation is derived from the plant's resinous wood, which has been used in some parts of its range as a source of fuel. Shoots of both species will burn readily and fragrantly and have also been used for torches.

Two species of torchwood are often listed as part of Florida's tree flora. Both are extremely similar in appearance. The balsam torchwood (*A. balsamifera*) is generally considered to be the more restricted of the two species and is purportedly found primarily in hammocks of the Keys and the lower peninsula, whereas *A. elemifera* is considered more widespread and extends up the eastern coast to about the center of the state. However, according to Dan Austin, professor of biology at Florida Atlantic University, some claim that the presence of balsam torchwood in Florida is questionable and might actually be attributed to a misidentification of *A. elemifera*. Hence, the former species is not included in the field descriptions that make up Part II. *Amyris elemifera* takes its specific epithet from Mexican elemi, a fragrant resin used in the production of both medicine and varnish.

The hop tree or wafer ash (*Ptelea trifoliata*) is a north Florida species with a rather wide distribution beyond the state. In addition to being a native understory tree of calcareous woodlands and rich forested slopes, it is also often sold as an ornamental plant, particularly in those nurseries that specialize in marketing Florida's native flora. It takes both of its common names from its bitter fruit which has sometimes been used in brewing as a substitute for hops. It is also known as stinking ash or skunk bush for its strongly scented foliage.

Five species of *Zanthoxylum* are found in Florida. Three species, including the Biscayne prickly ash (*Z. coriaceum*), wild lime (*Z. fagara*), and yellow heart (*Z. flavum*), are found only in the southern part of the state. The latter is a rare species that occurs solely in the Keys and is the only member of the genus in the state that does not have sharp spines along its branches. The northern prickly ash (*Z. americanum*) is found sparingly in a few locations in northern Florida. It is not a common tree in any part of its range but is more abundant along the central and northern seaboard. Hercules'-club (*Z. clava-herculis*) is the most wide-ranging *Zanthoxylum* species in the state and is found from about Hendry and Palm Beach counties northward. All five of these plants belong to a rather large genus of over 200 species that range mostly in tropical regions of the world. Only a few members of the genus extend into more temperate climes.

The scientific name for the *Zanthoxylum* genus derives from the combination of the Greek words *zanthos*, or yellow, and *xylum*, or wood, because of the color of its lumber. The common name yellowwood is even used for at least one species. A few other species, most notably the northern prickly ash and Hercules'-club, are also known by the common name toothache tree, probably due to their purported folk use in alleviating the pain of toothaches in children. Chewing the bark of these plants tends to deaden the tongue and increase the natural flow of saliva and also has the effect of a mild stimulant.

At least one member of the genus is known best for its wood. Although scarce in most of its range today, the yellow heart once enjoyed considerable commercial importance and was formerly one of Puerto Rico's most important timber exports. Its heartwood is yellow to yellowish brown, hard, fine grained, and highly valued. The wood is quite decorative and is prized in the construction of fine furniture as well as in the production of high-quality paneling and veneer. However, the demand for its wood has had a dramatic and detrimental impact on this tree. In Puerto Rico, for example, the tree was exploited so heavily that even the stumps and roots were removed and shipped to foreign markets. Today this slow-growing tree is not common in any part of its range and is particularly rare in Florida.

Florida's Rutaceae are probably best known for the nonnative members of the genus *Citrus,* a commercially important group of plants that yield such fruits as the orange, lemon, lime, tangerine, and grapefruit. The genus is of Asian origin but is little understood in its native form, probably due to its long history of cultivation and great num-

Table 16-1 Florida's *Citrus* Species

Common Name	Scientific Name
Citron	*Citrus medica*
Grapefruit	*Citrus paradisi*
Lemon	*Citrus limon*
Key Lime	*Citrus aurantifolia*
Sweet Orange	*Citrus sinensis*
Sour Orange	*Citrus aurantium*
Pummello	*Citrus grandis*
Tangerine	*Citrus reticulata*

ber of humanmade hybrids. Estimates of the actual number of natural species assigned to the genus range from as few as 16 to as many as 145.

Two species are currently considered to be part of the state's naturalized flora and are the only species included in Part II. However, other species may sometimes be found scattered along highways, in old fields, or in other disturbed sites. Table 16-1 lists the common and scientific names for all of Florida's citrus species.

The two naturalized *Citrus* species include the sour or seville orange (*C. aurantium*) and the Key lime (*C. aurantifolia*). The seville orange is widespread across much of central and southern Florida and is not difficult to find. Its fruit is acidic and bitter to the taste and has a thick rind and hollow core. The Key lime actually comes from southeastern Asia and is not native to any part of Florida. However, it is naturalized in the Keys and has been made famous by the tart-tasting Key lime pie in which it is the main ingredient.

The mock, or trifoliate, orange (*Poncirus trifoliata*) is the only other tree-sized member of Florida's rues. It is a native of China that was introduced for ornamentation and as grafting stock for citrus. It is a rare species in the state as well as across much of the eastern United States, where it generally persists only from cultivation.

Lignum Vitae

The lignum vitae (*Guaiacum sanctum*) is one of Florida's most unique and interesting trees. Native to the Keys, Bahamas, West Indies, and Central America, it was once more common than it is today. Much of its population has now been decimated by commercial exploitation, and the plant is considered to be an endangered species in Florida.

The lignum vitae's common name literally means "wood of life" and reflects a long-held belief that the tree's timber exhibits powerful medicinal properties. The plant was discovered during the early explorations of the New World. From the beginning of the 1500s large quantities were shipped back to the European continent. For over 200 years the plant was thought to be an effective remedy for venereal disease, and its heartwood became a sought-after product. The wood was sold by the pound for exorbitant prices, making it a lucrative commodity.

The wood of lignum vitae is very dense, very strong, has a heavy resin content, and is extremely resistant to decay and to attack by insects. This unique set of characteristics has made it very useful in applications calling for self-lubricating wood products and immunity to water damage. The wood was used in the early shipbuilding trade for bearings, propeller shafts, pins, hubs, pulleys and a variety of other small parts. Today, it is used in the fabrication of mallets, bowling balls, caster wheels, and other such items.

Guaiacum sanctum is part of the Zygophyllaceae or caltrop family. The family contains about 26 genera and approximately 250 species found chiefly in the warmer, drier regions of the world. The genus *Guaiacum* includes only four or five species distributed widely around the Caribbean basin. The lignum vitae is the only member of the genus found in the United States.

CHAPTER **17**

GUMBO LIMBO, MAHOGANY, QUASSIAS, AND BAY CEDAR

The Burseraceae, Simaroubaceae, Meliaceae, and Surianaceae are closely related families represented by only eight tree species in North America, all of which occur in Florida. Six are known in the United States only from southern Florida; the other two are nonnative species that range more widely across the eastern seaboard. All are unique and easy to recognize in the field.

Gumbo Limbo

The gumbo limbo, or torchwood, family (Burseraceae) is a mostly tropical collection of about 16 genera and 600 species. The family is represented in Florida by only one member. The gumbo limbo, or West Indian birch (*Bursera simaruba*), is native to the West Indies, Mexico, Central America, and northern South America. The northern limits of its range extend into the Florida Keys and the southern peninsula as far north as Pinellas and Brevard counties. It is particularly common in Florida's tropical hammocks but is also planted as an ornamental shade tree on south Florida lawns. The coppery colored trunk of the gumbo limbo is often seen along highways and turnpikes in southern Florida and is an easy tree to recognize, even at highway speed.

Gumbo limbo is easy to propagate. A branch thrust into the ground will take root quickly, in much the same way as the willow trees. As a result, the decaying trunks of fallen trees tend to produce several new individuals to replace the one that was lost. Its rapid growth and ease of propagation has made the gumbo limbo useful as a living fence post in tropical America. The seeds are also spread by birds and the resulting saplings may often be found in open areas near the parent tree.

The name gumbo limbo probably originated from an African phrase which means "slave's birdlime," a reference to a sticky glue made by slaves by boiling the tree's sap. The gluey substance was spread on the branches of trees to catch songbirds. The aromatic sap, which is sometimes called Chibou, Cachibou, or Gomart resin, has also been used medicinally, and in the preparation of incense and varnish.

Bursera simaruba is most easily recognized by its copper-colored bark which commonly exfoliates in thin layers, reminiscent of the birch trees. When taken in combination, the gumbo limbo's characteristic bark and pinnately compound leaves distinguish it from all other south Florida tree species.

Mahogany Family

The Meliaceae, or mahogany family, is composed of about 500 species in 50 genera, most of which are found in the tropical regions of Africa, Asia, Australia, and South America. Only one species in each of two genera occur in the United States.

The true mahoganies of the genus *Swietenia* constitute one of the family's smallest sub-divisions. There are likely only three species worldwide. All three tend to hybridize easily and are distinguished mainly by their geographic distributions and differing ecological requirements. At least two natural hybrids are recognized, and the species are still somewhat poorly defined.

Two species of *Swietenia,* including the one that occurs in Florida, are well known as sources of some of the world's finest timber. Both were discovered by Spanish conquistadors during their wide-ranging explorations of the New World, and both were introduced to the European continent by the early 1700s. The wood was probably first used, and made famous, by the well-known English cabinetmakers Thomas Chippendale and George Hepplewhite.

The precise etymology of the word mahogany is not well understood. Some authors suggest that the present term may have resulted from the corruption of the Jamaican word *Mogano.* Others believe that it may have originated from the Spanish word *Madera,* which literally means wood. Regardless of whether either of these suppositions is correct, the word has little botanical meaning today since it is applied equally to a range of Meliaceae species which often have little in common.

Florida's single true mahogany species (*S. mahagoni*) occurs naturally only in the more elevated hammocks of southern Florida and the Keys. However, it is widely used as a handsome street tree across much of the lower peninsula and is generally not a difficult species to find. Although it has the potential to become a relatively large tree approaching 20 m in height and 1 m in diameter, finding such specimens in the wild is rare. Mahogany Hammock in the Everglades National Park and North Key Largo State Botanical Site in the Florida Keys are two of only a few locations left where one can glimpse this tree in its former grandeur.

The chinaberry (*Melia azedarach*) is Florida's only other member of the Meliaceae. Its specific name, *azedarach,* derives from the Arabic and means free, or noble. The chinaberry is a nonnative species that is found most abundantly in the northern parts of the state but also often escapes from cultivation in peninsular Florida and the Keys. Also known as the Pride of India, purportedly because it is a scared tree in that country, the chinaberry is a fast-growing Asian tree that has been widely planted in the southern United States. It is most prized for its attractive clusters of purplish blue flowers that appear in early summer and for its rounded, yellowish berries that appear in the fall. Although the berries are poisonous to humans and some other mammals, they are relished by a variety of songbirds, who sometimes gorge themselves so heavily that they become temporarily intoxicated from the bitter juice. The leaves have insecticidal properties and have been used to protect stored clothing from insects.

Quassias and Bay Cedar

The quassia family (Simaroubaceae) is closely related to both the rue (see Chapter 16) and gumbo limbo families. The family consists of about 200 species in approximately 30 genera worldwide, most of which occur in the tropics. Only one species in each of three genera is native to southern Florida. A fourth species has been introduced but is found only sparingly in the state's northernmost counties. Some authors also include the bay cedar (*Suriana maritima*) within the Simaroubaceae. Others segregate it into the monotypic family Surianaceae. The latter convention is followed here.

Florida's native Simaroubaceae include the Mexican alvaradoa (*Alvaradoa amorphoides*), the paradise tree (*Simarouba glauca*), and the bitterbush (*Picramnia pentandra*). The nonnative species, commonly referred to as the tree of heaven (*Ailanthus altissima*), appears only sporadically in the northernmost counties of the state. The latter species has been planted widely across much of the southeast but has now become a troublesome weed for many towns and cities because it grows rapidly, spreads easily, and is difficult to eradicate. Ailanthus is the tree referred to in the title of Betty Smith's 1940's novel, *A Tree Grows in Brooklyn.* Smith used the tree's resiliency and hardiness as a metaphor for one of her story's central themes.

The alvaradoa is a rare member of the state's tropical hammock community. It is apparently restricted to the southern peninsula and is not reported from the Keys. The alvaradoa's precise taxonomic classification is somewhat obscure and has been subject to question. It was once placed with the Sapindaceae, or soapberry family (see Chapter 20). More recently, it has been shown to be closest in relationship to the genus *Picramnia* and is now generally considered to be part of the quassia family. Some of its leaves are somewhat similar in appearance to those of the necklace pod (*Sophora tomentosa*), but the two plants may be distinguished by their different habitats as well as by their very different flowers and fruit. Necklace pod is more likely to be found only in coastal scrub or along the edges of coastal hammocks whereas the alvaradoa occurs in the heart of the hammock community as well along its margins.

The paradise tree is a rather small tree of coastal and other high hammocks across southern Florida and the Keys. It is one of only six members of its genus, all of which are native to tropical America. It is a very attractive tree that has been cultivated as a source of oil as well as for its roots, which are said to provide an effective treatment for diarrhea. It is sometimes a dominant in the hammock canopy. It typically blooms in early spring from about February to April and produces a profusion of tiny yellow to cream-colored flowers in showy terminal clusters. Its fruit, which appears quickly after flowering, is a conspicuous oval drupe about 2 cm long that encloses a single, orange-brown, oily seed. The thin, purplish flesh surrounding the seed is an attraction to a variety of birds, and much of the fruit is consumed before ripening. The common name for this species probably resulted from the tree's similarity to a handful of others commonly called "paraiso" in Spanish.

Young specimens of paradise tree may sometimes be mistaken for the bitterbush, another small tree of south Florida hammocks. The bitterbush, too, has leaflets that are sometimes opposite, sometimes alternate, along the rachis. It is distinguished from the paradise tree by usually having nine or fewer leaflets, whereas the latter species usually has leaflets numbering between 10 and 18. The common name of the bitterbush stems from the bitter taste of its foliage, which has been used in Cuba as a remedy for fevers.

The bay cedar is a strictly coastal species found chiefly along beaches, sand dunes, and sandy thickets, and is one of the first plants to colonize newly stabilized beaches. The plant's scientific appellation commemorates the French physician and botanist Joseph Donat Surian. It takes its common name from the slight cedarlike fragrance that emanates from its crushed leaves. Bay cedar is particularly notable for its buoyant fruit which has the capacity to remain vital for long periods while floating with the ocean currents. It is chiefly this factor that accounts for this tree's wide but sporadic distribution along the seashores of both the New and Old World tropics.

CHAPTER 18

BAYBERRIES, CASHEWS, AND CORKWOOD

The Myricaceae, Anacardiaceae, and Leitneriaceae represent three botanical orders. Together, they include ten of Florida's tree species.

The Bayberries

The Myricaceae, or bayberry family, is a small, ancient family of only three genera and about 50, usually aromatic, species. Fossil records date the family to at least the Late Cretaceous period, or about 100 million years ago. Members of the family were apparently more numerous then and their distribution more widespread. Today, the family is composed primarily of trees and shrubs of midtemperate to subtropical distribution. Two genera are represented in the southeastern United States; only one genus with three species is found in Florida.

The wax myrtle or southern bayberry (*Myrica cerifera*), our most common member of this genus, occurs in many situations across the state including flatwoods, titi swamps, upland forests, and secondary woodlands, as well as the edges of saltwater environments. So varied are the habitats in which it thrives that it often seems the most omnipresent of our native flora. Its leaves are narrow at their bases and longer than wide. They are 3 to 15 cm long, irregularly toothed above the middle, and contain brownish orange dots in small depressions scattered across both their upper and lower surfaces.

The bayberry (*M. heterophylla*) is very similar to the wax myrtle in appearance. However, it is more limited in habitat preference and is common in Florida only in wetlands, flatwoods, and titi and bay swamp communities of the northern part of the state. The leaves of this species tend to be wider and less tapered than the wax myrtle, and the leaf lobes less pointed. One diagnostic difference between the two lies in the brownish dots scattered across the leaf surfaces. On the wax myrtle these dots are on both the upper and lower surfaces; on *M. heterophylla,* the dots are usually restricted to the lower surface. The leaves of both species are aromatic when crushed and give off a faint bayberry odor.

Our third member of the genus *Myrica* exhibits neither the fragrant foliage nor the wider range of the other two species. While those above enjoy a rather wide distribution across the southeastern coastal plain from New Jersey southward, the odorless bayberry (*M. inodora*) is limited to and found sparingly in Florida, Louisiana, Alabama, and Mississippi. In the Sunshine State it is restricted exclusively to the panhandle from about Leon and Wakulla counties westward. It, too, is a tree of bay swamps and bogs but is less common than its two relatives. The odorless bayberry has shiny green leaves with smooth edges and gray, smooth bark. The distinctive fruit of the species is black, round, less than 7 mm in diameter, and is covered with raised dots that give it a sandpapery appearance.

The wax myrtles are well-known species with a long history of popular and practical uses. Early colonists gathered the berries of these common plants and melted down their waxy coatings to produce delicate but fragrant candles. Today, the southern wax myrtle is often seen cultivated as a hedge along suburban lot lines.

Although bayberries most often grow as shrubs, they have the potential to become small trees, and specimens as tall as 13 m are known. Many of Florida's plants, however, do not exceed 6 m in height.

The Cashews

The Anacardiaceae, or cashew family, is well known for a large number of species with significant commercial value. The family is an important source of nuts, including the cashew and pistachio; of fruits, including the mango; and a host of other products such as dyes, lacquers, tannins, waxes, resins, varnishes, and timber.

In addition, the family is also well known for its numerous species with poisonous qualities. The most famous of these are probably poison ivy (*Toxicodendron radicans*), poison oak (*T. toxicarium*), and poison sumac (*T. vernix*). However, the family also includes south Florida's poisonwood (*Metopium toxiferum*), and mango (*Mangifera indica*). Even the rind of the mango causes a contact dermatitis in some individuals, and many people must have the fruit washed and peeled by someone who is not susceptible to the poison. It is known that many of the mango's wild relatives, which are commonly cultivated in Malaysia, are definitely poisonous.

Six tree-sized Anacardiaceae species in five genera occur in Florida. Only four of these are native to the state.

Three species in two genera bear the common name sumac. The winged, or shining, sumac (*Rhus copallina*) is the most widespread of the three and is found throughout the state, with the exception of the Keys. It is a fast-growing species that volunteers readily in a variety of circumstances, including suburban lawns and woodlands. It is most often recognized by the dense, conspicuous, terminal clusters of dark red fruit that matures in late summer and early fall. The plant is also an important wildlife food for a variety of animals. The fruits are consumed by a host of bird species, the leaves are savored by white-tailed deer, and the bark and branchlets are eaten by rabbits. It is most easily distinguished by its compound leaf with a winged rachis and its leaflets numbering more than nine.

The smooth sumac (*R. glabra*) is a close relative of the shining sumac. It, too, has compound leaves but lacks the winged rachis. The smooth sumac is found only in the central panhandle and, like its relative above, is a favored food of wildlife.

The poison sumac is the third Florida species referred to as sumac. It, too, was once assigned to the genus *Rhus* but, like its close relatives, poison oak and poison ivy, has been assigned to the genus *Toxicodendron*. Unlike the other sumacs, the poison sumac has white, waxy fruit rather than red fruit. It is generally distributed widely over the eastern United States but is found sparingly in Florida only in the northern panhandle and northeastern part of the state. It is another important wildlife food, but the oils that exude from all parts of the plant can cause a severe rash in humans.

The poisonwood is the only other tree-sized member of the Anacardiaceae that is native to Florida. As both its common name and specific epithet suggest, it is also poisonous. Like many members of its family, the toxic properties of its leaves and wood seem to be selective. Not all who come in contact with the tree experience symptoms. For those who are allergic, however, contact with any part of the plant can result in severe repercussions.

Like several other plants that are toxic to humans, the poisonwood does not appear to be detrimental to wildlife. This is particularly true for the white-crowned pigeon, a threatened species that is found in the Florida Keys. White-crowned pigeons thrive on the poisonwood's orange drupes and are highly dependent on the health and longevity of the hammocks in which these handsome trees grow.

The two nonnative members of the cashew family include the well-known and highly delectable mango as well as the extremely weedy Brazilian pepper (*Schinus terebinthifolius*). The former is an exotic tree that is cultivated in southern and south-central Florida as a fruit crop and shade tree. As with most commercialized fruit trees, there are now a number of mango varieties. The mango, which is thought to have been cultivated for over 4,000 years, probably originated in India and was a sacred tree to the Buddhists and Hindus. It was imported into Brazil in the 16th century and then spread to other parts of the American tropics. The dense foliage of narrow, sharp-pointed, deep green leaves and the attractive reds, yellows, and greens of its large and conspicuous fruits are often seen in many south Florida yards and fields.

The Brazilian pepper is a shrub or small tree that is native to Brazil but has been widely planted in southern Florida. Its genus name derives from the Greek word for the mastic tree and its specific epithet, *terebinthifolius,* refers to the turpentine odor of its foliage. It is an attractive plant for ornamental purposes and produces its bright red berries most spectacularly near the Christmas season. It was officially introduced to Florida by the U. S. Department of Agriculture in 1898 and was propagated and distributed widely. Since then, the Brazilian pepper has taken well to the southern and south-central peninsula where it forms nearly impenetrable thickets and has become a troublesome weed that threatens the state's native flora and fauna. Although the plant is a threat to all of south Florida's plant communities, it is particularly detrimental to the flatwoods, hammocks, and landward edge of the mangrove fringe. The fruit is relished by mockingbirds, robins, and cedar waxwings. A not insignificant portion of the pepper's rapid expansion can be attributed to the droppings of these birds. It does well in full sun and is extremely difficult to eradicate once established. The bark of larger trees is furrowed and often resembles the bark of mature specimens of the Carolina willow (*Salix caroliniana*).

Corkwood

The corkwood (*Leitneria floridana*) is one of Florida's more unique and interesting species. It is the only existing member of the family Leitneriaceae which is considered by most taxonomists to be the only existing family of the order Leitneriales. Fossil evidence indicates that the species may have once been found in Siberia and western

Russia. Today, however, it is confined entirely to several widely separated sites in the eastern and southeastern United States, including locations in southeastern Missouri, eastern Arkansas, southeastern Texas, and southern Georgia. In Florida, the plant seems to be restricted to only four locales: streams and estuaries associated with the lower Apalachicola River, the marshy edges of hammocks on St. Vincent Island and Cape St. George, sawgrass marshes in the St. Marks National Wildlife Refuge, and along the edges of the Waccasassa River in Levy County. Each of these populations is limited in extent and not easily visited.

The plant's common name comes from the use of its extremely lightweight wood in the fabrication of floats for fishing nets. It typically flourishes best along the edges of muddy rivers and their associated sawgrass marshes, an attribute which, no doubt, led to its use in the fishing industry. With the possible exception of *Stillingia aquatica*, a shrub which is also commonly referred to as corkwood, *Leitneria floridana* has, perhaps, the lightest wood of any species in the state.

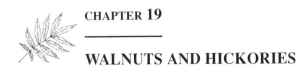

CHAPTER **19**

WALNUTS AND HICKORIES

The walnuts and hickories of the family Juglandaceae are important American trees that are well known for the commercial value of their wood and fruits. The lumber of both genera has long been respected for its beautiful grain and outstanding durability, and the value of the genera's tasty nuts has been recognized since the New World's earliest days. Historical accounts of colonial nutting parties indicate that the fruits of at least some of the hickories and walnuts were often collected and highly prized for their oily, sweet kernels. The fruit of the walnut is still used as a flavoring for commercially produced ice cream.

The Walnuts

There are about 20 species of walnuts in the world. Six species occur in the United States; only one in Florida. The walnuts are members of the genus *Juglans.* The name is derived from combining the words *Jovis glans,* an ancient Latin phrase which literally means "Jupiter's acorn" and reflects the historical name for the Persian walnut, *J. regia.* It is a name that obviously refers to the tree's distinctive nut.

The black walnut (*J. nigra*) is a potentially huge tree that is found widely across eastern North America. Historically, specimens were known to approach 2 m in diameter and reach heights of up to 50 m. However, few individuals reach such dimensions today, and no such trees are found in Florida's rather limited population.

The wood of the black walnut has been a favorite of cabinetmakers and furniture builders. In earlier times, when the tree was more plentiful, American colonists used solid walnut lumber to fashion a wide assortment of household furniture. Today, however, the tree is much less abundant, and its wood is more often made into a high-quality veneer used to cover woods of lesser quality and to display the fine-grained beauty of a highly polished walnut finish.

In its restricted range in the north-central panhandle, the black walnut can be confused with few other trees. It's alternate, pinnately compound leaves with many leaflets bear a resemblance only to the pecan and water hickory. However, the thick, deeply furrowed bark found on a mature black walnut distinguishes it from either of these latter species.

The Hickories

Hickories are large, handsome trees that range widely across the eastern United States. Collectively they are assigned to the genus *Carya,* which comes from a Greek word meaning walnut tree. Their common name probably derives from the English corruption of the Indian word *pocohicora,* a type of oily beverage concocted by native Americans by grinding up hickory nuts in water.

Hickory wood is highly valued for a variety of uses. Its strength and elasticity make it the perfect choice for such high impact tools as hammers, axes, and baseball bats, as well as for crutches, canes, and walking sticks. It is also a good fuel with slow-burning properties and is popularly used in charcoal cookers for smoking a wide assortment of meats.

The hickories are most often confused with the ash trees (*Fraxinus* spp.), although it is quite simple to distinguish the two groups. While both have pinnately compound leaves, meaning that each leaf is composed of several leaflets arranged on opposite sides of a central rachis, the leaf arrangement of each genus is quite different. Hickory leaves (not to be confused with the leaflets comprising each leaf) are arranged alternately with only one leaf borne at each point along the branch. Conversely, the leaves of the ash trees are arranged opposite one another along the branch.

The hickories often pose a significant challenge to field identification. Their bark, leaves, and nuts are quite similar in appearance, and many species overlap in distribution. In addition, they frequently grow to great heights, making access to their characteristic crown leaves difficult, if not impossible. The number of leaflets per leaf, the type of pubescence exhibited on the leaf surfaces, and the way in which the fruit husk splits upon maturing are some of the key features used in separating the species.

The hickories are part of a relatively small genus composed of only about 15 species worldwide. Most are native to eastern North America and southeastern Asia. Fossil evidence indicates that they were also present in the American West during Tertiary times, but they are absent from that region today.

There are seven hickories in Florida, two of which are confined predominantly to the panhandle, and one of which is found only in the white sand scrub of the central portion of the state. Our most widespread members of the genus *Carya* include the pecan tree (*C. illinoensis*), and the water (*C. aquatica*), pignut (*C. glabra*), and mockernut (*C. tomentosa*) hickories.

The pecan is a naturalized addition to north Florida. Its native range, which is somewhat difficult to determine today, appears to have been along the Mississippi River valley from southern Indiana and northern Illinois southward to Alabama, Mississippi, Louisiana, and Texas. It was probably first spread by the American Indians but has since been widely planted throughout the southeast and has become the source of one of the world's most important commercial nut crops. It is normally found in Florida only in fields, in yards, and along roadsides. The tree is easy to identify, even while driving along at highway speeds. Its dark green compound leaves with many leaflets and grayish, scaly bark is unmistakable. It is most similar in appearance to the water hickory but is never found in the same habitat as the latter species.

As its name suggests, the water hickory normally occurs along rivers and on floodplains. Like the pecan, it has scaly, grayish bark and numerous leaflets, the larger of which are found nearest the leaf's point of attachment to the branch. Upon first seeing a water hickory, the uninitiated might think it a pecan. It may be distinguished from the latter by the many tiny hairs that are evident when the lower surfaces of the leaves are examined with a hand lens. It is also not likely to be found in the disturbed uplands that are commonly associated with the pecan.

The leaves of the pignut and mockernut hickories are quite different from those of either the water hickory or pecan tree. Each leaf normally contains only five to seven leaflets, the larger of which are near the terminal end of the rachis. Their bark is gray with furrows that run together, forming a series of diamondlike patterns. Like distinguishing between the pecan and water hickory, the easiest way to separate the pignut from the mockernut is by using a hand lens to examine the leaflets. On the mockernut there is a dense covering of hairs on the petiole and rachis. The undersurface of each leaflet also contains scattered tufts of hairs. This will not be the case on the pignut. Along with at least two non-Florida species, the mockernut and the pignut are the main sources of hickory lumber.

The Florida or scrub hickory (*C. floridana*) is one of Florida's several endemic species. Found nowhere else in the world outside the white sand scrub of the central and southern peninsula, it is apparently adapted to growing only on dry, sandy soils and is a common constituent of the sand pine–evergreen scrub oak community.

The sand (*C. pallida*) and bitternut (*C. cordiformis*) hickories are of restricted occurrence in Florida. Although distributed widely across much of the southeastern United States, both are found in Florida only in sporadic locations within the northern panhandle. The former is a tree of well-drained sands in long leaf pine–scrub oak woodlands; the latter of floodplains, hammocks, and wet woodlands of the Chipola, Apalachicola, and Ochlockonee River drainage basins.

CHAPTER **20**

MAPLES, BUCKEYES, SOAPBERRIES, AND BLADDERNUT

The maples, buckeyes, soapberries, and bladdernuts constitute a closely related collection of distinctively leaved and easily identifiable trees. All have, at one time or other, been considered members of the order Sapindales, though not all are generally classified as such today. Some taxonomists believe that the buckeyes and bladdernuts more properly belong in the order Celastrales along with the hollies. Others think that they are more closely related to Anacardiaceae, Burseraceae, Meliaceae, Rutaceae, and Simaroubaceae, all of which are often thought of as Sapindales. No matter what the eventual outcome of this taxonomic vacillation might be, one thing is certain: all four of these families make up an interesting assemblage of Florida's native tree flora.

The Maples

The genus *Acer,* to which all of Florida's maples belong, is composed of about 150 species worldwide. Most are found in the north temperate zone, but a few are known to extend into the subarctic regions of Europe. The genus was more widely distributed during prehistoric times and was probably common across much of the European continent.

There has been some degree of confusion over just how many types of maple trees occur in Florida, and what scientific names should be applied to them. Although much of the dilemma has now been cleared up, a few of the former specific and subspecific names are still sometimes encountered. According to most authorities, there are actually only four maples in the state: box elder (*Acer negundo*), red maple (*A. rubrum*), silver maple (*A. saccharinum*), and sugar maple (*A. saccharum*).

Of these, the box elder is the only one that does not have simple leaves. Instead, its leaves are pinnately compound with three to five leaflets, each of which is usually recognizable by its generally maplelike shape. The box elder is not a widely known tree and is found in Florida only as a component of floodplains, river hammocks, and ravine slopes within about 50 miles of the coast from the Apalachicola River southeastward to Hernando County.

The most attractive member of Florida's Aceraceae is the aptly named red maple. In spring this tree first produces masses of delicate red flowers that offer the first splashes of color to late winter woodlands. Flowering is quite shortlived but is followed immediately by a profusion of two-winged, scarlet red seeds that hang in clusters from the naked limbs. Even the tips of the newly unfolding leaves are red. *A. rubrum* is our most common member of the maple family, and is a tree of swamps, hammocks, and floodplain woodlands across much of the state from about the Tamiami Trail northward. It also has the distinction of having the greatest continuous range along the east coast of any Florida tree, about 1600 miles from the tip of the state to southern Newfoundland.

The silver and sugar maples are less common in Florida than the red maple and are found only in the northern part of the state. The former is another of those species that has a generally northern distribution and is restricted in Florida to the banks, levees, and bottomlands of the central panhandle's Apalachicola and Choctawhatchee Rivers. It is most easily separated from all other Florida maple species by its deeply lobed leaves, with the terminal lobe being more narrow at its base than its middle. Its common name is taken from the silvery sheen that characterizes the undersurfaces of mature leaves.

The Florida, or southern sugar, maple was once believed to constitute two separate species. One was assigned the scientific name *A. barbatum,* the other *A. leucoderme.* Today, both are considered to be subspecies of *A. saccharum* and are known as the Florida maple (*A. saccharum* subsp. *floridanum*) and the chalk maple (*A. saccharum* subsp. *leucoderme*). Of the two, the Florida maple is the more widely distributed species across northern Florida. The chalk maple is restricted to the Apalachicola and Chipola River drainage areas. Both are characterized by leaves with squarish lobes.

The Buckeyes

The buckeye or horse chestnut family (Hippocastanaceae) is composed of two closely related genera, one of which is found in the north temperate zone, the other only from southern Mexico to northwestern South America. The best known member of the family is probably the Ohio buckeye (*Aesculus glabra*) which ranges from the northern portions of Alabama, Mississippi, and Texas to Iowa, Missouri, southern Michigan, and eastern Pennsylvania. However, several additional tree-sized buckeye species are native to the continental United States and another, the horse chestnut (*A. hippocastanum*), was introduced in colonial times and has become an oft-used and now naturalized ornamental.

Florida's only member of the genus is the red buckeye (*A. pavia*), a delicate and attractive tree confined in Florida almost entirely to the northern part of the state. Like all members of the genus, the red buckeye is distinguishable by its palmately compound leaves with five leaflets. It is the only tree in the state with such foliage.

The red buckeye takes its common name from the combination of its striking inflorescence and hard, reddish brown seeds. In the first throes of spring, sometimes even as early as mid-February, the plant produces a showy panicle of scarlet red, tubular flowers that are especially conspicuous in the dim light of a mature forest understory. The complete flowering appendage is held upright at the tip of the developing central stem. Later in the season the flowers give way to a large brownish capsule that eventually splits to expose the several kernellike seeds.

The Soapberries

The Sapindaceae, or soapberry family, is a large family of about 150 genera and 2000 species. It is most widely represented in the tropical and subtropical regions of the world.

The common name of the family refers primarily to members of the genus *Sapindus,* a collection of about 13 species, three of which are native to the United States. Both the common and scientific names for the genus refer to the presence of saponin in the soft pulp of the trees' fruits. Solutions made from this pulp produce a lather much like commercially manufactured soap and have been used as detergents in some tropical countries. While the several species of *Sapindus* are most often associated with this attribute, saponins are present in all members of the family.

Two species of soapberries are native to Florida. The Florida soapberry (*S. marginatus*) is a tree of northern Florida, while the tropical, or wingleaf soapberry (*S. saponaria*) is restricted to the state's more tropical, southern counties. There has been some confusion about the difference between these species, and some authorities still consider the two conspecific. However, most consider them as separate species, and this convention is followed here. Since the ranges of these species do not overlap, they are not likely to be confused and are relatively easy to distinguish in the field.

The other four Sapindaceae species that occur in Florida each represent separate genera and are found only in the tropical portions of the state. Two of these species, white ironwood (*Hypelate trifoliata*) and Florida cupania (*Cupania glabra*), are part of the state's listed flora and are not easily found. The other two, inkwood (*Exothea paniculata*) and varnish leaf (*Dodonaea viscosa*), are both more common and more widely distributed.

White ironwood has the distinction of being the sole member of its genus. It occurs mainly in high hammocks of the Florida Keys from about Big Pine Key to Key Largo. A small population is also known from the pinelands of Long Pine Key in the Everglades National Park. This tree is extremely difficult to find and generally occurs in very small populations of only a few trees at a time. Its trifoliate leaves with stalkless leaflets are discriminating field marks.

Cupania is limited in Florida to the Lower Keys and is more restricted in range than the white ironwood. It is most abundant on Big Pine Key but is known from a few adjacent keys as well. The easiest place to find the plant in a natural state is within the confines of the Key Deer National Wildlife Refuge. Otherwise, the plant is a common member of the flora of Jamaica, Cuba, and the West Indies.

Inkwood is a shrub or tree of hammocks and shell mounds from the Keys to as far north as Volusia County. Several specimens are easily found along the nature trails at Hugh Taylor Birch State Recreation Area in Ft. Lauderdale, the Gumbo Limbo Nature Center in Boca Raton, as well as in several hammocks of the Everglades National Park. Its common name may derive either from its sap, which turns black upon exposure to the air, or from its black, berrylike fruits which were once crushed and used as ink. Its pinnately compound leaf with only four leaflets is both unique and diagnostic.

Varnish leaf is an outlier species of a primarily Australian genus. Of the 60 species contained within the genus, all but five are restricted to the Australian continent. The varnish leaf is another of those plants that exhibits different growth forms in different habitats. In the pinelands, as on Long Pine Key in the Everglades National Park, it is typically a low-growing shrub. In the hammocks, however, it takes on the stature of a small tree. There is also evidence that the plant displays several different leaf forms. According to Roger Hammer, those in the pine rocklands of the southern mainland have relatively long, narrow, pointed leaves; those in the Florida Keys have shorter, blunt leaves that often have an indenled leaf tip; and those along the coastal mainland and on sand barrier islands, such as Key Biscayne, have leaves that are much larger than either of the other two populations.

Dodonaea takes its common name from the varnished appearance of its leaves. However, it is most easily recognized by its fruit which consists of a papery, three-winged (or occasionally four-winged) capsule which may be present at nearly any time of year.

Bladdernut

The Staphyleaceae is a small family of about six genera and 25 species. Only the American bladdernut (*Staphylea trifolia*) is native to eastern North America. A single western species, the sierra bladdernut (*S. bolanderi*), occurs in the foothills of northern California's Sierra Nevada.

The American bladdernut is a north Florida species that exists at the extreme southern limits of its range. It is found in Florida only along the upper reaches of the Apalachicola River, a stream that is well known for harboring the southernmost remnants of a typically ice age flora. The main part of the bladdernut's distribution extends from northern Georgia to Minnesota, Wisconsin, and Quebec, with only a few scattered localities in the lower elevations of Mississippi and Alabama.

The common name of the plant derives from its relatively large, bladderlike fruit pods which mature in the fall following a burst of showy spring flowers. The entire fruiting capsule is 3 - 6 cm long, inflated, predominantly egg shaped, and very distinctive.

The bladdernut is a rare component of Florida's flora and is not often encountered by the average tree enthusiast.

CHAPTER 21

BLOLLY, COCKSPUR, SEA GRAPES, AND CACTI

The blolly, cockspur, and sea grapes represent four tree species in two families. All occur in Florida only in the southern peninsula and the Keys and are strictly tropical in distribution. The sole member of the cactus family that reaches treelike proportions is found only in one hammock in the Florida Keys and is listed among Florida's rare and endangered plant species.

The Four-o'clock Family

The Nyctaginaceae, or four-o'clock family, consists of about 30 genera and 300 species worldwide. Most North American members of the family are herbaceous rather than woody, and the family may be best known in Florida for the bougainvillea (*Bougainvillea* spp.), a collection of colorful tropical vines that are used ornamentally in the southern part of the state. However, the family takes its common name from the four-o'clock, or marvel of Peru (*Mirabilis jalapa*), a temperate species that is cultivated for its bright red, tubular flowers. This latter species is quite showy and occurs as a frequent and weedy escape in the southwestern U. S. as well as in scattered localities throughout the southeastern coastal plain. With these two exceptions, however, the family is otherwise of little economic importance.

The blolly (*Guapira discolor*) and cockspur (*Pisonia rotundata*) are Florida's only tree-sized members of the Nyctaginaceae. Both appear quite closely related to each other and have, on at least two occasions, been assigned to the same genus. To complicate matters even further, the blolly has also undergone several transformations in its specific epithet. As a result of this somewhat fitful taxonomic evolution these species have acquired a rather long list of synonymous scientific names, and readers might still see either one referred to differently by different authors. The blolly may be found bearing any one of several scientific names, including *Guapira longifolia, Torrubia longifolia, T. discolor*, and *Pisonia discolor;* and the cockspur is sometimes, though generally only in older publications, referred to as *Torrubia rotundata*.

The blolly is the more widespread of the two. It is a small tree common throughout southern Florida from about Cape Canaveral southward and is not difficult to find. It is most easily recognized by the combination of its opposite to alternate, blunt-tipped, leathery leaves with yellowish and translucent central veins, its yellowish petioles, and its bright red, juicy fruit.

The name blolly derives from the English word loblolly, which refers to thickets growing in moist depressions. Blolly, then, actually means thicket, an apt appellation for this thicket-forming species.

The cockspur is much less common than the blolly and is restricted in Florida to the Lower Keys. It is also found outside of the state in both Cuba and the Bahamas. The plant's common name derives from its sticky seeds which readily attach themselves to birds or mammals, thus using these animals to insure adequate seed dispersal. Although currently limited to an essentially tropical distribution, members of this genus once ranged much farther north. Fossil evidence indicates that at least one, now extinct, species probably flourished in the area of what has become north Florida's Apalachicola River drainage basin. This latter plant appears to have existed near the end of the Oligocene Epoch, or about 25 million years ago, and offers convincing evidence of the radically different environmental circumstances that likely defined Florida's landscape in prehistoric times.

Sea Grapes

Few plants are more closely associated with southern Florida than the sea grape (*Coccoloba uvifera*) and pigeon plum (*C. diversifolia*). Both are members of the Polygonaceae, or buckwheat family, a rather large collection of about 30 genera and 800 species that display an interesting distributional pattern. Those found in the north temperate zones of the world, which include many species in the United States, are mostly nonwoody plants that often exhibit a somewhat weedy nature. Those found in the tropics, on the other hand, are more often woody species and include a number of shrubs and trees. Florida's two species of *Coccoloba* occupy an overlapping zone between these two growth forms and are North America's only two Polygonaceous trees.

The sea grape takes its name from its grapelike fruit. The reddish to purplish berries are eaten raw as well as fashioned into jellies and wines, and are often gathered by spreading a cloth under a fruit-laden tree, then shaking the trunk vigorously. The pigeon plum is also sometimes called the tie-tongue, probably due to the flavor of its fruit. Unlike the sea grape, the fruit of the pigeon plum is full of tannins, has an astringent taste, and is seldom used as food.

In addition to being an important part of our native flora, the Sunshine State's two *Coccoloba* species have also found wide use as ornamental and landscape plants. The sea grape, in particular, has been planted along seashores in many of the world's warmer regions and is prized for its hardiness, orbicular evergreen leaves, and attractive, grapelike pendants of green to reddish fruits.

The first use of *Coccoloba* in cultivation dates back to 1690 when two separate species, one of which was our sea grape, were brought to England by New World explorers. Through the years, a variety of specimens of several species, including both of Florida's representatives, have shown up in greenhouses, arboreta, and botanical gardens around the world. Within the last several decades, *Coccoloba uvifera* has even found use as a low-maintenance potted plant.

Probably nowhere is this genus used more extensively for ornamentation than in southern Florida, where both of our naturally occurring species are widely planted. Throughout the lower peninsula and the Keys, sea grape is often seen gracing lawns as well as decorating shopping centers, roadside medians, and driveway entrances, and the pigeon plum is used regularly to line city streets or provide shading for backyard patios. Although the former is adapted primarily to coastal scrub and the latter to tropical hammocks, both have proven themselves worthy landscape plants that require little care or maintenance.

Cacti

The typical plant enthusiast would certainly not expect to see a member of the Cactaceae included in a book about Florida's trees. Indeed, most of us likely know the native cacti only from the several species of prickly pears (*Opuntia* spp.) that thrive along the state's coastal strip or sandy uplands. Yet, there is one member of the family that is a true tree and meets all the criteria of the definition of a tree used in this book.

The tree cactus (*Cereus robinii*) is a rare member of Florida's flora and is probably most abundant in a single hammock on Big Pine Key. However, it is also known to grow on Long and Matecumbie Keys, and has also been recently discovered on Key Largo. The hammock on Big Pine Key, which is sometimes referred to as "cactus hammock," is located in Key Deer National Wildlife Refuge and is well protected from degradation. Like other members of its genus, *C. robinii* is considered a columnar cactus because its central stem and branches are cylindrical in shape and stand erect like columns. It is closely related to and grows in conjunction with at least two other members of its genus. Of these two, the prickly apple (*C. gracilis* var. *simpsonii*) is most easily confused with the tree cactus. Tips for separating these two species are suggested in Part II.

The lower trunk of the tree cactus is brownish to grayish in color and is similar in appearance to many of Florida's tropical hammock species. The upper trunk, however, leaves no doubt about the tree's family. It is green, succulent, ridged, and copiously covered with clusters of sharp spines. Making one's way safely through a large stand of tree cactus and prickly apples can be a challenging task.

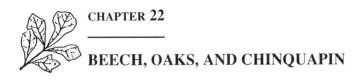

CHAPTER **22**

BEECH, OAKS, AND CHINQUAPIN

The beeches, oaks, and chinquapins are members of the family Fagaceae, a large and broadly distributed assemblage of hardwood trees that are as equally well known for the uses of their wood as for their beauty in the landscape. Worldwide, the family consists of about 8 genera and more than 500 species. The three genera native to Florida are represented by about 30 species, most of which are oak trees.

The American Beech

The American beech (*Fagus grandifolia*) is one of eastern North America's best known and most often recognized trees. It is one of not more than ten species of beech worldwide, and is the only representative of its genus in the United States. It is also one of only two beech trees found outside of the Eurasian continent. The American beech is a tree of rich woodlands and mesic slopes and is generally limited to the northern portions of the state from about Madison and Taylor counties westward. However, several outlier populations are also reported from Alachua and Columbia counties.

Fagus grandifolia is considered one of the three dominant species in the climax community of North America's eastern deciduous forests. Along with the yellow birch (*Betula lutea*) and sugar maple (*Acer saccharum*), the American beech was once distributed widely over the rolling hills and lower mountain slopes of much of the New England countryside and was probably well known to the New World's earliest settlers. Even today, the beech–birch–maple community maintains its status as an important forest-cover type over much of the White and Green Mountains of New Hampshire and Vermont.

In more southern climes, like the sloping ravines and magnificent bluffs of the Florida panhandle, this lush forest community takes on a somewhat different aspect. Although it retains the beech and maple as characteristic species, the maple's importance in the canopy is much reduced and the yellow birch is replaced by the huge flowered southern magnolia (*Magnolia grandiflora*).

The American beech is most easily recognized by its smooth, thin, almost silvery bark in combination with its glossy green leaves with sharply dentate margins. The leaves are particularly distinctive. Each of their 18 to 28 pinnately arranged, laterally ascending veins typically terminates in a marginal tooth. Although this is a feature shared by many members of the Fagaceae, it is most noticeable in the American beech.

The Chinquapin

The sometimes overlooked chinquapin (*Castanea pumila*) is a deciduous shrub or small tree that is closely related to the American beech. Unlike the beech, however, it is a tree of dry sandy soils and is often found as a low shrub on pine–oak ridges and other fire-dominated communities in the northern parts of the state. The chinquapin belongs to the same genus as the well-known American chestnut (*C. dentata*). Fortunately, however, the chinquapin is less susceptible to the blight that has all but eliminated its stately cousin.

The precise taxonomic classification of the chinquapin has, until recently, been subject to a degree of uncertainty. It is quite variable across its range and was previously considered to consist of several different species. As used here, the name *Castanea pumila* includes the synonyms *C. alnifolia, C. floridana,* and *C. ashei.*

As might be expected from the close relationship between these trees, the leaves of the chinquapin are similar to those of the beech, although they are usually more narrow in appearance. Like the beech they have dentate margins and lateral veins that terminate in the marginal teeth. However, differences between the two trees' habitats, sizes, and bark characteristics make them almost impossible to confuse in the field.

The Oaks

The oaks are heavy-wooded trees with furrowed bark and variously shaped, five-ranked leaves that are often borne in clusters near the ends of the branches. They are part of a genus of approximately 500 species and are known primarily from the warm temperate regions of the northern hemisphere. Between 50 and 60 species of oaks are native to the United States and Canada, and the numerous known hybrids only add to the confusion. All of the true oaks are classified in the genus *Quercus* which derives from combining the Celtic words *quer,* or beautiful, and *cuez,* or tree, an apt description for many oak species.

Not surprisingly, Florida's oaks are often thought of as being most characteristic of the northern parts of the state. Indeed, of the 24 species of oaks found in Florida, only one, the live oak (*Q. virginiana*), is found statewide including the Keys. Few others, with the possible exception of the diamond leaf oak (*Q. laurifolia*), extend beyond the south-central peninsula, and several are found only in the state's more northern reaches.

Learning to distinguish Florida's oaks is not an extremely difficult task. Several can be differentiated by leaf shape alone, others by the way in which they grow, some by the type of acorn they produce, and still others by their habitat. One should be cautioned that using leaf shape alone for making a positive identification of an oak tree is not preferred in many cases. The leaves of many oaks are quite variable and sometimes closely resemble those of other species. This is particularly true of leaves found on seedlings, sucker shoots, or poorly situated specimens. In such cases, a combination of factors should be used in making the identification.

The foregoing caution notwithstanding, two of our oaks have distinctive leaf shapes that aid in their identification. The swamp chestnut oak (*Q. michauxii*) is a common inhabitant of floodplains and low woods throughout northern Florida. Its leaves are large, obovate, and have shallowly lobed margins. Its bark is relatively light in color and scaly in appearance and its acorns are quite large, averaging about 4 cm in length.

The only other oak tree that can be confused with the swamp chestnut is the chinquapin or yellow oak (*Q. muehlenbergii*). The leaves of the chinquapin oak are very similar to those of the former species in appearance, but are generally smaller. The mature swamp chestnut exhibits many leaves that are well over 15 cm long. The length of chinquapin leaves, on the other hand, seldom exceeds this measurement. The chinquapin also grows farther up on bluffs than does the swamp chestnut.

There are at least four other oaks characteristic of lowland and floodplain woods. These include the overcup (*Q. lyrata*), diamond leaf (*Q. laurifolia*), willow (*Q. phellos*), and water (*Q. nigra*) oaks. With the exception of the water oak, which occurs in a wide variety of habitats, each of these trees is limited to the lowlands.

The overcup oak takes is name from its acorn, which is almost completely enclosed by its cup. The diamond leaf and willow oaks both take their names from the shape of their leaves, although in neither case do all their leaves justify these names. The diamond leaf is a large tree with a variety of leaf shapes. However, at least some of the leaves on every tree appear rhombic or diamond shaped. The willow oak's leaves are much less variable and are generally lanceolate in shape, resembling the leaves of the willow trees (*Salix* spp.) but being shorter and not exhibiting the finely serrated leaf margins of the latter species.

Some of our oaks are upland trees, occurring either on wooded bluffs, in pine–oak–hickory woods, or in well-drained stands of mixed hardwoods. The southern red oak (*Q. falcata*) is quite common in upland woods. It has dark, deeply ridged bark and conspicuously lobed leaves that are pointed at their tips. Probably the single most distinguishing characteristic of these leaves is their U-shaped base. The southern red oak is often accompanied by the post oak (*Q. stellata*). The latter also has lobed leaves. However, the tips of its lobes are blunt rather than rounded, and often appear even squarish.

The white oak (*Q. alba*) is a large tree of mixed hardwood sites. Its bark is light in color and scaly in appearance. Its leaves are divided into seven to ten narrow lobes and are whitish below. Taken together, these bark and leaf characteristics distinguish *Q. alba* from all other oak species.

The bluff oak (*Q. austrina*), although somewhat less common, is most like the white oak, with similar bark and leaf shapes. However, the undersurfaces of its leaves are green instead of white.

Two other upland oaks with limited distribution are the shumard (*Q. shumardii*) and black oaks (*Q. velutina*). Both of these trees have lobed leaves with bristle tips, the former having both more lobes and more bristles.

As implied previously, the laurel (*Q. hemisphaerica*) and live oaks (*Q. virginiana*) are our two most widely occurring oaks. They are large, handsome trees and are found in many habitats. The live oak occurs in a variety of situations from upland well-drained woods and pine–palmetto flatwoods to the edges of the saltmarsh. Live oaks only reach about 20 m in height but have massive trunks and widespreading crowns. An old live oak may support a trunk that is as much as 2 m in diameter with a crown spread of up to 50 m from drip line to drip line. Typically, live oaks branch quite low so that older trees appear to have short stubby trunks that are only one or 2 m high with several major branches extending into the crown. The leaves of the live oak are stiff and leathery, predominantly oblong in shape, dark green above and grayish below.

The laurel oak occurs from coastal dunes to upland woods across much of northern Florida. It typically has a tall, straight trunk and reaches heights of 20 to 30 m. The leaves are most easily confused with the less widely distributed willow oak mentioned above. However, the leaves of the former are usually widest above their middles, whereas those of the latter are usually widest at their middles.

Several oaks inhabit dry sandy ridges across northern Florida and are often referred to collectively as scrub oaks. These trees and shrubs include the turkey (*Q. laevis*), bluejack (*Q. incana*), sand-post (*Q. margaretta*), running (*Q. pumila*), Chapman (*Q. chapmanii*), myrtle (*Q. myrtifolia*), and sand live (*Q. geminata*) oaks. The first three seem to do well in areas that burn frequently and are often found in mixed communities on sites that are dominated by buff-colored, sandy soils. The running oak is actually a shrub with very thin, leathery leaves. Running oaks occur both in scrub oak territory as well as in the pine flatwoods. The running oak seldom exceeds 1 m in height and is not considered a tree for the purpose of this book.

Three of our oaks are common associates in the evergreen oak scrub of coastal dunes. The sand live oak is probably the most conspicuous. This oak is similar to the live oak, with which it sometimes hybridizes. However, the sand live oak does not attain such large dimensions. Its leaves are quite thick and leathery, often rolling downward on the edges. When a leaf is held upside down in the hand, it has the appearance of an elongated bowl. The upper surface of the sand live oak leaf is often described as rugose-veiny, meaning that it is rough to the touch and that the veins are conspicuously depressed into the leaf surface.

The chief associates of the sand live oak in the dune scrub are the myrtle oak and the Chapman oak. The former is most often a shrub with relatively short, predominately obovate leaves, with rolled-under edges. The latter has slightly larger leaves with flat, wavy edges and more often attains the stature of a small tree than the former species.

CHAPTER **23**

WITCH HAZEL, SYCAMORE, AND BIRCHES

The Hamamelidaceae, Platanaceae, and Betulaceae are loosely related families of two distinctive taxonomic orders. The first two belong to the order Hamamelidales; the latter to the order Fagales. All are composed of primarily temperate to north temperate species that are best known from the North American and European continents. Seven genera, each with a single species, occur in Florida. All are distributed primarily in the northern part of the state or southward to about the central peninsula.

Witch Hazel and Sweetgum

The witch hazel (*Hamamelis virginiana*) and sweetgum (*Liquidambar styraciflua*) are Florida's only two tree-sized members of the family Hamamelidaceae. Both exhibit a number of unique characteristics and are relatively easy to identify.

The sweetgum has the distinction of being one of only a few North American trees that were discovered in the New World by a Florida explorer. In 1528, traveling with de Soto on his Spanish expedition to the land of the flowers, fellow traveler Alvar Nunez Cabeza de Vaca listed the tree among several species that he found on a site near what is now the city of Apalachicola. He was able to recognize this tree, no doubt, by its similarity to the Turkish species of the same genus whose sap was widely used in Europe as perfume and incense, as well as in the treatment of diphtheria.

The genus name of the sweetgum literally means liquid amber and refers to the fragrant, yellowish liquid which exudes from the trunk when the tree is injured. Its common name, too, derives from this sweet-smelling sap. In the Old South, the sweetgum had many uses. Reputed for its medicinal value, it was selected by Confederate doctors as a treatment for dysentery and by mothers as an ointment for their children's sores and skin afflictions. Children also used dried bits of the tree's bitter-tasting rosin as chewing gum.

The sweetgum is an easy tree to recognize. It has rather large, star-shaped, light green, aromatic, five-lobed, deciduous leaves which transform into a beautiful crimson color before falling. The leaves alone are enough to identify the tree. Even in deep winter, when the branches are bare of foliage, the uniquely shaped leaves can usually be found on the ground nearby. The sweetgum's bark is light gray and deeply furrowed between rather narrow ridges, and there are usually a few of the dried, horn-tipped seedballs of the previous year still hanging from the branches.

The witch hazel is a much smaller tree than the sweetgum and more limited in its favored growing conditions. Nevertheless, it is a widely distributed species that ranges from Texas to Florida, across much of the eastern United States, and into the Canadian provinces of Ontario and Nova Scotia.

The common name for witch hazel originated in colonial America and likely resulted from the use of the tree's forked twigs as divining rods, reminiscent of the way hazel was used in England. However, it is for the purported medicinal value of its bark, leaves, and twigs that the plant is probably best known. Home-remedy experts extol the witch hazel for its astringent, hemostatic, and antiinflammatory properties, and cosmetic manufacturers sometimes incorporate its alcoholic extract in the formulation of women's makeup. The plant has been used in the treatment of dysentery, diarrhea, hemorrhages, bruises, and abrasions; and mixtures of witch hazel, bayberry bark, cayenne pepper, and the bark of prickly ash (*Zanthoxylum* spp.) have been used to relieve the discomfort of varicose veins.

The American Sycamore

The American sycamore (*Platanus occidentalis*) ranges from southern Maine to northern Florida, and from the Atlantic coast to Nebraska, Kansas, Oklahoma, and Texas. Along the Mississippi River, in the Ohio Valley, and probably elsewhere in the central parts of its range, it grows to huge proportions. Some individuals in these areas exceed 50 m in height and 13 m in girth, though trees of such dimensions are seldom found today.

The sycamore is sometimes planted as an ornamental in suburban yards. In its natural state, however, it is a tree of floodplains and river bottoms. In northern Florida, which is the only place it occurs in the Sunshine State, it is associated primarily with the low-lying edges of the Escambia, Choctawhatchee, and Apalachicola rivers and is often found as part of the pioneer community that invades newly deposited riverbanks. On these latter sites its chief associates are the willow trees (*Salix* spp.) and river birch (*Betula nigra*).

Platanus occidentalis is a striking tree. Its upper trunk, sometimes as white as the northern birch made famous in the poetry of Robert Frost, often varies sharply from its dappled and multicolored base. The lower bole commonly appears light green, with a mottling of browns, reds, and tans. The uniqueness of this color scheme is due to the sycamore's pattern of growth. As the tree enlarges, it sheds its outer bark in thin, irregular plates, exposing younger bark that has not yet attained its mature coloration, thus leaving a patchwork of contrasting hues.

The deciduous leaves of the sycamore are large and regularly measure as much as 15 cm wide. They are somewhat maplelike in shape, bright green above, ridged along the major veins, and normally have 3 to 5 coarsely toothed lobes. When young, the leaves are woolly with a whitish down that eventually sloughs off leaving the leaf blade smooth.

The Birch Family

The birch family (Betulaceae) consists of six genera and about 150 species. Most are found in the cooler climates of Asia, Europe, and North America, or the mountainous regions of Mexico, Central America, and northern Argentina. They belong to the same botanical order as the beeches and oaks and are generally believed to be rather closely allied with these latter plants. The family is relatively small, but a number of its members are well known and dominant components of temperate forest communities.

The Betulaceae compose a very old family with a fossil record extending at least as far back as the Upper Cretaceous period, or more than 70 million years ago. The origin of the family is not precisely known. Some believe its ancestors to be from the Fagaceae, or oak family; others have suggested that both the oaks and birches might have derived separately from a common ancestor of the order Hamamelidales. In either event, it is clear that all of the family's present-day species reach far back in time to very ancient stock.

Four members of the family inhabit various portions of northern Florida, all of which are classified in different genera. Only one Florida species bears the common name birch.

The river birch (*Betula nigra*) is most common only in that portion of Florida west of the Suwannee River. It is named for its preference for riverbanks and floodplains, and is a major component of the pioneer community that invades newly formed levees along the river's edge.

Betula nigra is easy to identify. Both its leaves and its bark are distinctive. The leaves are 3 - 10 cm long, nearly triangular in shape, and have doubly serrated margins. The bark is papery and scaly, and exfoliates in curly plates reminiscent of the more northern birch trees.

The hazel alder (*Alnus serrulata*) is also a plant of streambanks. It is found scattered throughout northern Florida but is considered common in only a few locations. Along some of the backwater creeks of the lower Apalachicola River, for example, it seems to be one of the most abundant species.

The hazel alder can be recognized at any time of year. In late winter, before the new leaves appear, it produces a profusion of long, yellowish brown catkins that are quite conspicuous. These catkins, or male flowers, first become evident in their early stages in the fall. The female flowers produce tiny "cones" that stand erect and in clusters on the tips of some of the branchlets. There are nearly always a few remnant cones on any given tree at any time of year that help confirm the tree's identity.

Our other two members of the birch family are the American hornbeam or ironwood (*Carpinus caroliniana*) and the eastern hophornbeam (*Ostrya virginiana*). Both of these species have alternate, two-ranked leaves with doubly serrated edges, and both trees sometimes occupy the same site. Their barks, however, are quite different. Ironwood bark is smooth, splotchy gray, and twisting, and often appears to encircle the trunk in long spirals. The bark of the hophornbeam, on the other hand, is brownish, flaky, and shredding. While both of these trees are common in the northwestern portions of the state, only the ironwood is found south of Marion County.

Both the ironwood and the hophornbeam are recognized as wildlife foods. Their seeds, catkins, or buds are eaten by the grey squirrel, turkey, and bobwhite, as well as by a variety of songbirds, and the leaves and stems of both are browsed by white-tailed deer. The ironwood is also sometimes used ornamentally.

CHAPTER **24**

ROSES AND COCO-PLUM

The roses and coco-plums are closely related families of the relatively large botanical order Rosales. This order encompasses about 20 families of flowering plants including the well-known and widely distributed Leguminosae, or bean family. Like the beans, both the roses and coco-plums exhibit rather distinctive familial characteristics that make assigning individual specimens to family a rather simple task. At least for the rose family, however, the high degree of intra-generic similarity that exists for a number of genera makes identifying some species a much more demanding challenge.

The Rose Family

The Rosaceae or rose family is well represented in Florida with a relatively large number of species in four genera. From the relatively uncommon downy serviceberry (*Amelanchier arborea*) to the haws, crabapples, cherries, and plums, these trees are noted for their beautiful white to pink flowers and their rounded, fleshy fruit.

The hawthorns, or haws, of the genus *Crataegus* constitute one of the most confusing groups of trees in eastern North America. Their many species are so closely related, so nearly similar, and hybridize so easily that even professional botanists are not agreed on the actual number of representatives in the genus. By current count, there are nine tree-sized hawthorns represented in Florida. However, they are part of a large and complex collection of plants that is sometimes said to include up to 150 species in North America. As might be imagined, learning to identify the haws can present a significant challenge to the amateur botanist. Many of us will have to be content with knowing these diminutive trees only by genus rather than by species.

The haws are small trees that do not normally exceed 12 m in height. They often have thorny branches, with the thorns usually arising at or near the leaf nodes. The leaves of the haw trees are characteristically small, green, and variously lobed and serrated. The flowers, which appear in early spring just before or with the new leaves, are typically small, white, and bunched together in clusters. The fruits are red, orange, or yellowish, appear in autumn, and sometimes remain on the tree long after the leaves have fallen. These fruits provide food for a wide variety of wildlife including white-tailed deer, raccoons, rabbits, rodents, and foxes.

The only other member of the Rosaceae that might be confused with the haws is the southern crabapple (*Malus angustifolia*). Like the haws, its leaves are small and variously lobed and serrated. However, its flowers are usually pink rather than white, and its fruit is about 2.5 cm broad, much larger than the haws and quite different in appearance. Without flowers or fruit, the easiest method to use in separating this species from *Crataegus* is to examine the thorns. On the crabapple the thorns contain leaves or leaf scars. This is never true of the hawthorns.

Our other members of the rose family include the plums and cherries of the genus

Prunus. Like a number of other Rosaceae, these trees have beautiful white flowers that bloom early in the spring. One of the primary observable differences between the plums and cherries is their method of blooming and fruiting. The flowers and fruits of the cherry trees are borne in racemes, or elongated stalks, whereas those of the plums are borne singly or in small umbels.

There are eight members of this genus found in Florida, only seven of which are native to the state. The only nonnative species is the peach tree (*Prunus persica*), a Eurasian import that is restricted to the northern part of the state. Of the other six species, three are cherries and three are plums.

The rose family is relatively large and quite well known. It encompasses more than 100 genera and over 3,000 species worldwide, many of which are of significant economic importance. Aside from the plums and cherries, the Rosaceae are the source of a number of other foods, including nectarines, apricots, almonds, blackberries, raspberries, strawberries, loquats, quinces, and rose hips. In addition, some rose species have also been used as home remedies for a variety of medical disorders, others in the manufacture of perfumes, and still others as outstanding ornamental and landscape plants.

Coco-plum

The coco-plum family (Chrysobalanaceae) is a mostly tropical collection of 17 genera and more than 400 species. Two genera, each with a single species, are found in the United States. Of these two, only the coco-plum (*Chrysobalanus icaco*) reaches tree stature. The other species is the gopher apple (*Licania michauxii*), a low, clonal shrub distributed from the lower Florida peninsula northward to at least South Carolina, and westward to Louisiana. The Chrysobalanaceae were formerly classified with the Rosaceae but are now considered by most taxonomists to constitute a clearly definable and quite natural family unit.

The coco-plum is an often-seen member of the south Florida flora and has adapted to a variety of growing conditions. It is a natural part of the shrubby vegetation that surrounds alligator holes, but is also found along canals, riverbanks, and roadways, on sandy beaches, and in low hammocks.

The coco-plum's leaves are its most distinctive feature. They are borne in two ranks, but are generally held erect so that they appear to arise solely from the upper side of the supporting branch. They are generally oval to round in shape and are usually notched at the tip, but they can be quite variable in shape and size, even on the same plant. Some taxonomists have used this leaf variation as the basis for splitting the coco-plum into several additional species. However, there is little evidence to support these additional species designations and *Chrysobalanus icaco* is still considered by most workers to be a single, albeit widely variable, species.

Chrysobalanus comes from two Greek words meaning "golden apple"; *icaco* probably derives from the Indian word *hicaco,* which is still used in some places. The appellation is an apt reference to the plant's distinctive fruit, which may be found on the tree at almost any time of year. The rounded drupes range in color from deep purple or black to yellowish or white. They may be up to 5 cm in diameter (although the larger sizes are rare), are very juicy, sweet to the taste, and enclose a single, hard, edible seed. Overall, the fruits resemble tiny plums and have long been used in the production of jellies and preserves, particularly in Venezuela and Colombia. Both the flesh and kernel are also eaten raw; the latter has a faint almondlike taste. The seeds of coco-plum are high in oil content, are relished by wildlife, and are widely scattered by a variety of animals. They are also known to be transported great distances by ocean currents, which may explain why the coco-plum is common in thickets along a number of tropical beaches.

CHAPTER 25

LEGUMES

Most of us know the legumes as variously sized herbaceous plants that provide a variety of common foods. Indeed, they constitute one of the most economically valuable families of plants and also one of the most diverse. Legumes are present on all of the world's continents except Antarctica and encompass about 500 genera and more than 14,000 individual species.

Florida's Genera of Leguminous Trees

At least 40 of North America's indigenous trees are from the legume family, and a large assortment of nonnative varieties have been introduced for ornamental purposes. Of these, at least 24 species in 16 genera now occur in Florida. A large number of these are native to the state; a few, however, are naturalized plants that have escaped from cultivation and are often enjoyed for their showy flowers or edible fruit.

In addition to the 24 leguminous species referenced above, there are many more tree-sized legumes that are used strictly as ornamentals. Most of these are found in the more tropical regions of southern Florida. It is likely that at least some of these species will eventually become established as components of Florida's flora. However, the following discussion does not include these latter plants.

The family Leguminosae (also sometimes referred to as the Fabaceae) is so large that some botanists have divided it into a number of subfamilies. The Mimosoideae is one of the largest of these subfamilies and is represented by a number of genera in Florida including the *Acacia, Albizia, Leucaena, Lysiloma,* and *Pithecellobium.*

The genus *Acacia* is one of the world's largest genera of flowering plants. Estimates suggest that the number of *Acacia* species may range from as few as 600 to over 1000. The genus is composed primarily of trees and woody shrubs, mostly of the tropical, subtropical, and, to a lesser degree, warm-temperate regions of the world. Six members of the genus are either native to or naturalized in Florida. However, many *Acacia* species, especially those from Australia, are cultivated in the southern portions of the state for their fragrant and appealing flowers.

All of our *Acacia* have bipinnately compound leaves and, with the exception of the tamarindillo (*A. choriophylla*), all also have very small leaflets and spiny branches. Of the six species found in Florida, only two are widespread. The sweet acacia (*A. farnesiana*) and pine acacia (*A. pinetorum*) are both found widely across much of the southern peninsula and the Keys. Both occur primarily in hammocks and pinelands along the coastal zone and are easy to differentiate. The sweet acacia has leaflets longer than 3 mm, and the pine acacia has leaflets shorter than 3 mm. The other four Florida *Acacia* are either highly localized in distribution or relatively uncommon in the state.

The genus *Albizia* is much smaller than the genus *Acacia*. Composed of approximately 100 species worldwide, it, too, is distributed primarily in the tropical and subtropical regions of the world. Both of Florida's *Albizia* species have been introduced to the state. The mimosa, or silk tree (*A. julibrissin*), is native to Asia from about Iran to China, Korea, and Japan but has been cultivated widely in the United States. It is quite common in the east from Washington, D.C., and Maryland southward to central Florida and west to Texas. Its attractive, bipinnate leaves, and delightful, pink and white cottony flowers are distinguishing field marks.

The woman's tongue (*A. lebbeck*), a close relative of the silk tree, is native to sub-tropical Asia. It has been introduced into southern Florida and has now become naturalized. Unlike the mimosa, its flowers are predominately creamy yellow. The two species are likely to be found together only in the central peninsula. They may be separated from each other by the silk tree's shorter leaflets and by the color of their flowers.

The lead tree, or jumbie bean (*Leucaena leucocephala*), is a small, spreading tree that is typically found in pinelands and hammocks along the coastal zone from about Tampa southward. It is an exotic species, but some authors still treat it as possibly native. It has spread widely in southern Florida due primarily to cultivation. The seeds of the jumbie bean have been used to fashion bracelets, necklaces, and other such trinkets, and the foliage has been used for the production of fertilizer as well as feed for livestock. Live plants are used as shade trees for coffee and cacao.

Wild tamarind (*Lysiloma latisiliquum*) is one of a small genus of about 35 species worldwide. It is a native plant and is a common component of several tropical hammocks of the upper Keys and Dade County. It is hardy, salt-tolerant, and has few natural enemies. It is also known to invade the pinelands that surround many of south Florida's hammocks. Frank Craighead, in the introduction to volume one of his *Trees of South Florida,* describes the wild tamarind as one of the more characteristic trees of the pine ridge hammock community.

Lysiloma latisiliquum is only one of two south Florida species referred to as tamarind. The other, *Tamarindus indica,* is a nonnative species that is cultivated in the state's southern counties. It probably originated in Africa but has been cultivated in India for many generations, hence its specific name. It is planted in fire breaks in India, but is best known for its fleshy, edible fruit that is often used in the production of candies, jellies, and beverages, as well as to spice up certain Indian recipes. *T. indica* is persistent in parts of southern Florida and can sometimes be seen along roadsides, especially near the coast.

Three of Florida's native or naturalized legumes are particularly noted for their ornamental value. Two of these are predominately tropical species and are found only in southern Florida, but one is common in the northern parts of the state.

The eastern redbud (*Cercis canadensis*) is one of north Florida's best known native species. It is a delicately branched and attractive tree that is scattered over most of the eastern United States and is generally found on rich, moist sites from southern Canada to Florida and Texas. Its exquisitely colored flowers range from light pink to magenta and normally appear in early spring, before the tree puts out new leaves. Its blooms are so beautiful and appear in such profusion along the naked branches that the tree is often considered to produce one of the most spectacular splashes of early spring color.

This factor alone explains why the tree is often found planted in yards and gardens, as well as alongside city streets.

In south Florida, the exotic orchid trees (*Bauhinia variegata* and *B. purpurea*) and royal poinciana (*Delonix regia*) rival the redbud in beauty and ornamental use. The former are common in the Miami area as well as the Keys, and are characterized by simple, two-ranked leaves with exquisite, purplish, orchidlike flowers. The flowers of *B. variegata* generally appear between January and March while the tree is leafless; those of *B. purpurea* appear more generally during the fall from about September to December, and the tree is more nearly evergreen. The two trees are difficult to distinguish and only the former species is included in Part II.

The royal poinciana undoubtedly takes its common name from its regal, bright red, frilly-petaled flowers that appear from early to midsummer. It, too, is a common ornamental that often decorates south Florida lawns. In addition to its showy flowers, it exhibits giant pods to about 50 cm long that hang on the tree nearly all year. The roots of this species grow very close to the surface and are known to break up sidewalks. Even so, the royal poinciana is still commonly used as a street tree throughout southern Florida and the tropics.

Three trees in two genera bear the common name locust. Of these, the water-locust (*Gleditsia aquatica*) and honey-locust (*G. triacanthos*) are most similar. Both are native species with even-pinnate, or occasionally bipinnate, leaves with many leaflets. The most distinguishing characteristic of these trees are the numerous sharp thorns found along their trunks and branches. Sometimes borne singly, these stiff, strong, extremely sharp, needle-tipped appendages are also often found in large masses along the lower trunk. The young, reddish colored thorns are also conspicuous among new leaf growth.

The water- and honey-locust are most readily differentiated by their fruits. The pods of the former are oval in shape and quite short, usually measuring less than 5 cm in length. Those of the honey-locust are much longer, ranging between 10 and 40 cm in overall length.

The black locust (*Robinia pseudoacacia*) is an introduced species to northern Florida. It is native to the Appalachian and Ozark mountains but has been cultivated in both the eastern and Pacific states as well as in portions of Europe. The black locust can be distinguished from our native locusts by its odd, rather than even, pinnate leaves and by the two sharp spines present at each leaf node.

The fishfuddle, or fish poison tree (*Piscidia piscipula*), has a long history of practical uses. Its common name derives from its utilization in a primitive system of fish gathering. According to reports of early observers, Jamaican natives were known to strip the fishfuddle's bark and throw it into shallow pools. The chemicals released from the bark were said to temporarily intoxicate any fish in the pool and cause them to turn belly up and float to the surface where they could be easily collected. These same narcotic properties also made the fishfuddle the source of an important anaesthetic. Near the turn of the century the tree's bark and roots were often used to relieve pain during surgical operations.

Piscidia piscipula is also referred to as Jamaica dogwood. This appellation is misleading in that the tree bears no relation to the Cornaceae, or true dogwood family. The name apparently arose from the tree's use in shipbuilding. Its strong, decay-resistant timber was often used as the central axis, or dog, of ships to insure the vessels' durability and longevity.

Two species of *Pithecellobium* are found in southern Florida. The genus name is Greek and refers to both species' twisted, sometimes spiral-shaped pods. The more common of the two is probably the blackbead (*P. guadalupense*). It grows best on sandy sites and is primarily a component of back-dune vegetation along the southeastern coast. It is found throughout southern Florida and is one of the most common plants in the Keys. Its bright red seeds appear in spring and early summer and are an attractive addition to the plant's dull green foliage.

Another of Florida's native legumes is classified as part of the subfamily Papilionoideae. The necklace pod (*Sophora tomentosa*) is a native of tropical Florida including the southern peninsula and the Keys, and thrives best only in bright sunlight. This attractive plant takes its common name from its interesting pods which are tightly pinched in between the seeds and take on the appearance of a beaded necklace. Its specific name, *tomentosa,* means densely woolly and refers to the copious covering of silvery hairs that coat the plant's young leaves. This same character has led some to call the plant silver bush. The seeds of the necklace pod are poisonous; ingesting them can cause headache, nausea, vertigo, and respiratory paralysis. Nevertheless, the plant is popular and easily cultivated, and is admired for its long, showy spikes of bright yellow flowers.

The coral bean (*Erythrina herbacea*) is one of Florida's more showy legumes. Typically a thin-trunked, multistemmed shrub, it is known to reach heights up to 5 m in the southern part of the state. Its genus name derives from the Greek word "erythros," which means red and refers to the plant's brightly colored, tubular flowers. Its specific name means herbaceous, which is not always accurate for this plant since the trunks of larger individuals are definitely woody. The seeds of the coral bean are poisonous if eaten and are used as rat poison in Mexico. Their colorful flowers are a favorite of the ruby-throated hummingbird, and the plant is often planted in suburban hummingbird gardens. The plant typically flowers in the summer and again in the fall and is easy to find when in bloom.

Shortcuts to Identifying Florida's Leguminous Trees

Florida's leguminous trees fall into three distinctive categories: those with simple leaves, those with pinnate leaves, and those with bipinnate leaves. Of these groups, those with bipinnate leaves are probably the most confusing for the beginning tree enthusiast. This confusion is particularly apparent for specimens that are neither in flower nor in fruit.

Tables 25-1 (p. 97) and 25-2 (p. 98) list the distinguishing characteristics of most of those species that exhibit bipinnate leaves. Table 25-1 differentiates among the spiny *Acacia,* all of which have relatively small leaflets; Table 25-2 treats the more easily confused of southern Florida's nonspiny legumes. When used in conjunction with the descriptions and distributional data found in Part II, these tables will prove extremely useful for making accurate field identifications.

Only two south Florida species with bipinnate leaves are not included in the tables. These omissions include *Pithecellobium guadalupense* and *P. unguis-cati*. Each of these latter trees is easily recognized by usually having a total of only four leaflets; neither tree bears a close resemblance to the other species listed in the tables. Distinguishing one of these species from the other, however, can be a taxing challenge.

Table 25-1 Spiny Acacia Species
Summary of Distinguishing Characteristics

Species	Number of Pinnae	Leaflet Length
Acacia farnesiana	mostly 4 - 10	3 - 6 mm
Acacia macracantha	20 - 34	about 3 mm
Acacia pinetorum	6 - 8	less than 3 mm
Acacia smalli	6 - 8	4 - 5 mm
Acacia tortuosa	mostly 10 - 16	3 - 4 mm

**Table 25-2 Non-spiny Leguminous Trees With Bipinnate Leaves
Summary of Distinguishing Characteristics**

Species	Leaf Length	Pinnae Number	Leaflet Number	Leaflet Length
Acacia choriophylla	10 - 20 cm	2 - 6	6 - 10	1 - 3 cm
Albizia julibrissin	10 - 35 cm	6 - 25	many	.5 - 1.5 cm
Albizia lebbeck	15 - 40 cm	4 - 10	10 - 24	2 - 4 cm
Delonix regia	20 - 50 cm	about 40	many	about 1 cm
Leucaena leucocephala	10 - 30 cm	8 - 16	20 - 40	.8 - 1.4 cm
Lysiloma latisiliquum	10 - 18 cm	4 - 8	16 - 30	.8 - 1.5 cm

CHAPTER 26

MANGROVES, BACCHARIS, AND BUTTONWOOD

The southwestern tip of the Florida peninsula is characterized by a vast jungle of salt-tolerant plants. Bordered on its outer edges by the wide expanse of shallow waters that make up Florida Bay, it is well protected from the onslaught of ocean waves and the erosional influence of powerful tidal currents. Unlike its sister coast that lies along the eastern edge of the state, much of the extreme southwestern seaside is nearly devoid of the wide, sandy beaches that are so often associated with the Florida shore. The typical attractions of sun and surf are replaced, instead, by an interconnected system of mangrove wetlands that stretch across a huge, flat plain and are never far from the influence of the advancing saltwater tides. Unfortunately, such areas are becoming increasingly rare in Florida today. Much of what remains north of the Ten Thousand Islands area is only a historical reminder of what was once a more expansive ecosystem.

The term mangrove is a comprehensive, and often somewhat confusing, expression. It is most appropriately used to denote those individual tree species which grow in a primarily saltwater environment. In common usage, however, the term is also often treated as a synonym for the characteristic plant community in which mangrove trees are most frequently found.

Even more confounding is the fact that the term is used to group plants together solely by similar ecological characteristics. Rather than being an all-inclusive term for closely related members of the same genus or family, as is the case for the hollies or oaks, for example, the name mangrove is used to symbolize the common association of several unrelated species in a similar habitat. As a result, mangroves often represent widely disparate plant families or genera, many of which also contain a variety of non-mangrove species.

Worldwide, the term mangrove is most accurately applied to those tropical and subtropical trees and shrubs that are typically found along muddy, saltwater shorelines. The chief characteristic that seems to bind them together is their apparent success in what would appear to be one of the earth's most hostile natural environments. Living at the edge of the sea, with its shifting substrate and daily dousing of tidal waters, the mangroves face environmental limitations to which few woody species have been able to adapt.

It is precisely the intolerance of other plants to such a hypersaline habitat that has helped the mangroves prosper. Although mangroves seem to grow equally well in fresh water as well as salt and do not appear to require saltwater for any critical metabolic purpose, they are often unable to successfully compete in nonmarine habitats and are usually crowded out by more aggressive, strictly freshwater, species. In their saltwater environment, however, they have carved out a specialized niche where competition is limited.

Mangrove species exhibit a variety of interesting ecological adaptations that have helped insure success in their primarily saline surroundings. At least two of these adaptations have to do with limiting the accumulation of salt into the plant's internal fluids. One adaptation functions to prevent too much salt from ever entering the plant's tissues; the other operates to expel excess salt before it can be assimilated.

Red mangroves, for example, are primarily salt excluders and have developed a remarkable facility for filtering out salt at the surface of the roots, thus insuring that predominately fresh water is taken into their systems. Black and white mangroves, on the other hand, are predominately salt excreters. Each is equipped with special salt glands on the surface of their leaves. These glands are specially adapted to excrete the plants' superfluous salts, as evidenced by the visible salt crystals that commonly decorate the plants' leaves. In reality, most mangrove species probably use a combination of both of these strategies, with one particular strategy being dominant for each particular species.

The mangroves have also developed a rather extraordinary method for insuring reproductive success. This, too, has probably evolved, at least partially, in response to harsh environmental conditions. Unlike most plants, whose seeds typically germinate only after falling from the plant and coming into contact with an appropriate growing medium, the seeds of many mangroves are viviparous, meaning that they actually germinate while still attached to the tree. In some species, particularly those that constitute the genus *Rhizophora* of which Florida's red mangrove is a member, even the seedlings develop from the still-attached fruit and are often evident as cigar-shaped appendages that hang pendently from the branch.

These odd-looking structures are often referred to as radicles, or propagules, and are intimately connected with the mangroves' mechanism for seed dispersal. After they reach sufficient development, the propagules drop from the tree and are carried by tides and currents to locations that are sometimes far distant from the mother tree. When they come into contact with an exposed muddy substrate in a protected body of quiet, shallow water, they put down roots and attach themselves firmly to the bottom.

Four tree species are typically referred to as part of Florida's mangrove zone. These include the red mangrove (*Rhizophora mangle*), the black mangrove (*Avicennia germinans*), the white mangrove (*Laguncularia racemosa*), and the buttonwood (*Conocarpus erectus*). However, only the first three are mangroves in the truest sense. The buttonwood is primarily a plant of the landward edge of the mangrove zone and thrives best in areas that are only occasionally subjected to tidal washing.

The red mangrove genus is a relatively small, pantropical collection of less than eight evergreen tree species of which *Rhizophora mangle* is the sole representative in Florida. It is the most easily recognized of Florida's native mangrove species and is a common constituent of the state's mangrove forests.

Red mangroves are generally recognized by the tangle of aerial prop roots that extend from the trees' trunks and lower branches. These roots are yet another adaptation to the saltwater environment and serve to counteract the anaerobic, or oxygen-poor, condition of coastal soils by allowing the trees to take in oxygen directly from the surrounding air. In older specimens these stilt roots, as they are sometimes called, also act as spreading buttresses and provide the trees with the additional support needed to remain upright in the muddy substrate.

The black mangrove is another of Florida's more salt-tolerant trees. Often described as inhabiting the intermediate portions of the mangrove zone, it is generally found in close association with the red mangrove and seems to thrive in even the most salt-rich soils. Its most distinctive feature is the massive system of cable roots and pneumatophores that cover the ground below many specimens. Pneumatophores are essentially the erect lateral branches of an otherwise horizontal root system. They commonly project above the ground and presumably serve the same aerating purpose as the prop roots of the red mangrove. In tropical climes the black mangrove is an important honey plant and produces clear white honey. It is also a source of salt which can be gathered from its leaf surfaces.

The white mangrove is a member of the Combretaceae, or combretum family. This is a primarily tropical family of about 500, mainly woody, species native to Central and South America. Only four species in four genera are found in Florida, two of which are native and two of which are introduced.

The white mangrove is typically the landward-most member of the true mangroves but is often found in mixed associations with the black mangrove. Like the black mangrove, it has the propensity to develop breathing roots, or pneumatophores, although such appendages are not nearly so commonplace with the white mangrove and are not always present. Specimens of this tree may be separated from the other two strictly mangrove species by the light green color of both leaf surfaces and by the generally oval shape of the blades.

The buttonwood is also a member of the Combretaceae, and is a brackish to freshwater species with a high degree of salt tolerance. Although commonly associated with the mangrove zone, it displays neither the specialized root structures nor the viviparous reproductive strategies of any of the true mangrove species. The buttonwood commonly forms a dense fringe along the landward edge of the mangrove zone and is one of south Florida's more prominent coastal trees. It takes its name from the button-like heads of tiny green flowers that appear on the tree from late spring to early fall. It is a favored host of epiphytic orchids and bromeliads and was known to be of commercial use to Florida's pioneers. There is evidence, for example, that the early inhabitants of Flamingo, the Florida mainland's southernmost village, once produced charcoal from buttonwood and shipped it to the inhabitants of Key West.

The two other combretums that inhabit southern Florida are introduced species that have become established components of Florida's flora. Although both species are considered mangrove associates in their native ranges, neither is closely tied to the mangrove zone in Florida. The oxhorn bucida (*Bucida buceras*) is a native of the West Indies that has been widely cultivated as an ornamental in the southern part of the state. It is a tall, straight tree with a spreading crown of nearly horizontal branches.

The odd-looking, long, twisted, hornlike galls that develop on its fruit are distinctive field marks.

The sea-almond (*Terminalia catappa*) is the other nonnative member of the combretum family. It was originally introduced as a shade tree but now volunteers readily in sandy soils and along beaches. It is a very salt-tolerant species that produces a dry, egg-shaped fruit containing a single edible nut. Its wood is not particularly useful except for posts and fuel, but its bark, roots, and fruit contain tannin and have been used in tanning. Sea-almond was once considered for its potential as a commercial nut producer, but the idea was later abandoned. It is one of the few south Florida trees whose leaves turn reddish before they fall.

The saltbush (*Baccharis halimifolia*) is included in this chapter with the mangroves only because of its presence in the coastal plant community. Although neither related to the mangroves nor so generally restricted to a coastal environment, it is a common component along many of Florida's more marshy shorelines. However, due to its weedy and opportunistic nature, it is also often found in disturbed sites far inland from its typical seaside habitat.

Baccharis is a member of the Compositae, or composite family (also often referred to as the Asteraceae, or aster family). The composites constitute a morphologically advanced group of plants that is probably best known for its numerous, low-growing, herbaceous species that burst into flower throughout the spring, summer, and fall.

The saltbush is commonly a bushy shrub that only rarely takes on the appearance of a tree. Its coarsely toothed, obovate leaves and numerous, white, densely packed, flowering heads are conspicuous field marks along Florida's coastlines.

CHAPTER **27**

CRAPE MYRTLE, STOPPERS, GUAVA, MELALEUCA, AND TETRAZYGIA

With the exception of the crape myrtle, the species presented in this chapter are all confined to southern Florida and the Keys. All are members of three closely related families of the order Myrtales, which also includes the Combretaceae, or combretum family, which is considered in Chapter 26.

Crape Myrtle

The crape myrtle (*Lagerstroemia indica*) is predominantly an ornamental landscape plant that has found wide use in gardens and lawns across much of Florida and the southeastern United States, as well as in Puerto Rico and the Virgin Islands. It is particularly well known as a roadside plant, and its beautiful white, pink, red, or purple flowers are often used to add an attractive border to many southern highways. It is native to Asia but has become established in Florida, particularly near the sites of old homesteads, along fencerows, or in old fields.

The crape myrtle is a member of the Lythraceae or loosestrife family, a collection of more than 20 genera and 450 species. Most members of the family are herbs or shrubs. The crape myrtle is Florida's only tree-sized member of this family that is counted as part of our naturalized flora. However, at least one other *Lagerstroemia* species is used for ornamental purposes.

Crape myrtle flowers are very showy and quite beautiful, which probably accounts for the plant's widespread popularity. They are borne in handsome panicles that extend well beyond the leafy branches and are present throughout the summer. The flowers typically have six clawed petals, each with a fringed outer edge. The entire inflorescence can be up to 30 cm long and nearly as wide, making the crape myrtle a conspicuous part of the landscape when in full bloom.

Tetrazygia

The tetrazygia (*Tetrazygia bicolor*) is Florida's only woody species of the Melastomataceae, or melastome family. The family is a rather large collection of about 200 genera and 4500 species of mostly tropical plants, many of which are native to South America. Only two of these genera occur naturally in the United States, both of which are represented in Florida. In addition to the state's single *Tetrazygia,* which is confined solely to the southern tip of the peninsula, the family is also represented in Florida by several species that are commonly referred to as meadow beauties. The latter plants, all of which are members of the genus *Rhexia,* are herbaceous species that are most often found in seasonally wet, acidic soils such as Florida's extensive pine flatwoods community.

The tetrazygia has two growth forms in southern Florida, probably owing to its occurrence in two distinctive vegetative communities. In the pinelands, like those found in the Long Pine Key area of the Everglades National Park, the plant seldom exceeds the stature of a small, single-stemmed shrub. In the adjacent hammocks, however, it is known to reach heights of 10 m with a trunk diameter of 6 - 10 cm.

Like many other members of its family, the tetrazygia is most often noticed in spring and early summer because of its conspicuous and showy flowers. The blossoms are borne in large terminal clusters that extend well beyond the top of the plant. Each one contains four or five bright white petals that sit atop a characteristic, urn-shaped calyx and encircle a mass of yellow stamens. When coupled with the plant's distinctive leaves, these flowers make the tetrazygia an easy plant to identify.

The Myrtle Family

The myrtle family, or Myrtaceae, is a complex and confusing collection of plants represented by at least seven genera in Florida, only some of which are native to the state. The family has undergone a rather long history of dramatic changes in taxonomic classification. Exacting distinctions have been difficult to define for many of the family's genera and species, resulting in a wide range of synonymous scientific names.

The stoppers of the genus *Eugenia* probably exhibit the most inconsistency in their historical names. Currently, it is generally agreed that four *Eugenia* species inhabit southern Florida. Two of these, the white stopper (*E. axillaris*) and Spanish stopper (*E. foetida*), are common and widespread. The red-berry stopper (*E. confusa*), with characteristically long-pointed leaves, is only an occasional resident of hammocks and is not common. The red stopper (*E. rhombea*), which is most similar in appearance to the white stopper, is a rare species found very sparingly in the Keys. All are noted for their opposite, evergreen leaves, a characteristic which helps immensely in separating them from all but a handful of south Florida trees.

The twinberry stopper, or simply twinberry (*Myrcianthes fragrans*), is closely related to the genus Eugenia and was, until recently, known as *Eugenia simpsonii*. The twinberry is part of a small genus of less than 50 species that ranges chiefly in South America and the West Indies. It is found in Florida in hammocks of the southern peninsula.

The only other south Florida tree commonly referred to as a stopper is the long-stalked stopper (*Mosiera longipes*). It, too, was once considered to be a part of the genus *Eugenia*, but was later classified in the same genus as the guava (*Psidium guajava*). However, the most recent revision places it in the genus *Mosiera*. Like the tetrazygia, it has two growth forms. Some maintain that this difference in form is largely dependent upon habitat. According to this theory, plants found growing in the pinelands seldom exceed 30 cm in height, while those in the hammocks tend to become trees up to about 4 m tall. In either event, *M. longipes* is a native species with a short trunk and wiry, spreading branches. It takes its common name from its conspicuously long flower stalks.

The guava is a nonnative species from Central America that has escaped from cultivation and has become naturalized in southern Florida. It is best known for its pear-shaped yellow fruit which is high in vitamin C and has been used in making jellies, preserves, and beverages. Although the fruit of cultivated plants is good tasting and an important fruit crop, that of escaped trees is usually of much poorer quality.

Two members of the myrtle family can be separated by the distinctive branching pattern of their leafy twigs. New branchlets of both the pale lidflower (*Calyptranthes pallens*) and the myrtle-of-the-river (*C. zuzygium*) are produced in pairs at each leaf node, resulting in only two oppositely arranged leaves per twig, both of which are borne at the terminus of the supporting branchlet. This unique forking arrangement sets these plants apart from all of the state's other opposite-leaved trees or shrubs. Neither of these plants is considered common, but both may be readily found in hammocks of south Florida and the Keys.

Several species of nonnative Myrtaceae are commonly known as bottle brushes and are widely used as ornamental species. The most widespread of these is the cajeput or melaleuca tree (*Melaleuca quinquenervia*); the others belong to the genus *Callistemon*.

The cajeput, which is distributed naturally primarily in Australia, was originally introduced into Florida as an ornamental species recommended for use in yards and parks to mark boundary lines or to add accent to woodland borders. It has since escaped from cultivation and is now extensively naturalized, often to the detriment of the state's native flora. It is particularly adapted to wet or moist areas and has become a troublesome weed species across much of the southern peninsula. To date, the species has been almost impossible to eradicate, but research is currently being conducted to find ways to control the species biologically. It will be interesting to observe what long-term effects this tree will have as our native flora attempts to recover from the impact of Hurricane Andrew.

The cajeput takes its common name from combining the two Malaysian words for tree and white, a name which refers to the cajeput's whitish, peeling bark. In like manner, Linnaeus used the two Greek works for tree and white to fashion the first part of its scientific name; the second part of its scientific name refers to its typically five- or sometimes seven-veined leaves. The curling bark, which is characteristic of the species, is somewhat reminiscent of the northern paper birch (*Betula papyrifera*) and has led to the additional common name paper bark tree. The melaleuca is easily seen along many south Florida highways and expressways and is not a difficult tree to identify.

Although the other bottle brush species are strictly ornamental plants and thus not included in Part II, it would be a major omission not to at least mention them here. At least four *Callistemon* species are cultivated widely in southern Florida. All are close relatives of the cajeput, but none have become naturalized or are considered a problem for our native vegetation. The most often-seen species are probably the showy bottle brush (*C. speciosus*) and the weeping bottle brush (*C. viminalis*). Both are bushy, evergreen trees that are commonly used to decorate lawns from about central Florida southward. They are characterized by narrow, drooping leaves and showy clusters of bright red flowers that encircle the branch and take on the appearance of a bottle brush, much like the white flowers of the cajeput.

CHAPTER **28**

MADDERS, BIGNONIAS, AND OLEANDERS

The madder and bignonia families encompass a large number of Florida's plant species, including 11 members that normally reach tree stature. Representatives of both families are found throughout the state and are easy to identify.

The Bignonias

Florida's Bignoniaceae are probably most noted for their showy, bell-shaped flowers and interesting fruit. Several native or naturalized species are represented in Florida, many of which have been cultivated for ornamental purposes. In addition, another strictly cultivated species is common in southern Florida.

At first glance, the fruit of at least two of Florida's bignonias would lead one to believe that they are part of the Leguminosae, or bean family. Both the southern catalpa (*Catalpa bignonioides*) and the yellow elder (*Tecoma stans*) bear long, cylindrical pods that split open to expose numerous dry, wind-scattered seeds. These fruits are quite reminiscent of several leguminous species and can lead to a quite frustrating search for their identity among members of the incorrect family of plants.

The southern catalpa is a north Florida species that has a rather limited distribution. It occurs naturally only on levees, in floodplains, and along riverbanks across a narrow strip of the southeast that includes the Florida panhandle, southwestern Georgia, southern Alabama, and southeastern Mississippi. The catalpa is well known by freshwater fishermen for the caterpillars that invade its foliage. It is most commonly found naturalized near dwellings, where it has been planted as a consistent source of fish bait. The catalpa is easily distinguished from all other north Florida trees by its large, heart-shaped leaves that are borne both opposite and whorled along the branch.

Yellow elder is a nonnative species that is naturalized and common in the Keys. It is a weedy plant that is often seen along roadsides and in yards. Its showy clusters of bright yellow flowers are eye-catching attractions and are likely to be seen on the tree at any time of year.

Only one tree is likely to be confused with the yellow elder. From February through early May, the very similarly flowered yellow tab (*Cybistax donnell-smithii*) is a common sight throughout southern Florida and the Keys. Although neither native nor naturalized, it is very conspicuous and certainly bears mention with the other members of its family, even though it is not described in Part II. The leaves of the yellow tab are palmately compound, and the five to seven, long-stemmed leaflets radiate in one plane from a central "hub" that looks quite similar to the center of a schefflera leaf. The leaf shape alone is enough to identify the plant, but the showy clusters of bright yellow flowers are usually what draws one's initial attention.

The fruit of the black calabash (*Amphitecna latifolia*), our other member of the bignonia family, is not as easily confounded with the beans as are those of the previous two species. Although seldom seen unless the flowers are artificially pollinated, it is no less distinctive than the fruit of the two plants mentioned above. It is large, green, hard-shelled, more or less egg shaped, and filled with a soft, seed-rich pulp. The fruit itself is not edible. However, when cleaned of the pulp mass, the hard, outer shell can be used as a small container and has found service as a drinking cup in the more central parts of its chiefly West Indies and South American range.

The black calabash is a tree of southernmost Florida and has sometimes been considered indigenous to the Florida Keys. There is question about whether this latter supposition is correct, but the species has been included here for completeness. The tree is sometimes planted as an ornamental, primarily for its interesting white to purple, rank-smelling flowers and odd fruit.

The Madders

The Rubiaceae, or madder family, is one of the largest families of flowering plants. It contains about 500 genera and over 7,000 species worldwide, most of which are herbaceous rather than woody. Only eight species regularly reach tree stature in Florida.

All of Florida's tree-sized Rubiaceae are unique and interesting plants. Several have a distinctive and showy inflorescence; others, a singular and easily identifiable leaf structure. None are particularly difficult to differentiate from Florida's other tree species.

Our most common representative of this family is the buttonbush (*Cephalanthus occidentalis*). Named for its ball-like heads of tubular white flowers, it is common across the whole of Florida and most of the eastern United States. Although it sometimes grows large enough to be called a small tree, it is more typically a shrub. It inhabits low areas along streams, rivers, swamps, lakes, and ponds and commonly grows in association with the willows, tupelos, and bays.

The buttonbush is an important plant for wildlife. White-tailed deer browse its large, glossy-green leaves and young twigs; ducks feed on its seeds, which mature in the autumn; and its dense foliage provides good cover for nesting birds.

The fever tree (*Pinckneya bracteata*) is perhaps the most unique of Florida's Rubiaceae species. Its oddly constructed flowers coupled with its purported pharmacological value have contributed significantly to its reputation. The plant's common name stems from its use as a medicinal herb in colonial America and during the Civil War when decoctions made from the tree's bark were used as a source of quinine to treat the high fever of malaria victims. Its flowers are composed of relatively small, greenish yellow, tubular corollas that are surrounded by four yellowish, pinkish, or whitish sepals, one of which may be much enlarged, very showy, and much more petallike than the petals themselves. When fully flowered in late spring and early summer, the fever tree is a delightful sight.

Six of Florida's Rubiaceae tree species are primarily tropical plants that are restricted to the southern peninsula or the Keys. These include two species of velvetseed (*Guettarda elliptica* and *G. scabra*), as well as the seven-year apple (*Casasia clusiifo-*

lia), princewood (*Exostema caribaeum*), firebush (*Hamelia patens*), and white indigo berry (*Randia aculeata*). Like the two species mentioned above, each of these latter plants exhibits at least one unique or characteristic feature that aids in its identification. The velvetseeds are noted for their velvety fruit; the seven-year apple for its large, shiny green leaves and egg-shaped fruit; the princewood for its delicate, showy, white to pinkish flowers; the firebush for its reddish orange, tubular blossoms and red-veined leaves; and the white indigo berry for its creamy white fruit with blackish pulp.

In addition to the foregoing eight trees, there are three other genera in Florida's madder family that contain woody plants. These include *Chiococca, Erithalis,* and *Psychotria.* All members of these genera are limited to the state's southernmost counties and are most often regarded as shrubs rather than trees. However, at least some observers have attributed arborescent qualities to a few of these plants. Of these, only black torch (*Erithalis fruticosa*) is included in Part II. All are addressed briefly below in the interest of completeness.

The snowberry (*Chiococca alba*) is a sprawling shrub that probably doesn't exceed about 3 m in height in its shrubby form. However, it sometimes takes on vinelike characteristics, extending to several meters in height. It takes its common name from the conspicuous clusters of bright white berries that appear in late summer and early fall. Its flowers are creamy white, bell shaped, and quite evident when in bloom. The snowberry is a common component of south Florida's tropical hammock community. It is easily seen in several locations along the roadway at Hugh Taylor Birch State Recreation Area in Ft. Lauderdale.

Black torch is typically a compact shrub with very dense foliage but sometimes reaches tree stature in hammocks of the Florida Keys. It is most common in the coastal scrub. Black torch often has a short trunk, many branches, and a rounded crown, at least in open coastal locations, and is typically less than 3 m tall. It produces small, distinctive, star-shaped flowers and black, berrylike fruit. The leaves are oval in shape, borne oppositely along the branch, clustered at the tips of branches, and usually do not exceed about 5 cm in length. The plant's common name apparently derives from its use as a long-burning torch in the West Indies.

There are three species of *Psychotria* in southern Florida, all of which are commonly referred to as wild coffee. These include *P. ligustrifolia, P. nervosa,* and *P. sulzneri.* All three are similar in appearance and are most easily recognized by their opposite leaves with conspicuously imbedded lateral veins that make the tissue between the veins appear raised. They are related to the true coffees but are not a substitute for it. The wild coffees are likely to be confused only with the Florida tetrazygia (*Tetrazygia bicolor*), a typically single-stemmed, shrubby plant of the Melastomataceae family that is generally restricted only to the pinelands and hammock edges of the Everglades keys.

Oleanders

The oleander family (Apocynaceae) is best known in Florida for a wide assortment of attractive ornamental species, none of which are native to the state. Many produce

colorful and conspicuous flowers that are widely recognized. These include the oleander (*Nerium oleander*), confederate jasmine (*Trachelospermum jasminoides*), crape-
jasmine (*Ervatamia coronaria*), frangipani (*Plumeria* spp.), heralds-trumpet
(*Beaumontia grandiflora*), lucky nut (*Thevetia peruviana*), and several species of allamanda of the genera *Allamanda* and *Mandevilla*. Florida's native Apocynaceae are
relatively few in number and consist chiefly of vines and herbs.

Only one native member of the family reaches tree stature, and even it seldom does.
The pearl berry or tear shrub (*Vallesia antillana*) is an attractive understory species
that is restricted in Florida to coastal scrub, dunes, and the edges of hammocks in the
extreme southern peninsula and the Keys. It is not common and is usually seen as a
low or moderately arborescent shrub. Its white, star-shaped flowers are borne in clusters that typically arise opposite a leaf stem. Its fruit is a pearly white, translucent
berry from which the plant takes one of its common names. Both the flowers and fruit
are usually present year-round and are good characteristics to use in identifying the
species.

CHAPTER **29**

ARALIA, DOGWOODS, HONEYSUCKLES, AND TUPELOS

The aralia, dogwoods, honeysuckles, and tupelos are closely associated families that exhibit a range of morphological and anatomical similarities. Likenesses in their wood, pollen, and floral structure as well as comparable characteristics of their cells and internal fluids have long led to disagreements about the taxonomic classification of some of these families. So nearly akin are the dogwoods and tupelos, for example, that it has been only within the last half century that the latter have been segregated into their own distinct family grouping. Such taxonomic uncertainty underscores the genetic relationship that exists between these families and suggests that many of their genera probably evolved from a common ancestral stock.

Aralia

The Araliaceae, or ginseng family, is a relatively large grouping of between 55 and 60 genera and nearly 800 species worldwide. Less than five of these genera are represented in Florida, and only one of these is classified as a tree.

The ginseng family is probably best known for the root of the Asiatic and American genus *Panax*. Reputed to have powerful medicinal properties with the capacity to cure such debilitating diseases as cancer, rheumatism, and diabetes, as well as to inhibit the physical deterioration sometimes associated with aging, the plant was revered by the ancient Chinese and later by 16th-century Europeans to whom it was introduced by explorers returning from the Orient. The English name for the family comes from the corruption of the Chinese term *schin-seng*. Roughly translated, the phrase means "essence of earth in the form of man" and apparently refers to the root's resemblance to the human form.

North America's sole tree-sized native of the ginseng family is *Aralia spinosa*, a diminutive and delicate tree that exhibits none of the medicinal properties associated with its more well-known relatives. Commonly referred to as the devil's walking stick because of the numerous sharp prickles that protrude from its trunk and leaf rachis, *A. spinosa* is an attractive plant that bears little resemblance to any of Florida's other native trees and shrubs. Its huge, bi-pinnately compound leaves are often clustered toward the top of its thin, straight trunk and make it an easy plant to pick out in the understory.

In addition to the devil's walking stick, one nonnative tree-sized member of the ginseng family is used as an outdoor ornamental in southern Florida or a potted indoor plant in the northern part of the state and is common enough to bear mention here. The well-known schefflera (*Brassaia actinophylla*), is a beautiful species with large, palmately compound leaves and a graceful stature. Although many visitors from the north know this plant only as an indoor shrub, in the southern peninsula it is often seen to reach tree stature. It is native to Australia and is most revered for its huge, deep red inflorescences that stand above the foliage in long, armlike appendages.

Dogwoods

The beauty and grace of the flowering dogwood (*Cornus florida*) has made it one of the state's most popular native ornamentals. Although naked of leaves in winter, its beauty in spring, summer, and fall is unsurpassed. Early in the year its showy white "blooms" cover the tree and provide a sure indication that spring has arrived. Following flowering, bright red, berrylike fruits appear amidst the attractive, bright green foliage. Although poisonous to humans, these fruits are a delicacy for songbirds, squirrels, and raccoons and have made the tree an effective natural feeding station for dooryards and gardens.

The magnificent blossoms of the flowering dogwood are a somewhat deceiving structure. What appear to be the petals of their handsome white flowers are actually enlarged bracts and not part of the flower at all. The real flowers are quite tiny and constitute the yellowish green, buttonlike cluster that lies at the center of these bracteal impostors.

Although the flowering dogwood is probably the best known of Florida's Cornaceae, it is certainly not the state's only member of the family. Four other species also inhabit various regions of the state, at least three of which reach tree stature.

Stiff cornel (*C. foemina*) is the most widespread of the remaining tree-sized species and is a common component of swamps, floodplains, and riverbanks across much of northern Florida and southward down the peninsula. Its tiny, cymose flowers, purplish fruit, and generally wetland habitat readily distinguish it from its more common cousin.

The rough leaf cornel (*C. asperifolia*) is very similar in appearance to the stiff cornel. However, it is a tree of well-drained rather than wetland woods. In addition, it has stiff hairs on the upper surfaces of many leaves which render them rough to the touch and provide an easy method for distinguishing them from those of the stiff cornel. The rough leaf cornel is typically a shrub with several trunks, but sometimes it reaches the stature of a small tree.

The other tree-sized dogwood is of limited occurrence in the state. Often referred to as the pagoda or alternate-leaved dogwood (*C. alternifolia*), it is typically a more northern tree that ranges from Maine, through the Great Lakes region, and down to the southern terminus of the Appalachians. Its leaf blades are similar to the flowering dogwood, but its range is quite restricted. It is found in Florida only in Gadsden and Calhoun counties and is considered rare in the state.

The state's shrubby dogwoods also include the swamp dogwood (*C. amomum*). Although it sometimes reaches heights of 5 m, it typically has several arching trunks and does not take on the form of a tree. It is mentioned only because its leaves are similar to one or more of the other dogwood species. It may be separated from the similar stiff cornel by its leaves, which reach 8 cm in width and are about twice as wide as those of the latter species, and by its fruit which is blue with irregular cream-colored spots.

Tupelos

The sour gum or tupelo family (Nyssaceae) is a small collection of only three genera and less than ten species. In prehistoric times the family was probably widely distributed worldwide, but today it is restricted almost solely to eastern North America and China. That the present-day members of the Nyssaceae are of ancient lineage is evident from a remarkable fossil record that places representatives of the family on most of the earth's major continents and in all major geologic time periods from the Eocene through the Pliocene.

With the exception of the upland-dwelling sour gum (*Nyssa sylvatica*), the tupelos are community-forming trees, often growing in mixed stands containing more than one species of the family. Most of the tupelos prefer wet sites and are able to remain inundated for long periods of time without harm. The water tupelo (*N. aquatica*) occurs from Leon and Wakulla counties westward, the ogeechee-lime (*N. ogeche*) from about Bay County eastward, and the blackgum (*N. biflora*) across nearly the entire state. There has been some disagreement about whether *N. biflora* is actually a separate species or a variety of the more wide-ranging *N. sylvatica*. The two trees are easily distinguished in the field and are treated as distinct species here.

Tupelo leaves are deciduous, alternate, and typically smooth on the edges, although some may have one to three large teeth. Of the swamp-dwelling tupelos, blackgum has the smallest leaves, none of which exceed 10 cm in length. Conversely, the leaves of the water and ogeechee tupelos are ordinarily greater than 15 cm in length and may even be much longer.

Tupelo trees have several uses. In April and May they bear clusters of small white flowers that produce an abundance of sweet nectar that makes them attractive to bees and other insects. The trees are famous in north Florida for the smooth-tasting "tupelo honey" that bees derive from this nectar. The fruits of all the tupelos are eaten by wildlife and the acidic juice of ogeechee fruit is sometimes even used by humans as a substitute for limes, hence one of its common names.

Honeysuckles

The family Caprifoliaceae is a divergent collection of trees, shrubs, and vines represented by 18 genera and perhaps 500 species. Members of the family are found worldwide in both temperate and tropical climatic regions. Four genera, two of which contain tree species, are found in Florida.

The elder-berry (*Sambucus canadensis*) is one of this family's best known and most often seen representatives. It is a common and conspicuous roadside plant and a prolific colonizer of wet clearings and disturbed sites throughout the state. It produces large, showy cymes of small white flowers that provide an attractive addition to the late spring and early summer landscape.

In addition to its flowers, the elder-berry is also known for its purplish black fruit which appears in mid- to late summer. Often used in the production of wines, jellies, jams, and pies, the elder-berry's shiny drupes have enjoyed a long history as the source of a variety of popular homemade recipes. Wildlife biologists also recognize them as an important food source for a large number of songbirds as well as for some of the state's more important mammals.

The viburnums constitute the other genus of Florida's treelike Caprifoliaceae. They are part of a complex genus of more than 150 species, most of which are found in the northern temperate regions of the world. Of the 15 or so species that occur in North America, five are represented in Florida, and only one does not exhibit a treelike stature.

The viburnums are most easily recognized in north Florida by their opposite leaves and five-lobed flowers. Only a limited number of other north Florida trees have opposite leaves, and none, except the dogwoods (*Cornus* spp.), have such showy flower clusters. Since the flowers of the dogwoods have only four lobes, the two can be readily separated when in flower. In addition, creasing and separating the leaf of a dogwood slowly across the central vein will produce threadlike strings of latex between the two leaf halves. This is not the case for the viburnums.

Our four viburnum species include arrow-wood (*Viburnum dentatum*), possum-haw (*V. nudum*), Walter or small viburnum (*V. obovatum*), and rusty or southern black haw (*V. rufidulum*). All are small, deciduous trees with simple leaves and showy clusters of tiny white flowers.

CHAPTER 30

GEIGER TREE, STRONGBARKS, AND FIDDLEWOOD

The geiger tree, strongbarks, and fiddlewood represent two families of the order Lamiales. All five of Florida's tree-sized members of these two families are primarily tropical species found only in the southern part of the state.

The Borage Family

The Boraginaceae, or borage family, is a relatively large assortment of perhaps 100 genera and more than 2,000 species. Most members of the family are herbaceous species, some of which are well known as ornamentals. The showy flowered scorpion-tail (*Heliotropium angiospermum*), puccoon (*Lithospermum caroliniense*), and forget-me-nots (*Myosotis* spp.) are some of the best-known representatives. Only three members of the family reach tree stature in Florida.

The genus *Cordia* is a mostly tropical genus that includes in excess of 250 species. Most are native to South America, but two occur in the United States. One of these is found only in southernmost Florida. The other (*Cordia boissieri*) occurs rarely in southwest Texas.

The geiger tree (*C. sebestena*) is a plant of the West Indies and is doubtfully native to the Florida Keys and hammocks of the Everglades. It is uncommon in the wild but has found wide use as an ornamental in both the Keys and the warmest regions of the southern peninsula. It does quite well in sun or partial shade, is tolerant of a range of soil conditions, and is used in suburban yards as well as along city streets. It blossoms in summer and produces showy terminal clusters of brilliantly colored, orange-red flowers that are very conspicuous. The plant's common name was reportedly conferred by John James Audubon in honor of John Geiger, an early Key West pioneer who earned his fortune by salvaging wrecked vessels. Audubon reportedly stayed in Geiger's home while visiting the Keys.

The strongbarks of the genus *Bourreria* are the other two tree-sized members of the borage family found in Florida. Both are known primarily from the Keys, but only one occurs with any regularity. The Bahama strongbark (*Bourreria ovata*) is a weedy species of hammock margins and is fairly common throughout the Keys. The other two members of the genus include the rough strongbark (*B. radula*) and the smooth strongbark (*B. cassinifolia*). The first of these two is a small tree of the lower Keys. The latter is a low, multistemmed shrub. Both of these latter plants are quite rare and their continued occurrence in their native habitats is very uncertain.

The genus *Bourreria* takes its Latin name from a corruption of the last name of Johann Ambrosius Beurer, a 16th-century pharmacist in Nurnberg, Germany. In 1732 Beurer helped German botanical illustrator Georg Dionys Ehret launch his career by introducing him to a well-known German botanist. Later, Ehret was asked to illustrate

Patrick Browne's *Civil and Natural History of Jamaica,* which appeared in 1756. During the course of this work, Ehret must have told Browne of the early assistance Beurer had given him. Browne undoubtedly misunderstood Buerer's name and later announced that he had founded the genus *Bourreria* in honor of "Mr. Bourer." The name later went through several revisions but was finally upheld by the International Botanical Congress in 1935, and is still with us today.

The Verbena Family

The Verbenaceae is a large family of about 75 genera and more than 3,000 species. Like the borage family, it is best known for its shrubby and herbaceous species, many of which are widespread components of Florida's flora. In addition to the two tree species included in this book, the family also encompasses such common plants as the popular shrubs American beauty berry (*Callicarpa americana*) and lantana (*Lantana camara*), the low-growing capeweed (*Phyla nodiflora*), and the conspicuously flowered glorybowers (*Clerodendrum* spp.) and vervains (*Verbena* spp.).

Florida's two tree-sized members of the Verbenaceae include the fiddlewood (*Citharexylum fruticosum*) and the golden dewdrop (*Duranta repens*). The former is a native species that is most common in the Keys but is also found on the east coast as far north as Brevard County. The latter is a nonnative ornamental, although it is sometimes claimed to be indigenous to the Keys. It is included here because of its popularity and because it sometimes volunteers from plantings.

The fiddlewood is a hammock species that has also become adapted to the pinelands. Like many plants, its common name is somewhat misleading and has apparently resulted from the corruption of similar words from separate languages. The French colonial name for members of this genus was "bois fidele," which literally translates as reliable or trustworthy wood, an accolade that likely refers to the tree's strength and toughness. The French word "fidele" was apparently misinterpreted as fiddle by the English, and the name has stayed with the plant. There is no history that the wood from this tree has ever been used in the manufacture of violins.

The golden dewdrop takes its common name from the yellow, drupaceous fruits that appear on the tree in summer and early fall. The fruits are poisonous to humans but are relished by birds. It is an easy tree to cultivate and requires little care once established, thus making it a useful street tree in those parts of the state that are not subjected to frost.

PART II

FIELD GUIDE TO FLORIDA'S TREES

This part includes a field guide to Florida's trees. It is divided into the gymnosperms and the angiosperms, the latter divided into monocots (the palms), and dicots (all the rest). The species within each of these categories are arranged in alphabetical order by family, genus, and species. All alphabetizing is based on scientific names. This organizing scheme will assist the reader in developing an appreciation of familial and generic similarities and differences. A total of 342 species are included in these descriptions.

Each entry includes a description of the species' key morphological characteristics, hints about how to distinguish the species from similar plants, and a note about the distribution of the species in Florida. In addition, many species are illustrated with line drawings or color photographs, sometimes in combination. Extremely similar species may be represented by an illustration of only one of the similar plants. In these latter cases, complete discussions of the plants' distinguishing characteristics are included in their descriptions.

Most field descriptions offer a range of measurements for each species' overall height, leaves, flowers, and fruit. It should be noted that these measurements generally represent maximum and minimum dimensions and are intended only as guides. Although care has been taken to insure that these measurements are accurate and inclusive, it is still possible that particular individuals may exceed the stated extremes. In these cases, other characteristics may prove more useful in making an identification. It should be further noted that identifying trees is not always an easy task. Many trees display a host of variable characters, characters very similar to other species, or diagnostic characters that are present at only certain times of the year. For these reasons, it may be impossible to make a positive identification of some individuals in only one visit.

In this section Photos refer to color photographs and Plates refer to the line drawings. It should be noted that the drawings are not to a single scale.

GYMNOSPERMS

Atlantic White Cedar

Chamaecyparis thyoides (L.) BSP **Photo #1**

Form: Evergreen tree to about 28 m in height; branchlets appearing flattened when viewed in cross-section.

Leaves: Tiny and scalelike, opposite, less than 3 mm long and held on branchlets so that all appear to be held in one plane.

Cones: Mature female cones leathery, rounded, 5 - 8 mm in diameter, borne singly near the tips of the branches.

Distinguishing Marks: Distinguished from red cedar (*Juniperus virginiana*) by combination of flattened branchlets, branchlets borne in one plane, and globular, woody cones, from the closely related variety *C. thyoides* var. *henryae* (Li) Little, by nearly all leaves (rather than just the central leaves of major branches) bearing a tiny gland that may require a 10x lens to see clearly.

Distribution: Swamps, wet woodlands, and woodlands along streams; mostly west of the New River in the Florida panhandle but also known from locations in northeast and north central Florida including impressive populations in Marion and Putnam counties.

Eastern Red Cedar

Juniperus virginiana L. **Photo #2**

Form: Typically a densely vegetated evergreen tree to about 30 m in height.

Leaves: Mature leaves scalelike, green, opposite, four-ranked, 2 - 3 mm long.

Cones: Male and female cones borne on separate trees, male cone clusters 3 - 6 cm long, yellowish, and often borne in great profusion, giving an overall golden cast to male trees in late winter, female cones only about 5 - 9 mm long, bluish, berrylike, often in great abundance on a given tree.

Distinguishing Marks: Distinguished from white cedar (*Chamaecyparis thyoides*) by branchlets quadrangular when viewed in cross-section and not appearing to grow all in one plane, and by differences in the cones of the two species.

Distribution: Found in a wide array of conditions from roadsides and old fields to moist hammocks; throughout northern Florida and south to about Sarasota County.

Sand Pine

Pinus clausa (Chapm. ex Engelm.) Vasey ex Sarg.

Form: Small to medium-sized evergreen tree to about 25 m in height; bark of young trunks smooth, that of older trunks also somewhat smooth but closely ridged and broken into small plates.

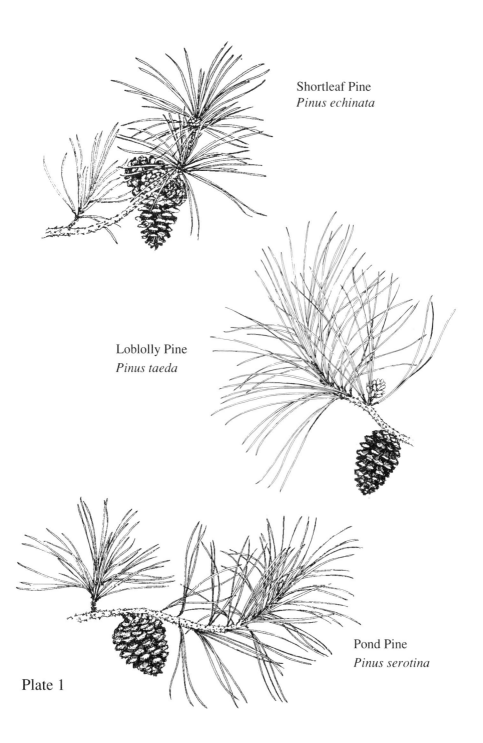

Shortleaf Pine
Pinus echinata

Loblolly Pine
Pinus taeda

Pond Pine
Pinus serotina

Plate 1

Leaves: Needles, short, mostly 4 - 8 cm long, borne predominately in fascicles of two.

Cones: Ovulate cones short, 5 - 8 cm long.

Distinguishing Marks: Most similar to the spruce pine (*P. glabra*), distinguished from it by occurring naturally only in deep coastal sands or along inland dune ridges, also by the inner surface of the cone scales bearing a dark brown band at the tip.

Distribution: Sporadic in natural stands along the panhandle coast, more common on inland sand ridges like those in and near the Ocala National Forest or along the central ridge in Highlands County, south to Broward and Collier counties; planted widely by forest product companies which makes identification by native habitat difficult.

Shortleaf Pine

Pinus echinata Mill.   **Plate 1**

Form: Medium or large evergreen tree to about 35 m in height with smooth, flat bark, often in large plates.

Leaves: Needles, borne mostly in fascicles of two, but some fascicles of three, 4 - 11 cm long.

Cones: Ovulate cones 4 - 6 cm long, very numerous on the tree, usually including old cones of several ages.

Distinguishing Marks: Distinguished from spruce pine (*P. glabra*) by having needles in fascicles of two and three and by bark being more characteristically pinelike.

Distribution: Generally restricted to upland woods of the northern panhandle and along the eastern side of the Apalachicola River southward to about Bristol.

Slash Pine

Pinus elliottii Engelm.   **Plate 2**

Form: Medium or large evergreen tree to about 40 m in height.

Leaves: Needles, 10 - 28 cm long, most commonly about 20 - 25 cm long, typically bound together in fascicles of two but often in twos and threes and extending brushlike from the branch.

Cones: Female cones 9 - 15 cm long; terminal buds brownish.

Distinguishing Marks: Distinguished from longleaf pine (*P. palustris*) by combination of brownish buds and comparatively shorter cones that are usually less than 15 cm in length.

Distribution: Statewide including the Keys; in south Florida this tree is more correctly known as *P. elliottii* var. *densa* Little & Dorman.

Spruce Pine

Pinus glabra Walt.   **Photo #3**

Form: Medium or large evergreen tree to about 40 m in height; bark tightly furrowed, broken into small plates, and more closely resembling the bark of a typical hardwood than a pine.

Leaves: Needles, 5 - 10 cm long, borne in fascicles of two.

Cones: Ovulate cones small, 5 - 10 cm long and very numerous on any given tree.

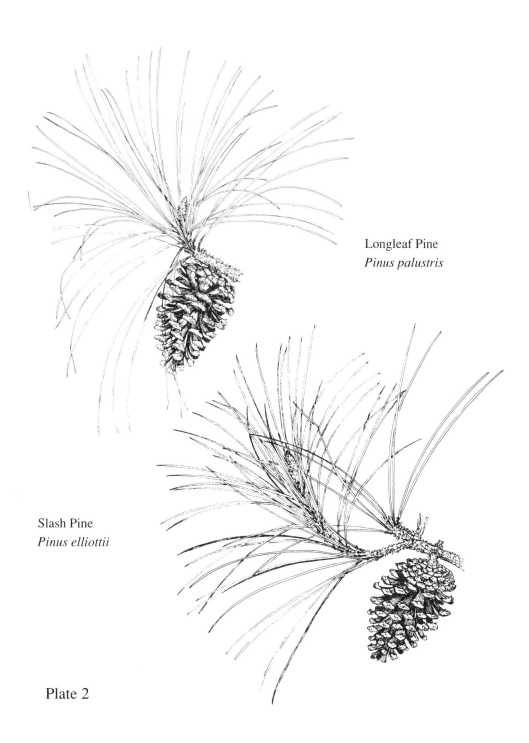

Longleaf Pine
Pinus palustris

Slash Pine
Pinus elliottii

Plate 2

123

Distinguishing Marks: Distinguished from the sand pine (*P. clausa*) by occurring intermixed with hardwoods in rich woodlands and calcareous bottomlands and by the inner surface of cone scales not bearing a brown band at the tip.

Distribution: Northwestern Florida, eastward to about Alachua County.

Longleaf Pine

Pinus palustris Mill. **Photo #4; Plate 2**

Form: Medium or large evergreen tree to about 40 m in height.

Leaves: Needles, largely borne in fascicles of three, 15 - 30 cm long (or longer), most commonly well over 20 cm long, extending from the branch in large globular clusters.

Cones: Female cones usually longer than 15 cm; terminal buds silvery white.

Distinguishing Marks: Distinguished from slash pine (*P. elliottii*) by silvery buds and cones generally longer than 15 cm.

Distribution: Statewide except the southern tip of the peninsula and the Keys; natural stands of this species are becoming increasingly scarce due largely to the practices of the forest products industry.

Pond Pine

Pinus serotina Michx. **Photo #5; Plate 1**

Form: Small to medium-sized evergreen tree to about 25 m in height; trunk sometimes twisted and appearing deformed, often bearing short adventitious branches.

Leaves: Needles, typically 6 - 20 cm long, predominately in fascicles of three though sometimes sparsely intermixed with those of both two and four.

Cones: Female cones 5 - 8 cm long, cone-shaped and resembling a toy top, often tightly closed and generally remaining on the tree for several years, old cones appearing to be sessile on the branch.

Distinguishing Marks: Most easily recognized by combination of adventitious branches and tightly closed, top-shaped cones.

Distribution: Throughout the panhandle to as far south as Osceola and Polk counties.

Loblolly Pine

Pinus taeda L. **Plate 1**

Form: Medium or large evergreen tree to about 40 m in height; bark often deeply furrowed and appearing to extend in vertical lines up the trunk.

Leaves: Needles, borne predominantly in fascicles of three but occasionally with only two per fascicle, ranging 8 - 22 cm long but averaging 12 - 15.

Cones: Female cones mostly sessile and mostly 6 - 10 cm long, at least a few cones on the tree at almost any time of year.

Distinguishing Marks: Distinguished from slash pine (*P. elliottii*) by needles predominately in fascicles of three, from longleaf (*P. palustris*) by overall shorter needles, shorter cones, and lack of silvery terminal buds.

Distribution: Widespread and common in uplands and old fields, as well as low woodlands; from the northern counties to just below the central part of the state.

Florida Yew

Taxus floridana Nutt. ex Chapm.

Form: Small evergreen tree to about 8 m in height with irregular branching.
Leaves: Dark green, needlelike, not exceeding about 2.5 cm in length and 2 mm in width, tips pointed but soft, not sharp to the touch.
Distinguishing Marks: Very similar in appearance to the torreya tree (*Torreya taxifolia*), pictured in Photo #6, distinguished from it by the yew's shorter, flexible leaves with soft-pointed tips, and irregular branching.
Distribution: Found chiefly on the bluffs and in ravines along the eastern edge of the upper Apalachicola River from just north of Bristol northward to Flat Creek and its tributaries, a few miles north of Torreya State Park.

Torreya, Stinking Cedar, Gopherwood

Torreya taxifolia Arn.   **Photo #6**

Form: Small evergreen tree to about 10 m in height, branches borne in whorls.
Leaves: Needlelike, glossy green, typically 3 - 5 cm long.
Distinguishing Marks: Distinguished from Florida yew (*Taxus floridana*) by whorled branching and by longer leaves with tips sharply pointed and piercing to the touch.
Distribution: Occurring naturally in the bluffs and ravines area of the upper Apalachicola River in the panhandle, in ravines of extreme southwestern Georgia, and in a small population of several sprouts on Dog Pond near Shady Grove in southeastern Jackson County; no mature specimens of this tree remain in native habitat; today's population consists chiefly of saplings and sprouts.

Pond-Cypress

Taxodium ascendens Brongn.   **Plate 3**

Form: Small to medium-sized deciduous tree, larger specimens to a maximum of about 40 m in height but usually not exceeding about 25 m.
Leaves: Mature leaves needlelike, green, 3 - 6 mm long (leaves on young trees sometimes much longer).
Distinguishing Marks: Leaves of mature trees differ from those of the bald-cypress (*T. distichum*) by being shorter and closely appressed to the supporting branchlets and by the short,

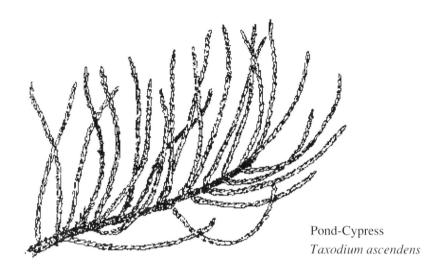

Pond-Cypress
Taxodium ascendens

Bald-Cypress
Taxodium distichum

Plate 3

126

leaf-bearing shoots being erect on their supporting twigs; leaves on young trees virtually indistinguishable from those of bald-cypress, particularly in the southern part of the state.

Distribution: Generally found in wet areas such as ponds, wet depressions, and shores of lakes; range generally the same as for bald-cypress, but slightly farther south.

Bald-Cypress

Taxodium distichum (L.) L. C. Rich   **Plate 3**

Form: Tall, straight deciduous tree to about 40 m in height; older trees often exhibiting a large buttressed base.

Leaves: Green, 8 - 20 mm long, typically spreading from their supporting shoots, thus featherlike in appearance.

Distinguishing Marks: Mature trees distinguished from mature pond-cypress (*T. ascendens*) by the featherlike leaves and by the short shoots spreading from their supporting twigs.

Distribution: Found in or along flowing water; generally statewide except for the southernmost counties and the Keys.

ANGIOSPERMS - MONOCOTS

Paurotis Palm or Saw Cabbage

Acoelorrhaphe wrightii (Griseb. & Wendl.) Becc.   **Photo #7**

Form: Delicate, slender-trunked, clump-forming tree to about 12 m in height; trunk typically matted with the remains of red-brown leaf bases for most of its extent.

Leaves: Fan shaped, green on both sides, about 60 cm across; petioles orangish, 20 - 90 cm long, armed with orange-colored, sawlike teeth along the edges.

Flowers: Yellow-green, borne on long stalks from among the leaves.

Fruit: Rounded, 5-8 mm in diameter, reddish orange when young but turning black with maturity.

Distinguishing Marks: Most easily identified by combination of slender, matted trunk and clump-forming growth habit.

Distribution: Native to south Florida, primarily the Everglades; planted as an ornamental in southern Florida and the Keys.

Coconut Palm

Cocos nucifera L.   **Plate 4**

Form: Attractive tree to about 20 m in height with a tall, leaning, often curved trunk that is topped by a cluster of long, plumelike leaves.

Leaves: Pinnate, to nearly 7 m in length; leaflets to about 1.5 m long, and 5 cm wide; petioles to nearly 2 m in length.

Flowers: Small, yellowish, borne in spikelike clusters to at least 1 m in length.

Fruit: Large, hard, three-sided, to about 40 cm long.

Distinguishing Marks: Distinguished from most other pinnate-leaved palms by characteristic coconut fruit and typically leaning trunk, from date palm (*Phoenix dactylifera*) by leaflets being opposite rather than extending from the rachis at various angles and by lacking sharp spines along the petiole.

Distribution: Naturalized and planted in much of south Florida, the Keys, and sparingly northward to about the Tampa area.

Silver Palm, Florida Silver Palm, Biscayne Palm, Seamberry Palm

Coccothrinax argentata (Jacq.) Bailey   **Photo #12**

Form: Small, slender, straight tree with a smooth trunk, not usually exceeding 6 m in height.

Leaves: Fan shaped, deeply divided almost to the point of attachment with the petiole, about 60 cm wide; segments shiny green above, conspicuously silvery white beneath; petioles unarmed, slender, flexible, to about 1 m long.

Flowers: White, fragrant, borne in long clusters.

Fruit: Rounded, deep purple to dark brown, 1 - 2 cm in diameter.

Distinguishing Marks: Distinguished from most other palms with fan-shaped leaves by the silvery white undersurfaces of the leaf segments, from Key thatch palm (*Thrinax morrisii*) by leaves being more deeply divided, darker green above, and having more narrow leaf segments.

Distribution: Coastal dunes and rocky pinelands; from north Palm Beach County southward including the Keys; the state champion for this species is found at Bahia Honda State Recreation Area.

Date Palm

Phoenix dactylifera L.

Form: Tree to about 30 m in height, topped with a sparse crown of 20 to 40 leaves, trunk often leaning and distinctively patterned with the scars of old leaf bases.

Leaves: Pinnate, to about 6 m in length or longer, petioles to about 45 cm long and bearing sharp spines; leaflets about 45 cm long, nearly flat, gray-green, sharp pointed, attached to the rachis at various angles.

Flowers: White, fragrant.

Fruit: The date of commerce, ovoid in shape, 2.5 - 7.5 cm in diameter, orange, edible and sweet to the taste.

Distinguishing Marks: Most likely confused only with the coconut palm (*Cocos nucifera*) but different from it by lacking the coconut fruit, by having leaflets being borne at various angles rather than being two-ranked, and by bearing sharp spines along the petiole.

Distribution: Nonnative palm cultivated and persistent in southern Florida, planted as far north as the Tampa area.

Coconut Palm
Cocos nucifera

Royal Palm
Roystonea elata

Washington Palm
Washingtonia robusta

Plate 4

129

Buccaneer Palm, Cherry Palm, Hog Palm

Pseudophoenix sargentii Wendl. ex Sarg.

Form: Tree to about 8 m in height with a smooth, gray-green trunk that is encircled with obvious rings and terminated by a smooth crown-shaft similar to that of the royal palm (*Roystonea elata*).

Leaves: Pinnate, unarmed, 2 - 3 m long, arching prominently, bases V-shaped; leaflets blue-green, stiff, to about 50 cm long with numerous threads suspended from the edges.

Flowers: Small, yellow-green, borne on short stalks.

Fruit: Bright red, rounded, to about 2 cm in diameter.

Distinguishing Marks: Distinguished from other palms with pinnate leaves by ringed trunk, from royal palm (which also has a trunk topped by a smooth, green crown-shaft) by the cherry palm's smaller, more delicate stature and shorter leaves.

Distribution: Well-drained rocky coastal areas of the Keys, thriving best in places with frequent saltwater inundation; very rare and nearly extinct in the wild, currently occurring naturally only on Elliott Key; cultivated but not native to the southern peninsula, most often seen as an ornamental.

Royal Palm

Roystonea elata (Bartr.) F. Harper   **Plate 4**

Form: Tall, stately tree to about 30 m in height with a massive, smooth, light gray trunk that is topped with a shiny, smooth, dark green and very conspicuous crown-shaft subtending a cluster of long, arching leaves.

Leaves: Pinnate, deep green, to about 4 m long; leaflets to about 1 m long, borne along the rachis in four distinctive rows.

Fruit: Blue, rounded, to a little more than 1 cm in diameter.

Distinguishing Marks: Most easily recognized by the concretelike appearance of the trunk in conjunction with the dark green crown-shaft.

Distribution: Native to southern Florida but not the Keys, though often seen in the Keys; often used in the southern part of the state to line streets and medians.

Cabbage Palm or Sabal Palm

Sabal palmetto (Walt.) Lodd. ex J.S. Schult. & J.H. Schult.   **Photo #8**

Form: Straight-trunked tree to about 18 m in height.

Leaves: Fan shaped, 1 - 2 m long, deeply divided and conspicuously V-shaped; segments shiny green above, gray-green below, with numerous threads suspended from the segment margins; petioles smooth, to about 2 m long.

Fruit: Round, black, borne in long, drooping clusters.

Distinguishing Marks: The V-shaped leaf is diagnostic for identification.

Distribution: Native throughout the state; Florida's state tree.

Saw Palmetto

Serenoa repens (Bartr.) Small
Photo #12

Form: Typically a low, prostrate shrub with most of the trunk more or less buried, but sometimes upright and having the dimensions of a small tree.
Leaves: Fan shaped, deeply divided into numerous segments, yellowish green to green; petioles 5 - 10 dm long, armed with sharp, curved spines reminiscent of a saw blade.
Flowers: Greenish white, 5 - 6 mm long, borne in spikelike clusters from among the leaves.
Fruit: An oblong drupe, yellowish at first but turning black at maturity, 15 - 25 mm long, 12 - 15 mm in diameter.
Distinguishing Marks: This is the common palmetto that ranges across much of Florida, most easily distinguished by the hard, sharp, recurved prickles that line both edges of its petiole; the photograph shows a shrubby specimen in flower at the base of a silver palm (*Coccothrinax argentata*).
Distribution: Sandy prairies, dunes, flatwoods, scrub oak ridges, and cabbage palm hammocks; throughout the state.

Key Thatch Palm, Brittle Thatch Palm, Key Palm, Small Fruited Thatch Palm

Thrinax morrisii Wendl.
Photo #10

Form: Tree, not normally exceeding about 7 m in height with a smooth gray trunk that is encircled by conspicuous leaf scars.
Leaves: Fan shaped, to about 1 m wide; segments green above, paler and whitish below; petioles unarmed, slender, to about 1.2 m long.
Flowers: Small, white turning to yellow.
Fruit: Rounded, white at maturity, 4 - 7 mm in diameter, borne essentially stalkless.
Distinguishing Marks: Distinguished from silver palm (*Coccothrinax argentata*) by white fruit and by leaf segments being wider and divided only about halfway to the leaf base, from Florida thatch palm (*Thrinax radiata*) by whitish leaf undersurface and stalkless fruit.
Distribution: A commercially exploited species that occurs in Florida only along the edges of hammocks and in pinelands of the Keys; readily seen on much of Key Deer National Wildlife Refuge.

Florida Thatch Palm, Jamaica Thatch Palm, Silk Top Thatch Palm

Thrinax radiata Lodd. ex J.S. Schult. & J.H. Schult.
Photo #18

Form: Tree to about 9 m in height with an exceptionally slender trunk.
Leaves: Fan shaped, to about 1 m wide, divided to about half the length of the leaf segments; segments green above with conspicuous yellow ribs, paler below; petioles slender, unarmed, to about 9 dm in length.
Flowers: Small, white, fragrant, borne in clusters.

Fruit: Smooth, white, rounded, 7 - 14 mm in diameter, borne on short stalks.

Distinguishing Marks: Distinguished from both the thatch palm (*Thrinax morrisii*) and silver palm (*Coccothrinax argentata*) by lacking the silvery white leaf undersurface, from cabbage palm (*Sabal palmetto*) by lacking the latter's V-shaped leaf.

Distribution: A commercially exploited species found naturally in shallow, coastal soils of the Florida Keys and the southernmost peninsula.

Washington Palm or Petticoat Palm

Washingtonia robusta Wendl.   **Plate 4**

Form: Tree to about 30 m in height with a brownish trunk; under natural conditions covered with a shaggy mass of dead leaves that looks like a skirt around the trunk.

Leaves: Fan shaped, 1 - 2 m wide, bright green; petioles reddish brown or orange-brown and covered with spines along the edges.

Flowers: Tiny, white, inconspicuous, borne in long clusters among the leaves.

Fruit: Rounded, shiny, black.

Distinguishing Marks: Distinguished from all other palms by its shaggy trunk, at least just below the leaves.

Distribution: Common as a cultivated plant in southern Florida, also sparingly planted as an ornamental in northern Florida.

ANGIOSPERMS—DICOTS

ACERACEAE

Box Elder or Ash-Leaved Maple

Acer negundo L.   **Plate 5**

Form: Small to medium-sized deciduous tree to about 20 m in height, typically branching quite close to the ground.

Leaves: Opposite, compound; leaflets typically three to five in number but very rarely as many as nine, 5 - 10 cm long, 5 - 7.5 cm wide, ovate to elliptic, margins coarsely toothed, each leaflet reminiscent of a single red maple (*A. rubrum*) leaf.

Flowers: Tiny, greenish yellow, borne in fascicles, appearing in early spring prior to new leaf growth.

Fruit: A two-winged samara typical of maple trees, each wing 2.5 - 3.5 cm long, generally appearing in midsummer.

Distinguishing Marks: Most easily distinguished from other north Florida trees by combination of opposite, compound leaves, leaflets with coarse serrations, and smooth, green twigs.

Distribution: Floodplains, wooded slopes, streambanks; from the vicinity of the Apalachicola River eastward and southward to Osceola County.

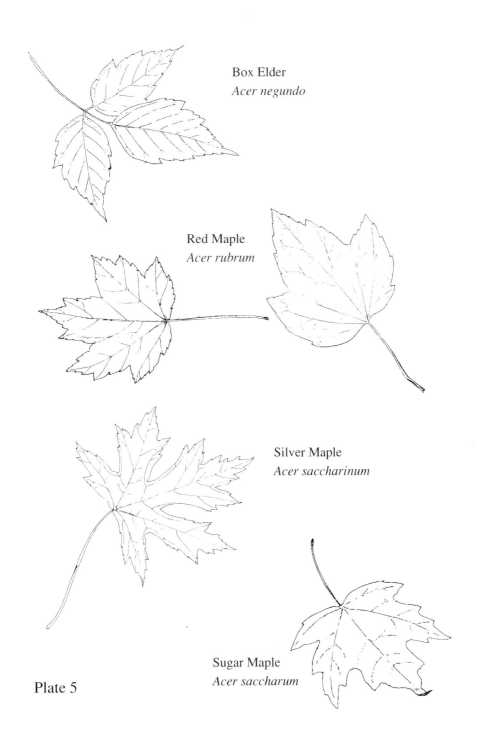

Box Elder
Acer negundo

Red Maple
Acer rubrum

Silver Maple
Acer saccharinum

Sugar Maple
Acer saccharum

Plate 5

Red Maple or Scarlet Maple

Acer rubrum L. **Photo #9; Plate 5**

Form: Small to large deciduous tree to 30 m in height with dark gray bark.
Leaves: Opposite, simple, mainly ovate, quite variable in size, 5 - 15 cm long, 3 - 10 cm wide, typically three- to five-lobed, margins serrate, upper surfaces green, lower surfaces typically grayish white, petioles and central leaf veins red.
Flowers: Tiny, red, borne in fascicles prior to the new leaves.
Fruit: A bright red, two-winged samara typical of other maple species, each wing 1 - 2.6 cm long.
Distinguishing Marks: Most easily distinguished by typical maple leaf shape with shallow rather than deep lobes in conjunction with its flowers, fruit, petioles, and central leaf veins all being red.
Distribution: Wet areas and moist woods throughout the northern part of the state and southward to about the Tamiami Trail.

Silver Maple or Soft Maple

Acer saccharinum L. **Plate 5**

Form: Medium-sized, rapidly growing deciduous tree to about 38 m in height.
Leaves: Opposite, simple, ovate, 6 - 20 cm long, green above, silvery white below, deeply and palmately five-lobed, the terminal lobe often with two lateral lobes, margins sharply serrate.
Flowers: Small, greenish yellow, borne in fascicles, appearing in early spring before new leaf growth.
Fruit: A two-winged samara typical of other maple species, each wing 3 - 6 cm long.
Distinguishing Marks: Most easily distinguished from other maples by the terminal leaf lobe of at least some leaves being more narrow at the base than at the middle and by the silvery color of the lower surfaces of leaves.
Distribution: A tree of the north-central panhandle; riverbanks, bottomlands, and slopes in Holmes, Jackson, Liberty, and Gadsden counties; often cultivated as a yard tree in other parts of northern Florida.

Sugar Maple, Southern Sugar Maple, Florida Maple

Acer saccharum Marsh. **Plate 5**

Form: Medium-sized deciduous tree to about 30 m in height.
Leaves: Opposite, simple, 3 - 9 cm long and wide, palmately three- to five-lobed, the three terminal-most lobes squarish, margins of lobes untoothed but sometimes themselves containing even smaller lobes.
Flowers: Small, borne in fascicles, typical of maple flowers.
Fruit: A two-winged samara typical of maple species, 1.5 - 3.5 cm long.
Distinguishing Marks: Distinguished as a maple by its leaf, distinguished from other maples by the obviously squarish lobes; there are two subspecies of this plant, *A. saccharum* Marsh.

subsp. *leucoderme* (Small) and A. *saccharum* Marsh. subsp. *floridanum* (Chapm.); the lower surfaces of the leaves are yellowish green on the former, whitish on the latter.

Distribution: Bluffs, ravines, upland woods of the northern part of the state; most common in the Chipola/Apalachicola River drainage basin.

Mango
Mangifera indica L.

Form: Medium-sized, densely compact evergreen tree to about 15 m in height.
Leaves: Lanceolate to long elliptic, averaging 10 - 25 cm long, 2 - 7 cm wide, reddish when young (following flowering), dark shiny green at maturity, lateral veins straight, parallel, in 20 to 30 pairs.
Flowers: Small, white, pinkish white, greenish, yellowish, or reddish, borne in long, conspicuous panicles on reddish, hairy branches and appearing from January to March.
Fruit: A large, fleshy drupe that is easily recognized as the common mango of commerce (contact with the fruit's outer surface causes a skin rash in some individuals).
Distinguishing Marks: Most easily recognized by its large leaf and the swollen base of the petiole.
Distribution: Imported from India and grown commercially in southern Florida where it sometimes volunteers from seeds; also used as an attractive street or dooryard tree.

Poisonwood or Florida Poison Tree
Metopium toxiferum (L.) Krug & Urban   **Photo #11; Plate 6**

Form: Evergreen tree to about 12 m in height with scaly, reddish brown bark that often exhibits blackish spots of poisonous sap that has exuded from the trunk.
Leaves: Alternate, pinnately compound; leaflets numbering three to seven, generally triangular in shape, 2 - 8 cm long, shining green above and often with characteristic blackish spots.
Flowers: Creamy white and borne in clusters.
Fruit: A yellow-orange drupe, 1 - 1.5 cm long, borne in spreading clusters.
Distinguishing Marks: Likely to be confused only with gumbo-limbo (*Bursera simaruba*) but differing from it by having dark green rather than yellow-green leaflets that are mostly triangular rather than ovate, and by the conspicuous black dots on older leaflets.
Distribution: Hammocks and pinelands; southern Florida (except the west coast) and the Keys.

Winged Sumac or Shining Sumac
Rhus copallina L.   **Photo #13; Plate 6**

Form: Deciduous shrub or small, slender tree to about 8 m in height.
Leaves: Alternate, pinnately compound with a winged rachis, to about 30 cm long; leaflets 9 to 23 in number, lanceolate to elliptic, 3 - 8 cm long, 1 - 3 cm wide, margins typically entire but

sometimes with a few teeth, lower surfaces pubescent, upper surfaces mostly glabrous except for a few scattered hairs along the main veins.

Flowers: Tiny, greenish yellow, borne in conspicuous clusters.

Fruit: A flattened drupe, each 3 - 5 mm in diameter, pubescent, dull reddish, borne in conspicuous clusters, mostly in the fall.

Distinguishing Marks: Distinguished from similarly leaved Brazilian pepper (*Schinus terebinthifolius*) by leaflets of the latter usually numbering less than nine, and fruits glabrous rather than hairy; from the soapberry (*Sapindus saponaria*), which also has a winged rachis, by the latter generally having only eight or fewer leaflets.

Distribution: Uplands and disturbed sites; statewide except for the Keys.

Smooth Sumac

Rhus glabra L.

Form: Slender deciduous shrub or small tree to about 7 m in height and very similar in general appearance to shining sumac (*R. copallina*).

Leaves: Alternate, pinnately compound, 12 to 14 cm in overall length; leaflets numbering 9 - 31, lanceolate, 5 - 14 cm long, 1 - 4 cm wide, upper surfaces bright green, lower surfaces grayish, margins toothed.

Flowers: Tiny, yellowish green, borne in large clusters at the tips of branches.

Fruit: Berrylike, rounded, borne in large, conical clusters at the tips of branches.

Distinguishing Marks: Similar to the winged sumac, pictured on p. 137, distinguished from it by lacking a winged leaf rachis and by the lower surfaces of leaflets having a grayish, waxy bloom.

Distribution: Woodland borders and disturbed sites; central panhandle from about Jefferson to Jackson counties.

Brazilian Pepper or Pepper Tree

Schinus terebinthifolius Raddi   **Photo #14; Plate 6**

Form: Evergreen shrub or small, attractive tree to about 8 m in height.

Leaves: Alternate, pinnately compound, to about 15 cm in overall length, with a narrowly winged rachis; leaflets typically numbering three to nine (rarely 11), lanceolate to elliptic, to 8 cm long, margins sometimes entire but often toothed; crushed foliage gives off a distinctive turpentine aroma.

Flowers: Small, white, borne in conspicuous clusters at the leaf axils.

Fruit: A bright red drupe, borne in conspicuous clusters, typically appearing from about November to February, but evident at almost any time of year.

Distinguishing Marks: Distinguished from winged sumac (*Rhus copallina*) by leaflets usually numbering less than nine and by fruits glabrous and bright red, rather than hairy and dark red.

Distribution: A troublesome weed in many habitats throughout central and southern Florida and the Keys.

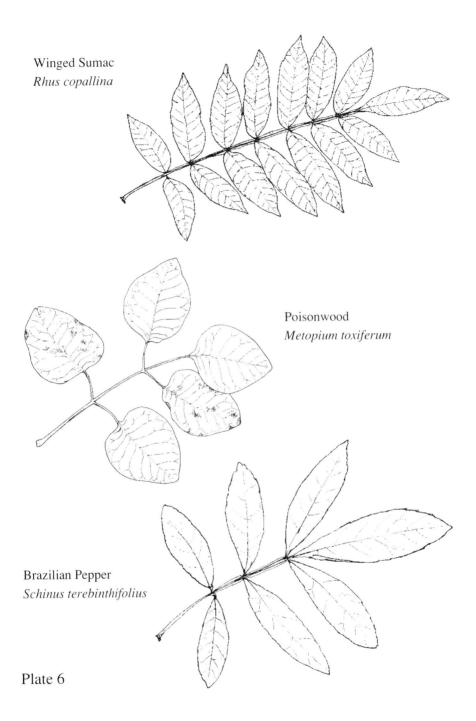

Winged Sumac
Rhus copallina

Poisonwood
Metopium toxiferum

Brazilian Pepper
Schinus terebinthifolius

Plate 6

Poison Sumac
Toxicodendron vernix (L.) Kuntze

Form: Slender, sparingly branched deciduous shrub or small tree to about 7 m in height.
Leaves: Alternate, pinnately compound, 18 - 35 cm long; leaflets numbering 7 - 15, ovate to elliptic, 3.5 - 10 cm long, 2 - 5 cm wide, smooth, shiny green above, sometimes wider on one side of the central leaflet vein than the other; leaf and leaflet stalks often reddish.
Flowers: Tiny, yellowish, borne in large, branching clusters from the leaf axils.
Fruit: A grayish white, berrylike, rounded drupe, to about 1 cm in diameter.
Distinguishing Marks: The compound leaves with reddish petioles, well-spaced leaflets, and inequilateral leaflet blades set this tree apart from all other wetland species in northern Florida.
Distribution: Uncommon in wet woodlands, bogs, and swamps throughout the panhandle, eastward and southward to about Marion County.

ANNONACEAE

Pond Apple
Annona glabra L.

Photo #15

Form: Small to medium-sized evergreen tree to about 16 m in height.
Leaves: Alternate, simple, entire, two-ranked, shiny green, leathery, 7.5 - 15 cm long, 3 - 7 cm wide, apices pointed, blade often reflexed upward in the shape of a V from the central axis.
Flowers: Borne hanging on short stalks, with six cream-white to pale yellow petals in two sizes, outermost petals 1.6 - 2 cm long, opening from a distinctive triangular bud, typically appearing March to August.
Fruit: Edible, large, 7 - 13 cm long, egg or heart shaped, pale yellow with brown spots.
Distinguishing Marks: Similar to some species of the genus *Ficus* but distinguished from them by its generally reflexed leaves and distinctive flowers.
Distribution: Banks of freshwater ponds and streams and wet hammocks; from about Brevard County southward and throughout the Keys.

Sugar Apple
Annona squamosa L.

Photo #16

Form: Tropical shrub or small tree to about 4 m in height, with branches that often droop toward their tips.
Leaves: Similar to pond apple in being alternate, two-ranked, simple, and entire, but more lance shaped, 5 - 13 cm long, less than 5 cm wide.
Flowers: Outer petals 1.6 - 2.6 cm long, the entire flower appearing longer and less rounded than pond apple.
Fruit: Rounded, yellowish green, 6.5 - 10 cm in diameter, knobby, very sweet to the taste and quite different in appearance from that of the pond apple.
Distinguishing Marks: The fruit is diagnostic.
Distribution: Introduced and persistent from cultivation, found only in the Keys.

Flag Pawpaw
Asimina obovata (Willd.) Nash

Form: Deciduous shrub that only occasionally reaches treelike proportions.
Leaves: Alternate, simple, entire, 4 - 12 cm long, 2 - 4 cm wide, oblong to oval in shape but somewhat narrowed near the base.
Flowers: White, fragrant, 6 - 10 cm wide, hanging from the tips of new shoot growth.
Fruit: A large, fleshy berry, 5 - 9 cm in length.
Distinguishing Marks: Distinguished from other tree-sized pawpaws by occurring only on coastal dunes and sand ridges and in coastal hammocks, and by young twigs, petioles, veins on lower surfaces of leaves, and peduncles conspicuously clothed with reddish pubescence.
Distribution: Coastal dunes, sand pine–scrub oak woods of eastern Florida; ranging from the northeastern to the southeastern peninsula.

Small-Fruited, Small-Flowered, or Dwarf Pawpaw
Asimina parviflora (Michx.) Dunal

Form: Shrub or small deciduous tree to about 6 m in height.
Leaves: Alternate, simple, entire, 6 - 15 (sometimes 20) cm long, reddish hairy on the lower surfaces when young, becoming sparsely reddish hairy on veins when mature.
Flowers: Maroon with a fetid aroma, less than 2 cm wide, appearing February - April.
Fruit: A fleshy berry, greenish yellow, 3 - 7 cm long.
Distinguishing Marks: Similar to dog banana (*A. triloba*) pictured on p. 140, differing from the latter mainly by having shorter leaves, smaller flowers, smaller fruits, and a generally smaller stature.
Distribution: Mesic woodlands, floodplains, and coastal hammocks; throughout the panhandle and northern Florida, extending down the eastern peninsula to about Orange and Brevard counties.

Dog Banana or Indian Banana
Asimina triloba (L.) Dunal   **Plate 7**

Form: Deciduous shrub or small tree to about 14 m in height.
Leaves: Alternate, simple, entire, 15 - 30 cm long (many on a given plant over 15 cm), widest at the tip then tapering to a narrowed base, apices mostly acuminate.
Flowers: Maroon, with a fetid aroma, 2 - 5 cm wide when opened, their stalks 1 cm long or more, appearing in May and June.
Fruit: Oblong, 5 - 15 cm long, greenish yellow.
Distinguishing Marks: Distinguished from dwarf pawpaw (*A. parviflora*) by flowers generally greater than 2 cm wide and leaves usually greater than 15 cm long.
Distribution: Mesic woodlands; limited to the central panhandle from Okaloosa to Liberty counties.

Dog Banana
Asimina triloba

Plate 7

APOCYNACEAE

Pearl Berry or Tear Shrub

Vallesia antillana Woodson   **Photo #17**

Form: Typically an evergreen shrub to about 4 m in height, sometimes obtaining the stature of a small tree; bark pale and furrowed.
Leaves: Alternate, simple, entire, elliptic to obovate, to about 8 cm long.
Flowers: Small, star shaped with five thin, white petals that spread laterally at the terminus of a tube-shaped corolla.
Fruit: A glossy, white, nearly translucent, pear-shaped drupe to a little more than 1 cm in length.
Distinguishing Marks: Both the fruits and the flowers may be seen on the plant throughout the year (sometimes in combination) and aid in identifying the plant.
Distribution: Hammocks and hammock edges of south Florida and the Keys.

AQUIFOLIACEAE

Carolina or Sand Holly

Ilex ambigua (Michx.) Torr. var. *ambigua*   **Photo #19**

Form: Normally a low, dioecious, deciduous shrub with light gray bark, sometimes treelike to about 6 m in height.
Leaves: Alternate, simple, with crenate to serrate margins, 2.5 - 10 cm long and 1 - 5 cm wide, marginal teeth generally only present from about the middle of the leaf upward.

Flowers: Male flowers borne in clusters, female flowers solitary.

Fruit: Green at first, turning red with maturity, berrylike, relatively large, 4 - 7 mm in diameter.

Distinguishing Marks: Distinguished from other deciduous hollies by having flower and fruit stalks less than 4 mm long, and by dry habitat (see *I. verticillata*).

Distribution: Upland mixed woods and sand ridges; throughout northern Florida and south to Lee County.

Sarvis Holly

Ilex amelanchier M. A. Curtis in Chapm.   **Plate 8**

Form: Typically a deciduous shrub but sometimes treelike to about 5 m in height.

Leaves: Alternate, simple, oblong, 5 - 9 cm long, 1.5 - 4.5 cm wide, margins entire to minutely serrate, lower surfaces of leaves copiously shaggy pubescent.

Flowers: Tiny, borne in small clusters at the leaf axils.

Fruit: Dull red, rounded, berrylike, 5 - 10 mm in diameter.

Distinguishing Marks: Distinguished from black-alder (*I. verticillata*) and possum-haw (*I. decidua*), the other two wetland hollies, by having leaves with margins entire, or with only minute teeth from about the middle upward, and by having pubescent leaves; very similar in appearance to downy serviceberry (*Amelanchier arborea*) but generally found in wetter habitats and retaining pubescence on the lower surfaces of leaves into maturity.

Distribution: Restricted to wetland habitats including gum and creek swamps and floodplain forests; known in Florida only from Escambia to Liberty counties; populations of this plant are scattered making the plant only locally common.

Dahoon

Ilex cassine L.   **Photo #20; Plate 8**

Form: Dioecious evergreen tree to about 12 m in height with smooth, light gray bark.

Leaves: Alternate, simple, 3 - 14 cm long, with mostly entire margins (a few to many on any tree with marginal teeth), apices tipped with a small bristle.

Flowers: White, small, with four petals.

Fruit: Red, yellow, or orange, 6 - 9 mm in diameter.

Distinguishing Marks: The smooth gray bark, bright red berries, and bristle-tipped leaves help set this species apart.

Distribution: Chiefly occurring close to the coast in the panhandle but found throughout the peninsula, south nearly to Flamingo in Dade County, to the Ten Thousand Islands in Collier County, not present in the Keys; often associated with cypress ponds and flatwoods depressions in the peninsular locations.

Sarvis Holly
Ilex amelanchier

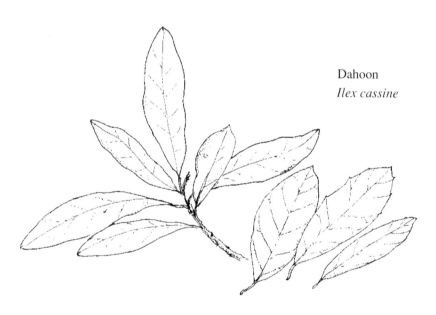

Dahoon
Ilex cassine

Plate 8

Large Sweet Gallberry

Ilex coriacea (Pursh) Chapm.

Photo #22

Form: Typically an evergreen shrub but sometimes growing into a tree.
Leaves: Alternate, simple, 3.5 - 9 cm long, 1.5 - 4 cm wide, with black dots on undersurfaces, margins entire or with a few spreading, short, bristlelike teeth.
Flowers: Small, borne in clusters at the leaf axils.
Fruit: A black, berrylike drupe, 7 - 10 mm in diameter.
Distinguishing Marks: Distinguished as the only widely distributed, tree-sized Florida holly with black fruits; distinguished from the shrubby gallberry (*I. glabra*) by the teeth on the leaf edges extending all the way to the base of the leaf or at least to below the middle of the leaf rather than just to the leaf's midsection, and by the teeth on the latter species being appressed-crenate rather than spreading.
Distribution: Commonly inhabiting bogs and wet areas from the western panhandle south to about Polk County; often in the wettest of such places.

Possum-Haw

Ilex decidua Walt.

Plate 9

Form: Small, deciduous, understory tree to about 10 m in height.
Leaves: Alternate (but sometimes crowded and appearing opposite toward the tips of branch-lets), simple, spatulate to obovate in shape, usually widest above the middle but sometimes elliptic, 2.5 - 8 cm long, .8 - 4.5 cm wide, margins obscurely to obviously crenate, each marginal tooth tipped with a tiny gland that is visible with magnification, bases cuneate.
Flowers: Male and female flowers borne in the leaf axils on separate trees.
Fruit: Red, yellow, or orange, 4 - 9 mm in diameter with pedicels up to 20 mm long.
Distinguishing Marks: Superficially similar to yaupon holly (*I. vomitoria*) but distinguished from it by being deciduous rather than evergreen and by having longer, more pliable leaves, from black alder (*I. verticillata*) and sarvis holly (*I. amelanchier*) by crenate leaf margins; also similar to Walter viburnum (*Viburnum obovatum*) but distinguished from it by having alternate rather than opposite leaves.
Distribution: Floodplains, secondary woods; throughout the panhandle eastward to the Suwannee River and southward to DeSoto County.

Tawnyberry Holly or Krug's Holly

Ilex krugiana Loesn.

Plate 9

Form: Small, evergreen tree to about 10 m in height.
Leaves: Alternate, simple, entire, 5 - 9 cm long, 3 - 5 cm wide, ovate to elliptic with a tapering tip.
Flowers: Male and female flowers borne on separate trees, produced in short clusters at the leaf axils.
Fruit: Round, 4 - 7 mm in diameter, sometimes red, tardily turning purplish to black.

Distinguishing Marks: Most easily recognized by inspecting the fallen leaves which shortly turn blackish.

Distribution: Rare and local; found chiefly in the Everglades hammocks of lower Dade County; considered threatened in Florida.

Myrtle-Leaved Holly

Ilex myrtifolia Walt.   **Photo #23**

Form: Dioecious evergreen shrub that sometimes assumes the stature of a scrubby tree to about 8 m in height.

Leaves: Alternate, simple, stiff, leathery, short, narrowly elliptic, .5 - 3 cm long, .3 - .8 cm wide.

Flowers: Borne in the leaf axils.

Fruit: Typically red but sometimes orange or yellow, 5 - 8 mm in diameter.

Distinguishing Marks: Most easily distinguished by its hollylike appearance in combination with its short, very narrow leaves.

Distribution: Commonly associated with cypress-gum ponds, savannas, flatwoods depressions, bay swamps, and open wetlands throughout the panhandle and south to about Union and Bradford counties.

American Holly

Ilex opaca Ait. var *opaca*   **Plate 9**

Form: Handsome evergreen tree with splotchy gray and whitish bark, to about 15 m in height.

Leaves: Alternate, thick, leathery, dark green, simple, 3 - 12 cm long, 2 - 5.5 cm wide, margins spiny toothed with bristles that are sharp to the touch.

Flowers: Male and female flowers borne on separate trees, both small and arising in the leaf axils.

Fruit: Rounded, bright red, 7 - 12 mm in diameter.

Distinguishing Marks: The spiny-edged, dark green leaves set this species apart.

Distribution: From the westernmost panhandle eastward and southward to about Polk and Hillsborough counties. (A shrubby variety, *I. opaca* Ait. var. *arenicola* (Ashe) Ashe, not described here, inhabits deep sands in the pine–oak scrub and extends slightly further down the peninsula into Highlands County.)

Black-Alder or Winterberry

Ilex verticillata (L.) A. Gray   **Plate 10**

Form: Dioecious deciduous shrub or small tree to about 8 m in height.

Leaves: Alternate, simple, elliptic to oval, typically 4 - 10 cm long, 1.5 - 5 cm wide, apices acuminate.

Flowers: Small, with four petals, borne in the leaf axils.

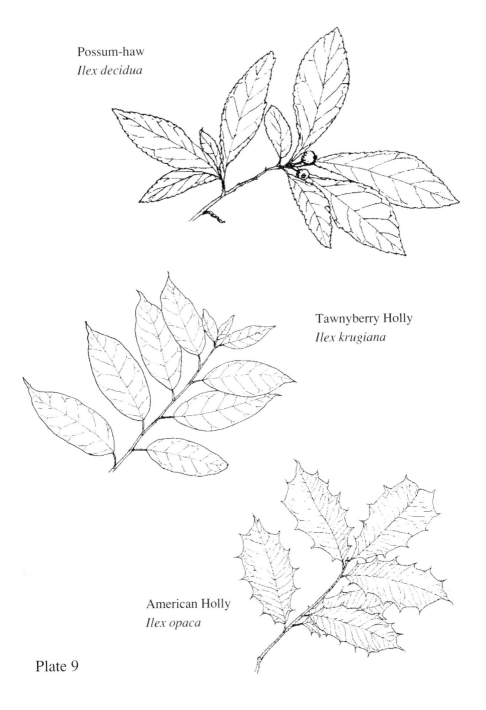

Possum-haw
Ilex decidua

Tawnyberry Holly
Ilex krugiana

American Holly
Ilex opaca

Plate 9

Fruit: Round, red, berrylike, 5 - 8 mm in diameter.

Distinguishing Marks: Distinguished from the Sarvis holly (*I. amelanchier*) and possum-haw (*I. decidua*), which also inhabit wetland communities, by having leaf margins with small but sharp teeth. (It should also be noted that distinguishing between this plant and *I. ambigua* is extremely difficult. In general the latter plant is not known to inhabit wetlands. However, at least one observer has reported it from such locations.)

Distribution: Generally limited and local in distribution, and uncommon; confined to wetlands including swamps, bogs, floodplains, and wet woodlands of the western panhandle and eastward to Liberty County.

Yaupon

Ilex vomitoria Ait. **Photo #21; Plate 10**

Form: Dioecious evergreen shrub or small bushy tree to about 8 m in height.

Leaves: Alternate, simple, dark green on the upper surfaces, stiff, elliptic to oval, .5 to 3 cm long, .5 - 2.5 cm wide.

Flowers: White, small (but conspicuous), appearing in spring and borne in leaf axils.

Fruit: Round, bright red, averaging 5 - 7 mm in diameter.

Distinguishing Marks: Distinguished as the only evergreen holly with leaves having crenate edges throughout their lengths; somewhat similar to both *Ilex decidua* and *Viburnum obovatum* by having leaves with crenate edges, but distinguished from the former by having generally shorter, stiffer leaves, from latter by leaves being alternate rather than opposite.

Distribution: Widespread and common in a variety of situations in northern Florida south to Sarasota County on the west coast, Brevard County on the east coast; a disjunct population once stood at a single location just east of Naples and was probably cultivated by the Seminoles.

ARALIACEAE

Devil's Walking Stick

Aralia spinosa L. **Photo #24**

Form: Deciduous shrub or small, single-trunked tree to about 10 m in height; trunk armed with short, stout, sharp-pointed thorns.

Leaves: Alternate, bipinnately compound (or sometimes tripinnately compound), triangular in overall outline, very large, .5 - 1.5 m long, arising from and clasping the main trunk; leaflets numerous, ovate, 3 - 10 cm long, margins serrate.

Flowers: Tiny, whitish, borne in long, showy, densely branched clusters, each inflorescence up to 1.2 m long.

Fruit: A rounded, purplish to purplish black drupe, 5 - 8 mm in diameter.

Distinguishing Marks: Distinguished from all other north Florida trees by large, triangular, bipinnately compound leaves.

Distribution: Understory in upland and lowland woods in the northern third of the state.

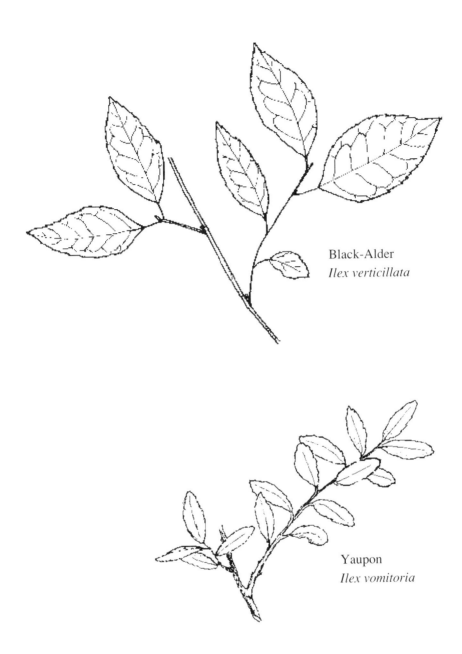

Black-Alder
Ilex verticillata

Yaupon
Ilex vomitoria

Plate 10

Black Mangrove

Avicennia germinans (L.),L. **Photo #25**

Form: Bushy evergreen tree of tidal flats and other shallow saltwater areas, potentially to about 25 m in height but usually shorter than this in Florida.

Leaves: Opposite, simple, elliptic to lanceolate, 5 - 12 cm long, 2 - 4 cm wide, upper surfaces green, lower surfaces copiously covered with a grayish pubescence, often with salt crystals evident on one or both surfaces.

Flowers: White, tubular, with four petals, borne in dense, conical heads at almost any time of year.

Fruit: A flat, shiny green pod, 3 - 5 cm long, asymmetrical in shape, apices pointed.

Distinguishing Marks: Distinguished from other mangroves by leaves with grayish undersurfaces, by green, flattened fruits, by dark to blackish bark, and by the presence of numerous short breathing roots, or pneumatophores, projecting from the ground in dense thickets below and around the tree.

Distribution: By far the most wide-ranging mangrove in Florida; most common on the lower southwest coast and the keys; found sparingly at least as far north as Shell Island off Panama City on the west coast and St. Johns County on the east coast; the more northern plants are often small, sometimes not exceeding but a few centimeters in height.

Hazel Alder

Alnus serrulata (Ait.) Willd. **Plate 11**

Form: Deciduous shrub or small tree to about 10 m in height with a crooked trunk and young twigs bearing a dense, brown pubescence.

Leaves: Alternate, simple, elliptic to obovate, 5 - 10 cm long, 2 - 5 cm wide, upper surfaces green, lower surfaces brownish, margins slightly wavy and unevenly toothed; veins conspicuously depressed on upper leaf surfaces and protruding on the lower.

Flowers: Male flowers tiny, borne in conspicuous, pendulous catkins, 4 - 8 cm long, appearing in middle to late fall.

Fruit: Reminiscent of a tiny pine cone, 7 - 12 mm long.

Distinguishing Marks: Distinguished from all other Florida trees but the river birch (*Betula nigra*) by tiny "cones," some of which commonly persist on the tree year-round, from river birch by lacking the latter's distinctly doubly serrate leaves and scaly, flaking bark.

Distribution: Swamps, rivulets, wet woods, alluvial streambanks and similar places; irregularly distributed throughout the panhandle and northernmost Florida.

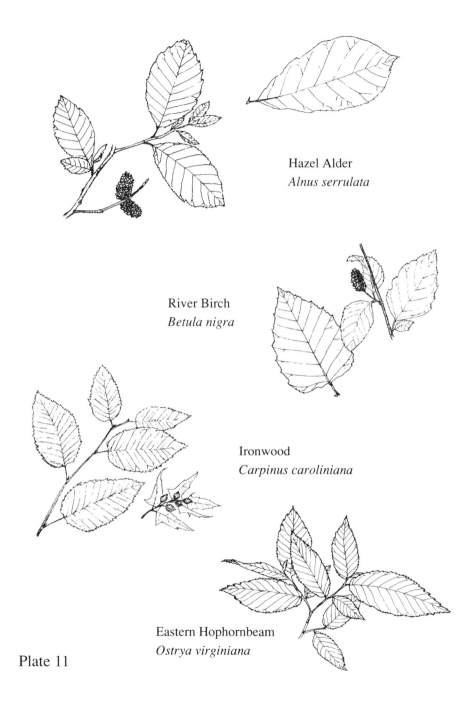

Hazel Alder
Alnus serrulata

River Birch
Betula nigra

Ironwood
Carpinus caroliniana

Eastern Hophornbeam
Ostrya virginiana

Plate 11

River Birch

Betula nigra L.   **Plate 11**

Form: Medium-sized deciduous tree to about 35 m in height with reddish to yellowish brown, scaly and flaking bark.
Leaves: Alternate, simple, nearly triangular in shape, 3 - 10 cm long, 1 - 3 cm wide, margins doubly serrate.
Flowers: Male flowers borne in pendulous catkins, female flowers in short, erect catkins, 5 - 7.5 cm long.
Fruit: Small, borne in small, conelike structures that are 2.5 - 4 cm long.
Distinguishing Marks: No other Florida tree has the combination of doubly serrate, nearly triangular leaves and scaly bark.
Distribution: Floodplains and wooded streambanks; throughout northern Florida.

Ironwood, American Hornbeam, Blue Beech

Carpinus caroliniana Walt.   **Plate 11**

Form: Small deciduous tree to about 10 m in height with hard, gray, smoothish, close-grained bark that often appears to spiral around the trunk.
Leaves: Alternate, simple, two-ranked, ovate, 2 - 10 cm long, 1 - 4.6 cm wide, bases slightly cordate, blades often slightly asymmetrical on either side of the central vein, margins doubly serrate.
Flowers: Male flowers tiny, borne in pendulous, cylindrical catkins, 2 - 4 cm long, catkins usually borne singly at the node.
Fruit: A small, brown, ribbed nutlet, 4 - 6 mm long.
Distinguishing Marks: Most easily confused with the closely related eastern hophornbeam (*Ostrya virginiana*) but differing from it by having smooth, gray, tightly compressed bark and a fluted trunk rather than the latter's generally brown, shredding bark.
Distribution: Wet woodlands, swamps, floodplains; northern part of the state southward to about Lake County.

Eastern Hophornbeam

Ostrya virginiana (Mill.) K. Koch   **Plate 11**

Form: Small deciduous tree to at least 20 m in height with thin, brown bark that often peels off in narrow shreds, young branches of the current growing season characteristically slightly zigzag.
Leaves: Alternate, simple, two-ranked, ovate, 5 - 13 cm long, 2 - 5 cm wide, margins serrate to doubly serrate.
Flowers: Male flowers borne in distinctive, light reddish brown, drooping catkins, 2 - 4 cm long, usually borne in clusters of two or three.
Fruit: An enlarged catkin with a succession of what appear to be overlapping bracts (reminiscent of hops' fruits), appearing in spring.
Distinguishing Marks: Distinguished from ironwood (*Carpinus caroliniana*), which has a similar leaf, by having brown, shredding bark rather than smooth, hard, gray, fluted bark; from

1. Atlantic White Cedar
    Chamaecyparis thyoides   *page 120*

4. Longleaf Pine
    Pinus palustris   *page 124*

2. Eastern Red Cedar
    Juniperus virginiana   *page 120*

3. Spruce Pine
    Pinus glabra   *page 122*

5. Pond Pine
    Pinus serotina   *page 124*

6. Torreya
   Torreya taxifolia   *page 125*

8. Sabal Palm
   Sabal palmetto   *page 130*

7. Paurotis Palm
   Acoelorrhaphe wrightii   *page 127*

9. Red Maple
   Acer rubrum   *page 134*

11. Poisonwood
    Metopium toxiferum   *page 135*

10. Key Thatch Palm
    Thrinax morrisii   *page 131*

14. Brazilian Pepper
    Schinus terebinthifolius   *page 136*

12. Silver Palm
    Coccothrinax argentata   *page 128*
    Saw Palmetto *Serenoa repens*   *page 131*

15. Pond Apple
    Annona glabra   *page 138*

13. Winged Sumac
    Rhus copallina   *page 135*

16. Sugar Apple
    Annona squamosa   *page 138*

17. Pearl Berry
 Vallesia antillana   *page 140*

19. Carolina Holly
 Ilex ambigua   *page 140*

18. Florida Thatch Palm
 Thrinax radiata   *page 131*

20. Dahoon
    Ilex cassine   *page 141*

22. Large Sweet Gallberry
    Ilex coriacea   *page 143*

21. Yaupon
    Ilex vomitoria   *page 146*

23. Myrtle-leaved Holly
   Ilex myrtifolia   *page 144*

25. Black Mangrove
   Avicennia germinans   *page 148*

24. Devil's Walking Stick
   Aralia spinosa   *page 146*

26. Catalpa
    Catalpa bignonioides   *page 151*

29. Bahama Strongbark
    Bourreria ovata   *page 152*

27. Yellow Elder
    Tecoma stans   *page 151*

28. Geiger Tree
    Cordia sebestena   *page 152*

30. Gumbo Limbo
    Bursera simaruba   *page 154*

TREES OF FLORIDA

31. Cinnamon Bark
    Canella winterana   *page 155*

34. Possum-haw
    Viburnum nudum   *page 157*

32. Elder-berry
    Sambucus canadensis   *page 156*

35. Walter Viburnum
    Viburnum obovatum   *page 158*

33. Arrow-wood
    Viburnum dentatum   *page 157*

36. Rusty Haw
    Viburnum rufidulum   *page 158*

37. Australian Pine
    Casuarina equisetifolia   *page 160*

39. Rhacoma
    Crossopetalum rhacoma   *page 161*

38. Papaya
    Carica papaya   *page 158*

40. False Boxwood
    Gyminda latifolia   *page 162*

43. Silver Buttonwood *Conocarpus erectus* var. *sericeus*   *page 166*

41. Florida Mayten
    Maytenus phyllanthoides   *page 163*

44. White Mangrove
    Laguncularia racemosa   *page 167*

42. Autograph Tree
    Clusia rosea   *page 164*

45. Black Titi
    Cliftonia monophylla   *page 172*

48. Common Persimmon
    Diospyros virginiana   *page 172*

46. Flowering Dogwood
    Cornus florida   *page 170*

49. Mountain Laurel
    Kalmia latifolia   *page 173*

47. Swamp Cyrilla
    Cyrilla racemiflora   *page 172*

50. Stagger Bush
    Lyonia ferruginea   *page 173*

51. Tung Tree
    Aleurites fordii   *page 176*

53. Milkbark
    Drypetes diversifolia   *page 177*

52. Highbush Blueberry
    Vaccinium corymbosum   *page 174*

54. Manchineel
Hippomane mancinella   *page 178*

57. Chapman Oak
Quercus chapmanii   *page 184*

55. Manihot
Manihot grahamii   *page 178*

58. Sand Live Oak
Quercus geminata   *page 185*

56. Popcorn Tree
Sapium sebiferum   *page 178*

59. Laurel Oak
Quercus hemisphaerica   *page 186*

60. Bluejack Oak
    Quercus incana   *page 186*

63. Live Oak
    Quercus virginiana   *page 196*

61. Scrub Oak
    Quercus inopina   *page 186*

64. Yellow Anise
    Illicium parviflorum   *page 199*

62. Blackjack Oak
    Quercus marilandica   *page 189*

65. Pignut Hickory
    Carya glabra   *page 200*

TREES OF FLORIDA

66. Camphor Tree
   Cinnamomum camphora   *page 204*

68. Lancewood
   Ocotea coriacea   *page 205*

67. Florida Anise
   Illicium floridanum   *page 198*

69. Red Bay
   Persea borbonia   page 206

72. Sweet Acacia
   Acacia farnesiana   page 208

70. Swamp Bay
   Persea palustris   page 206

73. Long Spine Acacia
   Acacia macracantha   page 209

71. Tamarindillo
   Acacia choriophylla   page 208

74. Twisted Acacia
   Acacia tortuosa   page 210

TREES OF FLORIDA

75. Mimosa
   Albizia julibrissin   *page 210*

78. Blackbead *Pithecellobium*
   guadalupense   *page 216*

76. Orchid Tree
   Bauhinia variegata   *page 212*

79. Crape Myrtle
   Lagerstroemia indica   *page 221*

77. Eastern Redbud
   Cercis canadensis   *page 212*

80. Southern Magnolia
   Magnolia grandiflora   *page 223*

TREES OF FLORIDA

81. Corkwood
    Leitneria floridana   *page 221*

82. Ashe Magnolia *Magnolia*
    macrophylla subsp. *ashei*   *page 223*

83. Sweetbay Magnolia
    Magnolia virginiana   *page 224*

84. Locust Berry
    Byrsonima lucida   *page 224*

85. Upland Cotton
    Gossypium hirsutum   *page 227*

86. Sea Hibiscus
    Hibiscus tiliaceus   *page 227*

87. Seaside Mahoe
    Thespesia populnea   *page 227*

89. Tetrazygia
    Tetrazygia bicolor   *page 228*

88. Chinaberry
    Melia azedarach   *page 228*

90. Common Fig
    Ficus carica   *page 231*

TREES OF FLORIDA

91. Shortleaf Fig
    Ficus citrifolia   *page 231*

93. Osage-orange
    Maclura pomifera   *page 233*

92. Strangler Fig
    Ficus aurea   *page 231*

94. Red Mulberry
    Morus rubra   *page 233*

96. Wax Myrtle
    Myrica cerifera   *page 234*

97. Swamp Candleberry
    Myrica heterophylla   *page 234*

95. White Mulberry
    Morus alba   *page 233*

98. Odorless Bayberry
    Myrica inodora   *page 235*

99. Marlberry
   Ardisia escallonioides   *page 235*

100. Blolly
   Guapira discolor   *page 242*

102. Long-stalked Stopper
   Mosiera longipes   *page 240*

101. Blackgum
   Nyssa biflora   *page 244*

103. Sour Gum
   Nyssa sylvatica   *page 246*

104. Gulf Graytwig *Schoepfia chrysophylloides*   *page 246*

105. Hog Plum
   Ximenia americana   *page 246*

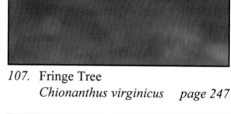

107. Fringe Tree
   Chionanthus virginicus   *page 247*

106. Wax-leaf Ligustrum
   Ligustrum lucidum   *page 252*

108. Wild Olive
   Osmanthus americanus   *page 254*

TREES OF FLORIDA

109. Pigeon Plum
     Coccoloba diversifolia   *page 256*

112. Carolina Buckthorn
     Rhamnus caroliniana   *page 258*

110. Wild Coffee
     Colubrina arborescens   *page 257*

113. Red Mangrove
     Rhizophora mangle   *page 260*

111. Soldierwood
     Colubrina elliptica   *page 257*

114. Cockspur Haw
     Crataegus crus-galli   *page 261*

115. Yellow Haw
Crataegus flava   *page 262*

118. Southern Crabapple
Malus angustifolia   *page 266*

116. Parsley Haw
Crataegus marshallii   *page 262*

119. American Plum
Prunus americana   *page 267*

117. Littlehip Hawthorn
Crataegus spathulata   *page 264*

120. Chickasaw Plum
Prunus angustifolia   *page 267*

121. Carolina Laurel Cherry
     Prunus caroliniana   *page 269*

124. Seven-Year Apple
     Casasia clusiifolia   *page 273*

122. Peach
     Prunus persica   *page 269*

125. Buttonbush *Cephalanthus*
     occidentalis   *page 273*

123. Black Cherry
     Prunus serotina   *page 270*

126. Black Torch
     Erithalis fruticosa   *page 273*

127. Rough Velvetseed
Guettarda scabra   *page 274*

130. Coastal Plain Willow
Salix caroliniana   *page 284*

128. Scarlet Bush
Hamelia patens   *page 277*

131. Florida Willow
Salix floridana   *page 286*

129. Pinckneya
Pinckneya bracteata   *page 277*

132. Florida Cupania
Cupania glabra   *page 288*

133. Varnish Leaf
  Dodonaea viscosa   *page 288*

136. Tough Bumelia
  Bumelia tenax   *page 293*

134. Gum Bumelia
  Bumelia lanuginosa   *page 291*

137. Satin Leaf
  Chrysophyllum oliviforme page 294

135. Smooth Bumelia
  Bumelia reclinata   *page 293*

138. Willow Bustic
  Dipholis salicifolia   *page 294*

139. Wild Dilly
     Manilkara bahamensis   *page 294*

142. Bitterbush
     Picramnia pentandra   *page 297*

140. Sapodilla
     Manilkara zapota   *page 295*

143. Paradise Tree
     Simarouba glauca   *page 297*

141. False Mastic *Mastichodendron*
     foetidissimum   *page 295*

144. Chinese Parasol Tree
     Firmiana simplex   *page 299*

145. American Snowbell
    Styrax americanum   *page 300*

148. Loblolly Bay
    Gordonia lasianthus   *page 303*

146. Bay Cedar
    Suriana maritima   *page 302*

149. Joewood
    Jacquinia keyensis   *page 304*

147. Horse Sugar
    Symplocos tinctoria   *page 302*

150. Winged Elm
    Ulmus alata   *page 308*

TREES OF FLORIDA

151. Lignum Vitae
     Guaiacum sanctum   *page 312*

153. Fiddlewood
     Citharexylum fruticosum   page 311

152. Cedar Elm
     Ulmus crassifolia   *page 309*

species of *Ulmus* by leaf bases being more nearly symmetrical and equilateral than asymmetrical and inequilateral.

Distribution: Mixed, moist woods throughout the northern part of the state and south to about Marion County; often growing intermixed with ironwood at the point of overlap in their habitats.

Black Calabash

Amphitecna latifolia (Mill.) Gentry

Form: Small evergreen tree to about 6 m in height.
Leaves: Alternate, simple, entire, leathery, dark green above, oval, 12 - 20 cm long, 3.5 - 10 cm wide, apices with a short but distinctive point.
Flowers: White to purplish white, bell shaped, to about 6 cm long, nearly hidden among the leaves and exhibiting a foul odor.
Fruit: Egg shaped, 7 - 12 cm long, 4 - 8 cm wide, dark green, covered with a hard, shell-like rind.
Distinguishing Marks: Most easily recognized by the distinctive, shell-like covering of the fruit.
Distribution: Formerly reported as native to southern Florida but this is doubtful; cultivated in south Florida and the Keys.

Catalpa, Southern Catalpa, Catawba Tree, Caterpillar Tree, Indian Bean

Catalpa bignonioides Walt.   Photo #26

Form: Small deciduous tree to about 15 m in height.
Leaves: Opposite or whorled, simple, entire, heart shaped, 10 - 26 cm long, bases 8 - 18 cm wide, petioles conspicuously long.
Flowers: White with conspicuous yellow and purple markings, bell shaped, borne in many-flowered, widely branched clusters.
Fruit: A long, brown, narrow pod, 10 - 38 cm in length.
Distinguishing Marks: The only north Florida tree with large, opposite, heart-shaped leaves.
Distribution: Occurring naturally on floodplains and riverbanks of the panhandle; often planted and frequently naturalized in urban locations.

Yellow Elder

Tecoma stans (L.) Juss.   Photo #27

Form: Evergreen shrub or small tree to about 8 m in height with furrowed, light gray bark.
Leaves: Opposite, pinnately compound, 10 - 25 cm long; leaflets 5 - 13 in number, lanceolate to elliptic, 4 - 10 cm long, margins serrate.

Flowers: Bright yellow, conspicuous and very showy, bell shaped, most about 5 cm long.
Fruit: A slender pod to about 20 cm long.
Distinguishing Marks: Distinguished as the only tree in the Keys with opposite, pinnately compound leaves with more than seven leaflets.
Distribution: Roadsides and hammock edges; naturalized in the Keys.

Bahama Strongbark or Strongbark

Bourreria ovata Miers   Photo #29

Form: Bushy, evergreen (leaves at least persistent) shrub or small tree to about 12 m in height with reddish brown, scaly bark.
Leaves: Alternate, simple, oval, entire, apices often notched, 6 - 12 cm long, 4 - 8 cm wide, yellowish green above, paler below.
Flowers: White, campanulate, to about 1.3 cm wide, borne in terminal clusters.
Fruit: A rounded drupe, to about 1.2 cm in diameter, green when new, turning red at maturity.
Distinguishing Marks: Similar to rough strongbark (*B. radula*) but having generally longer and glabrous leaves.
Distribution: Margins of hammocks in the Keys and the extreme southern peninsula.

Rough Strongbark

Bourreria radula (Poir. in Lam.) G. Don

Form: Evergreen shrub or small tree to about 12 m in height with reddish brown, scaly bark.
Leaves: Alternate, simple, entire, elliptic, 2.5 - 6.5 cm long, 1.2 - 3.5 cm wide, dark green above, paler below, apices either notched or rounded.
Flowers: White, campanulate, borne in terminal clusters.
Fruit: A rounded drupe to about 1.4 cm in diameter, turning red at maturity.
Distinguishing Marks: Very similar to the Bahama strongbark (*B. ovata*), pictured in Photo #29, but differing by having generally shorter leaves that are densely pubescent and rough to the touch.
Distribution: Very rare in the Lower Keys, perhaps close to extirpation in the wild.

Geiger Tree

Cordia sebestena L.   Photo #28; Plate 12

Form: Evergreen shrub or small, straight-trunked tree to about 9 m in height with very dark bark and green, pubescent twigs.
Leaves: Alternate, simple, stiff, ovate, 10 - 25 cm long, 5 - 13 cm wide, margins entire to irregularly toothed toward the apices, bases of at least some leaves cordate; upper surfaces of leaves dark green and rough to the touch due to a covering of short, stiff hairs; lower surfaces paler and also hairy; the blades of many leaves often appear tattered and in poor shape.

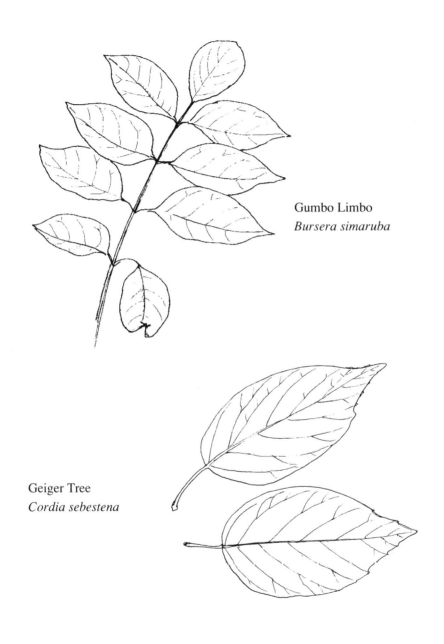

Gumbo Limbo
Bursera simaruba

Geiger Tree
Cordia sebestena

Plate 12

153

Flowers: Orange-red, showy, tubular or funnel shaped at the base but spreading into wavy-edged petals, 1 - 1.5 cm long, borne in compact, flattened, terminal clusters, appearing at almost any time of year.

Fruit: Egg shaped but completely enclosed in the enlarged, white calyx, 3- 5 cm long.

Distinguishing Marks: Most easily recognized by large, scabrid, cordate leaves and large, attractive flower clusters.

Distribution: Occurs naturally but sparingly in hammocks and coastal scrub of the Florida Keys; used as an ornamental plant in the extreme southern peninsula and the Keys.

BURSERACEAE

Gumbo Limbo or West Indian Birch

Bursera simaruba (L.) Sarg.   **Photo #30; Plate 12**

Form: Medium-sized, spreading, aromatic, deciduous tree, to about 20 m in height, with distinctive, smooth, copper-colored, resinous bark that has the aroma of turpentine and flakes off in strips to reveal a greenish brown underlayer.

Leaves: Alternate, pinnately compound, 15 - 20 cm long, 10 - 15 cm wide; leaflets three to nine in number, short stalked, entire, ovate to oblong, 6 - 7.5 cm long, 2 - 5 cm wide, shiny green above, paler below.

Flowers: Tiny, borne in elongated, terminal clusters that are 5 - 15 cm long, appearing in spring.

Fruit: Drupelike, slightly three-angled and diamond shaped, pointed at both ends, to about 1.5 cm long and 1 cm wide, arising in fall and winter.

Distinguishing Marks: Most easily recognized by combination of shiny, copper-colored bark and compound leaves.

Distribution: Coastal and tropical hammocks from Pinellas and Brevard counties southward; most common in the lower peninsula and Keys; often a conspicuous ornamental along roads, turnpikes, and interstate highways of the southern tip of the peninsula.

CACTACEAE

Tree Cactus or Column Cactus

Cereus robinii (Lemaire) Benson

Form: Sparsely branched cylindrical cactus with a distinct trunk, to about 10 m in height; lower trunk brownish and superficially appearing woody; upper trunk green, succulent, and bearing many clusters of yellowish spines.

Flowers: Bell shaped with purplish petals, appearing on the upper branches in late afternoon or evening and wilting shortly after sunrise.

Fruit: A fleshy, reddish, flattened, seed-laden drupe to about 5 cm in length.

Distinguishing Marks: Most easily recognized as the only cactus in Florida reaching such heights; distinguished from the prickly apple (*C. gracilis* var. *simpsonii*) by its upright growth habit and by the trunk usually exceeding 5 cm in diameter.

Distribution: Open hammocks; rare and likely found in quantity only in one hammock on Big Pine Key.

Cinnamon Bark

Canella winterana (L.) Gaertn.   **Photo #31**

Form: Small evergreen tree to about 10 m in height.
Leaves: Alternate, obovate, deep green, lustrous, entire, 7 - 13 cm in length, 1 - 5 cm wide, apices rounded.
Flowers: Small, with five deep red petals.
Fruit: A red berry, about 1 cm in diameter.
Distinguishing Marks: Distinguished by the cinnamonlike aroma of the inner bark of mature trees and by the fiery taste of its leaves.
Distribution: Hammocks of extreme southern Florida, especially near Cape Sable; more common in the Keys.

Jamaica Caper

Capparis cynophallophora L.

Form: Evergreen shrub or small tree to about 6 m in height with reddish brown bark.
Leaves: Alternate, simple, elliptic, slightly leathery, entire, quite variable in size, 5 - 10 cm long, 1.5 - 3.5 cm wide, apices blunt or commonly notched.
Flowers: Purplish, spreading, with clusters of long, brushlike stamens, inflorescence borne in clusters near the ends of branchlets, appearing in the evening in spring and summer.
Fruit: A pod with a long stalk, total structure 10 - 30 cm long and narrow between the seed cavities; seeds elliptic, shiny, brown, about 3 cm long.
Distinguishing Marks: Similar to the limber caper (*C. flexuosa*), pictured on p. 156, distinguished from it as well as other south Florida trees with notched leaves by lower surfaces of leaves having a dense covering of scales which impart a distinctive sheen.
Distribution: Coastal hammocks, shell middens; Brevard and Pinellas counties southward and throughout the Keys.

Bay-Leaved or Limber Caper

Capparis flexuosa L.   **Plate 13**

Form: Evergreen shrub or small tree to about 8 m in height.
Leaves: Alternate, simple, varying from oblong to elliptic to almost linear, leathery, entire, two-ranked, apices blunt or notched, pale green, predominately 4 - 10 cm long, 1 - 5 cm wide.
Flowers: Fragrant with white sepals, spreading white to yellow or pink petals, and clusters of white, threadlike spreading stamens, appearing in summer in loose terminal clusters, opening late in the day and in the evening, closing in the morning.
Fruit: A brown pod, 3 - 22 cm long, about 1.3 cm in diameter.
Distinguishing Marks: Distinguished from Jamaica caper (*C. cynophallophora*) by lower leaf surface lacking a dense covering of scales.

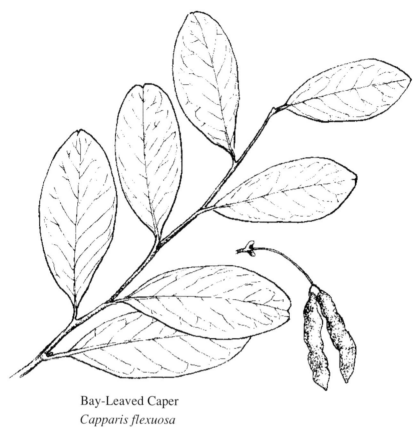

Bay-Leaved Caper
Capparis flexuosa

Plate 13

Distribution: Coastal hammocks and shell middens from Brevard and Lee counties southward along the coast and throughout the Keys.

CAPRIFOLIACEAE

Elder-Berry or Common Elder

Sambucus canadensis L.   **Photo #32**

Form: Deciduous shrub or very small tree to about 6 m in height.
Leaves: Opposite, pinnately (or occasionally bipinnately) compound, 15 - 25 cm long; leaflets, 5 - 15 cm long, lanceolate, five to seven in number, opposite except the terminal one, giving off a rank odor when crushed, margins serrate.

Flowers: Small, white, arranged in showy clusters and appearing in late spring and early summer.

Fruit: Purplish black and juicy, appearing in mid- to late summer.

Distinguishing Marks: Most easily recognized by opposite, compound, rank-smelling leaves and showy flower clusters; distinguished from Brazilian pepper (*Schinus terebinthifolius*) by lacking the latter's winged rachis and bright red berries.

Distribution: Found naturally in open wet areas and along the edges of wet woodlands, also in ditches, canals, and other disturbed sites throughout the state.

Arrow-Wood

Viburnum dentatum L.   **Photo #33; Plate 14**

Form: Slender-trunked deciduous shrub or small tree, seldom exceeding 3 m in height.

Leaves: Opposite, simple, generally ovate but terminal pair sometimes more nearly lanceolate, 3 - 12 cm long, 2 - 8 cm wide, margins generally dentate with coarse teeth, each tooth serving as the termination point for a lateral vein, both upper and lower surfaces somewhat rough to the touch.

Flowers: White, borne in spreading clusters.

Fruit: Green at first, turning blue-black with maturity.

Distinguishing Marks: Distinguished from other viburnum species and most other Florida trees by its coarsely dentate leaves.

Distribution: Found in a variety of situations, mostly in areas that are poorly drained such as the edges of rivers, bogs, bays, and flatwoods but sometimes also in well-drained woods; throughout the panhandle and eastward to the counties of the western central peninsula.

Possum-Haw

Viburnum nudum L.   **Photo #34**

Form: Deciduous shrub or small tree to about 6 m in height.

Leaves: Opposite, simple, lanceolate to elliptic or long-elliptic, usually 10 - 15 cm long but sometimes much shorter, upper surfaces dark, shiny green, lower surfaces copiously covered with tiny glandular dots, apices pinched to an abrupt point, margins typically entire but sometimes finely crenate to serrate and slightly revolute.

Flowers: Small, white, borne in showy, spreading clusters, each cluster to about 15 cm wide, appearing in March and April.

Fruit: Ellipsoid, initially red to pink but turning deep blue.

Distinguishing Marks: Distinguished from rusty haw (*V. rufidulum*) by punctate dots on lower leaf surfaces, from Walter viburnum (*V. obovatum*) by longer leaves, from wax-leaf ligustrum (*Ligustrum lucidum*) by the winged petiole; one of two species with the common name possum-haw, the other, *Ilex decidua,* distinguished from this species most quickly by its alternate rather than opposite leaves.

Distribution: Swamps, bay heads, and wet woodlands; throughout northern Florida, southward to about DeSoto County.

Walter or Small Viburnum

Viburnum obovatum Walt.   **Photo #35**

Form: Sometimes a shrub but often a small, deciduous to semievergreen tree to about 9 m in height.
Leaves: Opposite, simple, 2 - 5 cm long, 1 - 3 cm wide, margins entire or irregularly and minutely toothed, especially toward the apices, lower surfaces copiously covered with small brown dots.
Flowers: Small, white, borne in flat-topped clusters, each cluster 4 - 6 cm wide, appearing February to March, thus the earliest flowering *Viburnum*.
Fruit: An ellipsoid drupe, 6 - 10 mm long, red at first, turning black with maturity.
Distinguishing Marks: Distinguished from possum-haw (*V. nudum*) by generally smaller leaves; similar to *Ilex decidua* and *Ilex vomitoria* in leaf structure but distinguished from them by having opposite rather than alternate leaves.
Distribution: More common in wet areas such as flatwoods, streambanks, swamp margins, and hammocks, but also in dry uplands underlain by limestone; from about Washington County eastward and southward to about Hendry County.

Rusty Haw or Southern Black Haw

Viburnum rufidulum Raf.   **Photo #36; Plate 14**

Form: Deciduous shrub or small tree with blocky bark that resembles both common persimmon (*Diospyros virginiana*) and flowering dogwood (*Cornus florida*).
Leaves: Opposite, simple, 4 - 8 cm long, 3 - 6 cm wide, margins finely toothed, upper surfaces shiny green, lower surfaces exhibiting patches of shaggy, rusty pubescence, especially along the midvein.
Flowers: White, small, borne in spreading clusters, each cluster 5 - 10 cm wide.
Fruit: Purple, ellipsoid, 10 - 15 mm long, borne in spreading clusters.
Distinguishing Marks: Distinguished from Walter viburnum (*V. obovatum*) and possum-haw (*V. nudum*) by patches of rusty pubescence on the lower surfaces of leaves and lack of punctate dots.
Distribution: Upland, well-drained woods; throughout the panhandle, eastward and southward to about Hernando County.

CARICACEAE

Papaya

Carica papaya L.   **Photo #38**

Form: Herbaceous evergreen tree with smooth, greenish to grayish bark, to about 6 m in height.
Leaves: Alternate but clustered at the summit of the trunk, simple, deeply incised into seven to nine obvious lobes, upper surfaces green, lower surfaces whitish, leaf blade 20 - 60 cm long, with long petioles of 40 - 60 cm.

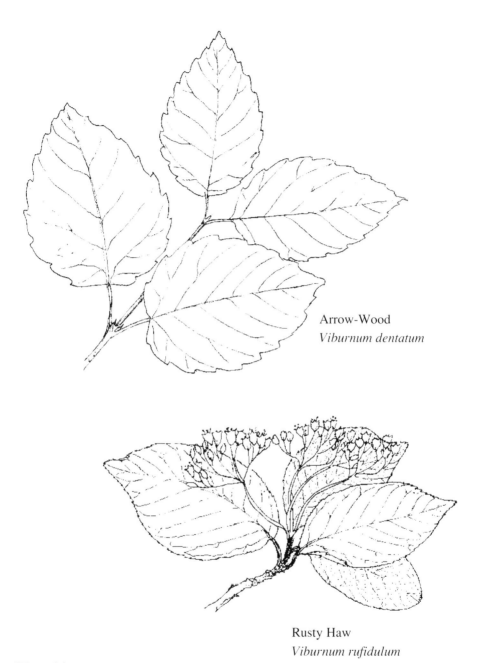

Arrow-Wood
Viburnum dentatum

Rusty Haw
Viburnum rufidulum

Plate 14

Flowers: Male flowers yellowish to white, borne in clusters, the clusters 15 - 60 cm long.

Fruit: Large, pear shaped, turning from green to orange with maturity, 15 - 45 cm long, fleshy, melonlike, sweet to the taste, very palatable.

Distinguishing Marks: The herbaceous trunk, deeply incised leaves, and large fruit set this species apart.

Distribution: Cultivated in the lower peninsula, escaped plants found along the east coast sometimes as far north as Duval County, more common in south Florida and the Keys.

CASUARINACEAE

Cunningham's Beefwood

Casuarina cunninghamiana Miq.

Form: Medium-sized, shaggy evergreen tree with an overall conical shape.

Leaves: Minute, scalelike, about 1 mm in length and encircling needlelike branchlets at regularly spaced nodes; branchlets having the appearance of pine needles.

Distinguishing Marks: Distinguished from other Australian pines by having eight to ten leaves in each whorl.

Distribution: A salt-intolerant species restricted to the south-central peninsula.

Australian Pine or Horsetail Casuarina

Casuarina equisetifolia L. ex J. R. & G. Forst.   **Photo #37; Plate 15**

Form: Potentially large, shaggy evergreen tree with an overall conical shape; bark of mature trees furrowed and splitting into strips.

Leaves: Minute, scalelike, about 1 mm in length and encircling needlelike branchlets at regularly spaced nodes; branchlets having the appearance of pine needles.

Distinguishing Marks: Distinguished from other Australian pines by having six to eight leaves in each whorl; highly salt tolerant.

Distribution: The most common of Florida's exotic Australian pines, weedy and pervasive throughout southern Florida and the Keys.

Brazilian Beefwood

Casuarina glauca Sieber ex K. Spreng.

Form: Medium-sized, shaggy evergreen tree with an overall conical shape.

Leaves: Minute, scalelike, about 1 mm in length and encircling needlelike branchlets at regularly spaced nodes; branchlets having the appearance of pine needles.

Distinguishing Marks: Distinguished from other Australian pines by having 10 - 16 leaves in each whorl; not at all salt tolerant.

Distribution: Throughout southern Florida and the Keys.

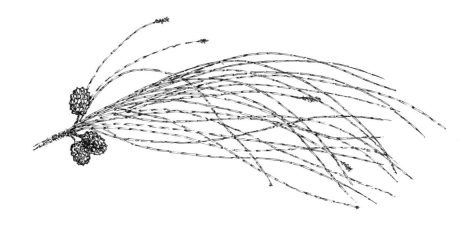

Australian Pine
Casuarina equisetifolia

Plate 15

CELASTRACEAE

Rhacoma or Florida Crossopetalum

Crossopetalum rhacoma Crantz   **Photo #39; Plate 16**

Form: Normally an evergreen shrub but sometimes a small, short-trunked, much-branched tree to about 6 m in height.
Leaves: Opposite, alternate, or whorled, simple, obovate to elliptic, 1 - 4 cm long, .5 - 2 cm wide, yellow-green in color, margins crenate with shallow, rounded teeth, or sometimes entire.
Flowers: Very small, petals reddish, borne in long-stalked clusters from leaf axils.
Fruit: A rounded, red to reddish purple drupe, 5 - 7 mm in diameter.
Distinguishing Marks: Distinguished from other hammock species by small, primarily opposite leaves that are definitely toothed or notched along the edges.
Distribution: Sun-loving species of southern Florida and the Keys; more common in pinelands, occasional in hammocks.

Eastern Wahoo or Burning Bush

Euonymus atropurpureus Jacq.

Form: Ordinarily a deciduous shrub in Florida, potentially a small, erect tree to about 8 m in height, often branching close to the ground.

161

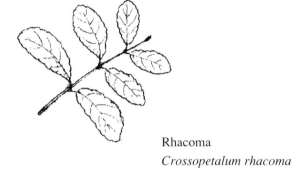

Rhacoma
Crossopetalum rhacoma

Plate 16

Leaves: Opposite, simple, elliptic, 5 - 12 cm long, 2 - 5 cm wide, margins finely serrate; leaf stalks 1 - 1.5 cm long.

Flowers: Maroon to purple in color, borne in few-flowered clusters on long, slender stalks, petals four in number and about 4 mm long, individual flowers about 10 mm wide when fully open.

Fruit: A four-winged capsule.

Distinguishing Marks: Most readily identified by its opposite, finely serrate leaves that are long-tapering at both the apices and bases; easily distinguished from the shrub hearts-a-bustin'-with-love (*E. americanus*), a close relative, by the distinctly petiolate leaves.

Distribution: Infrequent along streambanks, bluffs, and ravines, generally in conjunction with limestone soils; a tree of more northern distribution confined in Florida to the northern panhandle from about Jefferson County westward.

False Boxwood or Falsebox

Gyminda latifolia (Sw.) Urban   **Photo #40**

Form: Large evergreen shrub or small tree to about 8 m in height with gray to reddish brown bark; twigs angled or squared.

Leaves: Opposite, simple, light green in color, elliptic to obovate, 3.8 - 5 cm long, 2 - 3 cm

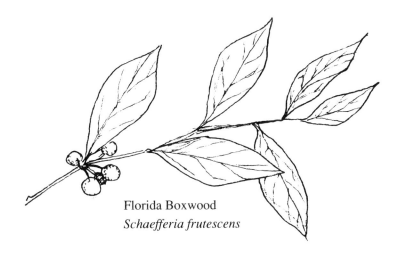

Florida Boxwood
Schaefferia frutescens

Plate 17

wide, margins entire to slightly crenate near the apices, sometimes revolute, apices rounded, veins inconspicuous.

Flowers: Small, white, borne in few-flowered clusters.

Fruit: Blue to black, rounded to ovoid, 5 - 8 mm in diameter.

Distinguishing Marks: Most easily recognized by combination of square twigs in conjunction with opposite leaves.

Distribution: Rare and restricted to only a few hammocks of the Florida Keys.

Florida Mayten, Mayten, Gutta-Percha Mayten

Maytenus phyllanthoides Benth.   **Photo #41**

Form: Evergreen shrub or small tree to about 6 m in height with a short trunk and smooth, gray bark.

Leaves: Alternate, simple, fleshy, leathery, oblong to elliptic, 2.5 - 4 cm long, 1.2 - 2 cm wide, margins entire but often wavy, apices blunt or notched.

Flowers: Greenish white, small, borne singly or in few-flowered clusters from the leaf axils, appearing primarily January to May.

Fruit: A bright red, four-angled, egg-shaped capsule, 6 - 12 mm long, may be seen on the tree at almost any time of year.

Distinguishing Marks: Most easily recognized by light green, fleshy leaves with notched apices and minute marginal scales.

Distribution: Coastal scrub and hammock edges; from Levy County southward along the west coast, Miami southward along the east coast, throughout the Keys.

Florida Boxwood or Yellowwood

Schaefferia frutescens Jacq. **Plate 17**

Form: Evergreen shrub or small tree to about 12 m in height with dark bark and angled, green twigs.

Leaves: Alternate, simple, leathery, elliptic to oval, 4 - 7 cm long, 1.2 - 2.5 cm wide, margins entire, usually revolute, apices with a small point.

Flowers: Greenish white, tiny, borne in clusters at the leaf axils.

Fruit: A rounded, fleshy, red drupe, 5 - 8 mm in diameter.

Distinguishing Marks: The green, angled twigs and ridged leaves help set this tree apart.

Distribution: Hammocks of the Keys and, to a lesser extent, of the southern peninsula.

CHRYSOBALANACEAE

Coco-Plum

Chrysobalanus icaco L. **Plate 18**

Form: Evergreen shrub or small bushy tree to about 5 m in height.

Leaves: Alternate, simple, leathery, dark green, shiny, oval to nearly round, 2 - 8 cm long, 1 - 6 cm wide, two-ranked on the stem but often borne erect so that all leaves appear to be on the same side of the branch, apices slightly notched.

Flowers: White, bell shaped, small, 5 - 7 mm long.

Fruit: A rounded, one-seeded, dark purple to yellowish (rarely white) drupe 1 - 4 cm in diameter.

Distinguishing Marks: The rounded, erect, two-ranked leaves in conjunction with the dark purple fruit that is evident at almost any time of year is diagnostic for identification.

Distribution: Low hammocks, beaches, sand dunes, cypress heads, and other wet habitats, primarily along the coastal zone but occasionally in inland swamps; Brevard and Charlotte counties southward and throughout the Keys.

CLUSIACEAE (GUTTIFERAE)

Autograph Tree, Pitch Apple, Balsam Apple

Clusia rosea Jacq. **Photo #42**

Form: Medium-sized evergreen tree potentially to about 18 m in height, more commonly not exceeding about 10 m.

Leaves: Opposite, simple, very stiff, 7 - 18 cm long, 5 - 13 cm wide, upper surfaces dull green,

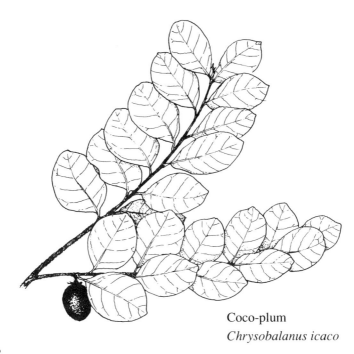

Coco-plum
Chrysobalanus icaco

Plate 18

lower surfaces yellow-green, margins entire but slightly turned under, apices notched; petiole distinctly grooved at the base.

Flowers: Lustrous, attractive, appearing mostly in the summer, petals white with tinges of pink, center of flower yellow.

Fruit: Large, globose, 5 - 6 cm in diameter, brown at maturity, splitting to expose large red seeds and orange arils.

Distinguishing Marks: Superficially similar only to the seven-year apple (*Casasia clusiifolia*) but differing from it by the latter having shiny, deep green leaves, rather than dull green leaves.

Distribution: Sometimes considered native, although questionably; often planted as an ornamental in south Florida and the Keys.

Sponge-Bark Hypericum or St. John's-Wort

Hypericum chapmanii Adams

Form: Typically a shrub with soft, spongy bark, sometimes takes on the appearance of a small tree to about 4 m in height.

Leaves: Small, needlelike, 8 - 25 mm long, crowded at nodes of branches and branchlets.

Flowers: Yellow, five-petaled, characterized by a mass of conspicuous stamens at the center.

Fruit: An ovate capsule that contains a tiny, peanutlike seed, capsule to about 6 mm long.

Distinguishing Marks: Similar to and difficult to distinguish from a number of five-petaled St. John's-worts that occur in similar habitats.

Distribution: Cypress ponds, wetter portions of flatwoods, flatwoods depressions, often in conjunction with cypress (*Taxodium* spp.), blackgum (*Nyssa biflora*), and sweetbay magnolia (*Magnolia virginiana*); endemic to the central panhandle from about Santa Rosa County to the Ochlockonee River.

Oxhorn Bucida or Black Olive

Bucida buceras L.   **Plate 19**

Form: Attractive, densely vegetated evergreen tree to about 25 m in height, with a broad crown of nearly horizontal branches.

Leaves: Alternate, obovate to elliptic, 2.5 - 9 cm long, 1 - 5 cm wide, clustered at the ends of erect roughened twigs that are separated by naked stem segments, upper surfaces green, lower surfaces yellow-green.

Flowers: Small, greenish white or light brown and crowded in lateral clusters.

Fruit: Egg shaped, 7 - 9 mm long but often deformed into long, twisted, hornlike galls (hence the name oxhorn) that are produced by the activity of mites; these galls can be up to 10 cm long.

Distinguishing Marks: Most easily recognized by leaves clustered on short twigs and the distinctive, twisted galls.

Distribution: Introduced and persistent in the southern peninsula; commonly planted along roadsides, in parking lots, and as a shade tree in south Florida and the Keys.

Buttonwood

Conocarpus erectus L.   **Photo #43**

Form: Evergreen shrub or tree to about 20 m in height.

Leaves: Alternate, simple, leathery, 2 - 10 cm long, 1 - 4 cm wide, apices often with a tiny, sharp-pointed tip.

Flowers: Tiny, green, borne in dense, rounded, compact heads (hence the name buttonwood), appearing from about March to September.

Fruit: Tiny, flattened, scalelike, borne in conspicuous conelike collections that are 1 - 3 cm in diameter and may be seen at almost any time of year.

Distinguishing Marks: Distinguished from all other south Florida trees by its buttonlike flowers and fruit; distinguished from the silver buttonwood (*C. erectus* var. *sericeus* Griseb.), pictured in Photo #43, by the latter having leaves conspicuously covered with a distinctive, silvery-gray pubescence.

Distribution: Generally coastal in distribution, normally found along the landward edge of the mangrove zone and along the edges of hammocks bordering the transition zone; southern Florida and the Keys, but also found in smaller numbers northward to Hernando County on the west coast and Merritt Island on the east.

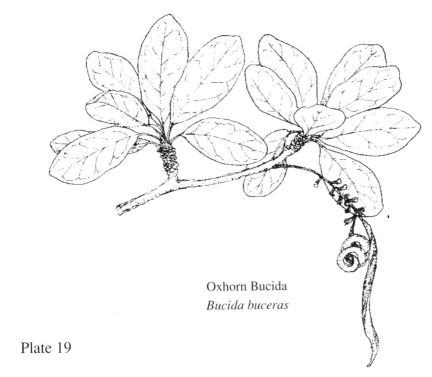

Oxhorn Bucida
Bucida buceras

Plate 19

White Mangrove

Laguncularia racemosa (L.) Gaertn. f.

Photo #44

Form: Evergreen shrub or small tree to about 18 m in height.
Leaves: Opposite, thick, leathery, smooth, succulent, oval, 2.5 - 8 cm long, 2.5 - 3 cm wide, apices often notched, both upper and lower surfaces light green with obscure veins; petioles with two conspicuous glands just below the base of the leaf blade.
Flowers: Tiny, white, velvetlike to the touch, borne at the tips of branches or in leaf axils.
Fruit: Greenish to reddish, narrow at the base and widening toward the apex, 1 - 1.5 cm long, with ten distinctive, lengthwise ribs, appearing in fall.
Distinguishing Marks: The two glands on the petiole in combination with the smooth, thick, oval leaves are diagnostic field marks.
Distribution: Coastal zone from about Brevard and Hernando counties southward and throughout the Keys.

Sea-Almond

Terminalia catappa L.

Plate 20

Form: Medium-sized deciduous tree to about 25 m in height with branches in horizontal circles at different levels along the trunk.

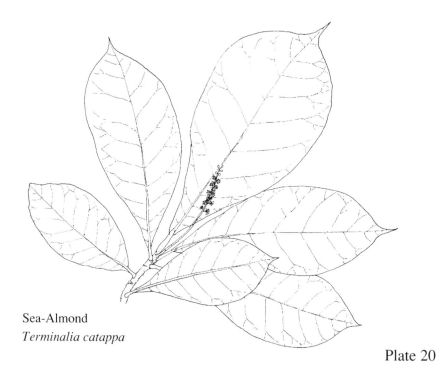

Sea-Almond
Terminalia catappa

Plate 20

Leaves: Alternate, leathery, entire, thick, dark green when mature, turning red just before falling, obovate, relatively large, 10 - 40 cm long, crowded together near the ends of twigs, upper surfaces rough to the touch, lower surfaces densely hairy and feltlike.

Flowers: Tiny, greenish, borne in elongated clusters among the leaves near the tips of the branches, each cluster 9 - 15 cm long.

Fruit: Almond shaped, flattened, fleshy, green, about 5 cm long, and containing a single edible nut.

Distinguishing Marks: Most easily distinguished by large, rough leaves clustered at the branch tips; distinguished from the larger-leaved magnolias by geographical range.

Distribution: Grown as a street tree and ornamental in south Florida; otherwise persistent in sandy sites and along beaches throughout south Florida and the Keys.

COMPOSITAE

Saltbush or Groundsel Tree

Baccharis halimifolia L.

Plate 21

Form: Freely branched evergreen shrub or small tree to about 4 m in height.

Leaves: Alternate, thick, pale green, 4 - 7 cm long, 1 - 4 cm wide, margins sometimes entire but often widely serrate with a few coarse teeth, particularly toward the apices.

Flowers: Small, greenish to white, borne in conspicuous heads.

Fruit: Small but with a mass of hairlike bristles that become very conspicuous as the fruit ma-

Saltbush
Baccharis halimifolia

Plate 21

tures and makes the entire plant look like a conglomeration of cottony appendages, even at a distance.

Distinguishing Marks: The distinctively toothed leaves, cottony fruit, and pale amber punctations on the leaf surfaces help in recognizing this species.

Distribution: Coastal areas such as the upper edge of marshes, along swales, and extending into sandy areas but also found in disturbed sites far inland; throughout the state including the Keys.

CORNACEAE

Pagoda or Alternate-Leaved Dogwood

Cornus alternifolia L. f.   **Plate 22**

Form: Small deciduous tree with smooth greenish bark, to about 9 m in height.

Leaves: Alternate, simple, entire, often closely set near the ends of the branches, oval to obovate, 5 - 12 cm long, 2.5 - 5 cm wide, apices acuminate.

Flowers: Creamy white, borne in open clusters.

Fruit: Bluish black, 4 - 8 mm in diameter.

Distinguishing Marks: A difficult tree to identify, distinguished from other dogwoods and members of the genus *Viburnum* by having alternate leaves.

Distribution: Spottily distributed along bluffs and ravine slopes of the upper Apalachicola River drainage basin; limited primarily to Gadsden and Jackson counties.

Rough Leaf Cornel

Cornus asperifolia Michx.

Form: Deciduous shrub, sometimes a small tree to about 5 m in height, with hairy twigs.
Leaves: Opposite, simple, entire, elliptic to lanceolate, 2 - 8 cm long, 1 - 4 cm wide, both surfaces pubescent, the upper surfaces of some leaves bearing stiff hairs that are conspicuously rough to the touch.
Flowers: Small, whitish, five-petaled, borne in conspicuous, flat-topped clusters.
Fruit: A light blue drupe to about 8 mm in diameter.
Distinguishing Marks: Similar in general appearance to the stiff cornel (*C. foemina*), pictured on p. 171, differing from it by at least some of the leaves having upper surfaces that are rough to the touch, and by typically occurring in well-drained rather than wetland habitats.
Distribution: Upland mixed woods generally on calcareous soils; throughout the panhandle southward to the central peninsula.

Flowering Dogwood

Cornus florida L.   **Photo #46; Plate 22**

Form: Small, attractive, deciduous tree to about 12 m in height, with grayish, blocky bark.
Leaves: Opposite, simple, entire, broadly elliptic, 3 - 10 cm long, 2 - 7 cm wide.
Flowers: Profuse and showy, appearing in the spring in compact, yellowish heads subtended by four enlarged, creamy white bracts that appear to be flower petals.
Fruit: An ellipsoid, bright red berry, 8 - 14 mm long.
Distinguishing Marks: Distinguished from stiff cornel dogwood (*C. foemina*) by broadly elliptic leaves and characteristic flowers and fruits; young trees of both rusty black haw (*Viburnum rufidulum*) and the common persimmon (*Diospyros virginiana*) may potentially be confused with this species due to their blocky bark.
Distribution: Well-drained woods, yards, roadsides, and highways of northern Florida, southward to about the central peninsula; often planted in northern Florida and also sometimes in south Florida.

Stiff Cornel Dogwood

Cornus foemina Mill.   **Plate 22**

Form: Deciduous shrub or small tree to 8 m in height.
Leaves: Opposite, simple, lanceolate to elliptic, 2 - 10 cm long, 1 - 4 cm wide, margins entire, but wavy.
Flowers: Small, cream colored, borne in spreading clusters, each cluster 3 - 7 cm wide.
Fruit: Globular, blue, 4 - 6 mm in diameter.
Distinguishing Marks: Easily distinguished from pagoda dogwood (*C. alternifolia*) by having opposite leaves and from flowering dogwood (*C. florida*) by generally wetland habitat, narrowly elliptic rather than broadly elliptic leaves, and flowers in open as opposed to compact clusters; most similar to rough leaf cornel (*C. asperifolia*) but distinguished from it by having smooth rather than rough leaf surfaces.
Distribution: Wet areas such as riverbanks, marshy shores, and swamp borders; throughout north Florida and southward to at least Lee and Hendry counties.

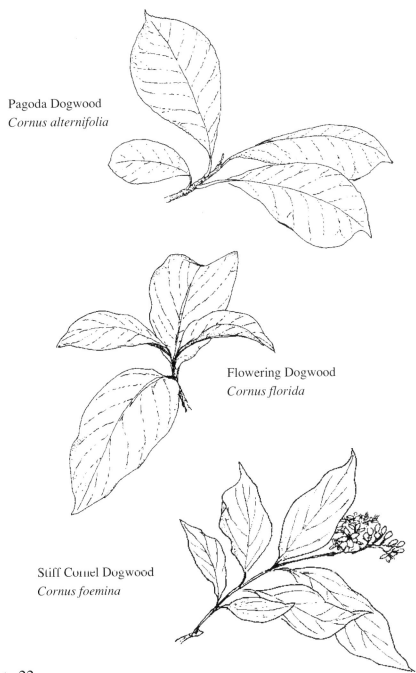

Pagoda Dogwood
Cornus alternifolia

Flowering Dogwood
Cornus florida

Stiff Cornel Dogwood
Cornus foemina

Plate 22

Black Titi

Cliftonia monophylla (Lam.) Britt. ex Sarg   **Photo #45**

Form: Medium-sized evergreen tree to about 8 m in height, with dark, sometimes blackish bark.
Leaves: Alternate, simple, entire, 2.5 - 10 cm long, normally sessile, rarely with short petioles.
Flowers: White, fragrant, appearing in early spring and borne in conspicuous, upright clusters.
Fruit: Four-winged, golden-amber in color, borne in conspicuous clusters.
Distinguishing Marks: Most easily recognized by its winged, buckwheat-type fruit, the darkened remains of which can be found on most specimens year-round; distinguished from swamp titi (*Cyrilla racemiflora*) by the veins on the lower surfaces of leaves not at all conspicuous.
Distribution: Bay swamps and edges of pine flatwoods; throughout the panhandle eastward to about Jefferson County.

Swamp Cyrilla or Titi

Cyrilla racemiflora L.   **Photo #47**

Form: Small, often twisted, thicket-forming tree to about 8 m in height, tardily deciduous and appearing evergreen.
Leaves: Alternate, simple, entire, quite variable in size from 1 - 10 cm long, .5 - 2.5 cm wide, individual trees having leaves predominately toward one of these extremes or the other.
Flowers: Appearing in late spring and early summer, borne in elongated, cylindrical clusters, trees with longer leaves also have longer flower clusters.
Fruit: Small and inconspicuous.
Distinguishing Marks: Most easily recognized by flowers in long clusters and by the remains of these clusters being present on the tree nearly year-round; distinguished from black titi (*Cliftonia monophylla*) by the veins on the lower surfaces of leaves being at least somewhat visible rather than not at all conspicuous.
Distribution: Swamps and wetlands; throughout north Florida and south to about Highlands County; more common in the northern part of its range.

Common Persimmon

Diospyros virginiana L.   **Photo #48**

Form: Medium-sized deciduous tree to about 20 m in height with bark eventually turning dark and breaking into small, regular blocks.
Leaves: Alternate, simple, entire, ovate to elliptic with rounded bases and acuminate tips, 7 - 15 cm long, 3 - 8 cm wide.
Flowers: Male flowers tubular, borne in clusters; female flowers white to greenish yellow, to about 2 cm long.
Fruit: Orange (when ripe), round, 4 - 5 cm in diameter.
Distinguishing Marks: Leaves somewhat similar to those of the sour gum (*Nyssa sylvatica*) but

distinguished from them by having whitish lower surfaces; the blocky bark, alternate leaves, and unisexual flowers are usually enough to distinguish this species.

Distribution: Wide ranging in a variety of habitats and communities throughout the state.

Mountain Laurel

Kalmia latifolia L. **Photo #49**

Form: Sometimes a small evergreen tree to about 9 m in height, more often a many-stemmed shrub.
Leaves: Very closely alternate, thick, firm, simple, entire, 2 - 10 cm long, 2.5 - 5 cm wide, elliptic to lanceolate.
Flowers: Borne in branched clusters, showy, cup shaped, pink to white, ten stamens, each held under tension in one of the tiny, reddish pouches that form a circle on the petals.
Fruit: A small, five-lobed capsule containing tiny seeds.
Distinguishing Marks: No other trees with a combination of the above characters is likely to be found in the mountain laurel's preferred habitat.
Distribution: Along woodland streams, wooded bluffs, and shady woodlands in the northern reaches of the panhandle from Escambia to Leon counties; one outlier population exists near the Suwannee River; considered rare in Florida.

Stagger Bush or Rusty Lyonia

Lyonia ferruginea (Walt.) Nutt. **Photo #50**

Form: Typically an evergreen shrub with several crooked trunks, sometimes to about 9 m in height and taking on treelike proportions.
Leaves: Mature leaves alternate, simple, 1 - 9 cm long, .5 - 5 cm wide, green above, paler and lightly pubescent below, margins entire, often wavy and revolute; young leaves copiously covered with rust-colored scales and pubescence.
Flowers: White and urn shaped, typical of many genera of the Ericaceae.
Fruit: A five-angled, pubescent capsule, 3 - 6 mm long, borne on a relatively long stalk.
Distinguishing Marks: Distinguished from the shrub *L. fruticosa* by having most leaves with revolute margins (although these two species are quite similar in south Florida and this latter distinction is less diagnostic) and by the lower surfaces of rusty lyonia bearing scales of two sizes (requires magnification) rather than only one size as in *L. fruticosa.*
Distribution: Wet pine flatwoods as well as dry sand pine–scrub oak woods from about Bay County southward to the northern edges of Lake Okeechobee in the central peninsula, much farther south along the coasts.

Sourwood

Oxydendrum arboreum (L.) DC.   **Plate 23**

Form: Slender, medium-sized deciduous tree to 18 m in height, bark gray tinged with red and longitudinally furrowed.
Leaves: Alternate, simple, elliptic, 12.5 - 18 cm long, 2.5 - 7.5 cm wide, margins finely serrate, upper surfaces medium-dark green, lower surfaces much paler, blades turning orange or scarlet-red in the fall and becoming quite obvious.
Flowers: White, urn shaped, borne in long, narrow racemes that extend beyond the leaves at the tip of the branches and appear from May to July.
Fruit: Borne in small capsules.
Distinguishing Marks: Distinguished from the black cherry (*Prunus serotina*), which has similar leaves, by leaves of the latter being generally more oval with abruptly narrowing apices and those of the former being more long-elliptic rather than elliptic with long, tapering apices, and by the black cherry's round, reddish to purplish fruit.
Distribution: Bluffs, ravines, well-drained hills; found chiefly in the northern half of the panhandle from about Escambia to Jefferson counties.

Sparkleberry, Farkleberry, or Tree Huckleberry

Vaccinium arboreum Marsh.   **Plate 23**

Form: Small tree to about 9 m in height, deciduous, but often appearing evergreen, outer bark scaling and flaking, inner bark smooth and reddish brown, trunk often appearing crooked and leaning.
Leaves: Alternate, simple, oval to broadly elliptic, somewhat stiff, margins entire (but sometimes with tiny serrations), commonly 1.5 - 7 cm long, 0.8 - 4 cm wide, apices tipped with an abrupt, short, very small point.
Flowers: Small, white, profuse, cup shaped, borne on long stalks.
Fruit: Typical of other blueberries, green at first, turning black, 5 - 8 mm in diameter, adorned at the apex with the tiny, five-pointed, star-shaped remains of the sepals.
Distinguishing Marks: Most easily recognized in its preferred habitat by its reddish brown bark, by its leaves with minutely pointed apices and marginal glands, and by the distinctive apices of its berries.
Distribution: Dry woodlands, hammocks, and clearings; throughout north Florida, southward to about Lee County; one stand is also known from Fakahatchee Strand State Preserve.

Highbush Blueberry

Vaccinium corymbosum L.   **Photo #52; Plate 23**

Form: Normally a deciduous shrub, rarely arborescent to about 5 m in height, widely branched when treelike.
Leaves: Alternate, elliptic to lanceolate or ovate, entire to serrate, to about 8 cm long, 5 cm wide, very variable in size and shape, individual plants tending toward one of these extremes or the other.

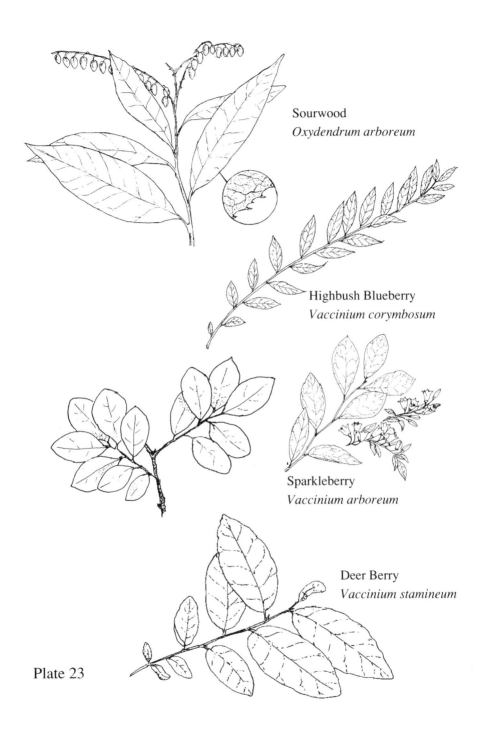

Sourwood
Oxydendrum arboreum

Highbush Blueberry
Vaccinium corymbosum

Sparkleberry
Vaccinium arboreum

Deer Berry
Vaccinium stamineum

Plate 23

Flowers: White, sometimes suffused with pink, cylindrical and similar in shape to those of sparkleberry (*V. arboreum*), borne in clusters.

Fruit: A dull (sometimes shiny) blue or black berry, 4 - 12 mm in diameter.

Distinguishing Marks: In general, the several species of highbush blueberries are quite variable, not well defined taxonomically, and are often difficult to distinguish from each other (for further discussion of this variation, and of the accompanying illustrations, the reader is referred to the closing paragraphs of Chapter 7, p. 32); the present species may be distinguished from the deer berry (*V. stamineum*) by lacking the latter's open, bell-shaped flowers, and from the sparkleberry by lacking the latter's reddish, scaling and flaking bark.

Distribution: Swamps, bogs, pinelands, upland woods; throughout northern Florida.

Deer Berry
Vaccinium stamineum L.   **Plate 23**

Form: Normally a deciduous shrub but sometimes taking on treelike proportions, to 5 m in height.

Leaves: Alternate, elliptic to obovate, simple, entire, 2 - 8 cm long, 1 - 3 cm wide, whitish below and often increasing in size toward the tips of the branches, margins with spreading hairs and appearing ciliate.

Flowers: Small, white, cuplike, with a mass of yellowish stamens that extend beyond the petals.

Fruit: Variously colored from whitish to blue-, reddish , or purplish black, 5 - 16 mm in diameter, typical of other blueberries.

Distinguishing Marks: Distinguished from sparkleberry (*V. arboreum*) by stamens extending far beyond the lip of the corolla; most easily recognized by leaves increasing in size toward the tip of the branches and whitish lower surfaces of leaves.

Distribution: Pine woods, mixed uplands, longleaf pine–scrub oak woodlands throughout northern Florida, southward to Martin County.

EUPHORBIACEAE
Tung Tree
Aleurites fordii Hemsl.   **Photo #51**

Form: Deciduous tree to about 10 m in height.

Leaves: Alternate, simple, generally heart shaped in overall outline but often with three pointed, terminal lobes, blades to about 30 cm long and wide but many much smaller, bases cordate; petioles long and bearing a pair of red glands on the upper side where it meets the leaf blade.

Flowers: Showy, borne in open clusters, petals five in number, white near the tips, bases reddish, measuring about 4 cm across when fully open.

Fruit: Green or red, rounded, 4 - 8 cm in diameter, borne on a long stalk and hanging pendently from the branch.

Distinguishing Marks: Distinguished from all other Florida trees by combination of leaf shape, pair of red glands on upper side of petiole, and five main veins arising from one place at the base of the leaf.

Distribution: Introduced and formerly heavily cultivated in the northern part of the state, now found mostly along roadsides and in other disturbed sites.

Crabwood or Oysterwood

Ateramnus lucidus (Sw.) Rothm.   **Plate 24**

Form: Evergreen shrub or small tree to about 10 m in height.
Leaves: Alternate, simple, elliptic, leathery, dark green, 5 - 10 cm long, 1 - 4 cm wide, margins wavy and irregularly toothed toward the apices, each tooth exhibiting a tiny, toothlike gland that is eventually shed; leaf base shouldered and extending minutely beyond the point of attachment with the petiole.
Flowers: Appearing in summer but remaining on the tree until the following spring, male flowers borne in yellow-green spikes up to 5 cm long, female flowers solitary on a long stalk.
Fruit: A rounded, multilocular capsule typical of the spurge family, to about 12 mm in diameter.
Distinguishing Marks: Easily distinguished from other south Florida hammock species by leaf base as described above.
Distribution: Hammocks of the extreme southern peninsula and the Keys.

Milkbark or Whitewood

Drypetes diversifolia Krug & Urban   **Photo #53; Plate 24**

Form: Evergreen shrub or small tree to 12 m in height with milk-white bark that is often partially covered with lichens.
Leaves: Alternate, simple, very stiff to the touch, dark green, elliptic to oval, 8 - 13 cm long, 2.5 - 5 cm wide (those of the crown smaller overall than those further down the trunk), margins of mature leaves entire, margins of leaves on very young plants lined with sharp teeth.
Flowers: Small, white, borne in tight clusters at the leaf axils.
Fruit: An ivory-white, ovoid drupe, 1 - 2.5 cm in diameter.
Distinguishing Marks: This tree is distinguished from other hammock species by its splotchy white bark and stiff, two-ranked leaves.
Distribution: Fairly common in hammocks of the Keys, occasional on the southern peninsula.

Guiana Plum

Drypetes lateriflora (Sw.) Krug & Urban   **Plate 24**

Form: Evergreen shrub or small tree to about 10 m in height with smooth, light brown bark.
Leaves: Alternate, simple, entire, leathery, shiny dark green, 8 - 10 cm long, lanceolate, tapering abruptly to a blunt point.
Flowers: White, small, borne in tight clusters in the leaf axils from spring throughout the summer.
Fruit: A round, bright red, fuzzy drupe, 7 - 10 mm in diameter, appearing in the fall.
Distinguishing Marks: Leaves somewhat similar in appearance to lancewood (*Ocotea coriacea*) of the Lauraceae but distinguished from it by lacking the distinctive fragrance that often emanates from the latter's crushed leaves.
Distribution: Common in hammocks of southern Florida, northward to about Brevard County, less common in the Keys.

177

Manchineel or Poison Guava

Hippomane mancinella L.

Photo #54

Form: Typically a deciduous shrub today, but known to reach a height of 15 m where undisturbed; known for its poisonous, bright white sap which can produce burnlike skin sores if handled.

Leaves: Alternate, simple, minutely and finely serrate, ovate, shiny, light green, 5 - 10 cm long, with long petioles.

Flowers: Individual flowers small and inconspicuous, greenish, borne in terminal spikes.

Fruit: Rounded, applelike, 2 - 4 cm in diameter, yellowish green when mature, extremely poisonous if ingested.

Distinguishing Marks: The light green, finely serrate leaves set this tree apart from all other hammock species.

Distribution: Quite poisonous, even to the touch in some people, and should not be handled; a tree of the seacoast, found naturally in brackish swamps just inside the mangrove zone of southern Florida and the Keys; infrequent today and considered threatened primarily because of attempts to eradicate the species.

Manihot or Cassava

Manihot grahamii Hook.

Photo #55

Form: Deciduous, monoecious tree to about 7 m in height.

Leaves: Alternate, deeply palmately incised into 5 - 11 long, narrow lobes that all originate near the point of the blade's attachment to the petiole, so deeply incised that the lobes take on the superficial appearance of leaflets; lobes 8 - 15 cm in length, the centermost lobes flared toward the apices then narrowing abruptly to a sharp point; petioles to about 20 cm in length.

Flowers: Yellowish green, attractive, borne in conspicuous spreading clusters.

Fruit: A rounded, three-sided capsule characteristic of the spurge family, about 1.5 cm in diameter.

Distinguishing Marks: The large palmately lobed leaves make this plant unlikely to be confused with any other tree in northern Florida.

Distribution: Occasionally cultivated, infrequently escaped; central panhandle, Tallahassee area, Polk County.

Popcorn Tree or Chinese Tallow Tree

Sapium sebiferum (L.) Roxb.

Photo #56

Form: Small to medium-sized, fast-growing, and attractive deciduous tree to about 15 m in height.

Leaves: Alternate, simple, entire, 3 - 6 cm both long and wide, generally broadly ovate and abruptly pinched and sharply pointed at the apices; petiole 2 - 5 cm long, with a pair of glands on the upper side at the point of attachment to the blade.

Flowers: Yellow, small, borne in long spikes to about 20 cm in length.

Fruit: A three-lobed capsule characteristic of the spurge family, 1 cm in diameter.

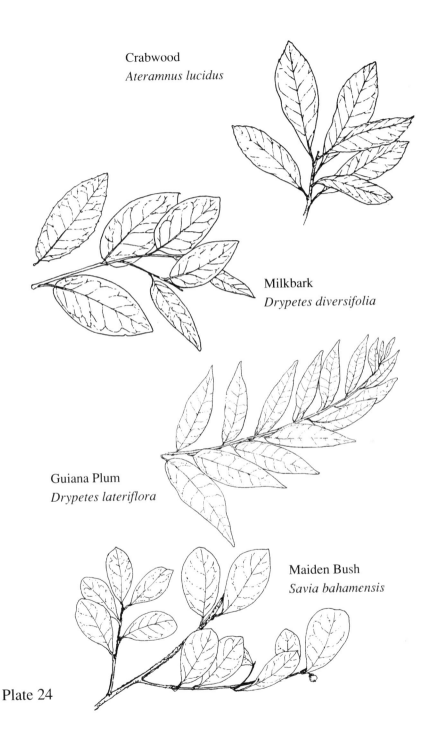

Crabwood
Ateramnus lucidus

Milkbark
Drypetes diversifolia

Guiana Plum
Drypetes lateriflora

Maiden Bush
Savia bahamensis

Plate 24

179

Distinguishing Marks: Easily recognized by characteristic fruit and by ovate leaves that are as wide as long; the milky sap of this species is poisonous.
Distribution: Various habitats including wet places and suburban yards; northern Florida.

Maiden Bush or Bahama Maiden Bush

Savia bahamensis Britt. **Plate 24**

Form: Low evergreen shrub with erect branches, or rarely a small tree to about 4 m in height.
Leaves: Alternate, simple, entire, ovate, leathery, shiny green with a light-colored central vein, 2 - 5 cm long, 1.5 - 4 cm wide, apices rounded or notched.
Flowers: Small, greenish white, appearing March through June, male flowers borne in dense clusters in the leaf axils, female flowers solitary.
Fruit: A round, three-locular capsule, 5 - 7 mm in diameter.
Distinguishing Marks: Most easily recognized by combination of upright branches, ovate leaves, and the conspicuous pair of brown stipules at each leaf base; the latter character in conjunction with all leaves being alternate easily separates this species from both blolly (*Guapira discolor*) and black torch (*Erithalis fruticosa*).
Distribution: Generally restricted to coastal thickets of the Keys.

FAGACEAE

Chinquapin

Castanea pumila (L.) Mill. **Plate 25**

Form: Deciduous shrub or small tree to about 20 m in height.
Leaves: Alternate, simple, two-ranked, typically elliptic to lance-elliptic but variable on a given tree, 4 - 18 cm long, 1 - 8 cm wide, margins dentate with the tip of each tooth being the terminating point for a single lateral vein.
Flowers: Male flowers white, borne in spikes 10 - 18 cm long and arising from the leaf axils.
Fruit: Enclosed in a round, densely spiny, sharp-pointed burr, 3 - 4 cm in diameter.
Distinguishing Marks: Most easily recognized by relatively long leaves with dentate margins in conjunction with the small, spiny burr that encloses the fruit.
Distribution: Throughout the panhandle, eastward to north-central Florida and southward to about Lake County.

American Beech

Fagus grandifolia Ehrh. **Plate 25**

Form: Medium to large deciduous tree with thin, smooth, grayish bark, to about 30 m in height.
Leaves: Alternate, simple, two-ranked, predominately oval to elliptic, 4 - 14 cm long, 2 - 7 cm wide, margins dentate, with 9 - 14 pairs of prominent lateral veins, each terminating at the tip of a marginal tooth.

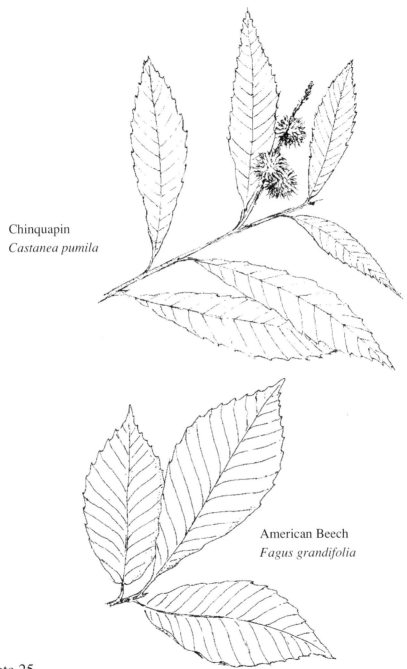

Chinquapin
Castanea pumila

American Beech
Fagus grandifolia

Plate 25

181

Flowers: Male and female flowers small and inconspicuous.

Fruit: Borne in a spiny enclosure that splits at maturity to expose one to three nuts.

Distinguishing Marks: Most easily recognized by smooth bark in combination with the lateral veins of leaves conspicuous and terminating in the tips of the marginal teeth.

Distribution: Mesic woodlands of the Florida panhandle, eastward to about Madison and Taylor counties; disjunct populations also exist in Alachua and Columbia counties.

White Oak

Quercus alba L.   **Plate 26**

Form: A potentially large, whitish, scaly barked deciduous tree to about 35 m in height.

Leaves: Alternate, 5 - 20 cm long, 3 - 10 cm wide, mature blades usually deeply cut into seven to ten rounded lobes.

Flowers: Male flowers borne in hanging catkins, 6 - 7.5 cm long.

Fruit: Acorn to about 3 cm in length, borne in a bowl-shaped cup covering about one-third of the nut.

Distinguishing Marks: Generally recognized by whitish, scaly bark and leaves with roundish lobes separated by deep sinuses; distinguished from bluff oak (*Q. austrina*) by generally longer leaves with the undersurfaces of leaves being whitish rather than green, by the leaf edges being regularly rather than irregularly lobed, and by the lobes generally numbering more than seven; from swamp chestnut oak (*Q. michauxii*) by the latter's leaves appearing more undulate than lobed.

Distribution: Hardwood forests of the Florida panhandle, eastward to about the Suwannee River.

Arkansas Oak

Quercus arkansana Sarg.   **Plate 26**

Form: Small, deciduous tree.

Leaves: Simple, alternate, mostly obovate, often as wide as long, typically 6 - 10 cm long, though some leaves to 15 cm, upper surfaces dark green and moderately shiny, sparsely covered with tiny, star-shaped hairs, margins unlobed or with three to five shallow lobes.

Fruit: Acorn small, 6 - 10 mm long, roundish with a very shallow cup that covers less than one-fourth of the nut.

Distinguishing Marks: Very similar in leaf structure to blackjack oak (*Q. marilandica*) but lacking the latter's rusty tomentose lower surfaces and firm, leathery feel.

Distribution: Local in well-drained, sandy, pine–oak–hickory woodlands of the western panhandle, eastward to Calhoun County.

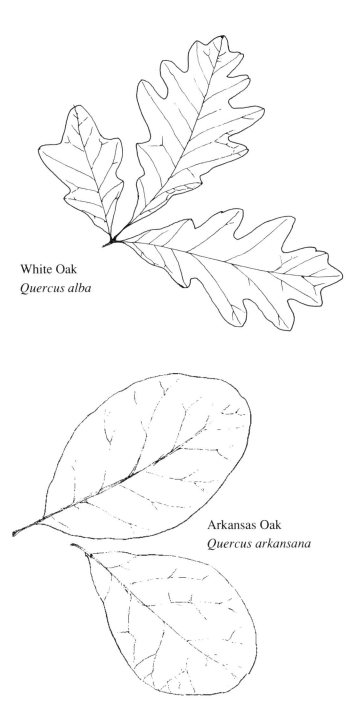

White Oak
Quercus alba

Arkansas Oak
Quercus arkansana

Plate 26

183

Bluff Oak

Quercus austrina Small

Form: Medium-sized deciduous tree with whitish, scaly bark similar in appearance to the white oak (*Q. alba*).
Leaves: Alternate, simple, 3 - 15 cm long, 2 - 8 cm wide, margins semishallowly and irregularly lobed, lobes numbering five to seven.
Fruit: Acorn 1.2 - 2 cm long and borne in a thin, shallow, bowl-shaped cup.
Distinguishing Marks: Distinguished from white oak, pictured on p. 183, by leaves being shorter and more shallowly lobed, the sinuses between the lobes usually not exceeding one-half the length of the lobe, the undersurfaces of leaves being green rather than whitish, and by the lobes on a given leaf generally being seven or less in number.
Distribution: Slopes, ravines, and bluffs; throughout the panhandle, eastward to the north-central counties.

Chapman Oak

Quercus chapmanii Sarg. **Photo #57**

Form: Small, shrubby, essentially evergreen tree to about 8 m in height.
Leaves: Alternate, simple, elliptic to sometimes obovate or spatulate, 2 - 10 cm long, 1 - 8 cm wide, upper surfaces dark green, shiny, and without pubescence, lower surfaces lightly pubescent, even if only on the veins, margins of at least some leaves entire, margins of others wavy to very shallowly lobed.
Fruit: Acorn 1.5 - 2.5 cm long, borne in a bowl-shaped cup 6 - 8 mm deep and enclosing about half the nut.
Distinguishing Marks: Distinguished from the myrtle and scrub oaks (*Q. myrtifolia, Q. inopina*), with which it frequently associates, by each of the latter having the lower surfaces of mature leaves without pubescence and at least some leaves with revolute margins.
Distribution: Coastal and inland sand pine–oak scrub; coastal areas of the panhandle and throughout the interior peninsula, southward to about Palm Beach County.

Southern Red Oak or Spanish Oak

Quercus falcata Michx. **Plate 27**

Form: Medium-sized to large, dark-colored deciduous tree with deeply fissured bark, to about 30 m in height.
Leaves: Alternate, simple, 12 - 23 cm long, 10 - 12 cm wide, margins with three to seven conspicuous lobes, each lobe typically with a bristle tip, undersurfaces gray or rusty tomentose, bases commonly and distinctly U-shaped.
Flowers: Male flowers borne in hanging catkins, 7.5 - 12.5 cm long.
Fruit: Acorn orange-brown, 1 - 1.5 cm long, borne in a bowl-shaped cup that encloses one-half to one-third of the nut.

Southern Red Oak
Quercus falcata

Plate 27

Distinguishing Marks: Distinguished from the turkey oak (*Q. laevis*) and most other oaks with sharply lobed leaves by U-shaped bases of leaves.
Distribution: Throughout the panhandle and the northern part of the state, southward to about Marion County.

Sand Live Oak

Quercus geminata Small   **Photo #58**

Form: Small to medium-sized, semievergreen tree with thick, roughly ridged, and furrowed bark.
Leaves: Alternate, simple, entire, thick, leathery, coarsely veined, 2 - 12 cm long, .5 - 4 cm wide, dark green above, dull gray beneath, margins extremely revolute, making an upsidedown leaf take on the appearance of an elongated bowl; petioles densely pubescent.
Fruit: Acorn 1 - 2 cm long, borne in a tapering cup 7 - 10 mm deep.
Distinguishing Marks: Recognized as the only tree-sized Florida oak with such conspicuously revolute leaves.
Distribution: Deep inland sands, dunes, sand pine–oak scrub, coastal hammocks; throughout northern Florida and southward to Dade and Collier counties.

Laurel Oak

Quercus hemisphaerica Bartr. ex Willd.   **Photo #59**

Form: Potentially large deciduous tree.
Leaves: Alternate, simple, entire, elliptic to lanceolate, 2 - 9 cm long, 1 - 3 cm wide, apices sometimes bristle tipped, upper surfaces dark green, lower surfaces bright green, both surfaces without pubescence.
Fruit: Acorn about 1 cm long, rounded at the apex, appearing somewhat squatty or flattened at the base.
Distinguishing Marks: Distinguished from the similar diamond leaf oak (*Q. laurifolia*), which was once thought to be the same species, by the latter species with at least some diamond-shaped leaves and being generally restricted to a wetland habitat, from the very similar willow oak (*Q. phellos*) by the latter's leaves being more nearly linear in shape and by their exhibiting tufted pubescence in the vein axils on their lower surfaces.
Distribution: Mixed woodlands, sand ridges, and other generally dry habitats from the panhandle eastward and southward to at least Palm Beach County.

Bluejack Oak

Quercus incana Bartr.   **Photo #60**

Form: Shrub or small, fast-growing, deciduous tree with dark gray to black, deeply furrowed bark, to about 12 m in height.
Leaves: Alternate, simple, elliptic to lanceolate, entire, 3 - 12 cm long, 1 - 3 cm wide, margins flat as opposed to revolute, upper surfaces bluish or ashy green when mature, lower surfaces silvery tomentose, apices tipped with a short bristle.
Flowers: Male flowers borne in slender, hanging catkins, 5 - 7.5 cm long.
Fruit: Acorn 1 - 1.5 cm long, rounded, borne in a shallow, reddish bro n cup.
Distinguishing Marks: Most easily distinguished from other oaks with entire leaves by the sandy habitat, and by leaves with ashy-green or bluish upper surfaces and silvery undersurfaces.
Distribution: Sand hills and ridges throughout northern Florida, southward to Lee County.

Scrub Oak

Quercus inopina Ashe   **Photo #61**

Form: Typically a single-stemmed evergreen shrub not exceeding about 2 m in height, previously reported to reach the stature of a small tree, occasionally found as such today.
Leaves: Alternate, simple, elliptical, 2 - 12 cm long, 1 - 7.5 cm wide, held erect on the branch, margins entire but strongly revolute, lower surfaces with a noticeable, powdery yellow fuzz.
Distinguishing Marks: Similar to the myrtle oak (*Q. myrtifolia*) but distinguished from it by having typically elliptic rather than obovate leaves.
Distribution: Sand pine scrub and scrubby flatwoods in association with sand live oak (*Q. geminata*) and Chapman oak (*Q. chapmanii*); found primarily in a restricted range from southernmost Orange to Highlands counties; also from a few locations in Hillsborough, Manatee, and Hardee counties.

Turkey Oak

Quercus laevis Walt. **Plate 28**

Form: Small scrubby deciduous tree to about 15 m in height or a little more, with dark gray, furrowed, and blocky bark.
Leaves: Alternate, simple, 7 - 30 cm long, with three to seven deeply cut, bristle-tipped lobes, bases tapered, lower surfaces hairy in the vein axils; petioles usually twisted so that leaf surfaces are held vertical to the ground.
Flowers: Male flowers borne from the tips of the branches in conspicuous, hanging catkins 8 - 12 cm long.
Fruit: Acorn 2 - 3 cm long, wide at the base and tapering to the apex.
Distinguishing Marks: Distinguished from other oaks of deep sandy ridges by sharply lobed leaves, from southern red oak (*Q. falcata*) by lack of rusty tomentose leaf undersurface and by the leaf base being tapered rather than U-shaped, from post oak (*Q. stellata*) and sand-post oak (*Q. margaretta*) by leaf lobes pointed rather than rounded or squarish.
Distribution: Well-drained, deep, sandy ridges in association with pine trees; throughout northern Florida, southward to Sarasota and Martin counties.

Diamond Leaf Oak

Quercus laurifolia Michx. **Plate 28**

Form: Large deciduous tree with dark, grayish bark, to about 30 m in height, bases of older specimens often buttressed, trunks of medium to large trees smoothish.
Leaves: Alternate, simple, entire, typically 5 - 10 cm long, 2 - 4 cm wide, obovate to oblanceolate, at least some leaves on each tree wider in the middle and tapering toward each end, thus appearing somewhat diamond shaped.
Fruit: Acorn 1 - 2 cm long, flattened at the base, rounded at the apex.
Distinguishing Marks: Recognized by at least a few leaves on any tree being diamond shaped.
Distribution: Floodplains, bottomlands, wet hammocks; throughout Florida except the Keys.

Overcup Oak

Quercus lyrata Walt. **Plate 28**

Form: Medium-sized deciduous tree to about 30 m in height.
Leaves: Alternate, simple, with five to nine shallow lobes, 7 - 25 cm long, 2.5 - 12 cm wide, lobes rounded, not bristle tipped.
Flowers: Male flowers borne in hanging, yellow catkins, 10 - 15 cm long.
Fruit: Acorn large, 1.5 - 2.5 cm long, rounded, borne in a thick cup that often nearly encloses the nut.
Distinguishing Marks: Distinguished from southern red oak (*Q. falcata*) and other species with similarly lobed leaves by generally wetland habitat and by distinctive acorns.
Distribution: Floodplain forests throughout the panhandle, eastward to about the Suwannee River.

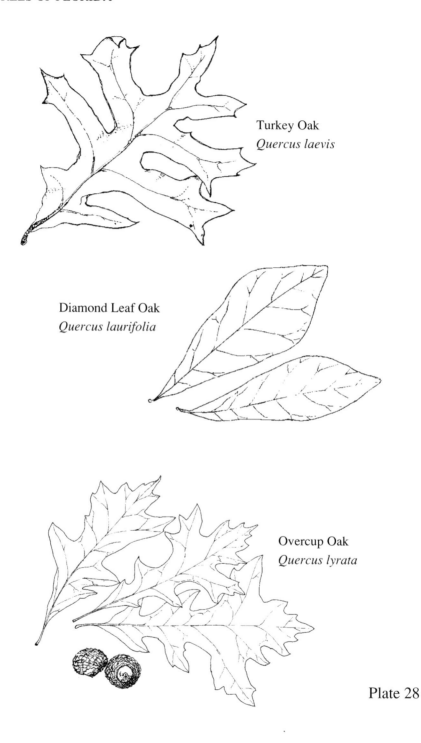

Turkey Oak
Quercus laevis

Diamond Leaf Oak
Quercus laurifolia

Overcup Oak
Quercus lyrata

Plate 28

Sand-Post Oak

Quercus margaretta Ashe   **Plate 29**

Form: Small, scrubby deciduous tree.
Leaves: Alternate, simple, 2 - 15 cm long, to 12 cm wide, typically with three to five lobes, lobes rounded or squarish.
Fruit: Acorn oblong, 1.5 - 2 cm long, borne in a cup that encloses about one third of the nut.
Distinguishing Marks: Distinguished from southern red oak (*Q. falcata*) and shumard oak (*Q. shumardii*) by smaller leaves with rounded lobes, from post oak (*Q. stellata*) by generally shorter leaves and glabrous twigs, from Arkansas oak (*Q. arkansana*) by having conspicuously lobed rather than shallowly lobed or unlobed leaves.
Distribution: Deep sand ridges and pine–oak scrub; throughout the panhandle, eastward and southward to the central peninsula.

Blackjack Oak

Quercus marilandica Muench.   **Photo #62**

Form: Small, attractive deciduous tree with thickened, blackish, deeply blocky bark, to about 12 m in height.
Leaves: Alternate, simple, stiff, with three to five lobes (if lobed at all), typically obovate or tri-angular in shape, normally 7 - 20 cm long, often as wide as long, upper surfaces shiny green, lower surfaces densely rusty-yellow or orange-brown tomentose and somewhat feltlike to the touch.
Flowers: Male flowers borne in hanging catkins, 5 - 12 cm long.
Fruit: Acorn 1.5 - 2 cm long, often borne in a wedge-shaped cup that tapers to a narrow base.
Distinguishing Marks: Distinguished from Arkansas oak (*Q. arkansana*) by the latter having more pliable and overall smaller leaves without rusty tomentose lower surfaces.
Distribution: Locally abundant in clay-type soils of open areas and woodland borders, chiefly west of the Suwannee River.

Swamp Chestnut Oak

Quercus michauxii Nutt.   **Plate 29**

Form: Large deciduous tree with scaly bark, to about 40 m in height.
Leaves: Alternate, simple, relatively large, 10 - 22 cm long, 7 - 15 cm wide, margins with nu-merous shallow lobes that often appear undulate rather than lobed.
Fruit: Acorn large, 2.5 - 4 cm long, enclosed in a scaly cup for one-third to one-half its length.
Distinguishing Marks: Distinguished from all Florida oaks but chinquapin oak (*Q. muehlen-bergii*) by distinctive leaf edges, from chinquapin oak by typically blunt rather than pointed lobes and generally larger size of mature leaves.
Distribution: Floodplain woods, slopes of bluffs and ravines, areas with limestone close to the soil surface; throughout the panhandle, eastward and southward to Hernando County.

Chinquapin Oak

Quercus muehlenbergii Engelm.   **Plate 29**

Form: Medium-sized deciduous tree to about 30 m in height.
Leaves: Alternate, simple, 5 - 15 cm long, 2 - 10 cm wide, margins with numerous shallow lobes.
Flowers: Male flowers borne in hanging catkins, 7 - 10 cm long.
Fruit: Acorn light brown, to about 1.5 cm long, borne in a knobby cup that encloses about one-third to one-half of the nut.
Distinguishing Marks: Distinguished from similarly leaved swamp chestnut oak (*Quercus michauxii*) by generally smaller leaves with pointed rather than rounded lobes.
Distribution: Limited to bluffs and slopes in the panhandle from Jackson to Leon counties.

Myrtle Oak

Quercus myrtifolia Willd.   **Plate 30**

Form: Dense, evergreen shrub or small tree to about 12 m in height.
Leaves: Alternate, simple, variously elliptic, oblong, or oval, 2 - 8 cm long, 1 - 5 cm wide, margins entire or lobed and revolute, upper surfaces dark green, lower surfaces dull to yellowish green, lower surfaces of at least the mature leaves without pubescence.
Distinguishing Marks: Distinguished from Chapman oak (*Q. chapmanii*) by leaves with revolute leaf margins and glabrous lower surfaces, from *Q. inopina* by the latter's leaves being generally elliptic rather than obovate and being held erect on the branch.
Distribution: Coastal regions of the panhandle, eastward to the central peninsula, southward to Dade County on the east coast and Collier County on the west coast.

Water Oak

Quercus nigra L.   **Plate 30**

Form: Medium-sized deciduous tree to about 25 m in height with smooth to shallowly furrowed bark.
Leaves: Alternate, simple, entire, extremely variable in shape, sometimes three lobed but more commonly spatulate, typically 5 - 15 cm long, 2 - 10 cm wide.
Flowers: Male flowers borne in narrow, hanging catkins, 5 - 7.5 cm long.
Fruit: Acorn .8 - 1.8 cm long, borne in a shallow cup that encloses only the base of the nut.
Distinguishing Marks: Distinguished from other oaks by always displaying at least some spatulate-shaped leaves with cobweblike hairs in the vein axils on the lower surfaces of leaves.
Distribution: Throughout the panhandle, southward to Hillsborough and Lake counties.

190

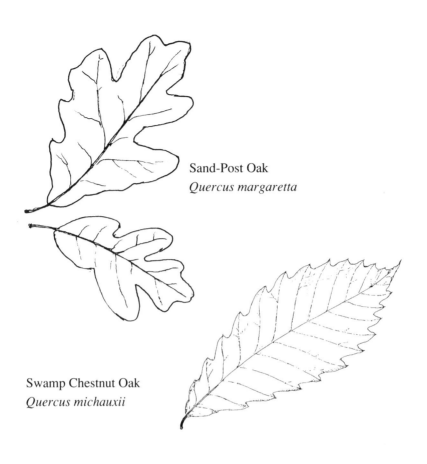

Sand-Post Oak
Quercus margaretta

Swamp Chestnut Oak
Quercus michauxii

Chinquapin Oak
Quercus muehlenbergii

Plate 29

Cherrybark Oak or Swamp Red Oak

Quercus pagoda Raf.

Form: Large deciduous tree.
Leaves: Alternate, simple, 8 - 20 cm long, five to seven lobes, lobes triangular and bristle tipped, bases truncate or wedge shaped.
Distinguishing Marks: Very similar to southern red oak (*Q. falcata*) pictured on p. 185 of which the cherrybark oak has long been classified a variety (*Q. falcata* var. *pagodaefolia*), distinguished from it by crown leaves lacking the typically U-shaped leaf bases of the latter species and the pubescence of the lower surfaces of leaves being more gray than reddish or rust colored.
Distribution: Floodplain forests and riverbanks; limited in Florida to the counties of the central panhandle.

Willow Oak

Quercus phellos L.

Form: Medium- or large-sized deciduous tree to nearly 30 m in height, with smooth to roughened bark depending upon age.
Leaves: Alternate, simple, entire, lanceolate, and willowlike in general shape but lacking the latter's marginal teeth, tapering toward both bases and apices, 6 - 13 cm long, generally less than 2 cm wide, upper surfaces light green and shiny, central vein extending beyond the leaf tip as a small toothlike structure.
Flowers: Male flowers borne in a narrow, hanging catkin, 5 - 7.5 cm long.
Fruit: Acorn solitary or borne in pairs, to a little more than 1 cm long, cup enclosing about one-fourth of the nut.
Distinguishing Marks: Similar in general appearance to the laurel oak (*Q. hemisphaerica*), pictured in Photo #59, differing from it by having most leaves much longer than wide and more linear in overall shape, and by exhibiting tufts of hairs in at least some of the vein axils on lower surfaces of leaves.
Distribution: Typically in bottomlands but sometimes in fields and along fence lines; western panhandle from Escambia to about Leon counties.

Shumard Oak

Quercus shumardii Buckl.   **Plate 30**

Form: Medium to large deciduous tree, 20 - 40 m in height.
Leaves: Alternate, simple, 7 - 15 cm long, 6 - 12 cm wide, mostly seven-lobed but sometimes nine-lobed or even more, each lobe with several smaller secondary lobes, each secondary lobe bristle-tipped, upper surfaces dark green, shiny and without pubescence, lower surfaces also shiny green but with small tufts of pubescence in the vein axils, old and fallen leaves with black spots on the surfaces.
Flowers: Male flowers borne in long, narrow catkins, 14 - 18 cm long.
Fruit: Acorn borne solitary or in pairs, 1.5 - 2.5 cm long, cup saucerlike and enclosing about one-third of the nut.

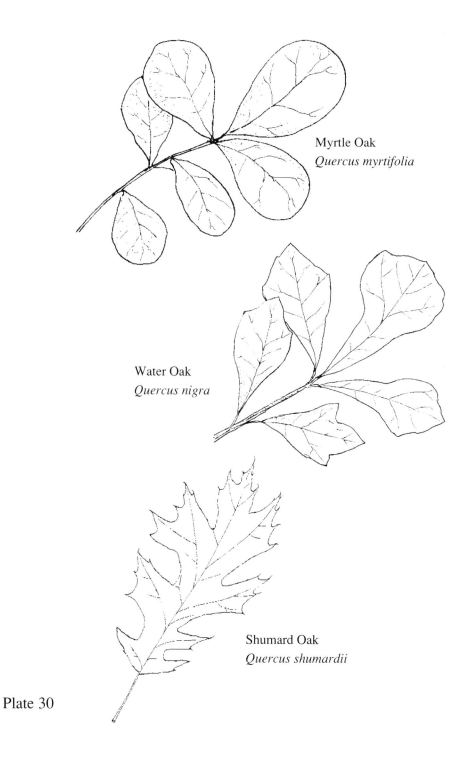

Myrtle Oak
Quercus myrtifolia

Water Oak
Quercus nigra

Shumard Oak
Quercus shumardii

Plate 30

Distinguishing Marks: Distinguished from other oaks with lobed, bristle-tipped leaves by combination of having only tufts of pubescence on lower leaf surface as described above and by having straight rather than twisted leaf petioles, from black oak (*Q. velutina*) by leaves typically with seven or more major lobes.

Distribution: Mesic woods, hammocks, riverbanks and other areas near water; throughout the panhandle and north Florida, southward to Marion County.

Post Oak

Quercus stellata Wangenh.   **Plate 31**

Form: Small to medium-sized deciduous tree, 10 - 20 m in height, with deep vertical furrows and reddish brown to grayish bark.

Leaves: Alternate, simple, 10 - 18 cm long, to about 15 cm wide, generally five-lobed, the terminal three lobes being squarish in shape and situated in such a way as to make the leaf take on the shape of a cross, the lower two lobes being smaller and often separated from the terminal lobes by relatively wide sinuses, upper and lower surfaces of leaves as well as petioles covered with tiny, star-shaped hairs.

Flowers: Male flowers borne on hanging catkins, 7.5 - 10 cm long.

Fruit: Acorn 1 - 2.5 cm long, rounded at the base and apex, borne in a bowllike cup that encloses about one-third of the nut.

Distinguishing Marks: Distinguished from other oaks with lobed leaves by leaves being distinctly cross shaped, from sand-post oak (*Q. margaretta*) by having overall larger leaves with lobes that are more squarish than rounded in outline.

Distribution: Upland woods, mixed hardwood forests, and sandy soils; throughout north Florida and the panhandle, south to about Hillsborough and Polk counties.

Black Oak

Quercus velutina Lam.   **Plate 31**

Form: Potentially medium-sized to large deciduous tree, to 25 m in height, generally smaller in Florida, older trees having dark brown to black, fissured bark.

Leaves: Alternate, simple, relatively large, wider above the middle, 10 - 20 cm long, 8 - 15 cm wide, margins typically with five (sometimes seven) major lobes; lobes bristle tipped, typically broad and separated by shallow, narrow sinuses, though some leaves on any tree not adhering to this description of lobes.

Flowers: Male flowers borne in hanging catkins, 10 - 15 cm long.

Fruit: Acorn oblong, 1.2 - 1.5 cm long, borne in a dark brown cup that encloses about one-half of the nut.

Distinguishing Marks: Distinguished from other oaks with bristle-tipped leaf lobes by combination of straight rather than twisted petioles and lower surfaces of leaves being sparsely pubescent; from similar shumard oak (*Q. shumardii*) by leaves typically having only five (or occasionally seven) main lobes.

Distribution: Upland mixed woodlands; north-central panhandle from Holmes to Leon counties.

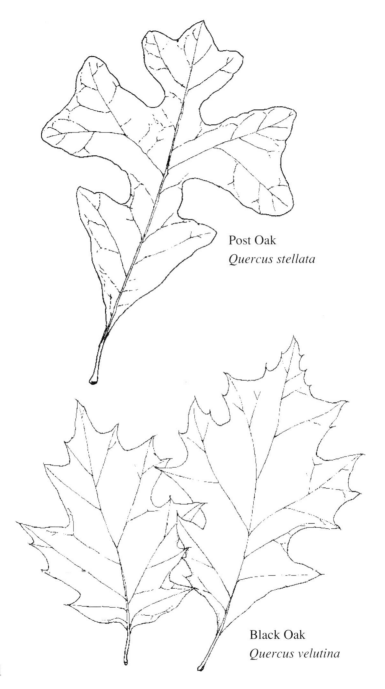

Post Oak
Quercus stellata

Black Oak
Quercus velutina

Plate 31

195

Live Oak

Quercus virginiana Mill.

Photo #63

Form: Spreading, bulky evergreen tree to about 20 m in height, with rough bark and a short central trunk that typically divides 2 or 3 m above the ground into several large branches.

Leaves: Alternate, simple, entire (except for leaves of saplings and new summer shoots which are sometimes toothed or shallowly lobed), leathery, stiff, 2 - 15 cm long, 1 - 5 cm wide, dark green and shiny above, pale gray and tightly tomentose beneath.

Flowers: Male flowers borne in hanging catkins, 5 - 7.5 cm long.

Fruit: Acorn shiny, dark brown, often black at the tip, oblong, 1 - 2.5 cm long, borne in a shallow cup that encloses about one-fourth of the nut.

Distinguishing Marks: Distinguished from sand live oak (*Q. geminata*) by leaves of the latter having a combination of leaf margins mostly revolute and veins on upper surfaces of leaves conspicuously depressed.

Distribution: Florida's most widespread oak, inhabiting a wide variety of sites throughout the state including the Keys.

HAMAMELIDACEAE

Witch Hazel

Hamamelis virginiana L.

Plate 32

Form: Deciduous shrub or small tree to about 8 m in height with a short, low-branching trunk and zigzag twigs.

Leaves: Alternate, simple, two-ranked, oval to obovate, 6 - 15 cm long, to 10 cm wide, margins undulate or scalloped, dull green in summer, turning pale yellow in autumn.

Flowers: Yellow and very distinctive with four ribbonlike petals, each 1 - 1.5 cm long, appearing in late fall and winter.

Fruit: A short, pubescent, four-pointed, two-valved capsule, 1 - 1.6 cm long.

Distinguishing Marks: The distinctive leaves, flowers, and fruit make it difficult to confuse this species with any other north Florida tree.

Distribution: Slopes, ravines, low woods, moist hillsides, mesic woods; throughout the panhandle and northern Florida, southward to about Lake County.

Sweetgum

Liquidambar styraciflua L.

Plate 32

Form: Potentially large deciduous tree to about 40 m in height with grayish, fissured, and interlacing bark.

Leaves: Alternate, simple, 10 - 18 cm long, star-shaped with five to sometimes seven straight, sharp-pointed lobes, each with serrated margins, leaves colorful in the fall.

Flowers: Male flowers borne in a compact, erect stalk; female flowers borne in a rounded cluster and hanging pendently from a relatively long stalk.

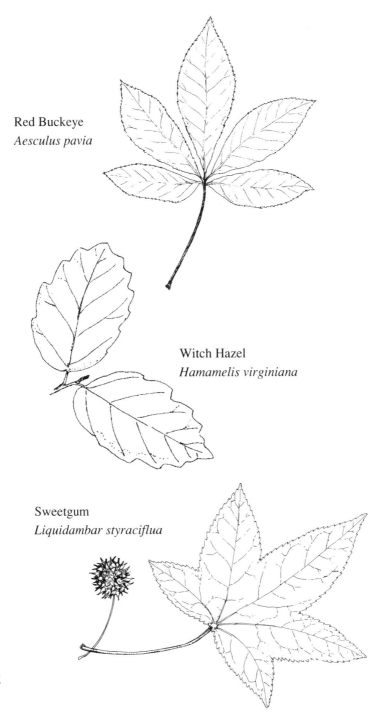

Red Buckeye
Aesculus pavia

Witch Hazel
Hamamelis virginiana

Sweetgum
Liquidambar styraciflua

Plate 32

197

Fruit: Hard, brown, spiny, and rounded, 2.5 - 4 cm in diameter, hanging on a relatively long stalk

Distinguishing Marks: The star-shaped leaves set this plant apart from all other Florida trees.

Distribution: Found in a variety of habitats from upland to lowland woods; throughout north Florida, southward to at least the Tampa area on the west coast, Brevard County on the east coast.

HIPPOCASTANACEAE

Red Buckeye

Aesculus pavia L.   **Plate 32**

Form: Deciduous shrub or small tree to about 12 m in height.

Leaves: Opposite, palmately compound with long petioles, overall leaf length 18 - 32 cm; leaflets five (occasionally seven) in number, elliptic, 5 - 15 cm long, margins finely toothed.

Flowers: Bright red, showy, borne in spreading clusters at the tips of the branches, each cluster 10 - 25 cm long.

Fruit: A light brown capsule 3 - 6 cm in diameter, splitting to expose several hard, reddish brown, poisonous seeds.

Distinguishing Marks: Distinguished as the only north Florida species with palmately compound leaves with five leaflets.

Distribution: Slopes, bottoms, ravines, bluffs, hammocks, rich mesic woods; throughout the panhandle and northern Florida, southward to Seminole County.

ILLICIACEAE

Florida Anise

Illicium floridanum Ellis   **Photo #67**

Form: Evergreen shrub or small tree to about 8 m in height.

Leaves: Alternate, simple, entire, elliptical with sharp-pointed tips, 6.5 to 15 cm long, 2 - 6 cm wide, usually clustered near the tips of the branches; the crushed foliage has a distinctive, pungent odor of anise.

Flowers: Ornate, crimson red, 2.5 - 6 cm wide, with as many as 30 petals, 15 pistils, and 30 stamens.

Fruit: Remains of the star-shaped spent fruit can be found on a few trees at almost any time of year.

Distinguishing Marks: The showy flowers and pungent odor of its crushed leaves set this tree apart.

Distribution: Moist ravines and steepheads; throughout the inner panhandle, eastward to the Ochlockonee River.

Yellow Anise
Illicium parviflorum Michx. ex Vent.   **Photo #64**

Form: Shrub or small tree.
Leaves: Similar to Florida anise, except lacking the sharp-pointed tip, exhibiting a strong aroma when crushed.
Flowers: Yellow, small, less than 2 cm wide, having 12 - 15 tepals, 6 - 7 stamens.
Distinguishing Marks: Distinguished from Florida anise (*I. floridanum*) by flowers smaller, yellow, and with fewer petals, and by geographic location.
Distribution: Hammocks and wetlands along spring-fed streams; endemic to several north-central counties, including Marion, Lake, and Volusia.

Water Hickory
Carya aquatica (Michx. f.) Nutt.   **Plate 33**

Form: Medium to large deciduous tree to about 35 m in height, with grayish, scaly bark.
Leaves: Alternate, compound, odd-pinnate, 15 - 30 cm long; leaflets usually 9 or 11 in number (but as few as 7 and as many as 17), mostly lanceolate in shape, 7 - 10 cm long, 1 - 3 cm wide, margins usually but not always evidently serrate.
Flowers: Male flowers borne in hanging catkins, 6 - 8 cm long.
Fruit: A nut, borne in a hard, four-ridged husk that splits to the base when mature.
Distinguishing Marks: Distinguished from similar pecan (*C. illinoensis*) by generally being in wetland rather than disturbed, upland habitats and by having pubescent leaf parts, from black walnut (*Juglans nigra*) by the scaly bark and larger terminal leaflet, and from ashes (*Fraxinus* spp.) by alternate leaves.
Distribution: Levees, riverbanks, floodplain woods; throughout northern Florida, southward to Lake Okeechobee.

Bitternut Hickory
Carya cordiformis (Wangenh.) K. Koch

Form: Medium to large deciduous tree to about 35 m in height with interlacing, diamond-patterned bark typical of hickories.
Leaves: Alternate, compound, odd-pinnate; leaflets typically 7 or 9 in number, rarely 5 or 11, mostly lanceolate, 10 - 15 cm long, 2 - 3 cm wide, with coarsely toothed margins.
Flowers: Male flowers borne in long catkins to about 10 cm long.
Fruit: A nut, borne in a thin, brown, only slightly four-angled husk.
Distinguishing Marks: The leaves of several hickories are extremely similar and virtually indistinguishable through casual observation; the leaves of the bitternut are similar in overall outline to those of the Florida hickory (*C. floridana*) pictured on p. 201, the bitternut may be most easily distinguished from it and all other hickories with seven to nine leaflets by being the only species in a predominately wetland habitat with the combination of the terminal buds at the ends

of branches being yellow or sulphur colored and by the pubescence of the leaf parts being evenly distributed rather than tufted (requires magnification).

Distribution: Floodplains, low woods, riverbanks; restricted in Florida to the drainage basins of the Chipola, Apalachicola, and Ochlockonee Rivers.

Florida or Scrub Hickory

Carya floridana Sarg.   **Plate 33**

Form: Small deciduous tree with grayish, interlacing, diamond-patterned bark that often contains grayish lichens similar to other scrub species, to about 25 m in height.
Leaves: Alternate, compound, odd-pinnate, 8 - 20 cm long; leaflets mostly five or seven in number, sometimes three, lanceolate to elliptic, margins serrate, lower surfaces often rust colored from a dense covering of rusty scales.
Flowers: Male flowers borne in greenish catkins, to about 4 cm long.
Fruit: A nut, borne in a thick, hard husk, splitting to the base when mature.
Distinguishing Marks: Most readily distinguished from other hickories by the rusty undersurfaces of its leaflets in conjunction with being the only Florida hickory likely to be encountered in the white sand scrub of the central peninsula.
Distribution: Endemic to the white sand scrub of central Florida, from Marion County southward to northern Palm Beach County on the east coast, Collier County on the west coast.

Pignut Hickory

Carya glabra (Mill.) Sweet   **Photo #65**

Form: Small to large deciduous tree with interlacing, diamond-patterned bark typical of hickories, varying from 25 to about 40 m in height.
Leaves: Alternate, compound, odd-pinnate, 15 - 40 cm long; leaflets usually numbering five or seven (sometimes three), lanceolate, elliptic, or ovate, 8 - 16 cm long, 3 - 5 cm wide, margins serrate.
Flowers: Male flowers borne in catkins, 5 - 7 cm long.
Fruit: A nut, borne in a thin, smooth husk that usually does not split to the base when mature.
Distinguishing Marks: Leaves similar in general outline to the Florida hickory (*C. floridana*) pictured on p. 201, most easily distinguished from it and all other hickories by all leaf parts being glabrous, except for occasional small tufts of hairs in the vein axils on the lower surfaces of at least some leaflets.
Distribution: Dry to moist woods throughout the northern part of the state, south to about Manatee, Hardee, and Highlands counties.

Pecan

Carya illinoensis (Wangenh.) K. Koch   **Plate 33**

Form: Large deciduous tree with grayish, scaly bark, to about 40 m in height.
Leaves: Alternate, compound, odd-pinnate, 10 - 50 cm long; leaflets usually 9 - 17 in number

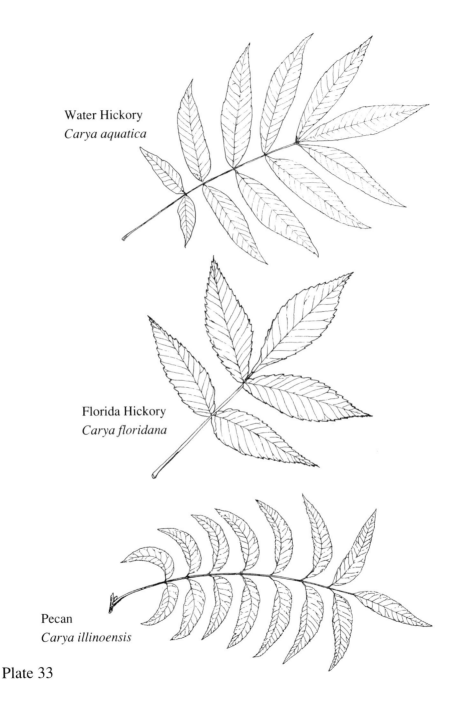

Water Hickory
Carya aquatica

Florida Hickory
Carya floridana

Pecan
Carya illinoensis

Plate 33

Leaves: Alternate, compound, odd-pinnate, 10 - 50 cm long; leaflets usually 9 - 17 in number and drooping, lanceolate in shape, 8 - 20 cm long, 2.5 - 7.5 cm wide, margins serrate.

Flowers: Male flowers borne in light green catkins to about 15 cm long.

Fruit: A nut borne in a smooth, thin-shelled husk, to about 5 cm long and shaped like a football.

Distinguishing Marks: Distinguished from water hickory (*C. aquatica*) by having glabrous leaf parts and by being restricted to disturbed upland habitats, from mature black walnut (*Juglans nigra*) by the grayish scaly bark and larger terminal leaflet.

Distribution: Introduced species found in disturbed upland sites across much of northern Florida where escaped from cultivation.

Sand or Pale Hickory

Carya pallida (Ashe) Engl. & Graebn.

Form: Small to medium-sized deciduous tree with interlacing, diamond-patterned bark typical of hickories, normally not exceeding about 15 m in height, but perhaps taller.

Leaves: Alternate, compound, odd-pinnate, 10 - 30 cm long; leaflets normally seven in number but as few as three and as many as nine, lanceolate to ovate, 7 - 15 cm long, 2 - 5 cm wide.

Flowers: Male flowers borne in slender, greenish yellow catkins, 5 - 13 cm long.

Fruit: Fruit a nut, borne in a thin, dark brown husk.

Distinguishing Marks: Leaves similar in general outline to the Florida hickory (*C. floridana*) pictured on p. 201, most readily distinguished from it and all other hickories as the only Florida hickory with upper surfaces of leaflets glabrous and lower surfaces bearing thin, silvery-yellow, dislike scales, and tufts of hairs that are not confined only to the vein axils (requires magnification).

Distribution: Found sporadically across the western panhandle primarily in association with longleaf pine–oak woods, but also in mixed woods along the upper slopes of bluffs and steepheads; from about Santa Rosa to Leon counties.

Mockernut Hickory

Carya tomentosa (Poir. in Lam.) Nutt.

Form: Medium to large deciduous tree with interlacing, diamond-patterned bark typical of most hickories, to about 35 m in height.

Leaves: Alternate, compound, odd-pinnate, 20 - 40 cm long; leaflets typically seven in number but sometimes five or nine, ovate to obovate; outermost leaflets 12 - 22 cm long, 7.5 - 12.5 cm wide, lowermost leaflets about one-third smaller.

Flowers: Male flowers borne in light green catkins, 10 - 20 cm long.

Fruit: A nut, borne in a thin, reddish brown husk.

Distinguishing Marks: Leaves similar in general outline to the Florida hickory (*C. floridana*) pictured on p. 201, most readily distinguished from it and all other upland hickories with five to nine leaflets by the tufted pubescence that is found on all parts of the leaf, including the rachis and the upper and lower surfaces of leaflets, in conjunction with the buff-colored hairs and tiny, globular, amber-colored granules of the lower surfaces of leaflets (requires magnification).

Distribution: Found primarily in well-drained upland woods; throughout north Florida, south to about Lake and Sumter counties.

Black Walnut
Juglans nigra

Plate 34

Black Walnut

Juglans nigra L.

Plate 34

Form: Large deciduous tree to about 40 m in height; bark on young trees grayish and scaly, on mature trees furrowed and very dark.

Leaves: Alternate, compound, 20 - 60 cm long, often appearing even-pinnate on mature trees due to lack of terminal leaflet, odd-pinnate on younger specimens; leaflets usually 15 - 23 in number, sometimes as few as eight, ovate to lanceolate, longest leaflets near middle of leaf, terminal leaflet absent or much reduced in size, margins serrate.

Flowers: Male flowers borne in greenish catkins, 5 - 10 cm long.

Fruit: Rounded, larger than those of the hickories, usually 3 - 4 cm in diameter.

Distinguishing Marks: Distinguished from water hickory (*C. aquatica*) and pecan (*C. illinoensis*) by dark, furrowed bark and apparently even-pinnate leaves, from other hickories by numerous leaflets.

Distribution: Bluffs, ravines, upland woods, limited in Florida to the north-central panhandle from about Walton to Leon counties; also used ornamentally.

Camphor Tree

Cinnamomum camphora (L.) Nees & Eberm.   **Photo #66**

Form: Small, attractive evergreen tree with green twigs.
Leaves: Alternate, simple, ovate, 4 - 10 cm long, 2 - 5 cm wide, upper surfaces shiny green, margins entire and wavy.
Flowers: Small, cream colored, borne in loose, spreading clusters.
Fruit: A rounded, black drupe to about 9 mm in diameter and borne atop a cup-shaped receptacle.
Distinguishing Marks: Distinguished by leaves that give off a strong aroma of camphor when crushed.
Distribution: Secondary woods, disturbed sites; naturalized in northern Florida, southward to the central peninsula.

Gulf Licaria

Licaria triandra (Sw.) Kostermans

Form: Small tree.
Leaves: Alternate, simple, entire, 5 - 11 cm long, widest in the middle with long pointed tips.
Flowers: Tiny and inconspicuous.
Fruit: A distinctive, deep blue drupe, about 2 cm in length and resting in a thick, red, double-rimmed cup.
Distribution: This tree is very rare and is likely still extant only at the City of Miami's Simpson Park; cultivated specimens may be seen at Fairchild Tropical Garden and at Metro Dade County's Arch Creek Park where an individual tree was planted by Brian Edmondson and Roger Hammer in honor of botanist George Avery who discovered the plant growing naturally there.

Spicebush

Lindera benzoin (L.) Blume   **Plate 35**

Form: Deciduous shrub, infrequently a very small tree with spicy and aromatic leaves and twigs.
Leaves: Alternate, simple, entire, ovate to elliptic, 6 - 12 cm long, 3 - 5 cm wide, upper surfaces dark green, lower surfaces grayish and pubescent at least along the central vein, but often pubescent throughout, apices often tapering to a point, margins fringed with hairs, larger leaves borne near the tips of branches, often with conspicuously smaller leaves below.
Flowers: Yellow, clustered along the branches, often at the point at which the leafy branchlets arise from the main branch, appearing in February.
Fruit: An oblong, red, aromatic drupe, 8 - 10 mm long.
Distinguishing Marks: Most readily recognized by the spicy aroma of crushed leaves (especially new ones) in conjunction with the tiny hairs that form a fringe along the leaf margin.
Distribution: Bluffs, slopes, hammocks, and floodplains; northeastern Florida as well as Jackson, Calhoun, Gadsden, and Liberty counties in the northern panhandle.

Spicebush
Lindera benzoin

Plate 35

Lancewood

Ocotea coriacea (Sw.) Britt.   **Photo #68**

Form: Small, evergreen understory shrub or tree to about 15 m in height.
Leaves: Alternate, simple, entire, lanceolate, 7 - 15 cm long, 2.5 - 5 cm wide, usually tapering to a long pointed tip, sharply fragrant when crushed.
Flowers: Creamy white, borne in clusters, each flower 5 - 7 mm in diameter.
Fruit: A dark blue, rounded drupe.
Distinguishing Marks: Distinguished from red bay (*Persea borbonia*) by leaf undersurface being green rather than grayish white.
Distribution: Most common in hammocks and pinewoods of southernmost Florida and the Keys but also found as far north as Cape Canaveral on the east coast.

Avocado

Persea americana Mill.

Form: Small tree with persistent to tardily deciduous leaves, to about 20 m in height.
Leaves: Alternate, simple, leathery, entire, elliptic to oblong, 10 - 30 cm long.
Flowers: Greenish yellow, fragrant, to about 7 mm long, borne in dense showy clusters.
Fruit: Particularly noted for its shiny, pear-shaped, edible, yellow-green fruit, 7 - 20 cm long.
Distribution: Cultivated and persistent from Brevard and Hillsborough counties southward.

Red Bay

Persea borbonia (L.) Spreng. **Photo #69**

Form: Evergreen shrub or small tree to about 20 m in height.
Leaves: Alternate, simple, entire, lanceolate, 2 - 15 cm long, 1.5 - 6 cm wide, aromatic when crushed.
Flowers: Small, greenish, borne in loose clusters in the leaf axils.
Fruit: A rounded, dark blue drupe, to about 1.2 cm in diameter.
Distinguishing Marks: Distinguished from other *Persea* and *Ocotea* by lower surface of leaves being grayish white below resulting from very short, appressed pubescence which cannot be seen without magnification and which appears like minute golden flecks; the regular occurrence of leaf galls also provides a helpful identification clue.
Distribution: Hammocks, bluffs, and scrub; common throughout the state including the Keys.

Silk Bay

Persea humilis Nash **Plate 36**

Form: Evergreen shrub or small tree with characteristically blackish trunk, branches, and twigs.
Leaves: Alternate, simple, entire, lanceolate, 3 - 10 cm long, 1 - 3 cm wide.
Fruit: A rounded drupe to about 1.5 cm in diameter.
Distinguishing Marks: Distinguished from other species of *Persea* by blackish branches in conjunction with leaf undersurface being covered with dense pubescence that is smooth and silky to the touch.
Distribution: Common component of the white sand scrub of central Florida, also rarely in southeastern Florida.

Swamp Bay

Persea palustris (Raf.) Sarg. **Photo #70**

Form: Evergreen shrub or small tree to about 12 m in height.
Leaves: Alternate, simple, entire, lanceolate or long-elliptic, 5 - 20 cm long.
Fruit: An oblong drupe to about 1 cm in length.
Distinguishing Marks: Similar in appearance to the red bay (*P. borbonia*) and lancewood (*Ocotea coriacea*), distinguished from both as well as spicebush (*Lindera benzoin*) by undersurfaces of leaves having dense, brownish, shaggy pubescence that is especially copious along the midrib (may require magnification); leaves also often contain galls, similar to red bay.
Distribution: Swamps, coastal swales, and spring margins; common throughout northern Florida and southward to the southern peninsula.

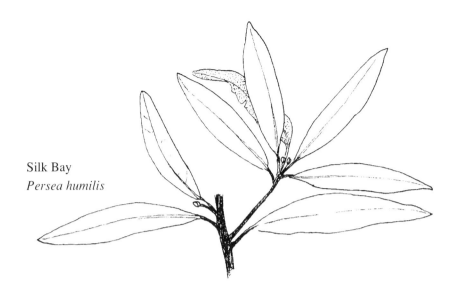

Silk Bay
Persea humilis

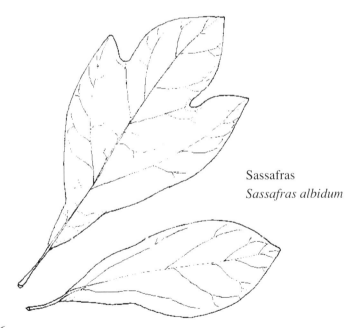

Sassafras
Sassafras albidum

Plate 36

Sassafras

Sassafras albidum (Nutt.) Nees   **Plate 36**

Form: Small, attractive, deciduous tree to about 15 m in height, bark with odor of root beer when crushed.
Leaves: Alternate, simple, 5 - 12 cm long, typically characterized by having two or three terminal lobes which often give the leaves the appearance of mittens or three-fingered gloves.
Flowers: Small, greenish yellow, 5 - 8 mm across at maturity, appearing in spring near the ends of naked branches.
Fruit: A fleshy, ovoid, dark blue drupe, 8 - 15 mm long.
Distinguishing Marks: Distinguished from all other species by the characteristic leaf shape.
Distribution: Dry bluffs, secondary woods, and disturbed sites; throughout the panhandle and northern part of the state, south to about Orange, Lake, Sumter, and Citrus counties.

LEGUMINOSAE

Tamarindillo

Acacia choriophylla Benth.   **Photo #71**

Form: Small, bushy tree lacking spines.
Leaves: Alternate, bipinnately compound, 10 - 20 cm in overall length, pinnae in one to three pairs; leaflets elliptic, numbering six to ten per pinna, 1 - 3 cm long, margins entire and revolute, apices rounded to notched.
Flowers: Bright yellow, globular, about 1 cm in diameter, appearing in spring and early summer.
Fruit: A flat pod about 5 cm long.
Distinguishing Marks: Distinguished from other *Acacia* by lack of spines and by having longer leaflets.
Distribution: Rare and restricted to the border separating high hammocks from the mangrove zone; found only in the Keys and considered endangered in Florida.

Sweet Acacia

Acacia farnesiana (L.) Willd.   **Photo #72**

Form: Deciduous shrub or small, much-branched tree to about 5 m in height, with slightly zigzag branches that are armed with paired, whitish spines.
Leaves: Alternate, often crowded on short spur twigs, bipinnately compound, pinnae in two to six pairs, overall leaf 2 - 10 cm long; leaflets linear, 3 - 6 mm long, numbering 10 - 25 pairs per pinna.
Flowers: Borne in rounded, bright yellow, headlike clusters, 1 - 1.3 cm in diameter, each held on stalks 1.5 - 2 cm long.
Fruit: A cylindric, purplish red pod, 5 - 8 cm long.
Distinguishing Marks: Distinguished from Small's acacia (*A. smallii*) by the latter species being found only in the western panhandle, from pine acacia (*A. pinetorum*) by larger leaflets.
Distribution: Shell middens, coastal hammocks, and pinelands; generally from about Citrus County southward but also rarely reported in northeastern Florida.

Long Spine Acacia or Steel Acacia

Acacia macracantha Humb. & Bonpl. ex Willd.   **Photo #73**

Form: Small, spreading tree to about 7 m in height, with conspicuous paired spines along its branches, spines to about 4 cm in length.
Leaves: Alternate, bipinnately compound, pinnae in 10 - 17 pairs, overall leaf to about 10 cm long; leaflets linear in shape, about 3 mm long and very narrow, 23 - 30 pairs on each pinna.
Flowers: Yellow, borne in globular heads that are less than 1 cm in diameter.
Fruit: A cylindrical pod to about 8 cm long.
Distinguishing Marks: Distinguished from other *Acacia* species by having pinnae in 10 to 17 pairs.
Distribution: Very rare and likely restricted only to one sandy ridge on Ramrod Key.

Pine Acacia

Acacia pinetorum Hermann

Form: Sprawling shrub or small tree with characteristically zigzag, spine-studded branches, spines in pairs, usually about 1 cm long.
Leaves: Alternate, bipinnately compound, barely exceeding 1 cm in length, pinnae in three to four pairs; leaflets linear, narrow, less than 3 mm long, 9 - 15 pairs per pinna.
Flowers: Yellow, borne in headlike clusters, less than 1 cm in diameter.
Fruit: A pointed, cylindric pod.
Distinguishing Marks: Very similar to the sweet acacia (*A. farnesiana*) pictured in Photo #72, but distinguished from it by having shorter leaves with leaflets less than 3 mm in length; distinguished from twisted acacia (*A. tortuosa*) pictured in Photo #74, by having smaller leaves and spines; distinguished from other *Acacia* by having zigzag branches.
Distribution: Pinelands, scrub, clearings in hammocks; locally common from about Lee County southward.

Small's Acacia

Acacia smallii Isely

Form: Deciduous shrub or small, broad-crowned tree to about 5 m in height, armed with pairs of very sharp spines.
Leaves: Alternate, bipinnately compound, pinnae in three to four pairs, overall leaf 3 - 5 cm long, 3 - 4 cm wide; leaflets linear, 4 - 5 mm long, commonly about 30 per pinna in 9 - 17 pairs.
Flowers: Golden-yellowish to orange, borne in ball-like heads, 8 - 10 mm in diameter, on stalks to about 1 cm in length.
Fruit: A linear pod, 3 - 10 cm long.
Distinguishing Marks: Similar in appearance to *A. farnesiana* pictured in Photo #72, but distinguished from it by having pinnae mostly in four pairs rather than having some with more than four pairs, by flower stalks generally being 1 cm or less in length, and by occurring in Florida only in the western panhandle.

Distribution: Sandy places near the edges of saltwater bays; found in Florida primarily in the extreme western panhandle near Pensacola but perhaps also in other places along the panhandle coast.

Twisted Acacia

Acacia tortuosa (L.) Willd.   **Photo #74**

Form: Shrub to small, spiny, wide-crowned tree with zigzag branches.
Leaves: Alternate but mostly clustered from spurs, bipinnately compound, less than 10 cm in overall length, pinnae in four to eight pairs, each pinna containing 15 - 20 pairs of leaflets; leaflets linear, narrow, 3 - 4 mm long.
Flowers: Borne in fragrant, globular, yellow heads, about 1 cm in diameter.
Fruit: A cylindric pod 8 - 10 cm long.
Distinguishing Marks: Distinguished from other *Acacia* with conspicuously zigzag branches by having longer spines and longer leaflets, from sweet acacia (*A. farnesiana*) by leaves mostly with more than ten rather than less than ten pinnae.
Distribution: Uncommon on shell mounds and along roadsides in southern Florida.

Mimosa or Silk Tree

Albizia julibrissin Durazz.   **Photo #75**

Form: Small, spreading, deciduous tree to about 15 m in height, with a short, grayish trunk that typically branches quite low to the ground.
Leaves: Alternate, bipinnately compound, overall leaf 10 - 35 cm long, to about 15 cm wide; pinnae numbering 6 to 25 and paired along the rachis; leaflets numerous, .5 - 1.5 cm long, 2 - 5 cm wide, notably asymmetric with central veins located along one edge of the leaflet rather than down the leaflet's center.
Flowers: Cottony, appearing in early summer with conspicuous clusters of numerous white and pink stamens.
Fruit: A flattened, yellowish green pod to about 15 cm long and 2 - 3 cm wide.
Distinguishing Marks: The pink and white flowers in early summer and the large, soft green, bipinnate leaves are distinctive in northern Florida.
Distribution: Planted as an ornamental in the northern half of the state and sometimes found escaped along roadsides and in disturbed sites.

Woman's Tongue or Lebbeck's Albizia

Albizia lebbeck (L.) Benth.   **Plate 37**

Form: Deciduous tree to about 12 m in height.
Leaves: Alternate to subopposite, bipinnately compound, overall leaf 15 - 40 cm long; pinnae in two to five pairs; leaflets 10 - 24 per pinna, oblong to elliptic, 2 - 4 cm long, often asymmetrical on either side of the midvein.

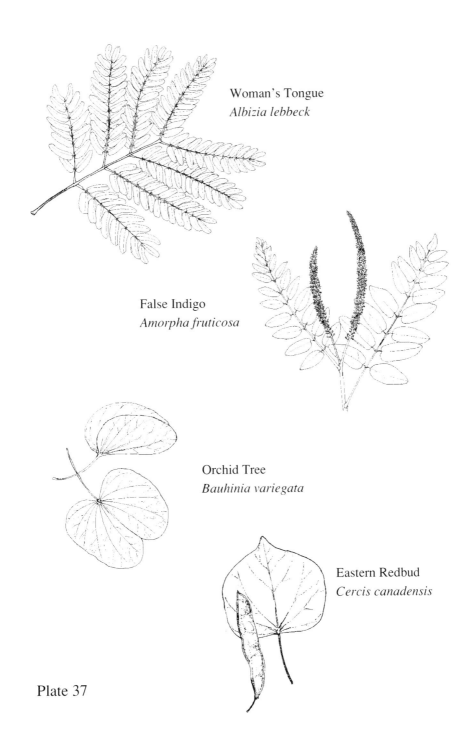

Woman's Tongue
Albizia lebbeck

False Indigo
Amorpha fruticosa

Orchid Tree
Bauhinia variegata

Eastern Redbud
Cercis canadensis

Plate 37

Flowers: Cream colored to light yellow, borne in loosely globose heads, 5 - 6 cm in diameter.

Fruit: A flat, thin, papery pod containing a single row of conspicuous seeds, each pod to about 20 cm long and tapering at each end.

Distinguishing Marks: Distinguished from silk tree (*A. julibrissin*) by being confined to southern rather than northern Florida, and by leaves and leaflets being generally longer and larger than the former species.

Distribution: Disturbed sites, yards, and escaped into hammocks from about central Florida southward and throughout the Keys.

False Indigo or Bastard Indigo

Amorpha fruticosa L.   **Plate 37**

Form: Typically a bushy deciduous shrub to about 4 m in height, sometimes treelike.

Leaves: Alternate, odd-pinnately compound, 1 - 3 dm long; leaflets numbering 9 - 35 per leaf, elliptic, 1 - 5 cm long, .5 - 3 cm wide, more or less glandular-punctate, often densely pubescent.

Flowers: Borne in dense, elongated racemes, with conspicuous golden anthers set against deep blue or purple petals.

Distinguishing Marks: The showy, purple and yellow flowers which appear in spring and early summer are distinctive.

Distribution: Wet woods, banks of river and streams, floodplain woods; throughout northern Florida, southward to about Lake Okeechobee and north Palm Beach County.

Orchid Tree

Bauhinia variegata L.   **Photo #76; Plate 37**

Form: Small, exotic, nearly evergreen ornamental tree to about 7 m in height.

Leaves: Alternate, simple, entire, two-ranked, palmately veined, 5 - 10 cm long, apices rounded and deeply notched, bases cordate.

Flowers: Orchidlike, fragrant, showy, with purplish petals, one petal usually displaying a darker purple streak, 7.5 - 10 cm wide.

Fruit: A flat pod 13 - 23 cm long and up to about 2 cm wide, less than 2 mm thick.

Distinguishing Marks: Not likely to be confused with any other Florida tree except *B. purpurea,* a close and extremely similar relative.

Distribution: Both of these species are cultivated in parks, along streets and roadsides, and in yards and are escaped from cultivation in some areas; from about Lee and Brevard counties southward.

Eastern Redbud

Cercis canadensis L.   **Photo #77; Plate 37**

Form: Small, attractive deciduous tree to about 8 m in height, with a short, grayish trunk.

Leaves: Alternate, simple, two-ranked, entire, typically heart shaped in overall form with cordate bases, 7.5 - 12.5 cm long.

Flowers: Appearing (often in great profusion) in spring before leaf growth, borne in clusters of four to eight separate flowers, dark magenta to purplish in color.

Fruit: A flattened pod, 6 - 10 cm long and shaped somewhat like the blade of a dinner knife.

Distinguishing Marks: The arresting flowers and heart-shaped leaves help in identifying this plant.

Distribution: Rich woods, roadsides, and yards from the central panhandle southward down the western peninsula to about Citrus County.

Royal Poinciana or Flamboyant Tree

Delonix regia (Bojer ex Hook.) Raf.

Form: Attractive deciduous tree to about 15 m in height with smooth to slightly furrowed brownish bark with many dots, and a broad, spreading crown.

Leaves: Alternate, bipinnately compound, overall leaf 20 - 50 cm long; pinnae numbering to 20 pairs per leaf, each pinna with numerous opposite, small, elliptic leaflets averaging about 1 cm in length.

Flowers: Ornate, showy, and conspicuous with bright red, frilly petals, appearing in profusion from May to July, making this one of south Florida's most attractive trees.

Fruit: A long, hard, blackish to dark brown pod 35 - 50 cm long, 4 - 6 cm wide, and nearly 1 cm thick.

Distinguishing Marks: Distinguished from other trees with bipinnate leaves by large leaves, characteristic flowers, and the giant pods, the latter of which remain on the tree nearly year-round.

Distribution: An exotic ornamental seen in yards, disturbed sites, and along streets from about Lee County (where found only sparingly) southward.

Coral Bean, Cardinal Spear, Cherokee Bean

Erythrina herbacea L.   **Plate 38**

Form: Deciduous shrub or small tree to about 5 m in height.

Leaves: Alternate, compound, trifoliolate, overall leaf 15 - 20 cm long, to about 6 cm wide; leaflets shaped like arrowheads or spearheads in overall outline, widest near the bases and tapering to pointed apices, each leaflet 2.5 - 8 cm long, dull green in color.

Flowers: Bright red, long, and tubular, 4 - 6.5 cm long, borne in showy, vertical racemes, appearing in late spring and summer.

Fruit: Pod narrow, 5 - 10 cm long, pinched in between the obvious seed pouches, splitting to expose hard, red seeds.

Distinguishing Marks: Distinguished from all other Florida trees by its uniquely shaped trifoliolate leaf.

Distribution: Nearly throughout the state but probably reaching tree stature only in southern Florida.

Water-Locust

Gleditsia aquatica Marsh.   **Plate 38**

Form: Deciduous tree to about 25 m in height, characterized by having large, branched thorns that are 7 - 15 cm long and borne along the trunk and branches.
Leaves: Alternate, pinnate to bipinnate, 15 - 20 cm long; pinnae on bipinnate leaves in four to seven pairs, each with 7 to 15 pairs of lanceolate leaflets.
Fruit: A short, thin, flattened, elliptic pod, 2 - 5 cm long, 2 - 3.5 cm wide.
Distinguishing Marks: Very similar in appearance to the honey-locust (*G. triacanthos*), distinguished from it by the much shorter fruit pod and by the lower surfaces of leaves being mainly glabrous or with only a few scattered hairs.
Distribution: Floodplains, river swamps, and low hammocks; throughout northern Florida, south to about Sarasota County.

Honey-Locust

Gleditsia triacanthos L.

Form: Deciduous tree to about 45 m in height, characterized by having large, branched thorns up to 40 cm long and borne along the trunk and branches.
Leaves: Alternate, pinnate to bipinnate, compound, 15 - 20 cm long, pinnae on bipinnate leaves in four to seven pairs, each with 7 to 15 pairs of lanceolate leaflets.
Fruit: A long, flattened, conspicuous pod, 15 - 45 cm long.
Distinguishing Marks: Very similar in appearance to the water-locust (*G. aquatica*) pictured on p. 215, distinguished from it by having much longer fruit pods, by being found in a generally drier habitat, and by the axes of the leaves, the stalks of leaflets, and the midveins on the lower surfaces of leaflets being conspicuously pubescent when seen with magnification.
Distribution: Upland, well-drained woods; sparsely distributed in the western panhandle, eastward to about Taylor and Jefferson counties.

Lead Tree or Jumbie Bean

Leucaena leucocephala (Lam.) de Wit   **Plate 38**

Form: Shrub or small, spineless tree to about 10 m in height.
Leaves: Alternate, bipinnately compound, overall leaf 10 - 30 cm long; pinnae in four to eight pairs, each with 10 - 20 pairs of opposite, oblong leaflets, 8 - 14 mm long.
Flowers: Borne in yellowish white to whitish globose heads to about 2 cm in diameter.
Fruit: A flat, reddish brown to brown pod, 8 - 15 cm long, 2 - 4 cm wide, often borne in dense, hanging clusters.
Distinguishing Marks: The whitish flowering heads and flattened pod set this species apart from most other south Florida trees.
Distribution: Exotic species established in hammocks and waste places of the coastal strand; Hillsborough County southward and throughout the Keys.

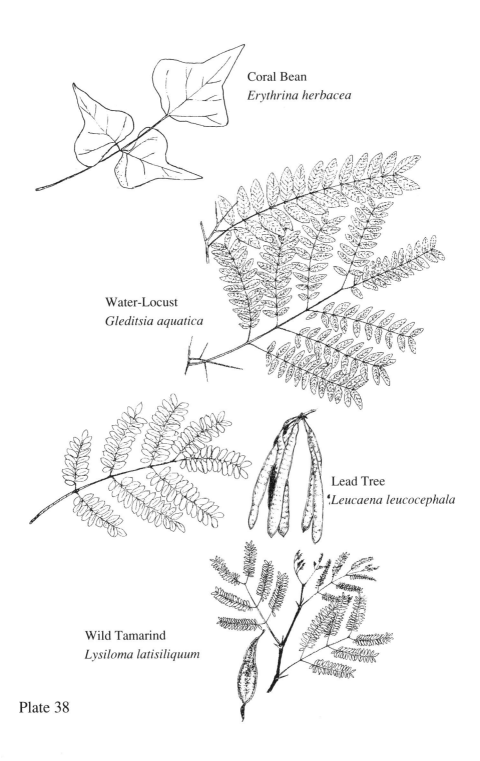

Coral Bean
Erythrina herbacea

Water-Locust
Gleditsia aquatica

Lead Tree
Leucaena leucocephala

Wild Tamarind
Lysiloma latisiliquum

Plate 38

215

Wild Tamarind or Bahama Lysiloma

Lysiloma latisiliquum (L.) Benth.   **Plate 38**

Form: Small to medium-sized deciduous tree (but considered large in comparison to other trees in the Keys), to about 10 m or even 20 m in height, with light grey or whitish bark.
Leaves: Alternate, bipinnately compound, overall leaf 10 - 18 cm long; pinnae numbering two to four pairs, each pinna with 8 - 15 pairs of leaflets; leaflets elliptic to oblong, 8 - 15 mm long, 3 - 5 mm wide, nearly symmetric.
Flowers: Small, borne in globular, greenish white heads, 1.5 - 2 cm in diameter, borne from the leaf axils in fascicles of one to three flowering heads.
Fruit: A flat pod, 6 - 10 cm long, 2 - 4 cm wide, usually remaining on the tree throughout the year.
Distinguishing Marks: Most easily recognized by its unarmed, zigzag branches, whitish bark, and distinctive pod.
Distribution: Disturbed sites, hammocks, pine–palmetto woodlands; native to the West Indies, Bahamas, southernmost Florida, and the Keys.

Jamaica Dogwood, Fishfuddle Tree, Florida Fish Poison Tree

Piscidia piscipula (L.) Sarg.   **Plate 39**

Form: Small, tardily deciduous tree to about 15 m in height with twisted branches and thin, gray bark.
Leaves: Alternate, odd-pinnately compound, 10 - 23 cm long; leaflets numbering 5 - 11 per leaf, oval, grayish green, 4 - 10 cm long, margins wavy and revolute (sometimes strongly revolute), veins obvious.
Flowers: White, lavender, or pink, 1.6 - 2 cm long, borne on long stalks in elongated clusters.
Fruit: A light brown pod, 7.5 - 10 cm long, 2.5 - 3.7 cm wide, with four papery wings.
Distinguishing Marks: Most easily distinguished in its south Florida locale by its fruit in conjunction with its compound leaves.
Distribution: Common in coastal areas but also occasionally found in hammocks; Hillsborough County southward, most abundant along Biscayne Bay and in the Keys.

Blackbead or Ram's Horn

Pithecellobium guadalupense (Pers.) Champ.   **Photo #78; Plate 39**

Form: Commonly a small, wide-spreading, rarely spiny evergreen shrub, reaching the stature of a small tree to about 6 m in height where it invades the hammocks.
Leaves: Alternate, bipinnately compound; pinnae numbering two, each with only two leaflets; leaflets obovate, oval to elliptic, commonly 2.5 - 5 cm long, 1.2 - 4 cm wide, apices often notched.
Flowers: Borne in whitish yellow heads, 1.5 - 2.5 cm in diameter, on stalks 2 - 3.5 cm long, appearing from February throughout the spring.
Fruit: A narrow, flattened, curving pod, 5 - 20 cm long, 7 - 10 mm wide.

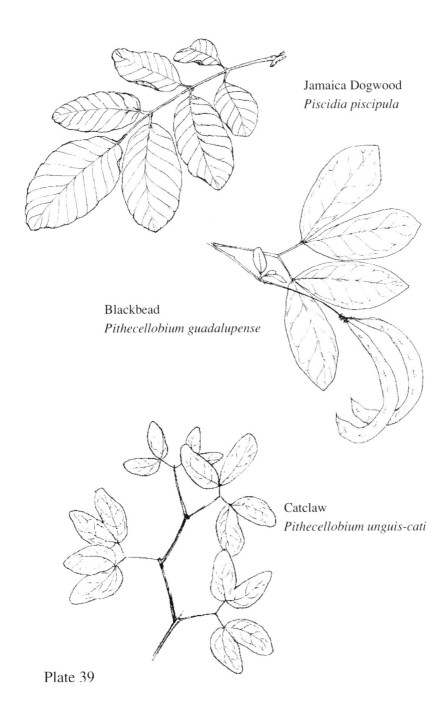

Jamaica Dogwood
Piscidia piscipula

Blackbead
Pithecellobium guadalupense

Catclaw
Pithecellobium unguis-cati

Plate 39

Distinguishing Marks: Distinguished from the catclaw (*P. unguis-cati*) by having leaf stems shorter than the leaflet stems and by less commonly exhibiting spines at the leaf bases.

Distribution: Sandy soils adjacent to beaches and hammocks; Lee, Palm Beach, and Broward counties southward and throughout the Keys.

Catclaw or Catclaw Blackbead

Pithecellobium unguis-cati (L.) Benth.   **Plate 39**

Form: Spiny evergreen shrub or small, multitrunked tree to about 7 m in height; stems slightly zigzag, often containing sharp spines to about 5 mm long.

Leaves: Alternate, bipinnately compound, overall leaf 2.5 - 8 cm long; pinnae numbering two, each with only two leaflets; leaflets bright green, obovate to elliptic, 1.5 - 6 cm long, 1 - 3.5 cm wide.

Flowers: Borne in whitish to yellow-green heads, 1 - 2 cm in diameter, borne from the leaf axils on stalks 1.5 - 2.5 cm long.

Fruit: An oblong, reddish, curving pod, 5 - 15 cm long.

Distinguishing Marks: Distinguished from *P. guadalupense* by having generally smaller leaves, by having leaf stems longer than the stems of the leaflets, and by more commonly having spiny branches and spines at the leaf bases.

Distribution: Shell mounds, roadsides, hammocks, sand ridges; from about Manatee County southward on the west coast, Dade County southward on the east coast, throughout the Keys.

Pongam

Pongamia pinnata (L.) Merrill   **Plate 40**

Form: Tardily deciduous tree to about 10 m in height with smooth, gray bark.

Leaves: Alternate, compound, odd-pinnate, overall leaf averaging about 10 cm long; leaflets ovate, numbering five to seven, brown to bright green when young, turning to lemon yellow with maturity.

Flowers: Fragrant, whitish, pinkish, or lavender, borne in clusters from the leaf axils.

Fruit: A flat, hanging, yellowish to brownish, one-seeded, semicircular pod, 3 - 4 cm long, about 2 cm wide.

Distinguishing Marks: Distinguished by flower and fruit, one of which can be found on the tree nearly year-round.

Distribution: Common street tree in the Miami area, also planted as an ornamental elsewhere in south Florida.

Black Locust

Robinia pseudoacacia L.   **Plate 40**

Form: Deciduous tree to about 25 m in height with a pair of spines at the leaf bases.

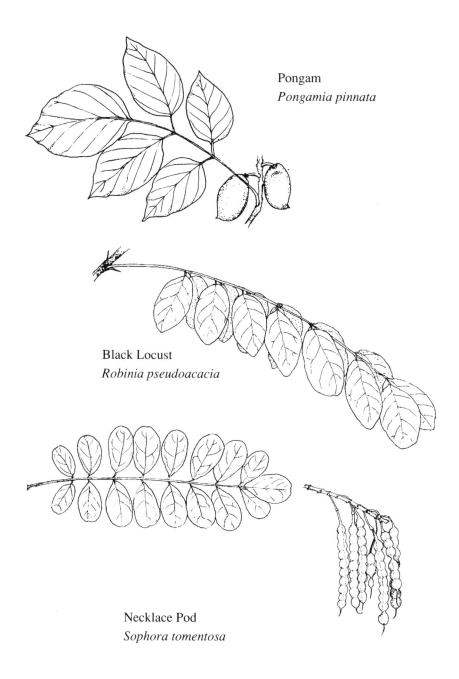

Pongam
Pongamia pinnata

Black Locust
Robinia pseudoacacia

Necklace Pod
Sophora tomentosa

Plate 40

Leaves: Alternate, odd-pinnately compound, 20 - 36 cm long; leaflets 7 to 19 in number, elliptic, 2 - 6 cm long, 1 - 2.5 cm wide, often drooping in the morning, more erect later in the day.

Flowers: Irregular, showy, creamy white with a yellow spot on the upper petal, borne from the leaf axils in drooping, fragrant racemes.

Fruit: A flattened pod, 5 - 10 cm long, about 1 cm wide.

Distribution: Disturbed sites, secondary woods, sometimes planted as an ornamental; native to the southern Appalachians and generally restricted in Florida to the vicinity of Leon, Gadsden, and Madison counties but also reported from Marion County.

Necklace Pod

Sophora tomentosa L.   **Plate 40**

Form: Commonly a thicket-forming shrub but sometimes reaching the stature of a small tree to about 6 m in height.

Leaves: Alternate, odd-pinnate, overall leaf to about 30 cm long; leaflets irregularly opposite, 11 to 21 in number, thick, bright green, obovate to elliptic, 2 - 5 cm long.

Flowers: Yellow, irregularly shaped, borne in long, racemose, terminal spikes, 10 - 33 cm long.

Fruit: A pod, 5 to 20 cm long, 5 - 10 mm in diameter, conspicuously pinched in between the seed cavities.

Distinguishing Marks: Similar to the Mexican alvaradoa (*Alvaradoa amorphoides*) but distinguished from it mainly by occurring only on the edges of hammocks and by having yellow flowers.

Distribution: Scrub and hammock margins of the coastal strand of southern Florida, more common in the Keys.

Tamarind

Tamarindus indica L.   **Plate 41**

Form: Tree to about 20 m in height with a massive, blackish trunk to about 1.5 m in diameter.

Leaves: Alternate, compound, even-pinnate, 6 - 12 cm long, borne on zigzag branchlets; leaflets elliptic, 10 - 20 mm long, borne in 10 - 15 pairs per leaf.

Flowers: Pale yellow, about 2.5 cm wide, petals three in number and streaked with red to pinkish veins.

Fruit: A brown, fleshy, edible pod, 5 - 12 cm long, deeply pinched in between the few seed cavities.

Distinguishing Marks: The pinnate leaves on zigzag branches help distinguish this species from other south Florida trees.

Distribution: Widely cultivated along the coastal strand; Broward and Lee counties southward and throughout the Keys.

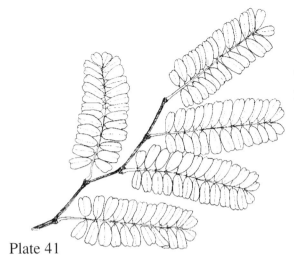

Tamarind
Tamarindus indica

Plate 41

Corkwood

Leitneria floridana Chapm.   **Photo #81**

Form: Single-stemmed deciduous shrub or small tree to about 8 m in height with a narrow, upright shape, few, if any, branches, and reddish brown bark; central stem with conspicuous, buff-colored spots of cork.

Leaves: Alternate, simple, elliptic, 5 - 20 cm long, 2 - 5 cm wide, upper surfaces of mature blades glabrous, lower softly pubescent.

Flowers: Tiny, borne from the central stem in cylindrical catkins to about 5 cm long.

Fruit: A smooth, brown, leathery, elliptic drupe, 1.5 - 2.5 cm long, flattened on one side, rounded on the other.

Distinguishing Marks: The upright, generally unbranched shape and corky bark are distinctive.

Distribution: Rare and scattered, known in Florida from only three general locations: in the vicinity of the tributaries, estuaries, and barrier islands of the lower Apalachicola River, in the St. Marks National Wildlife Refuge, and along the Waccasassa River in Levy County.

Crape Myrtle

Lagerstroemia indica L.   **Photo #79**

Form: Deciduous shrub or small tree to about 7 m in height with twisted branches and smooth, brownish orange bark that sometimes flakes off in large patches.

Leaves: Both opposite and alternate, simple, entire, predominately elliptic, 2 - 7 cm long, 1 - 4 cm wide.

Flowers: Inflorescence a large, showy panicle to 30 cm long and nearly as wide, individual

221

flowers white, pink, red, or purple; petals stalked, frilly, crinkled, generally numbering six per flower, each with a long, slender claw.

Fruit: A brown, woody, egg-shaped capsule that splits from the top.

Distinguishing Marks: The showy flowers that appear throughout the summer are distinctive.

Distribution: Widely planted throughout the state; naturalized in areas near dwellings or in fields.

MAGNOLIACEAE

Yellow Poplar or Tuliptree

Liriodendron tulipifera L.   **Plate 42**

Form: Large deciduous tree to about 50 m in height.

Leaves: Alternate, simple, 6 - 20 cm long, bases and apices truncate, the truncated tips often with a V-shaped notch, margins with four to six, normally pointed, lobes.

Flowers: Green with blotches of orange, tulip or bell shaped, appearing from late March through April.

Distinguishing Marks: Distinguished as Florida's only tree with squarish, truncated leaves.

Distribution: Bottomland woods, slopes, and bluffs; throughout northern Florida, southward to about Lake and Orange counties.

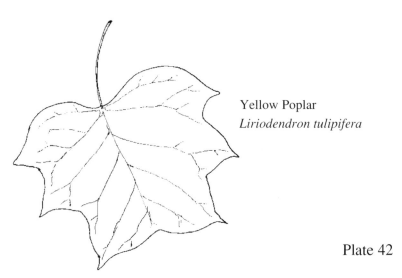

Yellow Poplar
Liriodendron tulipifera

Plate 42

Cucumber Tree

Magnolia acuminata (L.) L.

Form: Medium-sized deciduous tree to about 25 - 30 m in height.

Leaves: Alternate, simple, entire, oval, not stiff like the southern magnolia, large, 8 - 20+ cm long, 8 - 15 cm wide, tips pointed, bases rounded.

Flowers: Greenish yellow with petals usually not exceeding 7 - 8 cm in length, some much shorter.
Fruit: Fruiting bodies mostly 3 - 7 cm long, seeds red to reddish orange.
Distribution: Very rare; known as a shrub or small tree in Florida only from a few areas in Holmes and Walton counties.

Southern Magnolia or Bullbay

Magnolia grandiflora L.   **Photo #80**

Form: Medium-sized, attractive evergreen tree with beautiful smoothish bark, potentially to about 40 m in height but usually somewhat shorter.
Leaves: Alternate, simple, entire, stiff, elliptic to oval, generally 10 - 20 cm long (but sometimes longer), 6 - 10 cm wide, upper surfaces shiny, dark green, lower surfaces rust colored and covered with a dense mat of rusty brown, feltlike pubescence.
Flowers: Petals of flowers large, white to cream colored, very fragrant, entire flower 15 - 20 cm wide.
Fruit: Fruiting body conelike and bearing bright red berries.
Distinguishing Marks: The dark, shiny green, leathery leaves are unlike those of any other Florida tree.
Distribution: Upland forests, woodlands, coastal hammocks, bluffs; throughout northern Florida south to about Highlands and DeSoto counties along the western peninsula, Osceola and Brevard counties in the east.

Ashe Magnolia

Magnolia macrophylla Michx. subsp. *ashei* (Weatherby) Spongberg   **Photo #82**

Form: Deciduous shrub or small understory tree to about 6 m in height, recognized immediately by the huge leaves and flowers.
Leaves: Alternate, simple, entire, to about 60 cm long and 30 cm wide, green above, whitish beneath, bases eared or lobed.
Flowers: Huge, with purple suffused at the base of the petals, to 30 cm wide when fully opened.
Distinguishing Marks: Distinguished from all other Florida trees by huge leaves with eared, or cordate, bases.
Distribution: Rich hardwood forests of bluff and ravines; southern half of the panhandle, eastward to about Leon County; sometimes planted in north Florida as an ornamental.

Pyramid Magnolia

Magnolia pyramidata Bartr.   **Plate 43**

Form: Small to medium-sized, attractive deciduous tree with light gray bark, to about 20 m in height.

Leaves: Alternate, simple, entire, soft green in color, arising and spreading from the tips of the branches like a parasol, each leaf similar in shape to the Ashe magnolia, but much smaller, usually not exceeding 20 cm in length, tapering proximally then flaring into an eared or lobed base.
Flowers: White with narrow petals, fragrant, to 18 cm wide when completely opened.
Distinguishing Marks: Distinguished from Ashe magnolia (*Magnolia macrophylla* subsp. *ashei*) by smaller leaves with green rather than glaucous undersurfaces and petals without reddish purple bases.
Distribution: Slopes of bluffs and ravines of the panhandle, eastward to the Ochlockonee River.

Umbrella Magnolia

Magnolia tripetala L.

Form: Small deciduous tree usually not exceeding about 15 m in height in non-Florida locations.
Leaves: Alternate, simple, entire, elliptic, large, second in size only to the Ashe magnolia, to 45 cm long and 20 cm wide, tapering to a narrow base and lacking the eared or lobed base of the latter species.
Flowers: Large, petals white, each petal 8 - 12 cm long.
Distinguishing Marks: The huge, tapering leaves are distinctive.
Distribution: Very rare in Florida; restricted to one location in Okaloosa County if, indeed, it is still extant in the state.

Sweetbay Magnolia

Magnolia virginiana L.   **Photo #83; Plate 43**

Form: Medium-sized evergreen tree to about 30 m in height, with a straight trunk.
Leaves: Alternate, simple, entire, elliptic, 6 -15 cm long, 2 - 6 cm wide, green above, whitish beneath.
Flowers: Smaller than other magnolias but otherwise similar, petals white, 2.5 - 4.5 cm long, usually not exceeding 7 cm in width when fully open.
Fruit: A greenish, ovoid, knobby, conelike structure.
Distinguishing Marks: Distinguished from most other wetland species with long-elliptic leaves by having leaves with silvery-white undersurfaces that are quite obvious in a breeze.
Distribution: Swamps and wetlands; throughout Florida except the Keys; less common in Dade and Monroe counties.

MALPIGHIACEAE
Locust Berry or Key Byrsonima

Byrsonima lucida (Mill.) DC.   **Photo #84; Plate 44**

Form: Multitrunked evergreen shrub or small tree to about 6 m in height, with smooth, light brown bark, spreading branches, and jointed twigs.

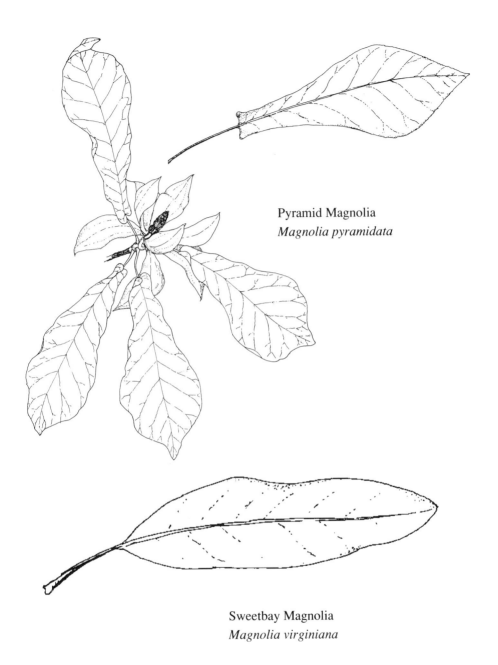

Pyramid Magnolia
Magnolia pyramidata

Sweetbay Magnolia
Magnolia virginiana

Plate 43

225

Leaves: Opposite, simple, entire, leathery, dark, shiny green above, dull yellow-green below, mostly oblanceolate to spatulate, 2 - 6 cm long, .5 - 2 cm wide, some leaves with acuminate apices, others rounded; base of petiole thickish and clasping the stem.

Flowers: White or pink but turning yellow or rose-red, borne in long, upright clusters of 5 - 12 individual flowers, each flower held on its own long stalk.

Fruit: Reddish brown, berrylike, round, 5 - 8 mm in diameter.

Distinguishing Marks: Most easily recognized by combination of jointed twigs (although sometimes obscurely so), opposite leaves, clasping petioles, and showy flowers.

Distribution: Primarily associated with the pinelands where it is normally a shrub, more often reaching tree stature in hammocks, particularly on the Keys; found only in southern Florida and the Keys.

Locust Berry
Byrsonima lucida

Plate 44

Upland Cotton or Wild Cotton

Gossypium hirsutum L. **Photo #85**

Form: Short, low-branched tree to about 4 m in height.
Leaves: Opposite, usually three- lobed, cordate at the base, 5 - 15 cm long, with long petioles.
Flowers: Showy, creamy white to pale yellow with a reddish spot at the base of each petal.
Fruit: A triangular capsule that exposes a cottony seed covering when opened.
Distinguishing Marks: Distinguished from both the portia tree (*Thespesia populnea*) and seaside hibiscus (*Hibiscus tiliaceus*) by having opposite rather than alternate leaves.
Distribution: Tropical thickets and disturbed sites along the extreme southwestern coast and the Keys; considered endangered in Florida.

Sea Hibiscus or Mahoe

Hibiscus tiliaceus L. **Photo #86; Plate 45**

Form: Evergreen shrub or small, spreading, sometimes crooked tree.
Leaves: Alternate, heart shaped, 10 - 30 cm long, apices pinching to a cuspidate point, margins entire to toothed.
Flowers: Large and showy, typical of hibiscus genus, yellow early in the day, turning red by evening.
Distinguishing Marks: Distinguished from the portia tree (*Thespesia populnea*) by leaves having mainly 9 to 11 veins rather than predominately 7 veins, by lower surfaces of leaves being copiously covered with whitish, stellate hairs, by leaves being generally more rounded, and by tips of leaves being cuspidate rather than tapering; from upland cotton (*Gossypium hirsutum*) by leaves borne alternate rather than opposite.
Distribution: Cultivated and reportedly naturalized in disturbed coastal sites of the southern peninsula and the Keys.

Seaside Mahoe or Portia Tree

Thespesia populnea (L.) Soland. ex Correa **Photo #87; Plate 45**

Form: Small, bushy evergreen tree to about 9 m in height.
Leaves: Alternate, simple, entire, heart shaped in overall form, 5 - 20 cm long, to about 12 cm wide, bases cordate.
Flowers: To about 8 cm in diameter, showy, characteristic of the hibiscus genus, yellow with a red center that turns darker near the end of the day.
Fruit: A leathery, nearly round capsule to about 4 cm in diameter, yellow at first but turning black at maturity and persisting on the tree as a dry husk.
Distinguishing Marks: Distinguished from sea hibiscus (*Hibiscus tiliaceus*) by leaves with usually 7 main veins rather than 9 to 11 as in the latter species, and by leaf blade lacking stellate hairs.

Distribution: Exotic species of coastal hammocks and beaches from about Lee County southward and throughout the Keys.

Tetrazygia or Florida Tetrazygia

Tetrazygia bicolor (Mill.) Cogn.   **Photo #89; Plate 45**

Form: Generally an evergreen shrub in the pinelands but reaching the size of a small tree to about 10 m in height inside hammocks.
Leaves: Opposite, lanceolate, curving, simple, 7.5 - 12 cm long, 2.5 - 4 cm wide, with three distinctive, lengthwise veins, upper surface conspicuously raised between depressed lateral veins, margins entire but rolled under.
Flowers: Inflorescence a showy, terminal cluster, flowers with five white petals encircling a mass of ten yellow stamens.
Fruit: Berrylike, black, rounded, 8 - 10 mm long.
Distinguishing Marks: This plant's distinctive leaf makes it unlikely to be confused with any other south Florida shrub or tree.
Distribution: Locally common and generally restricted to Everglades pinelands but also found in nearby hammocks.

Chinaberry or Pride of India

Melia azedarach L.   **Photo #88**

Form: Small to medium-sized, spreading, deciduous tree to about 15 m in height with smooth, purplish bark.
Leaves: Alternate, long-petioled, primarily bipinnately compound but sometimes tripinnately compound, overall leaf to about 50 cm long; leaflets dark green above, paler below, 2 - 7 cm long, 1 - 2 cm wide, pointed at the tip, margins sharply toothed, some leaflets with one or two deeply incised lobes at the base, some with stems 1 - 2 cm long, others sessile.
Flowers: With five narrow, purplish, slightly recurved petals, borne in conspicuous branched clusters.
Fruit: A rounded, fleshy, yellow or yellowish drupe, 1 - 1.5 cm in diameter.
Distinguishing Marks: The hanging fruit clusters persist throughout the winter and provide a distinctive means for separating this tree from other leafless trees.
Distribution: Fencerows, woodlands, disturbed places near dwellings; introduced and escaped throughout the state and reported sparingly from the Keys, more common in northern Florida and southward to the south-central peninsula.

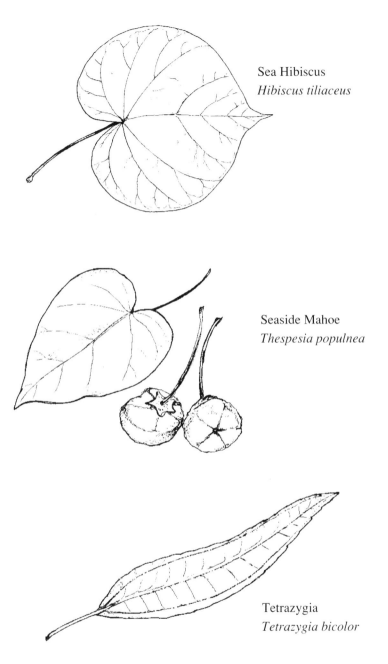

Sea Hibiscus
Hibiscus tiliaceus

Seaside Mahoe
Thespesia populnea

Tetrazygia
Tetrazygia bicolor

Plate 45

Mahogany

Swietenia mahagoni Jacq.   **Plate 46**

Form: Evergreen tree to about 15 m in height with rough, dark brown, coarsely fissured bark, a buttressed base, and large spreading branches.

Leaves: Alternate, attractive, pinnately compound, 10 - 19 cm long, with no terminal leaflet; leaflets typically in two to four pairs (sometimes more), ovate to lance shaped, 2 - 6 cm long, 1 - 2.5 cm wide, the blades of many leaflets curving backwards toward the base of the rachis.

Flowers: Small with tiny white or yellow petals, whole flower less than 7 mm wide.

Fruit: A large, woody, upright, egg-shaped capsule, 6 - 13 cm long, 3 - 7 cm wide, splitting into five parts from the base and releasing numerous winged seeds.

Distinguishing Marks: Unlikely to be confused with any other Florida tree.

Distribution: Occurs naturally in tropical hammocks of the southern tip of the state and the Keys but often planted as a handsome street tree throughout southern Florida.

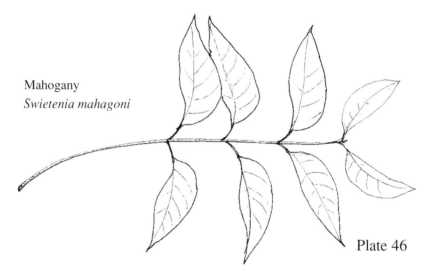

Mahogany
Swietenia mahagoni

Plate 46

MORACEAE

Paper Mulberry

Broussonetia papyrifera (L.) Vent.   **Plate 47**

Form: Small, thicket-forming, fast-growing deciduous tree with milky sap, to about 15 m in height.

Leaves: Alternate, opposite, or whorled on the same plant, simple, 6 - 20 cm long, 5 - 15 cm wide, margins toothed and sometimes lobed, upper surfaces of mature blades rough to the touch; petioles 4 - 15 cm long.

Flowers: Female flowers borne in round, hanging clusters; male flowers borne in drooping, elongated clusters.

Fruit: Orange to red and aggregated into globular clusters that are 2 - 3 cm in diameter.

Distinguishing Marks: Distinguished from other mulberries of genus *Morus* by leaf arrangement, from most other north Florida trees by leaf shape.

Distribution: Frequent in disturbed sites and near human habitations; northern half of the state south to the Tampa area.

Strangler Fig

Ficus aurea Nutt.   **Photo #92**

Form: Potentially large evergreen tree to about 20 m in height, often beginning life as an epiphyte on other trees and sending down long roots that frequently become latticelike on the trunk of its host, but eventually forming a single, twisted trunk that is actually a network of aerial roots.

Leaves: Alternate, simple, entire, thick, leathery, dark shiny green, 5 - 12 cm long, 3.5 - 7.5 cm wide.

Flowers: Small and inconspicuous at the leaf axils.

Fruit: Without stalks, globular, fleshy, 1.5 - 2 cm in diameter.

Distinguishing Marks: Distinguished from shortleaf fig (*F. citrifolia*) by stalkless fruits.

Distribution: Lower third of the state including the Keys from about DeSoto and Highland counties southward in the central peninsula and Brevard and Pinellas counties southward along the coasts.

Common Fig

Ficus carica L.   **Photo #90**

Form: Multitrunked deciduous shrub or tree to about 10 m in height.

Leaves: Alternate, large, broad, deeply incised into 3 - 5 lobes, each lobe with its own apparent central vein, upper surface rough to the touch due to the presence of stiff hairs.

Flowers: Produced in a receptacle near the ends of branches.

Fruit: Pear shaped, edible, tasty, recognized as those available at supermarkets and produce stands.

Distinguishing Marks: Most easily recognized by its deeply incised leaves.

Distribution: Planted for its fruit throughout the state, more common in the southern counties where it is sometimes seen in disturbed sites or along roadsides.

Shortleaf Fig or Wild Banyan Tree

Ficus citrifolia Mill.   **Photo #91; Plate 47**

Form: Evergreen tree; sometimes produces aerial roots from its branches.

Leaves: Similar to strangler fig (*F. aurea*), alternate, entire, leathery, smooth, dark green, 5 - 11 cm long and 3.5 - 9 cm wide.

Flowers: Small and inconspicuous.

Fruit: Rounded, to about 2.5 cm in diameter, yellow at first, dark red when ripe, borne on obvious stalks.

Distinguishing Marks: Differs from strangler fig by having fruits borne on elongated stalks rather than sessile.

Distribution: Dade, Collier, Broward, and Palm Beach counties southward and throughout the Keys.

Paper Mulberry
Broussonetia papyrifera

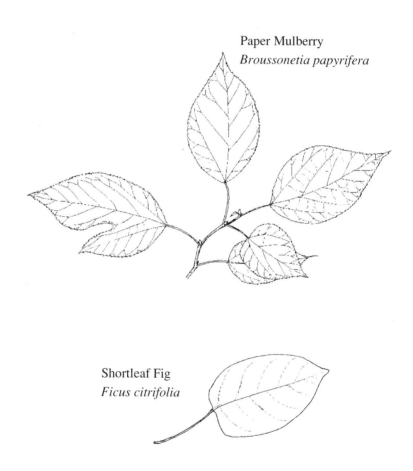

Shortleaf Fig
Ficus citrifolia

Plate 47

Osage-Orange

Maclura pomifera (Raf.) Schneid.

Photo #93

Form: Small to medium-sized deciduous tree to about 15 m in height; twigs often (but not always) having short, sharp spines.
Leaves: Alternate, simple, entire, ovate, 7 - 15 cm long, 5 - 8 cm wide, bases often rounded and appearing slightly heart shaped, surfaces dark green above, paler beneath, apices often tapering to a long point.
Flowers: Small, borne in rounded receptacles near the ends of branches.
Fruit: Distinctively collected into a large, compact conglomeration, 10 - 14 cm in diameter, superficially taking on the appearance of an orange, except green in color and somewhat more knobby.
Distinguishing Marks: The large, round, knobby fruit is an easy field mark in summer and early fall.
Distribution: Sporadic and uncommon across northern Florida and southward to about Marion County, probably most common in the central panhandle.

White Mulberry

Morus alba L.

Photo #95

Form: Small to medium-sized deciduous tree with glabrous, lustrous twigs, to about 25 m in height.
Leaves: Alternate, simple, very variable in size from about 6 to as much as 20 cm in length, some trees with most leaves tending toward once size or the other; margins toothed and variously lobed or unlobed, lobes more characteristic of small leaves and those leaves found on saplings rather than those on mature trees, lobes sometimes reaching nine in number but characteristically fewer; upper surfaces of leaves shiny green and smooth to the touch.
Flowers: Male flowers borne in elongated clusters; female flowers borne in rounded clusters.
Fruit: Usually white to pinkish but sometimes almost black, arising from the leaf axils, and held in globular clusters, 1 - 2 cm long.
Distinguishing Marks: Distinguished from red mulberry (*M. rubra*) by having smooth upper leaf surface.
Distribution: Native to Asia but widespread nearly throughout Florida except the southernmost counties, often in disturbed sites but also naturalized along streambanks and in bottomland woodlands.

Red Mulberry

Morus rubra L.

Photo #94

Form: Small deciduous tree to about 20 m in height.
Leaves: Alternate, simple, generally appearing large and heart shaped, 10 - 18 cm long, 6 - 13 cm wide, bases cordate, margins toothed and sometimes divided into lobes, similar in shape to leaves of the white mulberry (*M. alba*) but not shiny and usually not having more than three lobes per leaf.

Flowers: Greenish, borne in hanging clusters.

Fruit: Similar to white mulberry but more elongated, averaging more than 2 cm in length.

Distinguishing Marks: Distinguished from white mulberry by leaves with upper surfaces being dull green and scabrid, from most other trees with a similar leaf shape by broken leaf stems exuding a milky sap (see also *Broussonetia papyrifera*).

Distribution: Hammocks, floodplain and bottomland woods, pinelands, uplands; native understory tree found throughout the state except for the two southernmost counties and the Keys.

MYRICACEAE

Wax Myrtle or Southern Bayberry

Myrica cerifera L. **Photo #96**

Form: Evergreen shrub or small tree to 12 m in height, often with several trunks and dense foliage.

Leaves: Alternate, simple, narrowly oblanceolate, 3 - 15 cm long, 1 - 2 cm wide, typically toothed toward the apex, aromatic when crushed, upper and lower surfaces covered with amber-colored dots that often require a hand lens to see clearly.

Flowers: Borne in catkins at the leaf axils, catkins to about 2 cm long and often appearing in great profusion.

Fruit: A small but conspicuous, rounded, waxy, bluish drupe, 2 - 4 mm in diameter.

Distinguishing Marks: Likely to be confused in north Florida only with the swamp candleberry (*M. heterophylla*), but distinguished from it by the latter having larger leaves with amber dots only on the lower surface; leaves superficially similar to the crabwood (*Ateramnus lucidus*) of southern Florida but distinguished from it by the latter's distinctive, shouldered leaf base.

Distribution: Found in a wide variety of habitats throughout Florida including the Keys.

Swamp Candleberry or Evergreen Bayberry

Myrica heterophylla Raf. **Photo #97; Plate 48**

Form: Evergreen shrub or small tree to about 3 m in height.

Leaves: Alternate, simple, oblanceolate, 6 - 12 cm long, to about 5 cm wide, upper surface glabrous, lower dotted with amber-colored scales, margins often toothed toward the apex, aromatic when crushed.

Fruit: A rounded, knobby drupe, 2 - 4.5 mm in diameter.

Distinguishing Marks: Distinguished from the southern wax myrtle (*M. cerifera*) by generally larger, thicker leaves with only the lower surfaces of leaves being covered with amber-colored dots.

Distribution: Bogs, swamps, flatwoods depressions, and similar wet areas; throughout the panhandle and northern Florida.

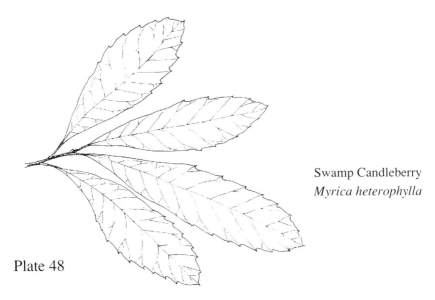

Swamp Candleberry
Myrica heterophylla

Plate 48

Odorless Bayberry

Myrica inodora Bartr.   **Photo #98**

Form: Evergreen shrub or small tree with smooth, glabrous twigs, to about 7 m in height.
Leaves: Alternate, simple, entire, slightly revolute, elliptic, leathery or somewhat rubbery to the touch, dark green above, 4 - 8 cm long, 2 - 3 cm wide, upper and lower surfaces copiously punctate, apices narrowed to a blunt point, bases tapered and appearing to extend a little ways down the petioles.
Fruit: A black, rounded drupe with a conspicuously roughened surface, 6 - 7 mm in diameter.
Distinguishing Marks: Most easily recognized in its habitat by roughened fruit typical of *Myrica* species in conjunction with entire, nonaromatic leaves.
Distribution: Bogs, swamps, flatwoods, and similar places; restricted in Florida to the panhandle from about Leon and Wakulla counties westward.

MYRSINACEAE

Marlberry

Ardisia escallonioides Schlecht. & Cham.   **Photo #99**

Form: Evergreen shrub or small tree to about 7 m in height.
Leaves: Alternate, simple, lanceolate, leathery, entire, often reflexed upward from the central axis, 10 - 15 cm long, 3 - 5 cm wide, arranged spirally along the branch, each blade often curving downward lengthwise, upper surfaces shiny green.
Flowers: White, arising in dense clusters and very conspicuous, appearing almost any time of year.
Fruit: A shiny, black drupe, 7 - 9 mm in diameter.

Distinguishing Marks: Potentially confused with myrsine (*Myrsine floridana*) but distinguished from it by young stem tips being brown rather than green.

Distribution: Hammocks and pinelands; from about Volusia and Hillsborough counties southward along the coast; from about Highlands and Okeechobee counties southward inland; throughout the Keys.

Myrsine or Rapanea

Myrsine floridana A. DC.   **Plate 49**

Form: Evergreen shrub or small tree with light gray bark, to about 6 m in height.

Leaves: Alternate but close together, simple, leathery, entire but margins often rolled under, crowded near the ends of the branches, 6 - 10 cm long, 1 - 4 cm wide, upper surfaces shiny green, apices often notched; flowering and fruiting generally along leafless portions of the branches.

Flowers: Small, white, appearing mainly in the winter.

Fruit: Rounded, dark blue to black at maturity, green when young, 4 - 7 mm in diameter, evident at almost any time of year.

Distinguishing Marks: Potentially confused with marlberry (*Ardisia escallonioides*) but distinguished from it by young stem tips being green rather than brown.

Distribution: Coastal hammocks and pinelands from about Manatee and Volusia counties southward; small populations also found in Levy and Citrus counties.

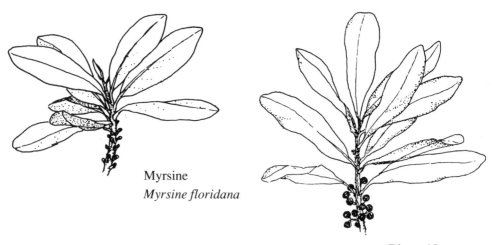

Myrsine
Myrsine floridana

Plate 49

Pale Lidflower

Calyptranthes pallens Griseb.

Form: Evergreen shrub or small tree to about 8 m in height with smooth gray to scaly bark and distinctive branching; branchlets produced in pairs at each leaf node, each branchlet then terminating at the next pair of leaves.

Leaves: Opposite, entire, aromatic, elliptic, 3 - 8 cm long, 1.2 - 2.2 cm wide, apices and bases tapering to long, blunt points.

Flowers: Small, greenish to white, borne in many-flowered clusters near the ends of twigs.

Fruit: A round, juicy berry, .5 - 1.2 cm in diameter, reddish at first, turning purplish black at maturity.

Distinguishing Marks: Very similar to myrtle-of-the-river (*C. zuzygium*), pictured on p. 239, distinguished from it by undersurfaces of leaves being finely hairy and by the central leaf vein not being ridged, from white stopper (*Eugenia axillaris*) by distinctive branching pattern of the branchlets.

Distribution: Coastal hammocks of Dade and Monroe counties including the Keys.

Myrtle-of-the-River

Calyptranthes zuzygium (L.) Sw.   **Plate 50**

Form: Evergreen shrub or small tree to about 12 m in height with smooth, light gray bark and distinctive branching; branchlets produced in pairs at each leaf node, each branchlet then terminating at the next pair of leaves.

Leaves: Opposite, simple, entire, elliptic to ovate with long, tapering apices, 3.5 - 6 cm long, 1.8 - 3.8 cm wide, central veins ridged and raised above the upper leaf surface.

Flowers: Borne in small clusters at the leaf axils with many stamens but no petals.

Fruit: A rounded berry, to about 1 cm in diameter.

Distinguishing Marks: Distinguished from pale lidflower (*C. pallens*) by having lower leaf surface glabrous rather than finely hairy at maturity and by the midvein being noticeably ridged and raised above the upper leaf surface, especially toward the base; from white stopper (*Eugenia axillaris*) by distinctive branching pattern of the branchlets.

Distribution: Hammocks of Dade and Monroe counties including the Keys.

White Stopper

Eugenia axillaris (Sw.) Willd.   **Plate 50**

Form: Evergreen shrub or small tree to about 8 m in height, with smooth, grayish white, scaly bark.

Leaves: Opposite, simple, leathery, entire, ovate, 3 - 7 cm long, 1.5 - 4 cm wide, upper surfaces dark green, lower surfaces paler with tiny black dots, petioles generally reddish in color, apices tapering to a blunt point.

Flowers: White, small, fragrant, borne in summer in axillary clusters.

Fruit: A juicy, reddish to black berry, 1 - 1.2 cm in diameter.

Distinguishing Marks: Similar to the rare spiceberry eugenia (*E. rhombea*) but distinguished from it by having flower stalks usually shorter than the flowers and by the bark of the trunk being whitish rather than brownish gray or clay colored.

Distribution: Common in coastal hammocks from the central peninsula southward and throughout the Keys.

Red-Berry Stopper

Eugenia confusa DC.   **Plate 50**

Form: Small evergreen tree to about 6 m in height with light gray, scaly bark and a straight trunk.

Leaves: Opposite, simple, entire, stiff, elliptic to ovate, 3 - 7 cm long, 2 - 4 cm wide, apices long tapered and curving downward, upper surfaces shiny, lower surfaces duller.

Flowers: White, small, approximately 6 mm wide.

Fruit: A bright red berry, 5 - 8 mm in diameter.

Distinguishing Marks: Most easily recognized by opposite, stiff, very shiny, long-pointed leaves with drooping apices.

Distribution: Hammocks of southernmost Florida and the Keys; not common.

Spanish Stopper or Box Leaf Eugenia

Eugenia foetida Pers.   **Plate 50**

Form: Small evergreen tree to about 6 m in height with smooth, gray, sometimes mottled, bark.

Leaves: Opposite, simple, entire, leathery, aromatic, elliptic to obovate, upper surfaces dark green, lower surfaces yellow-green and bearing tiny black dots, 2 - 6 cm long, 1.4 - 4 cm wide.

Flowers: White, small, borne in axillary racemes, mildly fragrant, with many white, threadlike stamens.

Fruit: A rounded berry, turning from reddish orange to black or brown at maturity, to about 8 mm in diameter.

Distinguishing Marks: Recognized as the state's only *Eugenia* with a rounded rather than tapered leaf apex; distinguished from long-stalked stopper (*Mosiera longipes*) by the latter having leaves mostly shorter than 2 cm.

Distribution: Hammocks of southern Florida, primarily from Collier and Palm Beach counties southward and throughout the Keys, but extending northward along the east coast at least to Brevard County; also found in pinelands of the Lower Keys.

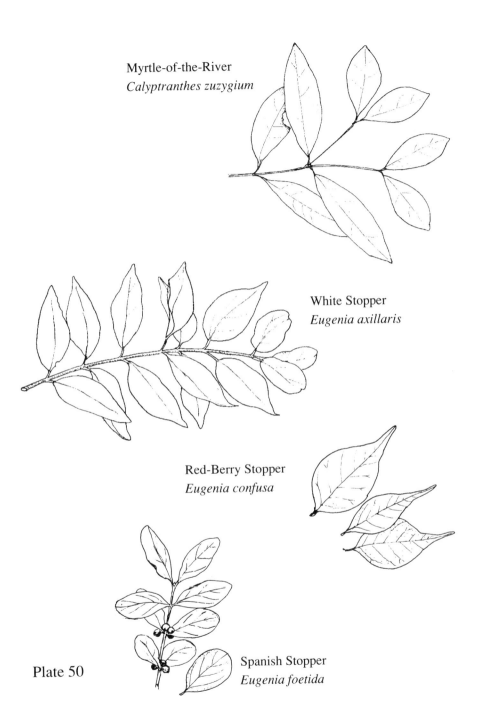

Myrtle-of-the-River
Calyptranthes zuzygium

White Stopper
Eugenia axillaris

Red-Berry Stopper
Eugenia confusa

Plate 50

Spanish Stopper
Eugenia foetida

239

Spiceberry Eugenia or Red Stopper
Eugenia rhombea (Berg) Krug & Urban

Form: Small, upright evergreen tree with smooth, brownish gray or clay-colored bark, to about 8 m in height in much of its range, to about 3 m in Florida.
Leaves: Opposite, simple, leathery, dark green above, yellow-green below, ovate, 3 - 6 cm long, 1.5 - 4 cm wide, apices tapering to a long, blunt point, margins entire and appearing to be outlined in yellow.
Flowers: Small, white, a little more than 1 cm wide, borne in few-flowered clusters.
Fruit: A rounded berry, orange-red at first but turning black at maturity, 7 - 9 mm in diameter.
Distinguishing Marks: Similar in appearance to the white stopper (*E. axillaris*), pictured on p. 239, distinguished from it by having flower stalks usually longer than the flowers, and brownish gray bark.
Distribution: Rare species found in its natural habitat only in one or two locations in the Florida Keys including a substantial and well-protected grove on North Key Largo; considered endangered in Florida.

Cajeput or Punk Tree
Melaleuca quinquenervia (Cav.) S.T. Blake   **Plate 51**

Form: Evergreen tree to about 15 m in height with characteristic thick, soft, white bark that sheds in thin layers, exposing a reddish inner bark.
Leaves: Alternate, simple, entire, lanceolate to narrowly elliptic, 4 - 12 cm long, 1.8 - 2.5 cm wide, with five to seven parallel veins running lengthwise along the blades.
Flowers: White, borne in clusters between groups of leaves and around the branchlets, giving the appearance of a bottle brush.
Fruit: A squarish capsule borne stalkless along the branchlets.
Distinguishing Marks: Most easily recognized by white, shedding bark in combination with narrow, linearly veined leaves.
Distribution: Exotic tree in Florida but found in many locations from about Pasco County southward where it has escaped from cultivation and become a troublesome weedy species; easily seen in disturbed wetlands along many of south Florida's roadways where its whitish trunk is unmistakable even at some distance.

Long-Stalked Stopper
Mosiera longipes (Berg) Small   **Photo #102**

Form: Typically an evergreen shrub in south Florida pinelands, sometimes forming a small tree to perhaps 4 m in height where it invades hammocks.
Leaves: Opposite, simple, entire, ovate to oval, usually less than 2 cm long, upper surfaces shiny green, lower surfaces paler, veins reddish.
Flowers: White to pink with four petals, to nearly 1.5 cm wide at maturity, produced singly on conspicuously long stalks.
Fruit: A round, black berry, 6 - 10 mm in diameter.

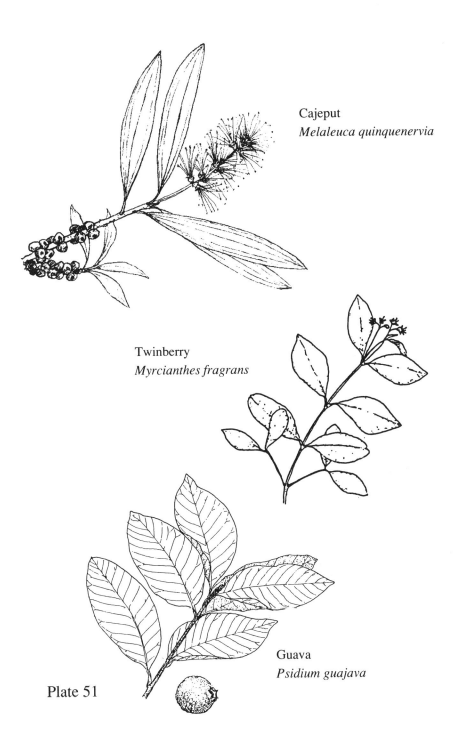

Cajeput
Melaleuca quinquenervia

Twinberry
Myrcianthes fragrans

Guava
Psidium guajava

Plate 51

241

Distinguishing Marks: The small, oval leaves and long-stalked fruit are diagnostic.
Distribution: Hammocks and pinelands; Dade and Monroe counties including the Keys.

Twinberry or Twinberry Stopper

Myrcianthes fragrans (Sw.) McVaugh   **Plate 51**

Form: Evergreen shrub or small tree to about 8 m in height with distinctive reddish, smooth, flaking bark similar to that of the guava.
Leaves: Opposite, simple, entire, aromatic, leathery, elliptic to ovate, 2 - 6 cm long, 1 - 4 cm wide, both surfaces covered with tiny, often blackish, dots.
Flowers: White, borne in long-stalked clusters, each flower with many spreading stamens.
Fruit: Rounded, 6 - 8 mm in diameter, red.
Distinguishing Marks: Most easily distinguished by reddish flaking bark in combination with opposite leaves.
Distribution: Hammocks from about Volusia County southward excluding the Keys.

Guava

Psidium guajava L.   **Plate 51**

Form: Evergreen shrub or low, spreading tree to about 10 m in height with angled twigs and scaly stems.
Leaves: Opposite, simple, coarse, entire, elliptic to oblong, dark green above, paler below, 4 - 15 cm long, with prominent, pinnately arranged veins.
Flowers: Fragrant, to about 4 cm wide at maturity, with white petals and a mass of white and yellow stamens, borne singly in the leaf axils.
Fruit: A large, yellow berry, 3 - 6 cm in diameter.
Distinguishing Marks: Easily distinguished by combination of coarse, opposite leaves with prominent venation, scaly bark, and angled twigs.
Distribution: Hammocks and disturbed sites where escaped from cultivation; from Brevard and Pinellas counties southward.

NYCTAGINACEAE
Blolly or Beefwood

Guapira discolor (K. Spreng.) Little   **Photo #100**

Form: Evergreen shrub or small, bushy tree to about 16 m in height, with smooth, gray bark.
Leaves: Opposite (sometimes subopposite to alternate), elliptic to obovate, light green in color, leathery, simple, 1 - 7 cm long, to about 2.5 cm wide, margins entire but thickened and often wavy, apices rounded, veins obscure except for the central vein which is yellowish green and translucent when held up to the light; petioles grooved.
Flowers: Tiny, greenish, tubular, borne in clusters, male and female flowers borne on separate trees and arising in spring and early summer.

Fruit: Bright red, juicy, berrylike, oval, to about 1.3 cm in diameter, usually appearing in summer and fall.

Distinguishing Marks: Most easily recognized by opposite leaves with yellowish green, translucent midveins, grooved petioles, and bright red, juicy berries.

Distribution: Hammocks and coastal scrub; Atlantic coast from about Cape Canaveral southward including the Keys.

Cockspur or Pisonia

Pisonia rotundata Griseb.   **Plate 52**

Form: Deciduous shrub or small, spreading tree with gray bark, to about 4 m in height.

Leaves: Opposite, simple, stiff, elliptic to obovate, 2.5 - 10 cm long, margins entire but somewhat revolute, dull green above with conspicuously depressed and light-colored veins.

Flowers: Tiny, green and white, without petals, borne in compact clusters.

Fruit: Rounded, 5 - 6 mm in diameter, quite sticky.

Distinguishing Marks: Most easily recognized by its opposite, elliptical leaves and conspicuously depressed veins.

Distribution: Native to hammocks and scrub of the lower Keys.

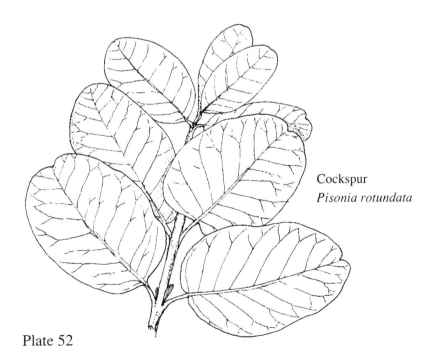

Cockspur
Pisonia rotundata

Plate 52

NYSSACEAE

Water Tupelo

Nyssa aquatica L.   **Plate 53**

Form: Medium-sized to large deciduous tree to about 35 m in height.
Leaves: Alternate, simple, entire, or with a few marginal teeth, ovate, 6 - 30 cm long (usually over 15 cm); petioles 3 - 6 cm long.
Flowers: Male flowers borne in rounded, compact clusters, 1 - 1.5 cm in diameter.
Fruit: A dark blue to purple drupe, 1.5 - 4 cm long, borne singly on a relatively long stalk.
Distinguishing Marks: Distinguished from other wetland tupelos by longer leaf stems, also from ogeechee tupelo (*N. ogeche*) by the length of the fruit stalk being generally longer than the length of the fruit.
Distribution: Floodplains, river swamps, and lake margins; chiefly from about Leon and Wakulla counties westward except for outlying communities in Duval County and along the lower Suwannee River.

Blackgum

Nyssa biflora Walt.   **Photo #101**

Form: Medium-sized to large deciduous tree to about 35 m in height; trunks with buttressed, swollen bases.
Leaves: Alternate, simple, entire, narrowly elliptic, 3 - 10 cm long, young leaves pale green, older leaves often darkly spotted, some leaves reddish to purplish in color, in general the leaves quite variable in coloration and tone from individual to individual.
Flowers: Male flowers small, borne in small clusters at the leaf axils.
Fruit: Green at first, turning dark blue, 8 - 13 mm long, typically borne in pairs on the fruit stalk.
Distinguishing Marks: Distinguished from other wetland tupelos by having shorter leaves and by fruit borne two to the stalk.
Distribution: Swamps, pond margins, bottomlands, bay heads; northern two-thirds of the state.

Ogeechee Tupelo or Ogeechee-Lime

Nyssa ogeche Bartr. ex Marsh.   **Plate 53**

Form: Typically a small deciduous tree with several leaning trunks, potentially medium-sized to about 20 m in height, often forming very dense stands.
Leaves: Alternate, simple, entire, elliptic, 8 - 15 cm long, 5 - 8 cm wide.
Flowers: Male flowers borne in rounded, compact clusters.
Fruit: A reddish, fleshy drupe, 2 - 4 cm long.
Distinguishing Marks: Distinguished from water tupelo (*N. aquatica*), with which it is most nearly similar, by having petioles less than 3 cm long and by the length of the fruit stalk being shorter than the length of the fruit.
Distribution: River swamps, bay heads, bottomland woods; from Walton to Hamilton counties.

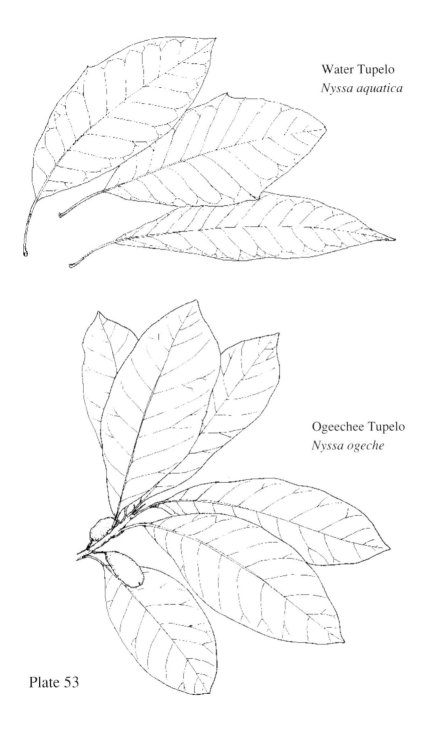

Water Tupelo
Nyssa aquatica

Ogeechee Tupelo
Nyssa ogeche

Plate 53

Sour Gum

Nyssa sylvatica Marsh.   **Photo #103**

Form: Medium-sized to large deciduous tree to about 42 m in height; branching low and at 90-degree angles from the trunk when provided adequate space for development; twigs and branchlets very tough and difficult to break.
Leaves: Alternate, simple, obovate, extremely variable in size and shape, often clustered near the ends of branches, 3 - 15 cm long, 2.5 - 10 cm wide, lustrous green when young, turning darker with purplish spots as the summer progresses, apices acuminate, margins of many leaves entire, margins of some leaves irregularly dentate with few to several teeth.
Flowers: Small, borne in small clusters at the leaf axils.
Fruit: A blue-black drupe, about 1 cm long and arising in clusters of two to five at the end of a longish stalk.
Distinguishing Marks: Some specimens potentially confused with the common persimmon (*Diospyros virginiana*) but distinguished from it by lacking the latter's whitish leaf undersurface, other specimens similar to the bigleaf snowbell (*Styrax grandifolia*) but distinguished from it by the latter having marginal teeth generally only above the middle of the leaf and by having lower leaf surface copiously and consistently covered with a soft, pale gray pubescence.
Distribution: Found in a variety of upland woodlands; throughout the panhandle and northern Florida, southward to the central peninsula.

OLACACEAE

Gulf Graytwig or Whitewood

Schoepfia chrysophylloides (A. Rich.) Planch.   **Photo #104**

Form: Evergreen shrub or small, erect tree to about 10 m in height, with crooked branches, zigzag branchlets, and whitish twigs.
Leaves: Alternate, simple, ovate to elliptic, entire, 3 - 7.5 cm long, 2 - 5 cm wide, with wavy edges, exhibiting a strong odor when crushed.
Flowers: Red to orange tinted, small, and sweet scented, appearing throughout the winter from about October to March.
Fruit: A red, ovoid drupe, 10 - 12 mm long.
Distinguishing Marks: Most easily recognized by the smooth, almost white, zigzag branchlets; the shape of some leaves are similar to those of the white stopper (*Eugenia axillaris*) but are alternate rather than opposite.
Distribution: Uncommon in hammocks of southern Florida, mainly on the Keys.

Hog Plum or Tallowwood

Ximenia americana L.   **Photo #105**

Form: Evergreen shrub or small tree to about 9 m in height with irregular, sometimes sprawling branches, and sharp spines in the leaf axils.

Leaves: Alternate, simple, entire, elliptic to ovate, 2.5 - 7 cm long, 1.2 - 2.5 cm wide, upper surfaces shiny green, lower surfaces paler.

Flowers: Yellowish white, fragrant, with four hairy petals, to about 12 mm wide.

Fruit: A rounded drupe, 2 - 3 cm long, at first green, then bright yellow at maturity, candylike to the taste and very palatable.

Distinguishing Marks: Distinguished from *Bumelia* by each leaf having a tiny tooth at its apex and a grooved petiole, both of which require magnification to see clearly.

Distribution: Hammocks and scrub from central Florida southward and throughout the Keys; also known from swamps in Fakahatchee Strand State Preserve.

Fringe Tree, Grandsie-Gray-Beard, Old Man's Beard

Chionanthus virginicus L.   **Photo #107; Plate 54**

Form: Deciduous shrub or small tree to about 10 m in height.

Leaves: Opposite, simple, entire, lanceolate to oval, variable in size, 10 - 20 cm long, 1.8 - 10 cm wide, upper surfaces dark green and glabrous, lower surfaces paler; petioles narrowly winged and often suffused with purplish red coloration.

Flowers: Unique, appearing in March, borne in showy pendent clusters, each with four conspicuous, linear, creamy white petals.

Fruit: An egg-shaped drupe, 1 - 2.5 cm long, dark blue to nearly black, fruiting clusters subtended by up to several pairs of leaflike bracts.

Distinguishing Marks: No other Florida tree has flowers that resemble this species.

Distribution: Found in a wide variety of habitats and often planted as an ornamental across the panhandle and northern Florida, southward to about Sarasota County.

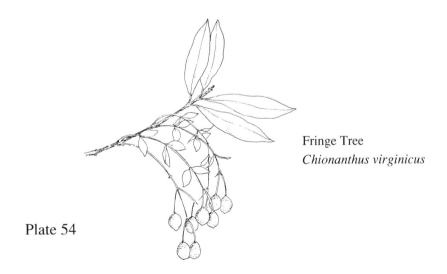

Fringe Tree
Chionanthus virginicus

Plate 54

Swamp Privet

Forestiera acuminata (Michx.) Poir. in Lam.   **Plate 55**

Form: Deciduous shrub or small tree to 13 m in height.
Leaves: Opposite, simple, lanceolate, 4 - 12 cm long, 2 - 3.5 cm wide, many leaves tapering to long-pointed apices and bases, margins serrate; petioles 5 - 20 mm long.
Flowers: Yellow, appearing in early spring, borne in small, axillary clusters.
Fruit: An ovoid to ellipsoid drupe, 10 - 15 mm long, 7 - 10 mm wide.
Distinguishing Marks: Distinguished from other opposite-leaved trees by long-tapering and distinctly sharply pointed leaf tip in conjunction with serrated leaf margins.
Distribution: Primarily found in river swamps and floodplains across the panhandle, eastward to the Suwannee River.

Godfrey's Privet

Forestiera godfreyi L. C. Anderson

Form: Deciduous shrub or small tree to about 5 m in height with rigid branches and a leaning trunk.
Leaves: Opposite, simple, ovate to elliptic, 5 - 8 cm long, 2.3 - 4 cm wide, margins finely serrate from about their middles to their apices; petioles 2 - 10 mm long and at least moderately pubescent.
Flowers: Yellowish green and tiny, borne in tight clusters in the leaf axils.
Fruit: A dark blue drupe, 10 - 12 mm long, 8 - 9 mm wide.
Distinguishing Marks: Leaves similar in appearance to *F. ligustrina*, pictured on p. 249, distinguished by being larger and by having uniform pubescence throughout their lower surfaces, from the leaves of Florida privet (*F. segregata*) by the latter's generally smaller size and the abundant punctations on their lower surfaces.
Distribution: Moist, calcareous woods; sporadically from about Liberty to Alachua counties.

Forestiera ligustrina (Michx.) Poir. in Lam.   **Plate 55**

Form: Most often described as a shrub with a leaning trunk, sometimes superficially appearing treelike to about 4 m in height.
Leaves: Opposite, simple, 2 - 5 cm long, less than 2 cm wide, lower surfaces sparsely to densely pubescent, margins inconspicuously toothed from their bases to their apices, apices blunt or rounded.
Flowers: Tiny, borne in clusters at the leaf axils, appearing mid to late summer or very early fall.
Fruit: A blue to black drupe, 7 - 8 mm long.
Distinguishing Marks: Similar to and easily confused with small viburnum (*Viburnum obovatum*) but distinguished by lacking punctations on the lower surfaces of leaves, distinguished from Godfrey's privet (*F. godfreyi*) by smaller leaves that are toothed throughout their margins.

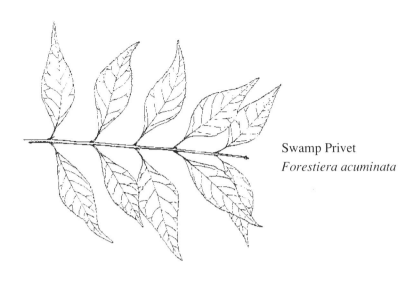

Swamp Privet
Forestiera acuminata

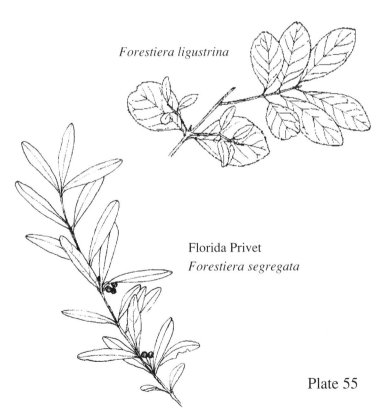

Forestiera ligustrina

Florida Privet
Forestiera segregata

Plate 55

249

Distribution: Upland mixed woods and in soils underlain closely by limestone; throughout the panhandle and eastward to the northwestern peninsula.

Florida Privet
Forestiera segregata (Jacq.) Krug & Urban   **Plate 55**

Form: Evergreen to tardily deciduous shrub or small tree seldom exceeding 3 m in height.
Leaves: Opposite, simple, elliptic to oblanceolate, entire, 1.5 - 5 cm long, 1.2 - 2 cm wide, lower and upper surfaces of blades glabrous.
Flowers: Small, borne in clusters from the leaf axils.
Fruit: A black, rounded drupe, 5 - 7 mm in diameter.
Distinguishing Marks: Distinguished from other treelike *Forestiera* with blunt-tipped leaves by leaves with entire margins and by lower surfaces of leaves being finely punctate.
Distribution: Most common in coastal hammocks, scrub, and thickets, southward from Dixie County on the west coast, Nassau County on the east coast; the only *Forestiera* species found in the Keys.

White Ash
Fraxinus americana L.

Form: Large deciduous tree normally to about 25 m in height but sometimes taller.
Leaves: Opposite, pinnately compound, overall leaf 20 - 30 cm long; leaflets numbering five to nine per leaf, but usually seven, ovate, 6 - 15 cm long, 3.5 - 7.5 cm wide, lower surfaces whitish, margins entire or bluntly serrate.
Fruit: A winged samara, 2.5 - 6.5 cm long.
Distinguishing Marks: Leaves very similar in outline to those of the Carolina ash (*F. caroliniana*) pictured on p. 251, distinguished from it and other ash trees by the whitish color of the lower surfaces of leaflets, and by inhabiting well-drained, upland woods; distinguished from upland hickories (*Carya* spp.) by having opposite rather than alternate leaves.
Distribution: Generally inhabiting rich soils in conjunction with other deciduous hardwoods; north-central Florida from about Jackson and Gulf to Marion and Lake counties.

Carolina Ash or Pop Ash
Fraxinus caroliniana Mill.   **Plate 56**

Form: Small, often crooked, deciduous tree to about 12 m in height, often with several trunks.
Leaves: Opposite, pinnately compound, 16 - 30 cm in overall length; leaflets numbering five to seven per leaf, rarely three or nine, commonly ovate to oval but also lanceolate to elliptic, 2.5 - 15 cm long, 2 - 8 cm wide, margins usually entire but sometimes serrate; stalks of lower leaflets winged.
Fruit: A samara 2 - 5 cm long, .5 - 3 cm broad, variable in shape but at least some being much the widest toward the middle and appearing diamond shaped.

Carolina Ash
Fraxinus caroliniana

Green Ash
Fraxinus pennsylvanica

Pumpkin Ash
Fraxinus profunda

Plate 56

Distinguishing Marks: Distinguished from other wetland ash trees by the generally flat, diamond-shaped samara; the only ash tree likely to be found south of Marion County.
Distribution: Throughout northern Florida, southward to about the Tamiami Trail on the west coast, Martin and Palm Beach counties on the east.

Green Ash or Red Ash

Fraxinus pennsylvanica Marsh.   **Plate 56**

Form: Large deciduous tree to 30 m in height.
Leaves: Opposite, pinnately compound, 20 - 30 cm in overall length; leaflets numbering five to nine, but commonly seven, elliptic to lanceolate, 4 - 15 cm long, 2 - 6 cm wide, margins entire to faintly serrate, upper surfaces dark green, lower surfaces paler; stems of lower leaflets winged.
Fruit: A samara, 3 - 6 cm long, 4 - 8 mm wide, mostly oblanceolate to spatulate, narrow at the seed, then abruptly widening, apex mostly tapering to a dull point.
Distinguishing Marks: Leaves similar in outline to those of the Carolina ash (*F. caroliniana*) pictured on p. 251, distinguished from it and other wetland ash trees by bearing mostly oblanceolate samaras.
Distribution: Swamps and floodplains; throughout northern Florida, southward to Marion County.

Pumpkin Ash

Fraxinus profunda (Bush) Bush   **Plate 56**

Form: Large deciduous tree to about 30 m in height.
Leaves: Opposite, pinnately compound, 12 - 30 cm in overall length; leaflets numbering five to nine, commonly seven, extremely variable in size, entire, ovate to lanceolate, 4 - 15+ cm long, 2 - 10 cm wide, lower surfaces pubescent along the midveins; stems of lower leaflets not winged.
Fruit: A samara, 4 - 8 cm long, to about 12 mm wide, many specimens uniformly wide for most of their length, apex often truncate.
Distinguishing Marks: Leaves similar in outline to those of the Carolina ash (*F. caroliniana*) pictured on p. 251, distinguished from it and other ash trees by stems of lower leaflets not being winged, in conjunction with samara body being generally rounded in cross section.
Distribution: River swamps and floodplains; from Walton to Marion counties.

Wax-Leaf Ligustrum, Glossy Privet, Tree Privet, Wax-Leaf Privet

Ligustrum lucidum Ait.   **Photo #106; Plate 57**

Form: Evergreen shrub or small tree to about 5 m in height.
Leaves: Opposite, simple, entire, coarse, dark green in color, 6 - 15 cm long, to about 5 cm wide, apices narrowing to sharp points.

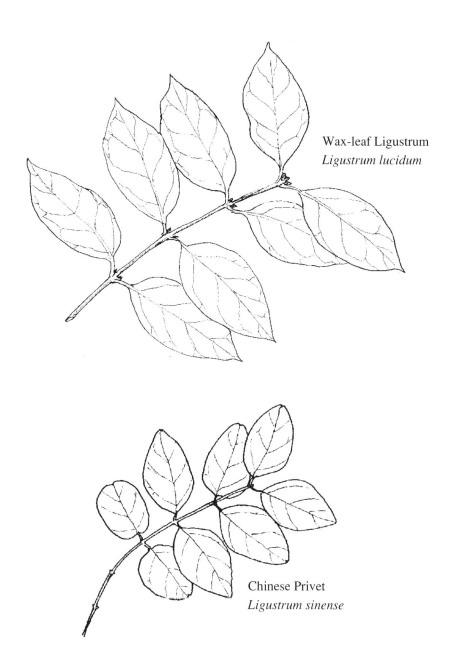

Wax-leaf Ligustrum
Ligustrum lucidum

Chinese Privet
Ligustrum sinense

Plate 57

Flowers: Small, white, fragrant, appearing in the spring, borne in terminal clusters.

Fruit: A black drupe, 4 - 8 mm long, evident on the tree for much of the year.

Distinguishing Marks: Distinguished from Chinese privet (*L. sinense*) by larger leaves and glabrous twigs.

Distribution: Asian species used as an ornamental throughout the state; rarely escaped and naturalized, mainly in upland woods.

Chinese Privet

Ligustrum sinense Lour.   **Plate 57**

Form: Tardily deciduous shrub or slender tree to about 10 m in height with pubescent twigs.

Leaves: Opposite, simple (but held on the branchlets so as to superficially appear compound), entire, oval to elliptic, 1.5 - 7 cm long, 1. 2 cm wide; petioles pubescent.

Flowers: Small, fragrant, appearing in April and May, borne in spreading, multiflowered clusters at the tips of branchlets.

Fruit: A rounded drupe, 4 - 5 mm in diameter.

Distinguishing Marks: Distinguished from glossy privet (*L. lucidum*) by smaller, nonleathery leaves and densely pubescent rather than glabrous twigs; distinguished from the several species of *Forestiera* by leaf margins being entire rather than at least partially serrate.

Distribution: Widely used as an ornamental, now naturalized and pestiferous along streams, in floodplains and in disturbed sites, often near plantings; Santa Rosa to Jefferson counties.

Wild Olive or Devilwood

Osmanthus americanus (L.) A. Gray   **Photo #108**

Form: Evergreen shrub or tree to about 15 m in height with a short trunk that typically branches close to the ground.

Leaves: Opposite, simple, entire, elliptic to obovate, 5 - 15 cm long, 1.8 - 5.5 cm wide, margins revolute.

Flowers: Small, creamy white, appearing February through April, borne in short, spreading clusters in the leaf axils, petals numbering four and fused together so as to form a tube 3 - 5 mm long.

Fruit: A distinctive, oval, dark blue to purple drupe, 1 - 1.5 cm long.

Distinguishing Marks: Distinguished from similarly leaved species of the Lauraceae, particularly those of the genus *Persea,* and from the superficially similar horse sugar (*Symplocos tinctoria*) by having opposite rather than alternate leaves.

Distribution: Found in a wide variety of habitats including flatwoods, bay swamps, scrub, coastal hammocks, floodplains, and wooded bluffs; throughout northern Florida, southward to Highlands County.

(Osmanthus megacarpa Small*)*

Form: Shrub or tree that is generally similar to the wild olive described above.
Distinguishing Marks: Distinguished as a separate species by some authors, as a variety of the wild olive (*O. americanus*) by others; distinguished from the latter by larger fruit that measures 2 - 2.5 cm in diameter.
Distribution: Sand pine scrub from about Marion County southward to Highlands and Desoto counties.

American Sycamore

Platanus occidentalis L.   **Plate 58**

Form: Large deciduous tree to 35 m in height or larger with mottled, scaling outer bark that sloughs off to reveal varying tones of inner bark ranging from green, tan, or brown to creamy white.
Leaves: Alternate, simple, 10 - 20 cm long, 8 - 20 cm wide, conspicuously lobed and toothed along the margins, long petiolate.
Flowers: Small, borne in dense globular heads.
Fruit: Conspicuous, round, 2.5 cm in diameter, borne on a stalk 8 - 15 cm long.
Distinguishing Marks: Distinguished from all other Florida trees by its large, distinctive leaves and mottled trunk.
Distribution: Abundant in floodplain and bottomland woods of large panhandle rivers including the Apalachicola, Choctawhatchee, and Escambia; sometimes planted as a yard tree.

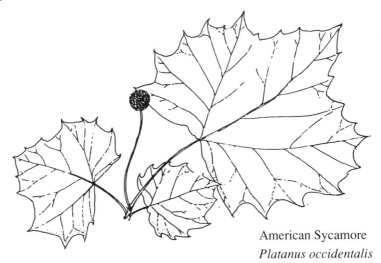

American Sycamore
Platanus occidentalis

Plate 58

Pigeon Plum, Dove Plum, or Tie-Tongue

Coccoloba diversifolia Jacq.   **Photo #109**

Form: Evergreen tree to about 20 m in height with smooth, mottled gray and brown, peeling bark; twigs ringed at each leaf node with a membranous sheath.

Leaves: Alternate, simple, entire, dull to shiny bright green above, leathery, varying widely in size and shape, typically 6 - 10 cm long, 3.8 - 5 cm wide (but those on sucker shoots and stump sprouts as much as four times this long).

Flowers: Whitish green and borne in longish racemes, male and female flowers borne on separate trees, appearing in spring.

Fruit: Rounded and somewhat egg shaped, dark red, 7 - 9 mm long, arising in summer and fall.

Distinguishing Marks: Most easily identified by combination of leaves and mottled bark.

Distribution: Common in hammocks; south Florida and the Keys.

Sea Grape

Coccoloba uvifera (L.) L.   **Plate 59**

Form: Varying widely in habit from a low, spreading evergreen shrub to a small tree about 6 m in height.

Leaves: Alternate, orbicular, to 27 cm long and wide, green above with reddish veins, bases typically cordate.

Flowers: Very small and borne in racemes nearly year-round.

Fruit: Egg shaped, fleshy, 1.8 - 2.5 cm long, hanging in long, grapelike clusters, turning from greenish to red to purple with maturity.

Distinguishing Marks: The large, orbicular leaves of the sea grape make it unlikely to be confused with any other south Florida tree.

Distribution: Coastal hammocks and dunes, often used as a landscape plant; from about Hillsborough and Brevard counties southward along the coasts and throughout the Keys.

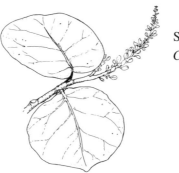

Sea Grape
Coccoloba uvifera

Plate 59

Wild Coffee, Coffee Colubrina, Snakebark

Colubrina arborescens (Mill.) Sarg.   **Photo #110**

Form: Evergreen shrub or small tree to about 8 m in height.
Leaves: Alternate, simple, entire, leathery, ovate, 5 - 14 cm long, 2.8 - 6.5 cm wide, upper surfaces dark green and glabrous, lower surfaces with reddish hairs.
Flowers: Greenish to yellowish, tiny, borne in clusters in the leaf axils, the entire cluster usually not exceeding about 12 mm in width.
Fruit: A capsule, rounded, purple to black, 6 - 10 mm in diameter, splitting at maturity to expose three seeds.
Distinguishing Marks: Most easily recognized, in conjunction with other characters, by rusty red pubescence on the younger stems and twigs.
Distribution: Hammocks, primarily of the Florida Keys but also occasionally in the southern Everglades.

Cuban Colubrina or Cuban Snakebark

Colubrina cubensis (Jacq.) Brongn.

Form: Evergreen shrub or small tree to about 9 m in height.
Leaves: Alternate, simple, leathery, long elliptic to oblong, 5 - 10 cm long, 1.5 - 4 cm wide, both upper and lower surfaces pubescent but lower more so, veins on upper surfaces conspicuously depressed, margins shallowly and irregularly crenate.
Flowers: Tiny, borne in small clusters in the leaf axils.
Fruit: A rounded capsule, 6 - 9 mm in diameter.
Distinguishing Marks: The conspicuously depressed veins on the upper surfaces of leaves help separate this species from the other two species of *Colubrina.*
Distribution: Uncommon in hammocks of the Miami Rock Ridge and Everglades keys.

Soldierwood

Colubrina elliptica (Sw.) Briz. & Stern   **Photo #111; Plate 60**

Form: Typically an evergreen shrub, sometimes a small tree with orange-brown bark, potentially reaching a height of 15 m.
Leaves: Alternate, simple, ovate to lanceolate, entire, soft to touch, 4 - 12 cm long, 4 - 6 cm wide, shiny dark green above, pubescent below with rusty hairs, margins with two conspicuous glands near the base of the blade.
Flowers: Greenish yellow, small, borne in clusters at the leaf axils.
Fruit: A rounded, reddish orange capsule, 6 - 9 mm in diameter.
Distinguishing Marks: Distinguished from other *Colubrina* by soft rather than leathery leaves and marginal glands, from Cuban colubrina (*C. cubensis*) by leaves lacking crenate margins.
Distribution: Widespread across the Caribbean basin, in Florida only in hammocks of the extreme southern peninsula and the upper Keys.

Black Ironwood or Leadwood

Krugiodendron ferreum (Vahl) Urban **Plate 60**

Form: Evergreen shrub or small tree to about 9 m in height with densely leafy and spreading branches.

Leaves: Opposite (rarely subopposite or slightly alternate), simple, entire, pliable, elliptic to oval, 2.5 - 4 cm long, 2 - 2.6 cm wide, margins wavy, apices rounded, blunt, and often notched.

Flowers: Small, yellowish green, borne in few-flowered clusters at the leaf axils, appearing in spring.

Fruit: A rounded to ovoid drupe, black, 5 - 10 mm in diameter, appearing in summer and fall.

Distinguishing Marks: Most easily distinguished from other hammock species by pliable, opposite leaves with notched apices and short, finely pubescent petioles.

Distribution: Hammocks of the Keys and southern peninsula, northward along the east coast to about Brevard County.

Darling Plum or Red Ironwood

Reynosia septentrionalis Urban **Plate 60**

Form: Evergreen shrub or small tree potentially to about 10 m in height but usually shorter.

Leaves: Opposite, simple, entire, oval to obovate, dark green above, stiff, leathery, 1.5 - 3 cm long, to about 1.5 cm wide, apices notched.

Flowers: Tiny, yellowish green, without petals, borne in clusters at the leaf axils.

Fruit: An egg-shaped, purple to black, edible drupe, 1 - 2 cm long, with a spiny tip.

Distinguishing Marks: Distinguished from black ironwood (*Krugiodendron ferreum*) by having stiff rather than pliable leaves, from both species of *Capparis,* which have leaves with a notched apex, by opposite rather than alternate leaves.

Distribution: Hammocks of southernmost Florida and the Keys.

Carolina Buckthorn

Rhamnus caroliniana Walt. **Photo #112**

Form: Deciduous shrub or small, unarmed tree, 10 - 14 m in height with young twigs that are reddish brown and pubescent.

Leaves: Alternate, simple, elliptic, 5 - 12 cm long, 3 - 5 cm wide, margins irregularly and minutely serrate, sometimes with small rounded teeth, lateral veins conspicuously parallel.

Flowers: Tiny, campanulate, yellowish to whitish, borne in small clusters in the leaf axils.

Fruit: A rounded berry, first red but turning black at maturity, to about 1 cm in diameter.

Distinguishing Marks: Most easily recognized by the parallel lateral leaf veins.

Distribution: Occasionally found in moist, deciduous forests, shell middens, and calcareous woods; north Florida southward to about Orange County.

Soldierwood
Colubrina elliptica

Black Ironwood
Krugiodendron ferreum

Darling Plum
Reynosia septentrionalis

Plate 60

Red Mangrove

Rhizophora mangle L.   **Photo #113**

Form: Evergreen shrub or small tree to about 25 m in height.
Leaves: Opposite, entire, leathery, elliptic, 4 - 15 cm long, 2 - 5 cm wide.
Flowers: With four yellowish to white petals, borne in clusters of two or three at the leaf axils.
Fruit: Brown, egg shaped, 2.4 - 3.6 cm long, germinating while still attached to the tree and sending out a distinctive, cigar-shaped seedling up to 30 cm long.
Distinguishing Marks: Distinguished from white mangrove (*Laguncularia racemosa*) by dark, shiny green upper surfaces of leaves, from black mangrove (*Avicennia germinans*) by pale green lower surfaces of leaves, from both by numerous reddish prop roots that arise from the lower trunk and branches, and the long radicles (or germinating seeds) that appear from early summer into the fall.
Distribution: Confined to shallow waters of coastal bays, lagoons, creeks, and rivers; from Levy and Volusia counties southward and throughout the Keys.

Downy Serviceberry

Amelanchier arborea (Michx. f.) Fern.   **Plate 61**

Form: Deciduous shrub or small tree with a smooth, gray trunk, to about 12 m in height.
Leaves: Alternate, simple, oval to ovate, 3 - 9 cm long, 2 - 4 cm wide, margins finely serrate, bases typically cordate; petioles conspicuous, averaging about 2 cm long.
Flowers: Star shaped with five white to pinkish, spreading petals, 1.5 - 2 cm long, appearing in early spring prior to the emergence of new leaves.
Fruit: Berrylike, reddish to dark purple, 5 - 10 mm in diameter.
Distinguishing Marks: Similar to several species of the genus *Prunus,* but distinguished from them and other trees with alternate, simple leaves with serrated margins by having longish petioles in conjunction with the lateral leaf veins being appressed to the central vein for a short distance before diverging to the leaf edges, the latter seen most easily on the upper surface, particularly near the base, but only with magnification.
Distribution: Streambanks and open woodlands; restricted in Florida to the panhandle.

May Haw or Apple Haw

Crataegus aestivalis (Walt.) Torr. & Gray

Form: Deciduous shrub or tree to about 8 m in height, often armed with sharp, conspicuous spines to about 4 cm long and borne at the leaf axils.
Leaves: Alternate, simple, shiny green, stiffish, 2 - 8 cm long, 1 - 3.6 cm wide, margins coarsely toothed to lobed; leaf blades with tufts of hair at least in the proximal vein axils beneath, or if uniformly pubescent then the pubescence copious, pale-grayish on very young leaves, rusty-brown on mature leaves.

Flowers: With five white to pinkish petals, borne individually or in clusters of two to four from leaf axils.

Fruit: Juicy, red, rounded, 8 - 10 mm in diameter, typical of haws with remains of the sepals evident at the distal end.

Distinguishing Marks: Some leaves on any plant superficially similar to Washington thorn (*C. phaenopyrum*), pictured on p. 265, but distinguished from them by having lateral veins terminating only at the tips of marginal teeth; other leaves similar in shape to those of the cockspur (*C. crus-galli*), pictured on p. 263, but distinguished from them by having tufts of hairs in the vein axils on the lower surface.

Distribution: Wet areas, in and near standing water; throughout the panhandle and southward to about the Gainesville area.

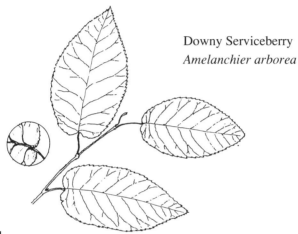

Downy Serviceberry
Amelanchier arborea

Plate 61

Cockspur Haw or Hog Apple

Crataegus crus-galli L.   **Photo #114; Plate 62**

Form: Small deciduous tree to about 10 m in height with thorny branches and clusters of thorns along the trunk.

Leaves: Alternate, simple, oblanceolate, 2 - 6 cm long, .8 - 3 cm wide, margins serrate to coarsely toothed, not lobed, upper surfaces glabrous, deep green and conspicuously lustrous.

Flowers: Roselike, with five white petals, .5 - 1.5 cm wide at full maturity.

Fruit: Dull red to reddish orange, to about 1 cm or a little more in diameter, borne on a long stem, typical of haws with remains of the sepals evident at the distal end.

Distinguishing Marks: Some leaves similar to the unlobed leaves of the littlehip hawthorn (*C. spathulata*), but differing from it slightly in habitat and by the latter having leaf veins terminating in both the marginal teeth and the sinuses between them, rather than just in the teeth; distinguished from May haw (*C. aestivalis*) by lacking tufts of hairs in the vein axils of the lower leaf surface.

Distribution: Open woodlands and upland woods; throughout northern Florida and the panhandle.

Yellow Haw
Crataegus flava Ait.   **Photo #115; Plate 62**

Form: Deciduous shrub or small tree to about 5 m in height with thorny branches, thorns measuring to about 6 cm long, branches sometimes drooping at their extremities; bark of young trees grayish, furrowed, blocky, and oaklike, bark of older trees also furrowed but often much darker.

Leaves: Alternate, simple, 2 - 5 cm long, 1 - 3 cm wide, widest above the middle, toothed and shallowly lobed, part of the blade often extending down the petiole in narrow wings.

Flowers: Fragrant, showy, borne individually or in three- to five-flowered clusters at the leaf axis, petals white at maturity, 10 - 16 mm wide when fully open.

Fruit: Red and berrylike, borne on long stems, variable in color from yellow to reddish to purplish, .8 - 1.5 cm in diameter, typical of haws with remains of the sepals evident at the distal end.

Distinguishing Marks: Leaves similar in appearance to those of the dwarf haw (*C. uniflora*) but distinguished by having conspicuous red glands at the tip of each marginal tooth when seen with magnification.

Distribution: Common in mixed woodlands, open woods, sandy pinelands; throughout northern Florida and the panhandle; perhaps the most easily found of Florida's hawthorns.

Parsley Haw
Crataegus marshallii Egglest.   **Photo #116**

Form: Small deciduous tree to about 8 m in height, usually with thorny branches and scaly, splotchy bark of grays and tans, larger specimens sometimes bear multipronged, often leafy thorns along the trunk, these thorns to about 5 cm long.

Leaves: Alternate, simple, triangular in overall outline, 1 - 5 cm long and wide, usually with several deeply incised lobes, each lobe with conspicuous teeth.

Flowers: White to pinkish with showy red anthers, 1.5 - 2 cm wide at full maturity.

Fruit: Rounded, bright red, 5 - 7 mm long, typical of haws with remains of the sepals evident at the distal end.

Distinguishing Marks: The small, distinctive, deeply incised, rather frilly leaves with truncated bases make this the easiest of the haws to separate from all other north Florida trees.

Distribution: Wooded slopes, moist woods, floodplains; throughout northern Florida, southward to about Hillsborough County.

Cockspur Haw
Crataegus crus-galli

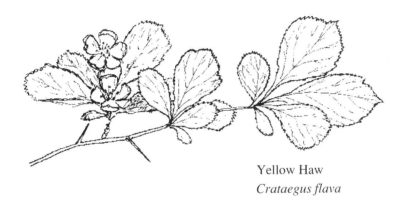

Yellow Haw
Crataegus flava

Plate 62

Washington Thorn

Crataegus phaenopyrum (L. f.) Medic.   Plate 63

Form: Deciduous shrub or small tree to about 10 m in height with sharp, reddish thorns to about 3 cm long.
Leaves: Alternate, simple, ovate, typically 1.5 - 2.5 cm long but variable and having several (to many) leaves to about 7 cm in length, 2 - 5 cm wide, upper surfaces dark green and smooth, margins lobed and toothed, lobes usually three in number, distal lobe narrowing to a sharp point at the apex.
Flowers: White, tiny, borne in many-flowered clusters.

Fruit: Bright red, rounded, 4 - 6 mm in diameter, typical of haws with remains of the sepals evident at the distal end.

Distinguishing Marks: At least some leaves have the appearance of miniature maple leaves with blunt rather than sharp-pointed serrations; somewhat similar to the may haw (*C. aestivalis*) but distinguished from it by having lateral leaf veins terminating in both the tips of marginal teeth and the sinuses between them rather than only in the tips of the teeth (requires magnification).

Distribution: Low woods; limited to only a few locations in the central Florida panhandle and Big Bend; fairly common along the drainage of the Choctawhatchee River in Washington and Walton counties, also reported in Wakulla County by Robert Godfrey.

Crataegus pulcherrima Ashe   **Plate 63**

Form: Small deciduous tree, branches with sharp thorns to about 2 cm long.

Leaves: Alternate, simple, variously shaped, lobed, and toothed, 2 - 6 cm long, 1 - 4 cm wide, margins coarsely to finely serrate, with dark purplish red glands (magnification required) on most petioles and on the tips of leaf serrations.

Flowers: White to pinkish, borne in few-flowered clusters, each flower to about 2 cm wide at maturity.

Distinguishing Marks: Similar in appearance to the green haw (*C. viridis*), but distinguished from it by lacking tufted pubescence in the vein axils of the lower surfaces of leaves, and by generally occurring in dry uplands rather than wetlands.

Distribution: Open upland woods; rather spottily distributed in Florida from Walton to Jefferson counties, and from northeast Florida southward to Alachua County.

Littlehip Hawthorn or Small Fruited Hawthorn

Crataegus spathulata Michx.   **Photo #117; Plate 63**

Form: Deciduous shrub or small tree to about 8 m in height, often with sharp thorns along slightly zigzag branches, bark brownish and stripping off in thin plates.

Leaves: Alternate, simple, oblanceolate to spatulate in shape and narrowing to a tapered base, 1 - 4 cm long, margins mostly crenate, leaves toward the extremities of the branches may be three-lobed and somewhat larger.

Flowers: White to pink, petals triangular, 7 - 10 mm wide when fully mature, borne in dense, showy clusters.

Fruit: Bright red, rounded, 4 - 7 mm in diameter.

Distinguishing Marks: Most easily distinguished from other haws by the presence of at least some spatulate leaves with strongly tapered bases.

Distribution: Bottomlands, floodplains, and wooded slopes; limited in Florida to the central panhandle.

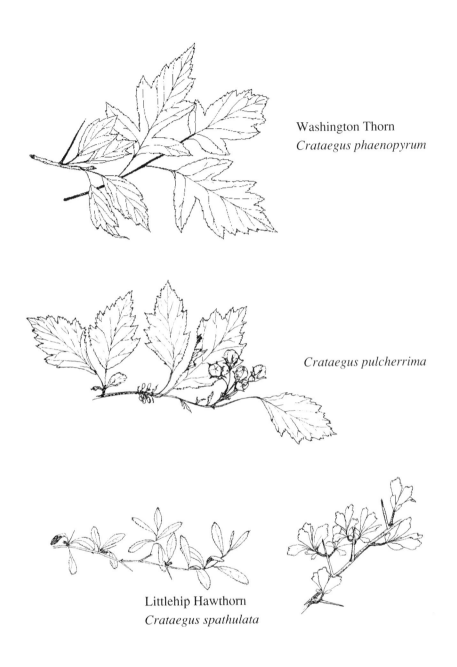

Washington Thorn
Crataegus phaenopyrum

Crataegus pulcherrima

Littlehip Hawthorn
Crataegus spathulata

Plate 63

Dwarf Haw or One-Flowered Hawthorn

Crataegus uniflora Muenchh.

Form: Typically a deciduous shrub to about 3 m tall in Florida, sometimes a small bushy tree in the more northern parts of its range; branches with thin spines to about 3 cm long.

Leaves: Alternate, simple, obovate to rounded, 1 - 3 cm long, margins irregularly serrate, upper surfaces shiny.

Flowers: White, usually borne singly, but sometimes in clusters of two or three, to about 1.5 cm wide when open.

Fruit: Rounded, brownish red, 1 cm in diameter, typical of haws with remains of the sepals evident at the distal end, margins of sepals generally serrate.

Distinguishing Marks: Leaves similar to those of the yellow haw (*C. flava*), pictured on p. 263, may be distinguished from the latter by lacking the conspicuous red glands at the tips of the marginal teeth (requires magnification).

Distribution: Open woods; Washington County to northeastern Florida, southward to Alachua County.

Green Haw

Crataegus viridis L.

Form: Deciduous shrub or small tree, largely spineless but sometimes with slender, sharp thorns.

Leaves: Alternate, simple, ovate to elliptic, 3 - 7 cm long, 1.5 - 5 cm wide, margins variously lobed, always toothed, lower surfaces with patches of pubescence at the points where the central and lateral veins intersect; petioles and marginal teeth, or lobes of blades, without glands.

Flowers: White to pink, borne in clusters, to about 1.5 cm wide or a little more at maturity.

Fruit: Red to orange, rounded to slightly elongated, 5 - 8 mm in diameter.

Distinguishing Marks: Similar to *C. pulcherrima*, pictured on p. 265, but differing from it by having tufted pubescence in the vein axils on the lower surfaces of leaves and by occurring primarily in wetland rather than dry upland habitats.

Distribution: Low woods, pond edges, swamps; across northern Florida and throughout the panhandle.

Southern Crabapple

Malus angustifolia (Ait.) Michx.   **Photo #118**

Form: Deciduous shrub or small tree to about 10 m in height, often with leafy thorns.

Leaves: Alternate but densely clustered on young twigs, simple, variable in shape and size, mostly elliptic, 2.5 - 5 cm long, 2.5 cm wide, margins serrate and sometimes lobed near the base.

Flowers: Fragrant, showy, five-petaled, typically rich pink in color, borne in clusters of three to five, to about 2.5 cm wide when open.

Fruit: Rounded, yellowish, resembling the crabapple of commerce, to about 2.5 cm in diameter.

Distinguishing Marks: Distinguished from haws by having leafy thorns rather than naked, axillary spines.
Distribution: Open, upland woods; limited in Florida to the panhandle.

Alabama Cherry or Alabama Chokecherry
Prunus alabamensis Mohr.   **Plate 64**

Form: Small deciduous tree.
Leaves: Alternate, simple, oval to obovate, 5 - 8 cm long, 3 - 5 cm wide, margins finely serrate and sometimes wavy, apices blunt.
Flowers: Borne in racemes to about 10 cm long and similar to those of the black cherry (*P. serotina*).
Fruit: Rounded, juicy, dark red to black when mature, to about 7 mm in diameter.
Distinguishing Marks: Leaves similar in color to those of the black cherry pictured in Photo #123, but distinguished from it by having pubescent petioles and branchlets, and by the typically obovate leaves with blunt apices.
Distribution: Uncommon in sandy, pine–oak woodlands; panhandle from at least the east side of the Apalachicola River westward.

American Plum
Prunus americana Marsh.   **Photo #119; Plate 64**

Form: Small deciduous tree to about 11 m in height, often with spine-tipped twigs borne along the branches and trunk; bark brownish, shaggy, exfoliating in curly plates.
Leaves: Alternate, simple, elliptic, 4 - 12 cm long, 2.5 - 5 cm wide, margins serrate or doubly serrate, apices tapered to narrow points.
Flowers: Fragrant, with five white petals that turn pink with age, bell shaped at the base, about 2 cm across when fully open, appearing in early spring, borne in clusters of two to five.
Fruit: Rounded, red, juicy, 1.8 - 2.5 cm in diameter, very tough, edible but sour.
Distinguishing Marks: This tree's fruit, strongly tapered leaf tips and shaggy, brownish bark are distinctive field marks.
Distribution: Woodlands, mostly in soils with a limestone subsurface; central and eastern panhandle.

Chickasaw Plum
Prunus angustifolia Marsh.   **Photo #120; Plate 64**

Form: Thicket-forming deciduous shrub or small tree to about 8 m in height.
Leaves: Alternate, simple, lanceolate, typically reflexed upward from the midrib, 3 - 8 cm long, 1 - 2.5 cm wide, margins finely serrate with tips of the teeth bearing tiny red or yellow glands.
Flowers: White, showy, fragrant, less than 1 cm wide when fully open.
Fruit: Red to yellow, oval, juicy, 1.5 - 2.5 cm long, edible but tart.

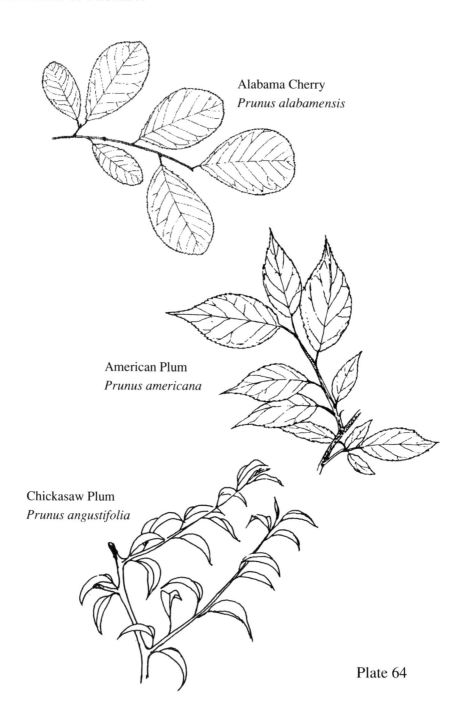

Alabama Cherry
Prunus alabamensis

American Plum
Prunus americana

Chickasaw Plum
Prunus angustifolia

Plate 64

268

Distinguishing Marks: Very similar to, and often difficult to distinguish from, the hog plum (*P. umbellata*), distinguished from it most readily by the gland-tipped leaf serrations (the latter seen only with magnification); the illustrations show the varying leaf forms.

Distribution: Woodland edges and fencerows; from north Florida southward to DeSoto County.

Carolina Laurel Cherry

Prunus caroliniana (Mill.) Ait.   **Photo #121**

Form: Small or medium-sized evergreen tree to about 12 m in height.

Leaves: Alternate, simple, leathery, elliptic, 5 - 12 cm long, upper surfaces dark green and lustrous, lower surfaces dull green, margins entire or with sharp teeth, some leaves on some plants more generously toothed than others; petioles of newer leaves reddish.

Flowers: White, fragrant, borne from the leaf axils in racemes to about 4 cm long, each flower less than .5 cm wide when open, appearing in late winter or early spring.

Fruit: A shiny black, oval drupe, 1 - 1.5 cm long.

Distinguishing Marks: Distinguished from other members of the genus by combination of stiff, mostly entire leaves and fruit borne in a short raceme.

Distribution: Found in a variety of habitats due to extensive use as an ornamental and distribution by birds; throughout north Florida, southward to about DeSoto County.

West Indian Cherry

Prunus myrtifolia (L.) Urban   **Plate 65**

Form: Small evergreen tree to about 12 m in height.

Leaves: Alternate, simple, entire, 5 - 11 cm long, 2.5 - 4 cm wide, margins wavy, exhibiting a strong aroma of bitter almond when crushed.

Flowers: With five petals, petals white tinged with yellow, appearing in November and December.

Fruit: A brownish orange drupe, 7 - 12 mm in diameter.

Distinguishing Marks: Most easily distinguished from other south Florida trees by distinctive aroma of crushed leaves.

Distribution: Uncommon in hammocks of southeastern Dade and Monroe counties including the Keys.

Peach

Prunus persica (L.) Batsch.   **Photo #122**

Form: Small deciduous tree to about 7 m in height.

Leaves: Alternate, simple, lanceolate to elliptic, 4 - 15 cm long, margins finely but sharply toothed, apices tapered and long pointed, petioles distinctly grooved and bearing two conspicuous glands just at or below the leaf base.

Flowers: Appearing before the leaves, showy, with numerous reddish purple styles, five reddish purple sepals, and five pink petals, each petal more deeply colored near the base, individual flowers to nearly 3.5 cm wide when fully open.

Fruit: The common peach of commerce.

Distinguishing Marks: Most easily recognized when not in fruit or flower by combination of toothed leaves and petioler glands.

Distribution: Native of China; irregularly distributed across much of northern Florida where escaped from cultivation or persisting near old home sites.

Black Cherry

Prunus serotina Ehrh.   **Photo #123**

Form: Medium-sized to large deciduous tree to about 30 m in height, bark brownish, smooth and shiny when young, changing to a conspicuous patchwork of small, dark, reddish brown to nearly black plates when mature.

Leaves: Alternate, simple, elliptic, shiny green above, 5 - 15 cm long, 2.5 - 4 cm wide, generally drooping from the branch, margins serrate, each serration tipped with a tiny, reddish gland; petioles grooved and with one to several conspicuous glands when viewed with magnification.

Flowers: Small, white, borne in long racemes to about 8 cm long.

Fruit: A shiny drupe, reddish at first, purplish black when mature, juicy, 7 - 10 mm in diameter.

Distinguishing Marks: Distinguished from the much less common Alabama cherry (*P. alabamensis*) by lacking pubescence on the petioles and branchlets.

Distribution: Mixed woods, uplands, fencerows, power lines, and other places where birds are likely to drop the seeds; throughout the panhandle and northern Florida, southward to about Brevard and Hillsborough counties.

Hog Plum or Flatwoods Plum

Prunus umbellata Ell.   **Plate 65**

Form: Deciduous shrub or small tree to about 6 m in height, often with a crooked trunk.

Leaves: Alternate, simple, oval to elliptic, serrate, 2 - 6 cm long, 1 - 3 cm wide, margins serrate, tips of serrations without glands, apices sharp pointed.

Flowers: White, showy, typically appearing before the leaves, 1.2 - 1.5 cm wide when fully open.

Fruit: A red or yellow drupe becoming dark purple at maturity, 1.5 - 2 cm in diameter.

Distinguishing Marks: Very similar to, and difficult to distinguish from the chickasaw plum (*P. angustifolia*), distinguished from it most easily by lacking glands at the tips of the leaf serrations (the latter seen only with magnification).

Distribution: Mixed woods, hammocks, pine woods; throughout northern Florida, southward to about Highlands County.

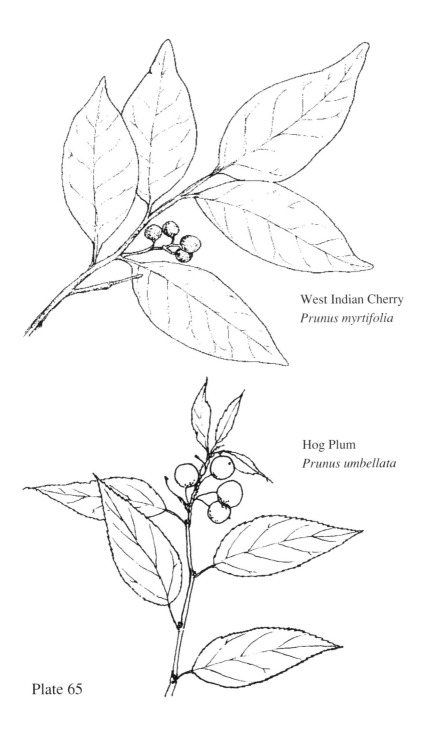

West Indian Cherry
Prunus myrtifolia

Hog Plum
Prunus umbellata

Plate 65

271

Red-Spire

Pyrus calleryana Decn.

Plate 66

Form: Small to medium sized, attractive, deciduous tree with leafy thorns.

Leaves: Widely alternate along the branch but closely set near the tips of fruiting twigs, simple, to at least 8 cm long and 5.5 cm wide, nearly triangular in shape, margins finely serrate; petioles 2 - 5 cm long, those clustered on fruiting twigs much the longest.

Flowers: White, sometimes tinged with pink, showy, borne in spring on slender stalks to about 5 cm long.

Fruit: A rounded, golden brown pome, very conspicuous, to about 2 cm in diameter.

Distinguishing Marks: This is one of two naturalized pears found in northern Florida, it is distinguished from the common pear (*P. communis* L.), another sparsely naturalized species that is found most often in yards and along roadsides, by having much smaller fruit and smaller flowers.

Distribution: Sparsely naturalized in northern Florida, generally near old homesites or former plantings.

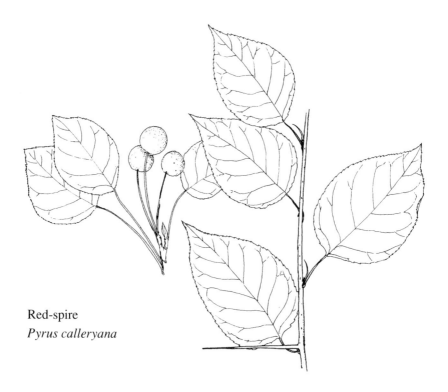

Red-spire
Pyrus calleryana

Plate 66

Seven-Year Apple

Casasia clusiifolia (Jacq.) Urban   **Photo #124**

Form: Evergreen shrub or small tree to about 6 m in height.
Leaves: Opposite, simple, obovate, entire, leathery, 5 - 15 cm long, 2.5 - 7.5 cm wide, shiny green above, clustered at the tips of branches.
Flowers: Bright white, star shaped.
Fruit: Green, hard, egg shaped, 6 - 10 cm long.
Distinguishing Marks: May be confused only with the balsam apple (*Clusia rosea*) but distinguished from it by having the upper surface of the leaf shiny rather than dull green.
Distribution: Occurs naturally in coastal hammocks and adjacent transition zone of Dade, Monroe, and Broward counties including the Keys; also planted as an ornamental.

Buttonbush

Cephalanthus occidentalis L.   **Photo #125**

Form: Deciduous shrub or small tree, potentially to about 15 m in height but usually much shorter.
Leaves: Opposite or in whorls of three to four, simple, lanceolate to elliptic, 6 - 18 cm long, 1.5 - 10 cm wide.
Flowers: Numerous, tiny, white, borne in a hanging, globular, compact, pincushionlike head, 2 - 4 cm in diameter.
Fruit: Small, produced in rounded heads.
Distinguishing Marks: Most easily recognized by its simple, elliptic, sometimes whorled leaves and showy, rounded flower heads; most similar to fever tree (*Pinckneya bracteata*) but distinguished from it by having at least some leaves in whorls of three or four.
Distribution: Wet areas and sites with standing water; throughout the state except the Keys.

Black Torch

Erithalis fruticosa L.   **Photo #126; Plate 67**

Form: Typically a low, much-branched shrub with very dense foliage, but sometimes more spindly and treelike, especially in hammocks of the Lower Keys; branchlets conspicuously and characteristically jointed.
Leaves: Opposite, entire, oval, 2 - 5 cm long, with blunt apices.
Flowers: Small, white, star shaped, with five petals, borne in clusters in the leaf axils.
Fruit: A rounded drupe to just under 1 cm in diameter, shiny black and conspicuous at maturity.
Distinguishing Marks: Most easily recognized by its opposite leaves that are closely clustered near the tips of the branches.
Distribution: Coastal scrub and hammocks of the southern peninsula and the Florida Keys.

Princewood

Exostema caribaeum (Jacq.) Roem. & Schult.   **Plate 67**

Form: Evergreen shrub or small tree to about 6 m in height with conspicuously jointed twigs.
Leaves: Opposite, simple, leathery, lanceolate to elliptic, entire, 3 - 8 cm long, 1 - 4 cm wide, dark green above, yellowish green below, often reflexed upward from the midrib.
Flowers: White, pinkish or orange colored, typically appearing from March to May, borne singly in the leaf axils, with a very long, tubelike corolla that spreads into five straplike petals near the apex.
Fruit: An upright, woody capsule which splits into two parts at maturity.
Distinguishing Marks: Most easily recognized when not in flower by combination of conspicuously jointed twigs and opposite, reflexed leaves.
Distribution: Hammocks and pinelands of the Florida Keys; also sparingly on the southern peninsula.

Velvetseed or Everglades Velvetseed

Guettarda elliptica Sw.   **Plate 68**

Form: Typically a small, spindly, arching evergreen tree to about 6 m in height.
Leaves: Opposite, simple, entire, oval to obovate, to about 7 cm long and 3 cm wide, dull green and soft to the touch.
Flowers: White to reddish pink, tubular, to about 1 cm long.
Fruit: A rounded, purple berry, 7 - 10 mm in diameter, covered with a velvetlike pubescence.
Distinguishing Marks: Somewhat similar in appearance to the rough velvetseed (*G. scabra*) but distinguished from it by having leaves that are soft to the touch and usually less than 7 cm long.
Distribution: Pinelands and hammocks; extreme south Florida and the Keys.

Rough Velvetseed

Guettarda scabra (L.) Vent.   **Photo #127**

Form: An evergreen shrub to about 1.5 m tall in the pinelands but reaching the stature of a small, sparsely branched, slender tree to about 5 m in height where it invades the hammocks.
Leaves: Opposite, simple, entire, oval, 5 - 15 cm long (though some leaves of hammock specimens may exceed this length), 2 - 8 cm wide, dark green and covered on both surfaces with short, stiff hairs making the leaf very rough to the touch.
Flowers: Tubular, 1 - 3 cm long.
Fruit: Red, rounded, berrylike, 6 - 12 mm in diameter, covered with a velvetlike pubescence.
Distinguishing Marks: Most easily recognized by its opposite, very rough leaves.
Distribution: Pinelands and hammocks of south Florida and the Keys; a disjunct population is known from Martin County.

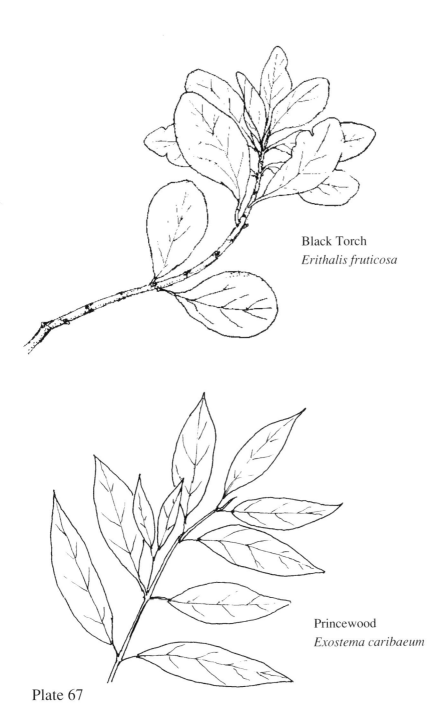

Black Torch
Erithalis fruticosa

Princewood
Exostema caribaeum

Plate 67

275

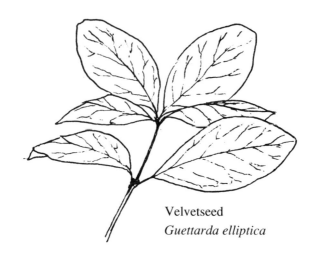

Velvetseed
Guettarda elliptica

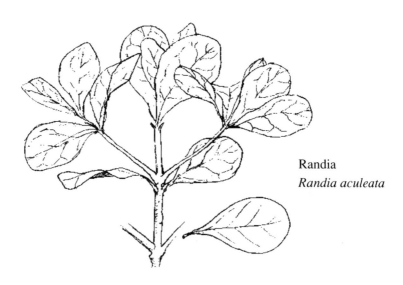

Randia
Randia aculeata

Plate 68

Scarlet Bush or Firebush
Hamelia patens Jacq. **Photo #128**

Form: Evergreen shrub or shrubby tree to about 5 m in height.
Leaves: Whorled with three to seven leaves at each node, simple, entire, elliptic, 5 - 15 cm long, 2 - 8 cm wide, blades often reflexed upward from the central vein, petioles and veins reddish.
Flowers: Red to reddish orange, tubular, 1.5 - 4 cm long, borne in axillary or terminal clusters.
Fruit: A rounded, juicy berry, 5 - 10 mm in diameter, red to purplish black.
Distinguishing Marks: Distinguished from other south Florida trees by whorled leaves with reddish veins and petioles.
Distribution: Hammocks, roadsides, disturbed sites; Highlands County southward and throughout the Keys.

Pinckneya or Fever Tree
Pinckneya bracteata (Bartr.) Raf. **Photo #129**

Form: Deciduous shrub or small tree to about 8 m in height.
Leaves: Opposite, simple, oval to elliptic, 4 - 20 cm long, 2.5 - 12 cm wide, often clustered toward the ends of branches, margins entire but sometimes slightly wavy.
Flowers: Bell shaped, greenish yellow, each with one, much enlarged, pinkish (rarely whitish) sepal that appears leaflike and is very showy, flowers appearing in late spring and early summer.
Fruit: A rounded capsule, 1 - 3 cm long.
Distinguishing Marks: Most easily recognized by rather large opposite, elliptic leaves and distinctive flowers; distinguished from the similarly leaved buttonbush (*Cephalanthus occidentalis*) by lacking whorled leaves.
Distribution: Wet areas of bogs, bay swamps, and low pinelands; from about Bay and Washington counties eastward across northern Florida.

Randia, Indigo Berry, White Indigo Berry
Randia aculeata L. **Plate 68**

Form: Typically a small evergreen shrub but very occasionally a short tree with opposite branches, to about 3.5 m in height.
Leaves: Opposite, simple, elliptic to obovate, light green in color, 1 - 5 cm long, blunt toward the apices but having a small, sharp point at the leaf tips, often exhibiting a pair of sharp spines just above the point of leaf attachment.
Flowers: Fragrant, white with five petals, borne along the branch or clustered at the leaf axils and a little more than 1 cm across.
Fruit: An oval, white to greenish white berry.
Distinguishing Marks: Most easily recognized by its distinctive opposite branching, by the leaves clustered at the terminus of the branchlets, and by the frequent pairs of wide-angled thorns along the stem.
Distribution: Found in a variety of habitats in southern Florida and the Keys.

Torchwood

Amyris elemifera L.   **Plate 69**

Form: Evergreen shrub or tree with light brown bark, to about 5 m in height.
Leaves: Opposite, compound; leaflets three to five in number, quite limber and drooping, 2.5 -
7.5 cm long, light green, ovate to ovate-lanceolate, with entire margins, long pointed tips, and
glandular dots on the upper surface.
Flowers: Tiny, white, borne in clusters up to 5 cm long.
Fruit: A purple to black, ovoid drupe with obvious glandular dots, about .5 - 1 cm long.
Distinguishing Marks: Most easily recognized by drooping, light green, and relatively small
compound leaves.
Distribution: Primarily found in wet coastal hammocks; southward along the east coast from
about the center part of the state and throughout the Keys.

Key Lime

Citrus aurantifolia (Christm.) Swingle

Form: Small, shrubby evergreen tree to about 5 m in height with thorny branches.
Leaves: Alternate, simple, ovate-elliptic, shiny, dark green, aromatic, 5 - 8 cm long, margins
crenate, petioles often conspicuously but narrowly winged (a character that is common to many
members of the *Citrus* genus).
Flowers: White, with four or five petals and up to 25 stamens but only one pistil.
Fruit: Rounded, 2.5 - 5 cm in diameter, turning from green to yellow as it ripens.
Distinguishing Marks: Leaves similar to those of *C. aurantium,* pictured on p. 279, distin-
guished from it by geographic range.
Distribution: Naturalized in coastal hammocks of southern Florida and the Keys.

Sour Orange or Seville Orange

Citrus aurantium L.   **Plate 69**

Form: Evergreen shrub or small tree to about 6 m in height, sometimes bearing sharp spines
along the twigs.
Leaves: Alternate, simple, entire, elliptic to ovate, 5.5 - 12 cm long, 3 - 10 cm wide, often bearing
a conspicuous wing on either side of the petiole (a character that is common to many members of
the *Citrus* genus).
Flowers: White, radially symmetrical, fragrant, borne in small, axillary clusters, petals numbering
four to eight.
Fruit: Like an orange, orange to reddish orange in color, 6 - 9 cm in diameter, rough on the surface and with a bitter taste.
Distinguishing Marks: Most easily recognized by combination of conspicuously winged petiole
and large, orangelike fruit.

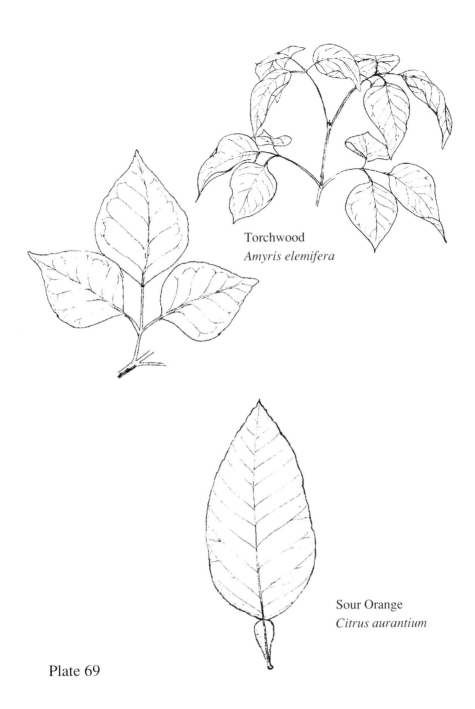

Torchwood
Amyris elemifera

Sour Orange
Citrus aurantium

Plate 69

279

Distribution: Cultivated but naturalized in many parts of the state; found growing wild in coastal shell middens of the more northern parts of the state, and hammocks of the southern peninsula.

Trifoliate Orange or Mock Orange
Poncirus trifoliata (L.) Raf.

Form: Deciduous shrub or small tree to about 7 m in height with sharp thorns along the twigs.
Leaves: Alternate, compound, with three leaflets and conspicuously winged petioles; leaflets obovate with minutely crenate margins, to about 8.5 cm long.
Flowers: White, rotate, conspicuous, 3 - 6 cm wide, with five to seven petals.
Fruit: Yellow in color and appearing orangelike, 4 - 5 cm in diameter.
Distinguishing Marks: Distinguished from all other species by combination of trifoliolate leaves with winged petioles, bright green stems, and sharp axillary thorns.
Distribution: Cultivated and occasionally escaped along woodland borders, and fence- and hedgerows in northern Florida.

Wafer Ash, Hop Tree, Stinking Ash, Skunk Bush
Ptelea trifoliata L.   **Plate 70**

Form: Small, spreading deciduous shrub or small tree to about 7.5 m in height with light brown to reddish brown, strongly scented bark.
Leaves: Alternate, compound, with long petioles; leaflets typically three in number but sometimes five, varying considerably in size and shape, exhibiting a musky odor when crushed; terminal leaflet elliptic to oval, margins entire to sometimes crenate or serrate; lateral leaflets ovate to lanceolate, typically inequilateral on either side of the central vein.
Flowers: Greenish white, borne in a widely branched panicle near the end of the branchlets.
Fruit: A flattened, winged, samara; samaras borne at the ends of branches in rounded clusters up to about 3 cm in diameter.
Distinguishing Marks: Most easily recognized by alternate, trifoliolate leaves with long petioles; similar to bladdernut (*Staphylea trifolia*) but having alternate rather than opposite leaves.
Distribution: Bluffs and rich woodlands across northern Florida, southward to about Orange County.

Prickly Ash or Toothache Tree
Zanthoxylum americanum Mill.

Form: Generally a deciduous shrub, rarely a small, slender tree to a maximum of about 10 m in height; branches with sharp thorns.
Leaves: Alternate, pinnately compound, 15 - 20 cm in overall length, rachis bearing sharp prickles; leaflets numbering 5 - 11, pubescent on their lower surfaces, ovate to oval, 1.5 - 6 cm long, 1.5 - 2 cm wide, margins entire to crenate.

Flowers: Borne in small, axillary clusters, petals green with red tips.

Distinguishing Marks: The leaves and thorns are similar to those of *Z. clava-herculis,* pictured on p. 283, the present species may be distinguished from the latter plant by having thorns primarily in pairs at nodes along the stem rather than scattered between the stem nodes.

Distribution: Mostly a tree of more northern climes; known in Florida only from Gadsden and Jackson counties.

Wafer Ash
Ptelea trifoliata

Plate 70

Prickly Ash or Hercules'-Club

Zanthoxylum clava-herculis L. **Plate 71**

Form: Deciduous shrub or tree to about 17 m in height with a short trunk and rounded crown.

Leaves: Alternate, deciduous, pinnately compound, 10 - 30 cm in overall length, rachis with sharp prickles; leaflets commonly numbering seven to nine, but sometimes numbering to nearly 20, broadly lanceolate, typically inequilateral on either side of the central vein, dark green above, glabrous, 2.5 - 7 cm long, margins crenate.

Flowers: Greenish yellow and borne in long clusters at the ends of branches.

Distinguishing Marks: Distinguished from *Z. americanum* by having prickles mostly between stem nodes rather than in pairs at stem nodes.

Distribution: Hammocks, wet woods, sand dunes, shell middens, usually near the coast; throughout northern Florida, southward to about Hendry and Palm Beach counties.

Biscayne Prickly Ash
Zanthoxylum coriaceum A. Rich. in Sagra

Form: Evergreen shrub or tree to about 7 m in height, usually with sharp prickles on the branches.
Leaves: Alternate, pinnately compound, 6 - 20 cm in overall length; leaflets usually even-pinnate in two to eight pairs, leathery, obovate to elliptic, 2.5 - 6 cm long, 1.5 - 2.5 cm wide, margins entire, apices rounded.
Flowers: Yellow, tiny, borne in long, many-flowered clusters.
Distinguishing Marks: Distinguished as the only member of its genus in Florida with usually even-pinnate leaves.
Distribution: Coastal hammocks from about Brevard County southward.

Wild Lime
Zanthoxylum fagara (L.) Sarg.   **Plate 71**

Form: Evergreen shrub or tree to about 10 m in height with sharp spines along the twigs.
Leaves: Alternate, pinnately compound, with a conspicuously winged rachis; leaflets numbering seven to nine, obovate to ovate, 1 - 3 cm long, .5 - 1.5 cm wide, margins crenate on at least the upper half of the leaflet.
Flowers: Yellow-green, very small, appearing in spring.
Fruit: A dry, black, shiny seed in a brownish husk, appearing in summer and fall.
Distinguishing Marks: Distinguished from other members of its genus and most other species by the relatively small leaflets in conjunction with its winged petiole and rachis.
Distribution: Hammocks from about Hernando, Orange, and Brevard counties southward.

Yellow Heart
Zanthoxylum flavum Vahl

Form: Small, essentially evergreen tree to about 12 m in height with pale gray bark and spineless twigs.
Leaves: Alternate, compound, about 20 cm long; leaflets numbering five to nine, ovate, entire, 2.5 - 7.5 cm long, 1.2 - 3.7 cm wide, light green in color.
Flowers: Greenish white, appearing in June and July, borne in wide-branched clusters at the ends of branches.
Distinguishing Marks: Distinguished from other members of its genus by its spineless twigs.
Distribution: A rare, endangered tree in Florida known only from two sites in the lower Keys including single trees on both Bahia Honda and Marquesas Keys; the former tree, which is the state champion, is contained within the Bahia Honda State Recreation Area; the tree occurs more widely in the West Indies and the Bahama Islands.

Prickly Ash
Zanthoxylum clava-herculis

Wild Lime
Zanthoxylum fagara

Plate 71

Eastern Cottonwood

Populus deltoides Bartr. ex Marsh.   **Plate 72**

Form: Large deciduous tree to about 30 m or more in height, with roughly and deeply fur-rowed, grayish bark.
Leaves: Alternate, simple, stiffish, deltoid (or pyramid shaped), often copper colored when first unfolding, 5 - 15 cm long, 10 - 12 cm wide, veins prominent, margins toothed, bases truncate, petioles long and flattened.
Flowers: Borne in catkins, 5 - 7.5 cm long.
Fruit: A capsule, 8 - 12 mm long.
Distinguishing Marks: Distinguished from most other Florida trees by combination of grayish bark and deltoid leaves.
Distribution: Primarily in bottomlands and wet woodlands along the Apalachicola River drainage basin; sparsely southward in the western peninsula to about Hernando County.

Swamp Cottonwood

Populus heterophylla L.   **Plate 72**

Form: Large deciduous tree with dark, deeply fissured, reddish brown bark.
Leaves: Alternate, simple, 10 - 20 cm long, 7.5 - 15 cm wide, long-petioled, blades widest near the middle, somewhat stiff, with a small patch of pubescence at the point at which the leaf stalk meets the leaf blade, bases often cordate or heart shaped, petioles rounded.
Flowers: Male and female flowers borne in separate catkins.
Fruit: A capsule, 1 - 1.5 cm long.
Distinguishing Marks: Distinguished from eastern cottonwood (*P. deltoides*) by rounded or an-gled rather than truncate leaf bases, and rounded petioles.
Distribution: Primarily in bottomlands and wet woodlands along the Apalachicola River drainage system; sparsely distributed in the western panhandle, eastward to about Leon County.

Coastal Plain or Carolina Willow

Salix caroliniana Michx.   **Photo #130**

Form: Small deciduous tree to about 10 m in height, often leaning over water, appearing densely vegetated and bushy.
Leaves: Alternate, simple, lanceolate, variable in size to about 20 cm (typically 6 - 14 cm) long and 3.5 cm (typically 1 - 3 cm) wide, about 12 times as long as wide, margins finely toothed, lower surfaces whitish.
Flowers: Male flowers borne in attractive catkins near the ends of branches, each catkin green-ish yellow, 2 - 9 cm long, arising with the new leaves.
Fruit: A capsule, 4 - 6 mm long.
Distinguishing Marks: Leaves similar in general outline to those of *S. nigra,* pictured on p. 287, but distinguished from them by being strongly glaucous or grayish white beneath.
Distribution: Florida's most widely distributed willow; from about Walton County eastward and throughout the rest of the state; rare in the Keys.

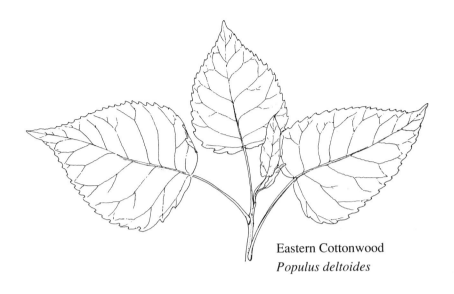

Eastern Cottonwood
Populus deltoides

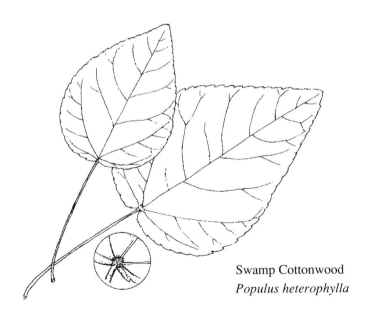

Swamp Cottonwood
Populus heterophylla

Plate 72

Heart-Leaved Willow

Salix eriocephala Michx. **Plate 73**

Form: Deciduous, often shrubby tree sometimes reaching 6 m or so in height in its Florida locations.
Leaves: Alternate, simple, lanceolate, dark green above, pale and silvery below, 8 - 15 cm long, 2 - 3 cm wide, margins finely toothed, petioles 5 - 8 mm long; stipules conspicuous, persistent, rounded, and leaflike.
Flowers: Appearing before the new leaves, borne in conspicuous woolly catkins.
Fruit: A capsule, 7 - 9 mm long.
Distinguishing Marks: Distinguished from other willows with similar leaves by having leaves with cordate or heart-shaped bases and comparatively large, rounded stipules.
Distribution: Wet areas, alluvial woods and along streambanks; found in Florida only in a very few locations in Gadsden and Jackson counties.

Florida Willow

Salix floridana Chapm. **Photo #131**

Form: Small deciduous tree to about 4 m in height.
Leaves: Alternate, simple, elliptic, usually widest near the middle, bases broadly rounded, normally 12 - 15 cm long, 4 - 5 cm wide, margins more nearly serrate.
Flowers: Male and female flowers borne in separate catkins.
Fruit: A capsule, 6 - 7 mm long.
Distinguishing Marks: Distinguished from other willows by being Florida's only tree-sized willow with elliptic to oblong rather than narrowly lanceolate leaves, and with more nearly serrate rather than finely toothed margins (particularly large-leaved specimens of the much more common *S. caroliniana* may potentially be confused with this species).
Distribution: Rare and local in wet areas along spring runs of Jefferson, Columbia, Levy, Lake, and perhaps other northeastern counties.

Black Willow

Salix nigra Marsh. **Plate 73**

Form: Medium-sized deciduous tree with brown, scaly bark, normally to about 20 m in height but potentially larger.
Leaves: Alternate, simple, narrowly lanceolate, 5 - 18 cm long, .5 - 3 cm wide, up to 12 times as long as wide, margins finely toothed.
Flowers: Male and female flowers borne in upright catkins on separate trees.
Fruit: A capsule, 3 - 8 mm long.
Distinguishing Marks: Leaves similar in overall outline to *S. eriocephala,* but lacking the cordate bases and enlarged stipules, distinguished from the similarly leaved coastal plain willow (*S. caroliniana*) by undersurfaces of leaves being green rather than glaucous.
Distribution: Found in the panhandle west of the Suwannee River, but most abundantly west of the Aucilla River; likely the only willow species in Escambia, Santa Rosa, and Okaloosa counties.

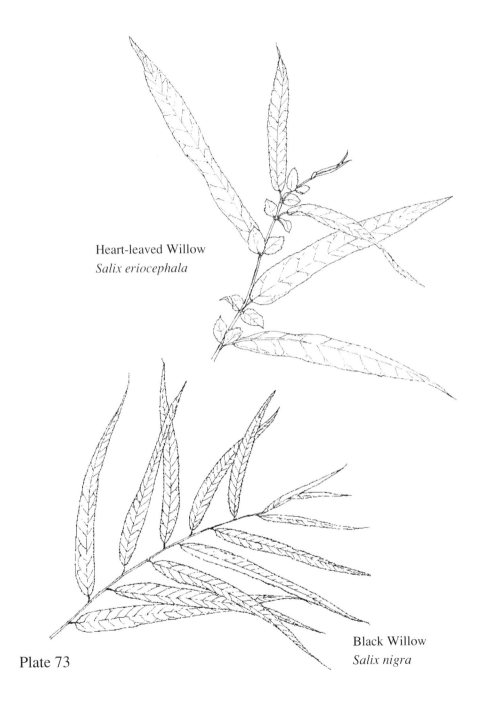

Heart-leaved Willow
Salix eriocephala

Black Willow
Salix nigra

Plate 73

Florida Cupania

Cupania glabra Sw.   **Photo #132**

Form: Evergreen shrub or small tree to about 10 m in height, with smooth, splotchy, gray and brown, closely striated bark that is very similar to that of inkwood (*Exothea paniculata*).

Leaves: Alternate, compound; leaflets numbering 5 to 15, oblong with rounded tips and coarsely toothed margins, 6 - 18 cm long, 2.5 - 8 cm wide, dark shiny green above, typically borne upright along the rachis, thus each pair of leaflets forming the shape of a V.

Flowers: White, borne in long branched clusters and appearing in the fall.

Fruit: A three-lobed, leathery capsule, 1.2 - 2 cm long.

Distinguishing Marks: Distinguished from soapberry (*Sapindus saponaria*) by lacking a winged rachis, from both Mexican alvaradoa (*Alvaradoa amorphoides*) and bitterbush (*Picramnia pentandra*) by coarsely toothed leaflets.

Distribution: Rare in hammocks of the lower Keys; most common on Big Pine Key.

Varnish Leaf or Florida Hop Bush

Dodonaea viscosa (L.) Jacq.   **Photo #133**

Form: Low evergreen shrub or small tree to about 3 m in height, typically a shrub in the pinelands but a tree in hammocks; bark of mature trees gray and shaggy, exfoliating in strips.

Leaves: Alternate, simple, narrowly to widely obovate depending upon geographic location (see pp. 78-79), entire, 2.5 - 15 cm long, .5 - 4 cm wide, surfaces yellowish green and sticky, often with a scaly texture and appearing varnished.

Flowers: Yellowish green, borne in small clusters at the tips of leafy branches.

Fruit: A distinctive three-winged and three-locular capsule, .6 - 2.5 cm long.

Distinguishing Marks: Most easily recognized by leaf shape in conjunction with the three-winged (or occasionally four-winged) fruit.

Distribution: Hammocks and pinelands; from Hillsborough and Pinellas counties southward, most common in the southernmost peninsula and the Keys.

Inkwood

Exothea paniculata (Juss.) Radlk.   **Plate 74**

Form: Small or medium-sized evergreen tree to about 15 m in height.

Leaves: Alternate, compound; leaflets usually four in number (rarely six, typically two on younger plants), entire, 5 - 12.5 cm long, apices rounded or slightly notched, upper surfaces dark, shiny green.

Flowers: White, five-petaled, borne in terminal or axillary clusters, appearing January to April.

Fruit: Berrylike, fleshy, red, turning to purplish black, 8 - 12 mm in diameter, ripening in June and July.

Distinguishing Marks: Recognized as the only south Florida tree with pinnately compound leaves and only four leaflets.

Distribution: Hammocks and shell mounds; Volusia County southward along the east coast and throughout the southern peninsula and the Keys.

White Ironwood

Hypelate trifoliata Sw.   **Plate 74**

Form: Evergreen shrub or small tree to 13 m in height with smooth, reddish gray bark.
Leaves: Alternate, palmately compound; leaflets three in number, all arising from the same place on the leaf stalk, 3.5 - 5 cm long, 1.5 - 3.5 cm wide, shiny green above.
Flowers: Small, white, borne in few-flowered, axillary clusters, appearing April through July.
Fruit: A rounded, black, fleshy drupe, 8 - 12 mm in diameter.
Distinguishing Marks: Recognized as the only south Florida tree with palmately trifoliolate leaves, the crown leaves on large specimens are often difficult to distinguish because of their small size and may require binoculars.
Distribution: Rare in hammocks of Everglades National Park and the Keys.

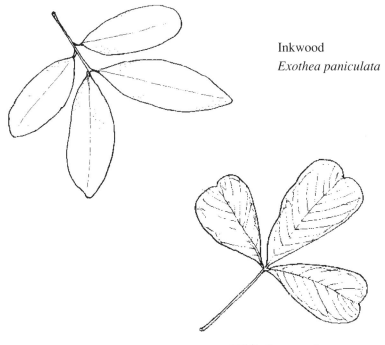

Inkwood
Exothea paniculata

White Ironwood
Hypelate trifoliata

Plate 74

Florida Soapberry

Sapindus marginatus Willd.

Form: Small deciduous tree to about 10 m in height with light brown bark.
Leaves: Alternate, pinnately compound, 15 - 32 cm in overall length; leaflets opposite or alternate, lanceolate, odd or even pinnate (both types appearing on a single tree), leaflets numbering 6 to 13, each leaflet 5 - 15 cm long, 2 - 7 cm wide, margins entire, both surfaces dark green.
Flowers: Creamy yellow, borne in loosely branched clusters at the branch tips.
Fruit: Irregularly rounded and drupelike, 1 - 2 cm in diameter.
Distinguishing Marks: Leaves similar in appearance to those of the tropical soapberry (*S. saponaria*), pictured below, but generally having more leaflets and lacking the latter's winged rachis; distinguished from all other north Florida trees with alternate, compound leaves by some leaves bearing alternate or subopposite leaflets.
Distribution: Coastal woodlands and hammocks; throughout the panhandle and northern Florida and south to Lee County.

Tropical Soapberry, Soapberry, Wingleaf Soapberry

Sapindus saponaria L. **Plate 75**

Form: Deciduous tree to about 15 m in height.
Leaves: Alternate, compound, with a conspicuously winged rachis; leaflets opposite or subopposite, six to eight and typically even in number, lanceolate, 8 - 18 cm long, margins entire.
Flowers: Tiny, white, borne in loosely branched clusters at the tips of branches, appearing from early summer into the fall.
Fruit: Rounded, brown, leathery, drupelike, 1 - 2 cm in diameter.
Distinguishing Marks: Distinguished from all other south Florida trees with compound leaves by combination of winged rachis and eight or less, typically even numbered and pointed, leaflets.
Distribution: Hammocks and coastal scrubby vegetation; Lee County southward and throughout the Keys.

Tropical Soapberry
Sapindus saponaria

Plate 75

Alachua Buckthorn

Bumelia anomala (Sarg.) R. B. Clark

Form: Small, tardily deciduous tree not usually exceeding 3 m in height with thorny, crooked branches typical of many *Bumelia* species; stems of shoots of the season with a definite pale gray or silvery hue.

Leaves: Alternate, simple, entire, elliptic, 5 - 6 cm long, 3 - 4 cm wide, upper surfaces dark green and glabrous, lower surfaces densely covered with silvery pubescence.

Distinguishing Marks: Leaves similar in shape to those of *B. lanuginosa,* pictured on p. 292, distinguished from it and other *Bumelia* by combination of young stems being glabrous and lower surfaces of leaves being silvery pubescent.

Distribution: Rare and restricted to several small populations in Alachua, Marion, and St. Johns counties.

Saffron Plum

Bumelia celastrina HBK.   **Plate 76**

Form: Small evergreen tree to about 6 m in height with slender, spreading branches.

Leaves: Alternate (but borne in fascicles and often appearing opposite), simple, slightly leathery, entire, oblanceolate, 1 - 4 cm long, .5 - 3 cm wide, quite variable in size from tree to tree, margins thick, lower surfaces pale, upper surfaces dull green.

Flowers: Small, white, with five petals, borne in clusters.

Fruit: Black, 10 - 25 mm long, sweet, edible.

Distinguishing Marks: Distinguished from the tough bumelia (*B. tenax*) by leaves being glabrous or only sparsely hairy rather than densely pubescent, from smooth bumelia (*B. reclinata*) by having leathery leaves and by occurring in coastal hammocks rather than uplands and pinelands; a variety of this species, *B. celastrina* var. *angustifolia,* is also reported and is distinguished by much smaller leaves and shorter thorns.

Distribution: Coastal hammocks and salt flats of the lower peninsula and the Keys.

Gum Bumelia

Bumelia lanuginosa (Michx.) Pers.   **Photo #134; Plate 76**

Form: Small deciduous tree, 6 - 12 m in height with thorny, crooked branches typical of many *Bumelia* species.

Leaves: Alternate but closely clustered, simple, entire, typically oblanceolate, 2 - 8 cm long (sometimes longer), 1 - 4 cm wide, upper surfaces pubescent at first, becoming dark green and shiny, lower surfaces densely pubescent with rusty- (or sometimes whitish-) colored hairs and feltlike to the touch, apices rounded.

Flowers: Small, borne in clusters in the leaf axils.

Fruit: A black, fleshy, berry, 6 - 15 mm in diameter.

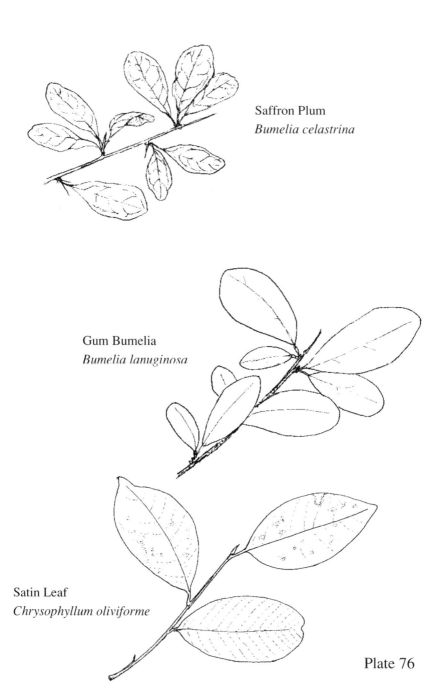

Saffron Plum
Bumelia celastrina

Gum Bumelia
Bumelia lanuginosa

Satin Leaf
Chrysophyllum oliviforme

Plate 76

Distinguishing Marks: Distinguished from other *Bumelia* species by combination of pubescent stems and copious covering of rust-brown pubescence on the lower surfaces of leaves.

Distribution: Dry, often sandy, upland woods throughout north Florida and sparingly southward to about Pinellas County.

Buckthorn
Bumelia lycioides (L.) Pers.

Form: Small, tardily deciduous tree, ordinarily to about 9 m in height but potentially reaching heights of 20 m, with thorny, crooked branches typical of many *Bumelia* species.

Leaves: Alternate, simple, entire, oblong-elliptic to elliptic, 8 - 15 cm long, 1 - 5 cm wide, upper surfaces bright green and glabrous.

Flowers: Small, bell shaped, borne in clusters.

Fruit: A black, egg-shaped berry, 1 - 2 cm long, about 1 cm in diameter.

Distinguishing Marks: Distinguished from other *Bumelia* species by having stems and both leaf surfaces glabrous in conjunction with longer leaves exceeding 8 cm in length.

Distribution: Known predominately from natural silt levees along the eastern bank of the Apalachicola River; considered rare in Florida.

Smooth Bumelia
Bumelia reclinata (Michx.) Vent. **Photo #135**

Form: Commonly a deciduous shrub but sometimes treelike in unburned pinelands of southern Florida, reaching heights of 5 m, branches often with thorns at the leaf axils, leafy shoots often thorn-tipped.

Leaves: Alternate (but sometimes crowded at the tips of leafy shoots and appearing opposite or fascicled), simple, entire, oblanceolate to spatulate, 1 - 6 cm long, .4 - 2 cm wide, leaf surfaces glabrous, apices rounded.

Fruit: A shiny, black, elongated berry, 5 - 8 mm long.

Distinguishing Marks: Distinguished from other *Bumelia* by stems and upper surfaces of leaves glabrous in combination with the longer leaves usually being much shorter than 7 cm.

Distribution: Bluffs, ravines, and riverbanks; northern and central peninsula, southward to at least Highlands Hammock State Park.

Tough Bumelia
Bumelia tenax (L.) Willd. **Photo #136**

Form: Evergreen shrub or small tree to about 8 m in height with reddish brown, fissured bark.

Leaves: Alternate, simple, oblanceolate, entire, 2 - 7 cm long .5 - 3 cm wide, lower surfaces covered with dense, silvery, golden, coppery or brownish pubescence, often contrasting sharply with the dark green upper surfaces.

Flowers: Small, white, borne in clusters at the leaf axils.

Fruit: A black berry, inversely egg shaped, 10 - 14 mm long.

Distinguishing Marks: Distinguished from other *Bumelia* with pubescent leaves by pubescence of lower surfaces of leaves being densely matted rather than just copious.

Distribution: Coastal dunes and interior scrub across northern Florida and southward to about the central peninsula; most common along the east coast, rather spottily distributed along the Gulf Coast.

Satin Leaf

Chrysophyllum oliviforme L.   **Photo #137; Plate 76**

Form: Small, handsome evergreen tree to about 9 m in height with reddish brown bark.

Leaves: Alternate, simple, oval, entire, 3 - 13 cm long, apices ending in abrupt points, upper surfaces dark green and smooth, lower surfaces covered by dense, velvety, copper-colored pubescence and contrasting sharply with upper surfaces.

Flowers: Tiny, white, with five petals.

Fruit: A one-seeded berry resembling an olive, to about 2 cm long and edible.

Distinguishing Marks: Not likely to be confused with any other Florida tree except, perhaps, the cultivated and closely related *C. cainito* which has larger, multiseeded fruits that are 5 - 8 cm in diameter.

Distribution: Hammocks of the Everglades and the Keys; formerly along the coast from about Brevard County southward but now mostly eliminated through poaching and urbanization.

Willow Bustic or Bustic

Dipholis salicifolia (L.) A. DC.   **Photo #138**

Form: Small evergreen tree to about 9 m in height; flowers and fruits arising in clusters along leafless sections of branches.

Leaves: Alternate, simple, lanceolate, entire, 7.5 - 13 cm long, tapering to a distinct petiole.

Flowers: Tubular, five-petaled, white.

Fruit: A black, globular to oblong berry, to about 7 mm long.

Distinguishing Marks: Most easily recognized by the flowers and fruit, when present, being borne on the older, leafless portions of the branches.

Distribution: Common in hammocks and the edges of pinelands; from Martin and Palm Beach counties southward on the east coast, Fakahatchee Strand State Preserve southward on the west coast, throughout the Keys.

Wild Dilly

Manilkara bahamensis (Baker) Lam & Meeuse   **Photo #139**

Form: Low, dense, salt-tolerant evergreen shrub or small tree to about 13 m in height.

Leaves: Alternate but crowded near the ends of branches, leathery, dull grayish green, simple, elliptic, entire, 5 - 10 cm long, lower surfaces covered with brownish pubescence, apices conspicuously notched.

Flowers: Yellowish, arising in drooping clusters in leaf axils.

Fruit: Brownish, globular, to about 4 cm in diameter, edible.

Distinguishing Marks: Most easily recognized by pale, grayish green leaves clustered near branch tips and brownish, rounded fruit.

Distribution: Common in hammocks of Cape Sable and the Keys.

Sapodilla

Manilkara zapota (L.) Royen   **Photo #140**

Form: Evergreen tree to about 15 m in height with dark brown, attractive, striated to deeply furrowed bark.

Leaves: Alternate, clustered near the tips of the branches, simple, elliptic, entire, 5 - 13 cm long, apices blunt pointed.

Flowers: White, drooping on long stalks, with six petals.

Fruit: Globular, light to dark brown, 5 - 10 cm in diameter, edible and very tasty, similar in appearance to fruit of wild dilly (*M. bahamensis*) but larger.

Distinguishing Marks: Most easily recognized by combination of leaves clustered near branch tips and tan-colored rounded fruit; distinguished from wild dilly by larger fruit and darker leaves.

Distribution: Cultivated; extreme south Florida and the Keys.

False Mastic

Mastichodendron foetidissimum (Jacq.) H. J. Lam   **Photo #141**

Form: Evergreen tree to about 25 m in height.

Leaves: Alternate, simple, elliptic, yellow-green in color, 5 - 20 cm long, margins entire and conspicuously wavy.

Flowers: Yellowish green, bell shaped, 6 - 7 mm wide, typically appearing about March to May.

Fruit: Bright yellow, olive shaped, about 2.5 cm long, appearing primarily in summer and fall.

Distinguishing Marks: Most easily recognized in its hammock habitat by its long-petioled, wavy-edged, yellowish green leaves.

Distribution: Coastal hammocks from about Volusia County southward and into the Keys; most common in the extreme southern part of its range.

Tree of Heaven or Ailanthus

Ailanthus altissima (Mill.) Swingle

Form: Small or medium-sized, irregularly branched deciduous tree to about 25 m in height.

Leaves: Alternate, pinnately compound, 15 - 90 cm long, with petioles 2 - 15 cm long; leaflets typically opposite or subopposite, to 41 in number, 2 - 15 cm long, borne on short stalks, generally lanceolate with variously shaped bases, margins with one or two (sometimes as many as five) prominently gland-tipped teeth located near the base, terminal leaflet often of a different shape than the lateral leaflets.

Flowers: Greenish yellow, borne in branched clusters in the axil of the uppermost leaf, appearing in summer.

Fruit: A winged samara.

Distinguishing Marks: The very long leaves and tooth pattern of the leaflets set this tree apart.

Distribution: Introduced and naturalized, vacant lots and other disturbed sites, uncommon and found mostly in the eastern panhandle.

Mexican Alvaradoa or Alvaradoa

Alvaradoa amorphoides Liebm.   **Plate 77**

Form: Small to medium-sized evergreen tree to about 15 m in height.

Leaves: Alternate, pinnately compound, 10 - 30 cm long; leaflets to 41 per leaf, elliptic, entire, 1 - 2 cm long, less than 1 cm wide, arranged alternately to oppositely along the rachis.

Flowers: Male and female flowers borne separately in long, hanging spikes, to 40 cm long, normally appearing in early winter from about November through December.

Distinguishing Marks: Distinguished from other south Florida trees by combination of compound leaves with small, elliptic leaflets and hairy, jointed twigs, likely to be confused only with the necklace pod (*Sophora tomentosa*), but distinguished from it by occurring primarily within, rather than on the edges of, hammocks.

Distribution: Rare in tropical hammocks of Dade County, not found in the Keys.

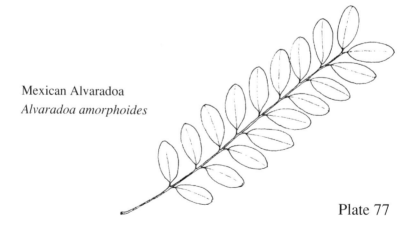

Mexican Alvaradoa
Alvaradoa amorphoides

Plate 77

Bitterbush

Picramnia pentandra Sw.   Photo #142

Form: Evergreen shrub, rarely reaching tree stature, potentially to about 6 m in height.
Leaves: Alternate, pinnately compound, 20 - 36 cm long, with or without terminal leaflets; leaflets elliptic to ovate, entire, numbering five to nine, arranged either alternately or oppositely along the rachis, 5 - 10 cm long, 2 - 5 cm wide, apices acuminate.
Flowers: Minute, green with a reddish tinge, less than 3 mm wide, borne in clusters, often appearing in summer from June to August, but appearing other times of the year as well, male and female flowers borne on separate trees.
Fruit: A fleshy berry, borne on slender red stalks, round to elliptic or oblong, 1 - 1.5 cm in diameter, turning from red to black at maturity.
Distinguishing Marks: Superficially similar to young specimens of the paradise tree (*Simarouba glauca*) but differing from it by usually having fewer than nine leaflets.
Distribution: Hammocks and sandy soils of Dade County.

Paradise Tree or Bitterwood

Simarouba glauca DC.

Form: Small, straight-trunked, sparsely branched tree to about 15 m in height.
Leaves: Alternate, pinnately compound, 15 - 30 cm long; leaflets dark and shiny green above, gray below, stiff, entire but often conspicuously revolute, elliptic to oval, 4 - 8 cm long, numbering 10 - 14 per leaf, borne both alternately and oppositely along the rachis.
Flowers: Small, radially symmetrical, yellow to cream colored, borne profusely in axillary or terminal clusters, appearing February to May.
Fruit: An oval drupe, 2 - 2.5 cm long, turning from red to purple to black upon maturing, often numbering as many as five on one fruit stalk, typically arising in early summer.
Distinguishing Marks: Distinctive and not easily confused with any other south Florida tree, young specimens superficially similar to bitterbush (*Picramnia pentandra*) but differing by generally having more than ten leaflets per leaf.
Distribution: Coastal hammocks; from Cape Canaveral southward on the east coast, more common from Martin County southward and into the Keys.

Potato Tree or Mullein Nightshade

Solanum erianthum D.Don   Plate 78

Form: Evergreen shrub or small tree to 5 m in height with thin, warty bark and densely pubescent branches.
Leaves: Alternate, simple, entire, oval to elliptic, light green, 10 - 30 cm long, 4 - 14 cm wide, both surfaces pubescent (the lower copiously so), margins often wavy.
Flowers: Borne in terminal clusters, star shaped with five white petals encircling showy, bright yellow pollen sacs.

Fruit: Juicy, rounded, yellow, 1 - 2 cm in diameter.

Distinguishing Marks: Easily distinguished by pale-colored, relatively large leaves that are woolly to the touch and copiously covered with star-shaped hairs which require magnification to see clearly; the closely related canker-berry (*S. bahamense*) may occasionally approach tree stature but may be distinguished from the present species by having leaf surfaces that lack the woolly pubescence and are rough to the touch, and by having blue rather than white flower petals.

Distribution: Thickets, waste places, edges of hammocks; from Brevard County southward on the east coast, Hillsborough County southward on the west coast, throughout the Keys.

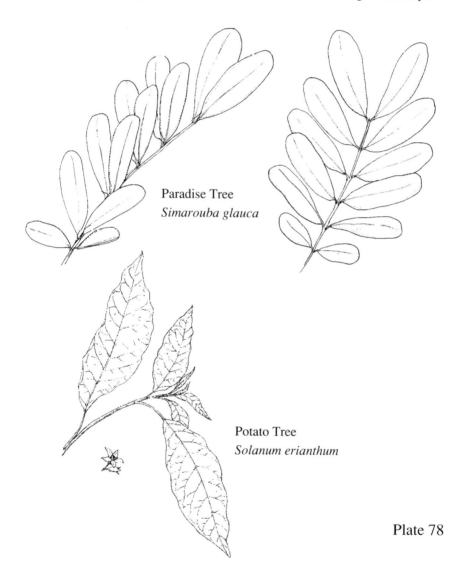

Paradise Tree
Simarouba glauca

Potato Tree
Solanum erianthum

Plate 78

Bladdernut

Staphylea trifolia L.

Form: Typically a deciduous shrub but sometimes reaching the stature of a small tree to about 8 m in height.
Leaves: Opposite, compound; leaflets three in number, elliptic, 3 - 10 cm long, 2 - 5 cm wide, margins serrate.
Flowers: Showy, creamy white, bell shaped, borne in drooping clusters that are 5 - 10 cm long.
Fruit: Three-parted, inflated, and bladderlike, similar in appearance to a Japanese lantern, 3 - 6 cm long.
Distinguishing Marks: Leaves similar to those of wafer ash (*Ptelea trifoliata*) pictured on p. 281 but distinguished from them by being borne opposite rather than alternate along the branch.
Distribution: Floodplains and wooded slopes; uncommon and confined to rich woodlands along the upper Apalachicola River.

Chinese Parasol Tree or Varnish Tree

Firmiana simplex (L.) W. F. Wright   **Photo #144**

Form: Small or medium-sized deciduous tree to about 20 m in height with smooth, greenish to grayish bark and green twigs.
Leaves: Alternate, simple, palmately veined and lobed, 10 - 30 cm long, petioles 20 - 50 cm long, lobes three to five (rarely seven) in number, bases conspicuously cordate.
Flowers: With reflexed petals, yellowish green turning orange or red, borne in long, upright, terminal clusters, each cluster 15 - 60 cm long (or sometimes even longer).
Distinguishing Marks: Easily recognized by large, distinctive leaves.
Distribution: Naturalized ornamental, sparsely and rarely distributed in mixed woodlands in northern Florida.

Carolina Silverbell or Little Silverbell

Halesia carolina L.   **Plate 79**

Form: Small deciduous tree usually not exceeding 12 m in height, bark tight with yellowish to whitish streaks.
Leaves: Alternate, simple, elliptic, entire or finely serrate, 7 - 18 cm long, 3 - 7 cm wide, apices acuminate.
Flowers: White, bell shaped, 1 - 1.5 cm long.
Fruit: Four-winged, 2 - 4 cm long, less than 1.5 cm wide.
Distinguishing Marks: Distinguished from two-winged silverbell (*H. diptera*) by four-winged fruit and more narrowly elliptic leaves, from horse sugar (*Symplocos tinctoria*) by having stel-

late pubescence on the lower surfaces of leaves, from loblolly bay (*Gordonia lasianthus*) by differing habitat preference and by the latter's stiff, leathery leaves.

Distribution: Bluffs, hammocks, and floodplains; from the panhandle to the north-central peninsula.

Two-Winged Silverbell

Halesia diptera Ellis   **Plate 79**

Form: Small, attractive deciduous tree normally not exceeding 10 m in height.
Leaves: Alternate, simple, unevenly dentate, oval, 6 - 16 cm long, 4 - 10 cm wide, apices abruptly pinched to a point.
Flowers: White, bell shaped, divided nearly to the base, to about 1.5 cm long, hanging in loose, pendant clusters.
Fruit: With two large wings.
Distinguishing Marks: Distinguished from Carolina silverbell (*H. carolina*) by two-winged rather than four-winged fruit, typically wider leaves, and by the bark lacking the yellowish to whitish streaks characteristic of the latter species.
Distribution: Bluffs, hammocks, and floodplain woodlands; northern panhandle from about Escambia to Leon counties.

American Snowbell

Styrax americanum Lam.   **Photo #145; Plate 79**

Form: Deciduous shrub or small tree to about 5 m in height with thin, smooth, dark gray bark, typically displaying larger leaves at the tips of branches and smaller leaves proximally.
Leaves: Alternate, simple, elliptic to obovate, to about 8 cm long, 1 - 4 cm wide, margins very variable from entire to irregularly dentate, apices rounded or tipped with a short point.
Flowers: Normally borne individually in leaf axils, white, with petals typically recurved and spreading, stamens yellow and conspicuous.
Fruit: A pubescent capsule that resembles in shape the fruit of the hollies, 6 - 8 mm in diameter.
Distinguishing Marks: Distinguished from big leaf snowbell (*S. grandifolia*) by leaves not usually exceeding 8 cm in length and flowers borne individually.
Distribution: Wet places such as swamps, wet woods, edges of cypress ponds; throughout northern Florida southward to about Charlotte County on the west coast, Brevard County on the east coast.

Big Leaf Snowbell

Styrax grandifolia Ait.   **Plate 79**

Form: Deciduous shrub or small tree to about 12 m in height with thin, smooth, streaked, dark brown bark.

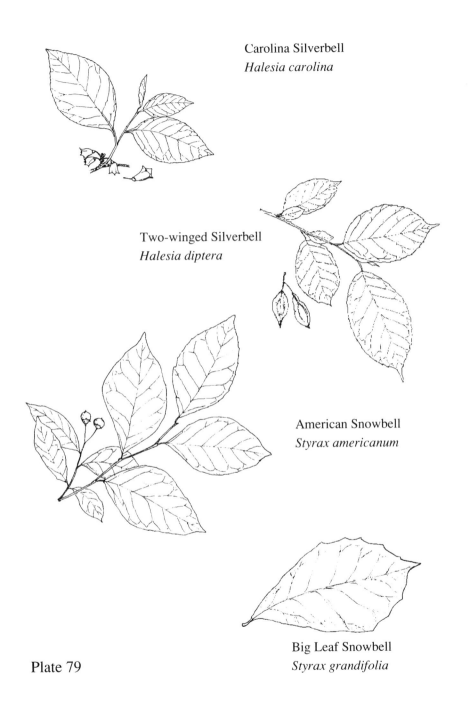

Carolina Silverbell
Halesia carolina

Two-winged Silverbell
Halesia diptera

American Snowbell
Styrax americanum

Big Leaf Snowbell
Styrax grandifolia

Plate 79

301

Leaves: Alternate, simple, oval to obovate, margins entire to irregularly dentate (especially toward the apices), 6 - 18 cm long, 4 - 15 cm wide.

Flowers: White, borne in racemes, petals often spreading to occasionally recurved.

Fruit: An oval capsule, 7 - 9 mm in diameter.

Distinguishing Marks: Distinguished from American snowbell (*S. americanum*) by leaves usually longer than 8 cm, and by larger flowers borne in racemes.

Distribution: Bluffs, ravines, and well-drained woods; northern panhandle and central ridge of northern Florida southward to about Alachua County.

SURIANACEAE

Bay Cedar

Suriana maritima L.

Photo #146

Form: Evergreen shrub or small tree to about 5 m in height.

Leaves: Alternate but densely crowded near the tips of branches and branchlets, linear, simple, entire, 2.5 - 6 cm long, apices rounded.

Flowers: Yellow, borne solitary or in short terminal clusters among the leaves, 1 - 1.5 cm across when open, sepals 6 - 10 mm long, petals 7 - 10 mm long.

Fruit: Dry and nutlike, to about 4 mm long.

Distinguishing Marks: Most easily recognized by dense clusters of linear, gray-green leaves.

Distribution: Beaches and dunes; coastal strand from about Brevard and Pinellas counties southward including the Keys.

SYMPLOCACEAE

Horse Sugar or Sweetleaf

Symplocos tinctoria (L.) L'Her.

Photo #147

Form: Deciduous understory shrub or small tree to about 10 m in height.

Leaves: Alternate, simple, elliptic, leathery, 5 - 15 cm long, 2 - 6 cm wide, sometimes deformed with whitish, tumorlike growths, upper surfaces dark shiny green, margins mostly entire but sometimes with small teeth.

Flowers: Yellow, fragrant, borne in rounded clusters along the leafless portions of older twigs.

Fruit: A green drupe to about 1 cm in length.

Distinguishing Marks: Distinguished from the little silverbell (*Halesia carolina*) by being evergreen and by lacking the stellate pubescence of the latter species, from loblolly bay (*Gordonia lasianthus*) by preferred habitat and by the latter's crenate to serrate leaf margins.

Distribution: Often in sandhills and flatwoods, but also ravines, floodplains, and bottomlands; panhandle and northern Florida southward to about Alachua County.

Tamarisk, French Tamarisk, Salt-Cedar

Tamarix gallica L.

Form: Spreading, deciduous shrub or small tree to about 10 m in height.
Leaves: Alternate, minute, scalelike, simple, entire.
Flowers: Tiny, pink, borne in compact racemes at the tips of leafy branches.
Fruit: A dry capsule, 4 - 5 mm long.
Distinguishing Marks: Distinguished as the only tree along Franklin County beaches with such leaves.
Distribution: Beaches and dry coastal areas; known in Florida from Franklin County and perhaps the northeast Florida coast.

Loblolly Bay

Gordonia lasianthus (L.) Ellis   **Photo #148**

Form: Small or medium-sized, handsome evergreen tree to about 20 m in height.
Leaves: Alternate, simple, oblong to elliptic, leathery, dark green above, 8 - 16 cm long, 3 - 5 cm wide, with distinctive crenate to serrate edges.
Flowers: White, rotate, with five petals encircling numerous, showy, yellow stamens, appearing in May and June.
Fruit: An ovoid capsule that splits open at maturity.
Distinguishing Marks: Most easily distinguished from the sweetbay magnolia (*Magnolia virginiana*) by the latter's leaves having silvery-white undersurfaces, from swamp bay (*Persea palustris*) by the crenate to toothed leaf margins.
Distribution: Swamps, bogs, edges of wet flatwoods; all of northern Florida south to about Highlands, Okeechobee, and Martin counties.

Silky-Camellia

Stewartia malacodendron L.   **Plate 80**

Form: Usually a deciduous shrub with several stems, sometimes a small tree to about 6 m in height.
Leaves: Alternate, elliptic, growing in two ranks along the stems but sometimes appearing clustered near the tip of branchlets, 5 - 10 cm long, 3 - 5 cm wide, margins minutely serrate and ciliate.
Flowers: Rotate, showy, to about 8 cm wide when fully open, with five white petals that are somewhat crinkly at their edges and encircle a mass of purple filaments, appearing in April and May.
Fruit: A capsule to about 3 cm long.
Distinguishing Marks: Most easily distinguished by the attractive flowers, the silky white pu-

bescence along the central vein on the lower surface of young leaves, and the tiny hairs that line the minutely serrated leaf edges.

Distribution: Restricted in Florida to ravine slopes in the panhandle; listed as threatened in Florida.

Joewood
Jacquinia keyensis Mez.   **Photo #149; Plate 80**

Form: Evergreen shrub or small tree to about 6 m in height, with thin, blue-gray bark.
Leaves: Alternate on lower portion of branches, clustered in multileaved whorls near the ends of branches, simple, thick, leathery, 2 - 8 cm long, 1.5 - 3.5 cm wide, margins entire and often rolled under, upper surfaces yellowish green, apices often notched.
Flowers: White to pale yellow, funnel shaped, fragrant.
Fruit: A rounded, yellow to orange-red berry, 8 - 10 mm in diameter.
Distinguishing Marks: The small brown spots on the light tan stem help to differentiate this species from others with notched, thickish leaves.
Distribution: Coastal scrub of the Florida Keys and extreme tip of the southern peninsula.

American Basswood or Linden
Tilia americana L.   **Plate 80**

Form: Medium or large deciduous tree with brownish to grayish bark, to about 25 m in height.
Leaves: Alternate, two-ranked, simple, ovate, margins serrate, 5 - 20 cm long, 5 - 12 cm wide, bases heart shaped and often unequal on either side of the central leaf axis.
Flowers: Borne in long-stalked clusters subtended at the leaf axil by a long, linear, leaflike bract that has the appearance of a leaf and is quite distinctive.
Fruit: Dry, hard, reddish, round, 5 - 7 mm in diameter.
Distinguishing Marks: Leaves similar to unlobed leaves of the mulberries (*Morus* spp.) but distinguished by lacking the latter's milky sap.
Distribution: Mixed moist woodlands throughout the panhandle and north Florida, south to about Polk and Osceola counties.

Sugarberry or Hackberry
Celtis laevigata Willd.   **Plate 81**

Form: Medium-sized deciduous tree to about 28 m in height with smooth, gray bark that often exhibits irregular, prominent, corky outgrowths.
Leaves: Alternate, simple, 3 - 15 cm long, lanceolate, 1.5 - 6 cm wide, margins entire or

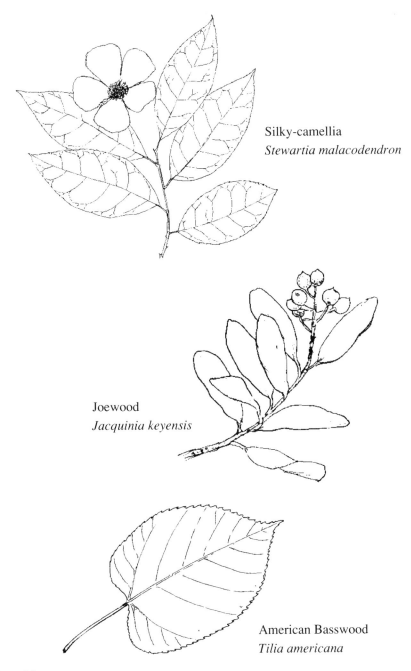

Silky-camellia
Stewartia malacodendron

Joewood
Jacquinia keyensis

American Basswood
Tilia americana

Plate 80

toothed, teeth sometimes few and irregularly spaced, sometimes regular and conspicuous except near the base, blades unequal in width on either side of the central axis, upper surfaces of mature leaves smooth, those of young leaves often rough to the touch, apices tapering and long pointed.

Flowers: Tiny, borne singly or in small clusters in the leaf axils.

Fruit: Fleshy, rounded, orange to red, typically 6 - 8 mm in diameter, sometimes a little smaller, normally appearing in the fall.

Distinguishing Marks: Most easily recognized by narrow, long-tapering leaves and bark with corky outgrowths.

Distribution: Found in a wide variety of habitats; throughout the state except the Keys.

Georgia or Dwarf Hackberry
Celtis tenuifolia Nutt.   **Plate 81**

Form: Normally a scraggly deciduous shrub, sometimes to 10 m in height.

Leaves: Alternate, entire or serrate, triangle shaped, 2.5 - 7 cm long, 1.5 - 4.5 cm wide, widest near the base, bases rounded or truncate, upper surfaces rough to the touch; the two lowermost lateral leaf veins arising with, and being nearly equal in size with, the central leaf vein.

Flowers: Tiny, borne singly or in small clusters along the branchlets.

Fruit: Orange to reddish, globular, 5 - 8 mm in diameter.

Distinguishing Marks: Leaves similar in overall outline to sugarberry (*C. laevigata*), distinguished from it by being darker, dull green above, by being less tapered toward the apex, and by having leaf surfaces that are slightly rough to the touch.

Distribution: Sporadic in northern Florida, predominately along the upper Apalachicola River and the northern portions of Walton and Holmes counties.

Planer Tree or Water Elm
Planera aquatica Walt. ex Gmel.   **Plate 82**

Form: Small deciduous tree to about 18 m in height, trunk often short with scaly and flaky, grayish brown outer bark and reddish inner bark, branches spreading.

Leaves: Alternate, simple, typically ovate, two-ranked along the branch, 2 - 8.5 cm long, 2 - 4 cm wide, upper surfaces dark green, bases rounded, apices tapering to a point, margins serrate.

Flowers: Small, borne in dense clusters at the leaf axils.

Fruit: A soft, burrlike drupe, to 1 cm in diameter.

Distinguishing Marks: Most easily recognized by combination of two-ranked and serrated leaves, scaly bark, and wetland habitat; potentially confused with eastern hophornbeam (*Ostrya virginiana*) and ironwood (*Carpinus caroliniana*) but distinguished from them by lacking doubly serrated leaf margins.

Distribution: Riverbanks, backwaters, and oxbow lakes in a wide band across the northernmost border of the state, extending southward down the courses of major rivers such as the Choctawhatchee, Apalachicola, and Suwannee.

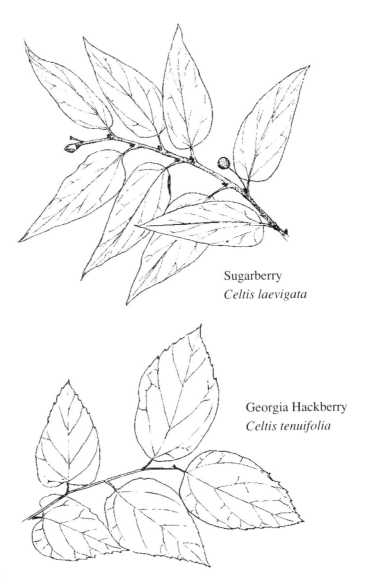

Sugarberry
Celtis laevigata

Georgia Hackberry
Celtis tenuifolia

Plate 81

West Indian Trema

Trema lamarckiana (R. & S.) Blume **Plate 83**

Form: Small, shrublike evergreen tree to about 6 m in height.
Leaves: Alternate, simple, two-ranked, lanceolate, usually not exceeding 5 cm in length, hairy and rough to the touch on both surfaces, margins finely toothed and turned under.

Flowers: Small and greenish.

Fruit: Pink, rounded, crowded around the leaf axils, measuring about 3 mm in diameter.

Distinguishing Marks: Distinguished from *T. micrantha* by smaller leaves that are rough to the touch on both the upper and lower surfaces.

Distribution: Uncommon at the southernmost tip of the peninsula, more plentiful in the Keys.

Florida Trema

Trema micrantha (L.) Blume   Plate 83

Form: Small to medium-sized evergreen tree to about 10 m in height, with smooth, light brown bark and long, horizontally spreading branches.

Leaves: Alternate, simple, broadly lanceolate, 7 - 15 cm long, two-ranked, margins finely toothed.

Flowers: Small, greenish yellow to whitish, borne in the leaf axils.

Fruit: Round, orange, 2 - 3 mm in diameter.

Distinguishing Marks: Most easily distinguished from other south Florida species by serrated, two-ranked leaves in conjunction with flowers and fruits, which are evident during much of the year; distinguished from *T. lamarckiana* by leaves being larger and rough to the touch only on the upper surfaces.

Distribution: From about the Broward/Palm Beach County line southward on the east coast, Pinellas County (where it is rare) southward on the west coast, throughout the Keys.

Winged or Cork Elm

Ulmus alata Michx.   Photo #150

Form: Medium-sized deciduous tree to about 20 m in height; twigs often with corky wings.

Leaves: Alternate, simple, lanceolate, two-ranked, relatively small, typically 6 - 10 cm long (but sometimes much shorter), 1 - 4 cm wide, upper surface dark green but turning yellow in the fall, margins doubly serrate.

Flowers: Tiny and bell shaped, borne in clusters.

Fruit: A dry, hairy samara, to about 1 cm long.

Distinguishing Marks: Distinguished from American and slippery elms (*U. americana, U. rubra*) by characteristic lanceolate leaves with acute tips rather than oval or elliptic leaves with acuminate tips and by conspicuous, corky, winged appendages that run along the edges of at least some of the twigs and branchlets.

Distribution: Floodplains, slopes, and well-drained woodlands across much of northwestern Florida to just west of the Atlantic coastal zone and south to about Lake and Orange counties.

American Elm

Ulmus americana L.   Plate 82

Form: Medium-sized or large deciduous tree to at least 40 m in height.

Leaves: Alternate, simple, two-ranked, oval in shape, 2 - 15 cm long, 1 - 10 cm wide, margins doubly serrate, bases asymmetrical, blades unequal on either side of the central vein, apices acuminate.

Flowers: Small, clustered in long, drooping catkins.

Fruit: A flattened samara, about 1 cm long.

Distinguishing Marks: Distinguished from the similar slippery elm (*U. rubra*) by leaf upper surfaces and twigs generally smooth to only slightly rough to the touch (except on leaves of root sprouts), and by buds being chestnut brown, nearly glabrous, and pointed rather than purplish-brown, prominently redhaired, and blunt.

Distribution: Throughout northern Florida and southward to about Lake Okeechobee.

Cedar Elm

Ulmus crassifolia Nutt.   **Photo #152**

Form: Small or medium-sized deciduous tree to about 20 m in height, with scaly, cedarlike bark; some twigs on some trees with winged outgrowths similar to those of the winged elm (*U. alata*), pictured in Photo #150.

Leaves: Alternate, simple, doubly serrate, small, 1 - 8 cm long, 2 - 3 cm wide, two-ranked, with upper surfaces that feel like fine sandpaper, petioles 1 - 3 mm long.

Flowers: Small, borne in clusters.

Fruit: A hairy, winged samara about 1 cm long.

Distinguishing Marks: Distinguished from the winged elm by combination of overall shorter leaves, cedarlike bark, and upper surfaces of leaflets being generally scabrid as opposed to smooth.

Distribution: A rare tree in Florida; confined chiefly to the floodplain of the central portions of the Suwannee River but also reported from Gulf Hammock in Levy County; easily found along the trails at Suwannee River State Park where one small specimen is marked with a sign.

Slippery or Red Elm

Ulmus rubra Muhl.   **Plate 82**

Form: Medium-sized deciduous tree usually not exceeding about 25 m in height; new twigs rough to the touch.

Leaves: Alternate, simple, doubly serrate, 3 - 18 cm long, 4 - 8 cm wide, leaf bases asymmetrical, apices acuminate.

Flowers: Small, borne in clusters.

Fruit: A flattened samara, nearly rounded in outline, to about 2 cm wide.

Distinguishing Marks: Distinguished from the similar American elm (*U. americana*) by upper surfaces of leaves always harshly scabrid, by scabrid to mildly scabrid twigs, and by samara lacking hairs; from hophornbeam (*Ostrya virginiana*) by leaf bases typically being inequilateral and asymmetrical rather than equilateral and symmetrical.

Distribution: Of limited distribution in Florida; found along wooded bluffs and in calcareous woodlands only in the northern and western panhandle.

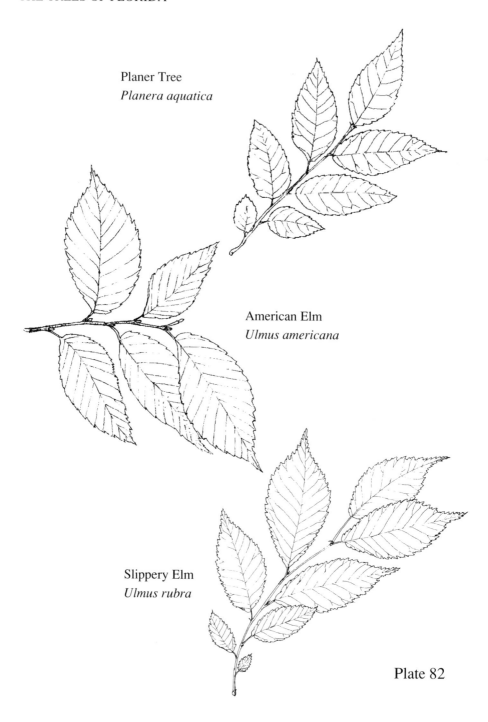

Planer Tree
Planera aquatica

American Elm
Ulmus americana

Slippery Elm
Ulmus rubra

Plate 82

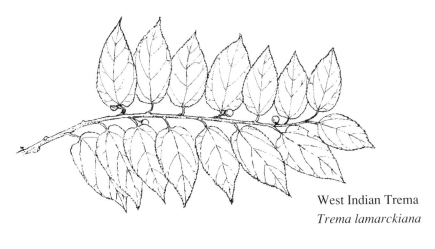

West Indian Trema
Trema lamarckiana

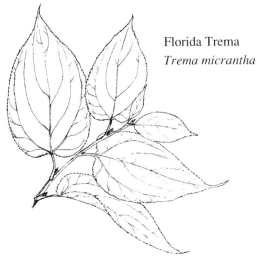

Florida Trema
Trema micrantha

Plate 83

VERBENACEAE

Fiddlewood

Citharexylum fruticosum L.   **Photo #153**

Form: Evergreen shrub or small, slender tree to about 12 m in height with smooth, light brown bark and square twigs.

Leaves: Opposite, simple, predominately elliptic to obovate but variable, leathery, thick, 5 - 17 cm long, 1 - 6 cm wide, upper surfaces shiny, yellow-green and pubescent, lower surfaces dull, margins entire (or rarely toothed on younger branchlets), petioles and midribs orange to pinkish, midribs especially so toward the leaf base.

Flowers: White, fragrant, tubular, borne in terminal or lateral racemes to about 30 cm in length, each flower to about 1.2 cm long.

311

Fruit: A rounded, red-brown drupe, 8 - 12 mm in diameter.

Distinguishing Marks: Most easily recognized by opposite, shiny leaves with orange midribs, borne on square twigs.

Distribution: Hammocks and pinelands from Brevard and Manatee counties southward and throughout the Keys.

Golden Dewdrop, Pigeon Berry, Sky Flower
Duranta repens L.

Form: Evergreen shrub or small tree, sometimes vinelike, to about 6 m in height with light gray bark.

Leaves: Opposite, simple, ovate to elliptic, 2.5 - 7.5 cm long, upper and lower surfaces dull light green, apices short pointed, margins entire or serrate.

Flowers: Tubular, light blue to purple to white with five petals, to about 1.3 cm across, borne in terminal or lateral racemes to 15 cm long.

Fruit: A rounded yellow drupe from which the plant takes its common name, to about 1.3 cm in diameter.

Distinguishing Marks: The bright yellow fruit and blue to purple flowers, which may appear on the tree at the same time, are distinctive.

Distribution: Purportedly native to the Keys but more likely an introduced ornamental; available from commercial nurseries and used as a landscape plant primarily in southern Florida but also further north.

ZYGOPHYLLACEAE
Lignum Vitae, Holywood, Tree of Life
Guaiacum sanctum L.   **Photo #151**

Form: Short, essentially evergreen tree to about 10 m in height with chalky white bark and a gnarled trunk; twigs light gray and enlarged at the nodes.

Leaves: Opposite, pinnately compound; leaflets in three to four pairs, the lower pair being largest, dark green, 2.5 - 3 cm long, less than 2 cm wide, inequilateral on either side of the central vein (particularly toward the leaf base), apices tipped with a small point, each pair of leaflets sometimes folding together during the hottest part of the day.

Flowers: Radially symmetrical with five blue petals, borne in clusters.

Fruit: A bright, orange-yellow capsule that splits open to expose dark black seeds.

Distinguishing Marks: Most easily recognized by its even-compound leaves with small leaflets, and by each leaflet bearing a small tooth at the apex.

Distribution: Found only in tropical hammocks of the Keys, particularly on Lignumvitae Key State Botanical Site; once somewhat more common than today but now found in limited numbers and considered endangered in the state.

APPENDIX: WHERE TO FIND TREES

Floridians are blessed with an outstanding assortment of preserved natural and seminatural areas, many of which provide abundant opportunity for studying the Sunshine State's native flora. A number of these locations are especially attractive to tree enthusiasts. Following is a brief list of some of the more important of Florida's parks, forests, refuges, and preserved natural areas. It should be noted that the following list is not exhaustive and is intended to serve only as a beginning point for further exploration.

State Parks

Florida's park system encompasses over 100 installations with a variety of outdoor recreation opportunities. While most of these parks preserve at least some small part of the state's natural environment, the following 11 should be on the trip list for anyone interested in learning about Florida's trees. For further information about these or any of Florida's parks, write to the Department of Natural Resources, Division of Recreation and Parks, 3900 Commonwealth Blvd., Tallahassee, FL 32399-3000.

Ponce de Leon Springs State Recreation Area. This small park is located just off U.S. Highway 90, near the little town of Ponce de Leon in the heart of the panhandle. A short but interesting nature trail passes through the park. Part of the path follows alongside a spring run and provides a good location for studying many of the panhandle's trees. Look for mountain laurel in the lawn adjacent to the parking lot.

Fred Gannon/Rocky Bayou State Recreation Area. Fred Gannon is on the north side of Choctawhatchee Bay, near Niceville in the panhandle. A very nice nature trail passes though natural sand pine scrub and offers plenty of opportunity to study northwest Florida's coastal plant community. A variety of tree species may be found on the trail including fringe tree, chinquapin, Chapman oak, and sourwood.

Florida Caverns State Park. One of the panhandle's most important plant preserves, this park is located just north of Marianna on Florida Highway 167. Several outstanding nature trails wind through the park and offer plenty of opportunity to study the plethora of tree species that thrive on the rich, calcareous soil that overlies the subsurface limestone. Look especially for silverbells, elms, wafer ash, ironwood, eastern hophornbeam, hickories, Carolina buckthorn, spruce pine, and several members of the rose family.

Torreya State Park. This park encompasses one of Florida's most unique and interesting plant communities. It is located north of Bristol on Florida 271, off Florida 12. A number of restricted species are found here including the torreya, Florida yew, Ashe magnolia, pyramid magnolia, and black walnut; others include sycamores, elms, beeches, hickories, tupelos, maples, and oaks.

Washington Oaks State Gardens. This park is located along Florida A1A near Marineland. A coastal hammock trail passes through a palm, hickory, oak, and magnolia woodland and provides a good place to study the flora of northeastern Florida.

Wekiwa Springs State Park. Most people visit here to swim or canoe. However, the hardwood hammock and lush edges of the spring run offer plenty of opportunity to study central Florida's trees. The park is located east of Apopka and north of Orlando. The park offers a well-done plant list that includes a separate accounting of the park's trees and shrubs. A copy can usually be obtained by asking at the entrance station. Several walking paths make the park very accessible.

Highlands Hammock State Park. Located just west of Sebring in the heart of Florida's white sand scrub, Highlands Hammock offers a variety of opportunities for the tree enthusiast. A well-designed system of walking trails passes through the center of the hammock and includes upland pathways as well as a boardwalk through the wetter areas. The park supports a number of huge live oaks, several citrus species, and an outstanding selection of the typical white sand scrub species including *Quercus inopina,* Florida scrub hickory, and sand pine. A well-done plant species list has been developed for the park but is only available by special request.

Hugh Taylor Birch State Recreation Area. This park is located in the center of Ft. Lauderdale. It was the former home of Hugh Taylor Birch, an early Florida pioneer, and has been planted with a number of subtropical species. Many of south Florida's tree species can be found along the roadway or walking paths. The park offers an outstanding brochure that lists all the plants in the park; copies may be obtained at the entrance station.

Collier-Seminole State Park. In some ways this park marks the beginning of Florida's subtropical plant community as one drives along the west coast south from Naples. It is best known for its dense tangle of mangroves but also offers an interesting trail through a hardwood hammock that supports a variety of south Florida trees. Once called Royal Palm Hammock, the park is also good place to see this latter species. It is located along the Tamiami Trail.

John Pennekamp Coral Reef State Park. This park is best known for its skin diving opportunities. Located on U.S. 1 in Key Largo, it is host to hundreds of snorkeling enthusiasts each year. However, it is also a good stop for those in search of the Keys' native flora. One trail leads through the mangrove fringe; the other through a typical upper Keys hammock. Ranger Joseph Nemec has established a small grove of representative tree species near the entrance to the latter trail which is especially useful to those just learning the identity of the state's tropical plants. The park also offers a well-done list of the native, naturalized, and exotic plants that appear within the park.

Long Key State Recreation Area. This is another excellent location for studying the trees of the Florida Keys. Located on U.S. 1 about halfway between Key Largo and Key West, it is easy to find. A nature trail leads through the hammock, mangroves, and coastal scrub transition zone. A variety of trees are abundant here, and the hammock portion of the trail even includes several specimens of gulf graytwig. The park also has prepared a list of the plant species included within the park, so be sure and request a copy.

Blackwater River State Forest

Florida supports several state forests. The Blackwater River State Forest, located in the western panhandle northeast of Pensacola and northwest of Crestview, along

Florida Highway 4, provides outstanding opportunities for studying the trees of the panhandle. Several of the state's more restricted oaks occur there, including the sand-post, blackjack, and Arkansas oaks, as well as such species as Florida anise, Atlantic white cedar, sour gum, and mountain laurel. The Sweetwater Trail is a good place to search for some of these species, as are the woodlands near the Krul Recreation Area campground. For more information, write to the forest headquarters at Route 1, Box 77, Milton, FL 32570.

National Parks, Forests, and Wildlife Refuges

Few people lack knowledge of Everglades National Park. For those attempting to learn Florida's subtropical flora, a visit to this outstanding natural resource is a must. A number of important hammocks are accessible off the main road to Flamingo and offer opportunities to see mahogany, gumbo limbo, strangler fig, shortleaf fig, tetrazygia, rough velvetseed, pigeon plum, willow bustic, long-stalked stopper, paurotis palm, and a variety of other species. Stops along the Tamiami Trail and the Loop Road also provide good locations to look for trees. A wide array of publications that focus on Everglades National Park are available. Many of these publications list or describe the plant species found there. Be sure and request a list of publications during your visit.

In addition to its one-of-a-kind national park, Florida also encompasses three national forests: the Apalachicola, Osceola, and Ocala. All offer a mosaic of native plant communities and are productive places to search for Florida's trees. The Apalachicola National Forest is located southwest of Tallahassee and offers many opportunities to study north Florida flatwoods, bay swamps, alluvial swamps, and high pinelands. The Osceola is located along Interstate 10 just north and west of Lake City. It is seldom visited except by hunters but offers the plant lover an outstanding assortment of native flora. The Ocala is located in the north central peninsula along Highways 19 and 40. It is a good location for seeing sand pine and is also known as a prime location for small populations of Atlantic white cedar and yellow anise. There is an excellent map for each of Florida's national forests. Information may be obtained by writing: National Forests in Florida, 325 John Knox Rd., Tallahassee, FL 32303.

Florida also encompasses several national wildlife refuges. Although all are outstanding natural resources, perhaps none are more enticing to the tree lover than Key Deer National Wildlife Refuge. Key Deer supports one of the few extensive pinelands in the Florida Keys as well as several hammocks and some very good examples of coastal scrub. Such species as Key byrsonima, mayten, jocwood, poisonwood, silver palm, Key thatch palm, long-stalked stopper, wild dilly, and pisonia are relatively easy to find. In addition, the refuge also preserves the state's finest population of tree cactus. The refuge's address is: P.O. Box 510, Big Pine Key, FL 33043.

Florida Native Plant Society

The Florida Native Plant Society (FNPS) is a statewide organization dedicated to the preservation, conservation, and restoration of Florida's native plants. The organization supports about two dozen local chapters which offer guided field trips to some of the locations mentioned above as well as to a variety of Florida's other special places. FNPS also publishes The Palmetto, a quarterly journal that focuses on Florida's native plants as well as activities of the association. Information about FNPS may be obtained by writing the association headquarters at: 2020 Red Gate Rd., Orlando, FL 32818.

REFERENCES

Alexander, Taylor R. 1968. *Acacia choriophylla,* A Tree New to Florida. *Quarterly Journal of the Florida Academy of Sciences,* 31(3) 197-198.

Anderson, Loran C. 1985. *Forestiera godfreyi* (Oleaceae), A New Species From Florida and South Carolina. *Sida,* 11:1-5.

Argus, George W. 1986. The Genus *Salix* (Salicaceae) in the Southeastern United States. *Systematic Botany Monographs,* 9:1-170.

Ashby, William Clark. 1964. A Note on Basswood Nomenclature. *Castanea,* 29(1) 109-116.

Barrett, Mary F. 1956. *Common Exotic Trees of South Florida.* Gainesville, FL: University of Florida Press.

Bell, C. Ritchie, and Brian J. Taylor. 1982. *Florida Wildflowers and Roadside Plants.* Chapel Hill, NC: Laurel Hill Press.

Bogle, A. Linn. 1974. The Genera of Nyctaginaceae in the Southeastern United States, *Journal of the Arnold Arboretum,* 55: 1-37.

Brizicky, George K. 1962. The Genera of Anacardiaceae in the Southeastern United States. *Journal of the Arnold Arboretum,* 43: 359-375.

Brizicky, George K. 1962. The Genera of Rutaceae in the Southeastern United States. *Journal of the Arnold Arboretum,* 43: 1-22.

Brizicky, George K. 1962. The Genera of Simaroubaceae and Burseraceae in the Southeastern United States. *Journal of the Arnold Arboretum,* 43: 173-186.

Brizicky, George K. 1963. The Genera of Sapindales in the Southeastern United States. *Journal of the Arnold Arboretum,* 44: 462-501.

Brizicky, George K. 1964. The Genera of Celastrales in the Southeastern United States. *Journal of the Arnold Arboretum,* 45: 206-234.

Brizicky, George K. 1964. The Genera of Rhamnaceae in the Southeastern United States. *Journal of the Arnold Arboretum,* 45: 439-463.

Brizicky, George K. 1966. The Genera of Sterculiaceae in the Southeastern United States. *Journal of the Arnold Arboretum,* 47: 60-74.

Carlton, Jedfrey M. 1975. *A Guide to Common Salt Marsh and Mangrove Vegetation.* Florida Marine Research Publications, No. 6. St. Petersburg, FL: Florida Department of Natural Resources.

Channell R. B., and C. E. Wood, Jr. 1962. The Leitneriaceae in the Southeastern United States. *Journal of the Arnold Arboretum,* 43: 435-438.

Clewell, Andre F. 1971. *The Vegetation of the Apalachicola National Forest: An Ecological Perspective.* Tallahassee: Unpublished manuscript prepared under contract 38-2249, U. S. Department of Agriculture, U. S. Forest Service.

Clewell, Andre F. 1985. *Guide to the Vascular Plants of the Florida Panhandle.* Tallahassee: University Presses of Florida, Florida State University Press.

Clewell, Andre F. 1986. *Natural Setting and Vegetation of the Florida Panhandle,* Mobile, AL: U.S. Army Corps of Engineers.

Collingswood, G. H., and Warren D. Brush. 1947. *Knowing Your Trees.* Washington DC: The American Forestry Association.

Craighead, Frank C., Sr. 1971. *The Trees of South Florida. Volume I. The Natural Environments and Their Succession.* Coral Gables, FL: University of Miami Press.

DePhilipps, R. 1969. Parasitism in Ximenia (Olacaceae). *Rhodora,* 71: 439-443.

Duncan, Wilbur H., and Marion B. Duncan. 1988. *Trees of the Southeastern United States.* Athens: The University of Georgia Press.

Elias, Thomas S. 1971. The Genera of Myricaceae in the Southeastern United States. *Journal of the Arnold Arboretum,* 52: 305-318.

Elias, Thomas S. 1974. The Genera of Mimosoideae (Leguminosae) in the Southeastern United States. *Journal of the Arnold Arboretum,* 55: 67-118.

Elias, Thomas S. 1980. *Trees of North America.* New York: Van Nostrand Reinhold Company.

Elias, Thomas S. 1987. *The Complete Trees of North America.* New York: Gramercy Publishing Co.

Ernst, Wallace R. 1963. The Genera of Hamamelidaceae and Platanaceae in the Southeastern United States. *Journal of the Arnold Arboretum,* 44: 193-210.

Eyde, Richard H. 1966. The Nyssaceae in the Southeastern United States. *Journal of the Arnold Arboretum,* 47: 117-125.

Ferguson, I. K. 1966. The Genera of Caprifoliaceae in the Southeastern United States. *Journal of the Arnold Arboretum,* 47: 33-59.

Ferguson, I. K. 1966. Notes on the Nomenclature of Cornus. *Journal of the Arnold Arboretum,* 47: 100-105.

Ferguson, I. K. 1966. The Cornaceae in the Southeastern United States. *Journal of the Arnold Arboretum,* 47: 106-116.

Fernald, M. L. 1950. *Gray's Manual of Botany. New York:* D. Van Nostrand Company.

Furlow, John J. 1990. The Genera of Betulaceae in the Southeastern United State. *Journal of the Arnold Arboretum,* 71: 1-67.

Godfrey, Robert K., and Jean W. Wooten. 1979. *Aquatic and Wetland Plants of Southeastern United States. Monocotyledons.* Athens: University of Georgia Press.

Godfrey, Robert K., and Jean W. Wooten. 1981. *Aquatic and Wetland Plants of Southeastern United States. Dicotyledons.* Athens: University of Georgia Press.

Godfrey, Robert K. 1988. *Trees, Shrubs, and Woody Vines of Northern Florida and Adjacent Georgia and Alabama.* Athens, GA: University of Georgia Press.

Graham, Shirley A., and C. E. Wood, Jr. 1965. The Genera of Polygonaceae in the Southeastern United States. *Journal of the Arnold Arboretum,* 46: 91-121.

Graham, Shirley A., 1966. The Genera of Araliaceae in the Southeastern United States. *Journal of the Arnold Arboretum,* 47: 126-136.

Green, C. H. 1939. *Trees of the South.* Chapel Hill: University of North Carolina Press.

Grimm, W. C. 1983. *The Illustrated Book of Trees.* Harrisburg, PA: Stackpole Books.

Hardin, James W. 1972. Studies of the Southeastern United States Flora. III. Magnoliaceae and Illiciaceae. *Journal of the Elisa Mitchell Society,* 87: 30-32.

Hawkes, Alex D. 1965. *Guide to Plants of the Everglades National Park.* Coral Gables, FL: Tropic Isle Publishers.

Hickok, L. G., and J. C. Anway. 1972. A Morphological and Chemical Analysis of Geographical Variation in Tilia L. of Eastern North America. *Brittonia,* 24: 2-8.

Howard, Richard A. 1958. A History of the Genus Coccoloba in Cultivation. *Baileya.* 6: 204-212.

Hume, H. H. 1953. *Hollies.* New York: Macmillan.

Isley, Duane. 1969. Legumes of the United States: I. Native Acacia. *Sida,* 3(6): 365-386.

Johnson, Ann F., and Warren G. Abrahamson. 1982. *Quercus inopina:* A Species to be Recognized from South-Central Florida. *Torreya,* 109(3): 392-395.

Kral, R. 1960. A Revision of Asimina and Deeringothamnus (Annonaceae). *Brittonia,* 12: 233-278.

Kurz, Herman, and Robert K. Godfrey. 1962. *Trees of Northern Florida.* Gainesville: University of Florida Press.

Lakela, Olga, and Richard P. Wunderlin. 1980. *Trees of Central Florida.* Miami: Banyan Books.

Leitman, Helen M., J. E. Sohm, and M. A. Franklin. 1984. *Wetland Hydrology and Tree Distribution of the Apalachicola River Flood Plain, Florida.* U. S. Department of the Interior, U. S. Geological Survey Water-Supply Paper 2196.

Lippincott, Carol. 1992. Return of the Native: Restoring Sargent's Cherry Palm on the Florida Keys. *Fairchild Tropical Garden Bulletin,* 47(1): 12-21.

Little, Elbert L., Jr., 1978. *Atlas of United States Trees.* Volume 5. Florida. Miscellaneous Publication No. 1361, Washington, DC: U. S. Department of Agriculture, Forest Service.

Little, Elbert L., Jr., 1980. *The Audubon Field Guide to North American Trees—Eastern Region.* New York: Alfred A. Knopf.

Little, Elbert. L., Jr., and F. W. Wadsworth. 1964. *Common Trees of Puerto Rico and the Virgin Islands.* Agricultural Handbook 249, Washington, DC: U.S. Department of Agriculture.

Little, Elbert L., Jr., R. O. Woodbury, and F. H. Wadsworth. 1974. *Trees of Puerto Rico and the Virgin Islands.* Vol. 2, Agriculture Handbook 449, Washington DC: U.S. Department of Agriculture.

Long, R. W., and Olga Lakela. 1976. *A Flora of Tropical Florida.* Miami: Banyan Books.

Mell, C. D. 1922. The Early Uses of Yaupon. 1922. *American Forestry,* 28: 531.

Miller, R. F. 1975. The Deciduous Magnolias of West Florida. *Rhodora,* 77: 64-75.

Myers, Ronald L., and John J. Ewel, eds. 1990. *Ecosystems of Florida.* Orlando: University of Central Florida Press.

Peattie, Donald C. 1950. *A Natural History of Trees of Eastern and Central North America.* Boston: Houghton Mifflin.

Pennington, Terrence D., Brian T. Styles, and D. A. H. Taylor. 1981. *Flora Neotropica: Meliaceae*. Monograph 28. New York: New York Botanical Garden.

Phipps, J. B. 1988. Crataegus (Maloideae, Rosaceae) of the Southeastern United States, I. Introduction and Series Aestivales. *Journal of the Arnold Arboretum*, 69: 401-431.

Platt, Rutherford. 1962. *American Trees: A Book of Discovery*. New York: Dodd, Mead.

Porter, Duncan M. 1972. The Genera of Zygophyllaceae in the Southeastern United States. *Journal of the Arnold Arboretum*, 53: 531-552.

Prance, Ghillean T. 1970. The Genera of Chrysobalanaceae in the Southeastern United States. *Journal of the Arnold Arboretum*, 51: 521-528.

Price, R. A. 1990. The Genera of Taxaceae in the Southeastern United States. *Journal of the Arnold Arboretum*, 71: 69-91.

Richens, R. H. 1983. *Elm*. Cambridge: Cambridge University Press.

Robertson, Kenneth R. 1972. The Malpighiaceae in the Southeastern United States. *Journal of the Arnold Arboretum*, 53: 101-112.

Robertson, Kenneth R. 1974. The Genera of Rosaceae in the Southeastern United States. *Journal of the Arnold Arboretum*, 55: 303-332.

Robertson, Kenneth R. 1974. The Genera of Rosaceae in the Southeastern United States. *Journal of the Arnold Arboretum*, 55: 611-662.

Robertson, Kenneth R. 1982. The Genera of Olacaceae in the Southeastern United States. *Journal of the Arnold Arboretum*, 63: 387-399.

Rudd, Velva E. 1969. A Synopsis of the Genus *Piscidia* (Leguminosae). *Phytologia*, 18(8): 473-499.

Scurlock, J. Paul. 1987. *Native Trees and Shrubs of the Florida Keys*. Pittsburg: Laurel Press.

Spongberg, Stephen. 1971. The Staphyleaceae in the Southeastern United States. *Journal of the Arnold Arboretum*, 52: 196-203.

Stearn, William T. 1971. Taxonomic and Nomenclatural Notes on Jamaican Gamopetalous Plants. *Journal of the Arnold Arboretum*, 52: 614-627.

Stern, William L., George K. Brizicky, and Francisco N. Tamolang. 1963. The Woods and Flora of the Florida Keys: Capparaceae. *Contributions from the United States National Herbarium*, 34(2): 25-43.

Tomlinson, P. B. 1980. *The Biology of Trees Native to Tropical Florida*. Allston, MA: Bound and Printed by the Harvard University Printing Office.

Tomlinson, P. B. 1986. *The Botany of Mangroves*. Cambridge: Cambridge University Press.

Walker, Laurence C. 1984. Trees. *An Introduction to Trees and Forest Ecology for the Amateur Naturalist*. Englewood Cliffs, NJ: Prentice-Hall, Inc.

Ward, Daniel B. 1967. *Acacia macracantha*, A Tree New to Florida and the United States. *Brittonia*, 19: 283-284.

Ward, Daniel B. 1978. *Rare and Endangered Biota of Florida. Volume 5*. Plants. Gainesville: University Presses of Florida.

Ward, Daniel B. and Andre F. Clewell. 1989. Atlantic White Cedar (*Chamaecyparis thyoides*) in the Southern States. *Florida Scientist.* 1(52): 8-47.

Webster, Grady L. 1967. The Genera of Euphorbiaceae in the Southeasten United States. *Journal of the Arnold Arboretum,* 48: 303-430.

Wilson, Kenneth A., 1960. The Genera of Myrtaceae in the Southeastern United States. *Journal of the Arnold Arboretum,* 41: 270-278.

Wilson, Kenneth A., and Carroll E. Wood. 1959. The Genera of Oleaceae in the Southeastern United States. *Journal of the Arnold Arboretum,* 40: 369-384.

Wolfe, Steven H., Jeffrey A. Reidenauer, and D. Bruce Means. 1988. *An Ecological Characterization of the Florida Panhandle.* FWS Biological Report 88(12), OCS Study MMS 88-0063, Washington, DC: Fish and Wildlife Service.

Wood, Carroll E., Jr. 1958. The Genera of the Woody Ranales in the Southeastern United States. *Journal of the Arnold Arboretum,* 39: 296-346.

Wood, Carroll E., Jr. 1961. The Genera of Ericaceae in the Southeastern United States. *Journal of the Arnold Arboretum,* 42: 10-80.

Wood, Carroll. E., Jr., and R. B. Channell. 1960. The Genera of the Ebenales in the Southeastern United States. *Journal of the Arnold Arboretum,* 41: 1-35.

Wunderlin, Richard P. 1982. *Guide to the Vascular Plants of Central Florida.* Tampa: University of South Florida.

Wunderlin, Richard P., and James E. Poppleton. 1977. The Florida Species of Ilex (Aquifoliaceae). *Florida Scientist,* 40: 7-21.

Wurdack, John J., and Robert Kral. 1982. The Genera of the Melastomataceae in the Southeastern United States. *Journal of the Arnold Arboretum,* 63: 429-439.

INDEX TO COMMON NAMES

Note: Illustrations are indicated by bold-face type. CP refers to the color plates between pages 142 and 143.

Acacia
  long spine 209, CP 73
  pine 93, 208, 209
  Small's 208, 209
  steel 209
  sweet 93, 208, 209, 210, CP 72
  twisted 209, 210, CP 74
Ailanthus 295
Alabama chokecherry 267
Alder
  black- 141, 143, 144, **147**
  hazel 89, 148, **149**
Allamanda 110
Alvaradoa 296
  Mexican 67, 220, 288, **296**
American hornbeam 89, 150
Anise
  Florida 20, 198, 199, CP 67
  star 20
  yellow 20, 199, CP 64
Apple
  balsam 39, 164, 273
  gopher 91
  hedge 50, 51, 52
  hog 261
  pitch 164
  pond 19, 138, CP 15
  prickly 82, 154
  seven-year 108, 165, 273, CP 124
  star 34
  sugar 20, 138, CP 16
Arrow-wood 114, 157, **159**, CP 33
Ash 74
  Biscayne prickly 62, 282
  Carolina 59, 250, **251**, 252
  green 59, **251**, 252
  northern prickly 62

pop 59, 250
prickly 62, 88, 280, 281, **283**
pumpkin 59, **251**, 252
red 252
stinking 62, 280
wafer 62, 280, **281**, 299
white 58, 250
Autograph tree 164, CP 42
Australian pine 7, 11, 160, **161**, CP 37
Avocado 22, 23, 205
Bahama lysiloma 216
Bahama nightshade 55
Bahama maiden bush 180
Basswood
  American 46, 304, **305**
Bastard indigo 212
Bay 37
  loblolly 18, 300, 302, 303, CP 148
  red 22, 205, 206, CP 69
  silk 22, 206, **207**
  swamp 18, 22, 206, 303, CP 70
Bayberry 69
  evergreen 234
  odorless 38, 69, 235, CP 98
  southern 69, 234
Beautyberry
  American 116
Beech
  American 83, 180, **181**
  blue 150
Beefwood 242
  Brazilian 160
  Cunningham's 11, 160
Birch
  paper 105
  river 88, 89, 148, **149**, 150
  West Indian 65, 154
  yellow 83
Bitterbush 67, 288, 297, CP 142
Bitterwood 297
Black calabash 107, 151
Black olive 166
Black torch 109, 180, 273, **275**, CP 126

Blackbead 96, 216, **217**, CP 78
Blackgum 29, 113, 166, 244, CP 101
Bladdernut 280, 299
   American 79
   Sierra 79
Blolly 80, 180, 242, CP 100
Bottlebrush
   showy 105
   weeping 105
Bougainvillea 80
Box elder 132, **133**
Boxwood
   false 57, 162, CP 40
   Florida 57, **163**, 164
Brazilian pepper 71, 136, **137**, 157, CP 14
Buckeye 77
   Ohio 77
   red 77, **197**, 198
Buckthorn 35, 293
   Alachua 35, 291
   Carolina 54, 258, CP 112
Buckwheat tree 28
Bullbay 223
Bumelia
   gum 35, 291, **292**, CP 134
   smooth 35, 291, 293, CP 135
   tough 35, 291, 293, CP 136
Burning bush 57, 161
Bustic 35, 294
   willow 35, 294, CP 138
Buttonbush 108, 273, 277, CP 125
Buttonwood 100, 166
   silver 166, CP 43
Byrsonima
   Key 61, 224
Cactus
   column 154
   tree 82, 154
Cajeput 105, 240, **241**
Camphor tree 22, 204, CP 66
Canker-berry 55, 298

Caper
   bay-leaved 40, 155, **156**
   Jamaica 40, 155
   limber 155
Capeweed 116
Cardinal spear 213
Cassava 178
Casuarina
   horsetail 11
   equisetum-leaved 11
Catalpa 151, CP 26
   southern 107, 151
Catawba tree 151
Catclaw **217**, 218
Catclaw blackbead 218
Caterpillar tree 151
Cedar
   Atlantic white 5, 120, CP 1
   bay 67, 302, CP 146
   eastern red 5, 120, CP 2
   salt- 41, 303
   stinking 3, 125
Cherokee bean 213
Cherry
   Alabama 267, **268**, 270
   black 174, 267, 270, CP 123
   Carolina laurel 269, CP 121
   ground 55
   West Indian 269, **271**
Chestnut
   American 84
   horse 77
Chinaberry 66, 228, CP 88
Chinese parasol tree 46, 299, CP 144
Chinese tallow tree 54, 178
Chinquapin 83, 180, **181**
Christmasberry 56
Cinnamon bark 24, 155, CP 31
Cockspur 80, **243**, 261
Coco-plum 91, 164, **165**
Colubrina
   coffee 55, 257
   Cuban 257
Confederate jasmine 110

Coral bean 96, 213, **215**
Corkwood 71, 72, 221, CP 81
Cotton
    upland 227, CP 85
    wild 227
Cottonwood
    eastern 44, 284, **285**
    swamp 44, 284, **285**
Crabapple
    southern 90, 266, CP 118
Crabwood 53, 177, **179**
Crape-jasmine 110
Crape myrtle 103, 221, CP 79
Cucumber tree 18, 222
Cupania, Florida 78, 288, CP 132
Cypress 29, 166
    bald- 4, 125, **126**, 127
    pond- 4, 125, **126**, 127
Cyrilla, swamp 28, 172, CP 47
Dahoon 25, 26, 27, 141, **142**, CP 20
Deer berry 32, **175**, 176
Devil's walking stick 111, 146, CP 24
Devilwood 59, 254
Dilly, wild 35, 294, 295, CP 139
Dog banana 19, 139, **140**
Dogwood
    alternate-leaved 112, 169
    flowering 112, 158, 170, **171**, CP 46
    pagoda 112, 169, 170, **171**
    stiff cornel 170, **171**
    swamp 112
Downy serviceberry 90, 141, 260, **261**
Eastern hophornbeam 89, **149**, 150, 306, 309
Eastern redbud 94, **211**, 212, CP 77
Eastern wahoo 57, 161
Egg fruit 34
Elder-berry 113, 156, CP 32
Elder
    box 76, 132, **133**
    common 156
    yellow 107, 151, CP 27

Elm
    American 48, 308, 309, **310**
    cedar 49, 309, CP 152
    cork 49, 308
    red 309
    slippery 48, 49, 308, 309, **310**
    water 49, 306
    winged 49, 308, 309, CP 150
    Wyche 48
Eugenia
    box leaf 238
    spiceberry 238, 240
False indigo **211**, 212
False mastic 295, CP 141
Falsebox 162
Farkleberry 174
Fever tree 108, 273, 277
Fiddlewood 116, 311, CP 153
Fig
    common 51, 231, CP 90
    shortleaf 51, 231, **232**, CP 91
    strangler 51, 231, 232, CP 92
Firebush 109, 277
Fishfuddle tree 95, 216
Fish poison tree 95
Flamboyant tree 213
Florida crossopetalum 57, 161
Florida fish poison tree 216
Florida Hop bush 288
Florida poison tree 135
Florida tetrazygia 228
Forget-me-not 115
Frangipani 110
Fringe tree 59, **247**, CP 107
Gallberry 26, 143
    large sweet 25, 26, 143, CP 22
Geiger tree 115, 152, **153**, CP 28
Glorybower 116
Golden dewdrop 116, 312
Gopherwood 3, 125
Grandsie-gray-beard 59, 247
Ground cherry 55

Groundsel tree 168
Guava 104, 105, **241**, 242
Gulf graytwig 58, 246, CP 104
Gulf licaria 22, 24, 204
Gumbo limbo 65, 135, **153**, 154, CP 30
Hackberry 304
  dwarf 50, 306
  Georgia 50, 306, **307**
Haw 90
  apple 260
  cockspur 261, **263**, CP 114
  dwarf 262, 266
  green 264, 266
  May 260, 262, 264
  parsley 262, CP 116
  rusty 114, 157, 158, **159**, 170, CP 36
  southern black 114, 158
  yellow 262, **263**, 266, CP 115
Hawthorn 90
  littlehip 261, 264, **265**, CP 117
  one-flowered 266
  small fruited 264
Hearts-a-bustin'-with-love 57, 162
Heralds-trumpet 110
Hercules'-club 62, 281
Hickory
  bitternut 75, 199
  Florida 75, 199, 200, **201**, 202
  mockernut 74, 75, 202
  pale 202
  pignut 74, 75, 200, CP 65
  sand 75, 202
  scrub 75, 200
  water 74, 199, **201**, 202, 203
Highbush blueberry 32, 174, **175**, CP 52
Holly
  American 25, 26, 144, **145**
  Carolina 27, 140, CP 19
  Krug's 27, 143
  myrtle-leaved 25, 26, 27, 144, CP 23
  sand 27, 140
  sarvis 27, 141, **142**, 143, 146
  tawnyberry 25, 27, 143, **145**

  yaupon 143
Holywood 312
Hop tree 62, 280
Horse sugar 37, 254, 299, 302, CP 147
Horsetail casuarina 160
Indian banana 19, 139
Indian bean 151
Indigo berry 277
Inkberry 26
Inkwood 78, 288, **289**
Ironwood 89, **149**, 150, 306
  black 55, 258, **259**
  red 258
  white 78, **289**
Jamaica dogwood 95, 216, **217**
Joewood 39, 304, **305**, CP 149
Jumbie bean 94, 214
Lancewood 22, 23, 177, 205, CP 68
Lantana 116
Lead tree 94, 214, **215**
Leadwood 258
Lebbeck's albizia 210
Lignum vitae 64, 312, CP 151
Ligustrum, wax-leaf 59, 157, 252, **253**,
  CP 106
Lime
  Key 63, 278
  ogeechee- 113, 244
  wild 62, 282, **283**
Linden 304
Locust berry 61, 224, **226**, CP 84
Locust
  black 95, 218, **219**
  honey- 95, 214
  water- 95, 214, **215**
Lucky nut 110
Magnolia 37
  Ashe 18, 223, 224, CP 82
  pyramid 18, 223, **225**
  southern 17, 83, 223, CP 80
  sweetbay 17, 29, 166, 224, **225**, 303,
    CP 83
  umbrella 18, 224

Mahoe 227
  seaside 45
Mahogany 66, **230**
Maiden bush 53, **179**, 180
Manchineel 53, 178, CP 54
Mango 70, 71, 135
Mangrove
  red 100, 260, CP 113
  white 100, 101, 167, 260, CP 44
  black 100, 101, 148, 260, CP 25
Manihot 54, 178, CP 55
Maple
  ash-leaved 132
  chalk 77
  Florida 77, 134
  red 76, 132, **133**, 134, CP 9
  scarlet 134
  silver 76, 77, **133**, 134
  soft 134
  southern sugar 77, 134
  sugar 76, 77, 83, **133**, 134
Marlberry 38, 235, 236, CP 99
Marmalade plum 34
Marvel of Peru 80
Mastic 36
Matrimony vine 56
Mayten 57, 163
  Florida 163, CP 41
  gutta-percha 163
Meadow beauty 103
Melaleuca 105
Mexican elemi 62
Milkbark 53, 177, **179**, CP 53
Mimosa 94, 210, CP 75
Mountain laurel 30, 173, CP 49
Mulberry 304
  paper 51, 230, **232**
  red 50, 233, CP 94
  white 50, 233, CP 95
Mullein nightshade 297
Myrsine 38, **236**
Myrtle-of-the-river 105, 237, **239**
Nakedwood 54

Necklace pod 67, 96, **219**, 220, 296
Oak
  Arkansas 182, **183**, 189
  black 85, 194, **195**
  blackjack 182, 189, CP 62
  bluejack 86, 186, CP 60
  bluff 85, 182, 184
  Chapman 86, 184, 186, 190, CP 57
  cherrybark 192
  chinquapin 85, 189, 190, **191**
  diamond leaf 84, 85, 186, 187, **188**
  laurel 85, 86, 186, 192, CP 59
  live 84, 85, 196, CP 63
  myrtle 86, 184, 186, 190, **193**
  overcup 85, 187, **188**
  post 85, 187, 189, 194, **195**
  running 86
  sand live 86, 185, 186, 196, CP 58
  sand-post 86, 187, 189, **191**, 194
  scrub 184, 186, CP 61
  shumard 85, 189, 192, **193**, 194
  southern red 85, 184, **185**, 187, 189, 192
  Spanish 184
  swamp chestnut 84, 182, 189, 190, **191**
  swamp red 192
  turkey 86, 185, 187, **188**
  water 85, 190, **193**
  white 85, 182, **183**, 184
  willow 85, 186, 192
  yellow 85
Ogeechee lime 113, 244
Old man's beard 59, 247
Oleander 110
Orange
  mock 63, 280
  seville 63, 278
  sour 63, 278, **279**
  trifoliate 63, 280
Orchid tree 95, **211**, 212, CP 76
Osage-orange 50, 51, 233, CP 93
Oxhorn bucida 101, 166, **167**
Oysterwood 177

Pale lidflower 105, 237
Palm
  Biscayne 128
  brittle thatch 131
  buccaneer 15, 130
  cabbage 130, 132
  Canary Island date 16
  cherry 130
  coconut 15, 127, 128, **129**
  date 15, 128
  Florida silver 128
  Florida thatch 131, CP 18
  hog 130
  Jamaica thatch 131
  Key 131
  Key thatch 128, 131, CP 10
  paroutis 127, CP 7
  petticoat 132
  royal 13, 15, **129**, 130
  sabal 13, 130, CP 8
  Sargent's cherry 15
  seamberry 128
  silk top thatch 131
  silver 128, 131, 132, CP 12
  small fruited thatch 131
  Washington **129**, 132
Palmetto
  sabal 13
  saw 9, 131, CP 12
Papaya 40, 158, CP 38
Paper bark tree 105
Paradise tree 67, 297, **298**, CP 143
Pawpaw
  dwarf 19, 139
  flag 19, 139
  small-flowered 19, 139
  small-fruited 139
Peach 91, 269, CP 122
Pear, common 272
Pearl berry 110, 140, CP 17
Pecan 74, 199, 200, **201**, 203
Pepper tree 136

Persimmon, common 34, 158, 170, 172, 246, CP 48
Pieris, climbing 5
Pigeon berry 312
Pigeon plum 81, 256, CP 109
Pinckneya 277, CP 129
Pine 37,
  Australian 7, 160, **161**, CP 37
  loblolly 11, **121**, 124
  longleaf 8, 122, **123**, 124, 125, CP 4
  pond 10, **121**, 124, CP 5
  sand 10, 120, 124
  shortleaf 10, **121**, 122
  slash 8, 122, **123**, 124
  spruce 10, 122, CP 3
Pisonia 243
Planer tree 49, 306, **310**
Plum
  American 267, **268**, CP 119
  chickasaw 267, **268**, 270, CP 120
  darling 55, 258, **259**
  dove 256
  flatwoods 270
  guiana 53, 177, **179**
  hog 57, 246, 269, 270, **271**, CP 105
  pigeon 81, 256, CP 109
  saffron 35, 291, **292**
Poison guava 178
Poison ivy 70
Poison oak 70
Poisonwood 70, 71, 135, **137**, CP 11
Pongam 218, **219**
Popcorn tree 54, 178, CP 56
Portia tree 45, 227
Possum-haw 26, 27, 114, 141, 143, **145**, 146, 157, 158, CP 34
Potato tree 55, 297, **298**
Prickly pear 82
Pride of India 66, 228
Princewood 109, 274, **275**
Privet 59
  Chinese 59, **253**, 254

Privet (*cont'd.*)
   Florida 248, **249**, 250
   glossy 59, 252, 254
   Godfrey's 248
   swamp 248, **249**
   tree 252
   wax-leaf 252
Puccoon 115
Punk tree 240
Ram's horn 216
Randia **276**, 277
Rapanea 38, 236
Redbud, eastern 94, **211**, 212, CP 77
Red-spire **272**
Redwood 4
Rhacoma 161, **162**, CP 39
Rough leaf cornel 112, 170
Royal poinciana 95, 213
Rusty lyonia 31, 173
Saltbush 102, 168, **169**
Sapodilla 34, 35, 295, CP 140
Sapote 34
Sassafras 22, 23, **207**, 208
Satin leaf 35, **292**, 294, CP 137
Saw cabbage 127
Scarlet bush 277, CP 128
Schefflera 111
Scorpion-tail 115
Sea-almond 102, 167, **168**
Sea grape 81, **256**
Sea hibiscus 45, 227, **229**, CP 86
Seaside mahoe 45, 227, **229**, CP 87
Sequoia 4
Silk tree 94, 210, 212
Silky-camellia 29, 303, **305**
Silver buttonwood 166, CP 43
Silverbell
   Carolina 299, 300, **301**
   little 36, 299, 302
   two-winged 36, 299, 300, **301**
Skunk bush 62, 280
Sky flower 312
Snakebark 257
   Cuban 257

Snowbell
   American 36, 300, **301**, 302, CP 145
   big leaf 36, 246, 300, **301**
Snowberry 109
Soapberry 77, 136, 288, 290
   Florida 78, 290
   tropical 78, **290**
   wingleaf 78, 290
Soldierwood 55, 257, **259**, CP 111
Sorrel tree 31
Sour gum 113, 172, 246, CP 103
Sourwood 31, 174, **175**
Sparkleberry 32, 174, **175**, 176
Spicebush 22, 24, 204, **205**, 206
Sponge-bark hypericum 39, 165
St. John's-wort 39, 165
Stagger bush 31, 173, CP 50
Stiff cornel 112
Stopper
   long-stalked xii, 104, 238, 240, CP 102
   red 104, 240
   red-berry 104, 238, **239**
   Spanish 104, 238, **239**
   twinberry 104, 242
   white 104, 237, **239**, 240, 246
Storax 36
Strawberry bush 57
Strongbark 152
   Bahama 115, 152, CP 29
   rough 115, 152
   smooth 115
Sugarberry 49, 50, 304, 306, **307**
Sumac
   poison 70, 138
   shining 70, 135, 136
   smooth 70, 136
   winged 70, 135, 136, **137**, CP 13
Swamp candleberry 234, **235**, CP 97
Sweetgum 87, 196, **197**
Sweetleaf 37, 302
Sycamore, American 88, **255**
Tallowwood 57, 246
Tamarind 94, 220, **221**

Tamarindillo 93, 208, CP 71
Tamarisk 3, 303
   French 41, 303
Tear shrub 110, 140
Tetrazygia 103, 109, 228, **229**, CP 89
Tie-tongue 81, 256
Titi 28, 172
   black 28, 172, CP 45
Toothache tree 280
Torchwood 62, 65, 278, **279**
   balsam 62
Torreya 3, 125, CP 6
Tree huckleberry 174
Tree of heaven 67, 295
Tree of life 312
Trema 48, 49, 50
   Florida 50, 308, **311**
   West Indian 50, 307, **311**
Tuliptree 18, 222
Tung tree 54, 176, CP 51
Tupelo
   ogeechee 244, **245**
   water 113, 244, **245**
Twinberry 104, **241**, 242
Upland cotton 45, CP 85
Varnish leaf 78, 288, CP 133
Varnish tree 299
Velvetseed 108, 274, **276**
   Everglades 274
   rough xii, 274, CP 127
Vervain 116
Viburnum
   small 114, 158, 248
   Walter 114, 143, 157, 158, CP 35

Wahoo 57, 161
Walnut
   black 73, 199, 202, **203**
   Persian 73
Washington thorn 261, 263, **265**
Wax myrtle 69, 234, CP 96
White indigo berry 109, 277
Whitewood 177, 246
Wild banyan tree 231
Wild coffee 109, 257, CP 110
Wild olive 59, 254, 255, CP 108
Wild tamarind 94, **215**, 216
Willow
   black 43, 286, **287**
   Carolina 43, 71, 284
   coastal plain 43, 284, 286, CP 130
   Florida 43, 286, CP 131
   heart-leaved 43, 286, **287**
   pussy 42
Winterberry 27, 144
Wire grass 9
Witch hazel 87, 196, **197**
Woman's tongue 94, 210, **211**
Yaupon 143, 146, **147**, CP 21
Yellow heart 62, 282
Yellow poplar 18, **222**
Yellow tab 107
Yellowwood 164
Yew
   American 3
   Florida 3, 125

INDEX TO SCIENTIFIC NAMES

Note: Illustrations are indicated by bold-face type. CP refers to the color plates between pages 142 and 143. Italics refer to outdated or invalid names.

Acacia 93, 96
  choriophylla 93, 208, CP 71
  farnesiana 93, 208, 209, 210, CP 72
  macracantha 209, CP 73
  pinetorum 93, 208, 209
  smallii 208, 209
  tortuosa 209, 210, CP 74
Acer 76
  barbatum 77
  leucoderme 77
  negundo 76, 132, **133**
  rubrum 76, 132, **133**, 134, CP 9
  saccharinum 76, **133**, 134
  saccharum 76, 83, **133**, 134
  subsp. floridanum 77, 134
  subsp. leucoderme 77, 134
Aceraceae 132
Acoelorrhaphe wrightii 14, 127, CP 7
Aesculus
  glabra 77
  hippocastanum 77
  pavia 77, **197**, 198
Ailanthus altissima 67, 295
Albizia 93, 94
  julibrissin 94, 210, 212, CP 75
  lebbeck 94, 210, **211**
Aleurites fordii 54, 176, CP 51
Allamanda spp. 110
Alnus serrulata 89, 148, **149**,
Alvaradoa amorphoides 67, 220, 288, **296**
Amelanchier arborea 90, 141, 260, **261**
Amorpha fruticosa **211**, 212
Amphitecna latifolia 107, 151
Amyris 61
  balsamifera 62

elemifera 62, 278, **279**
Anacardiaceae 69, 70, 76, 135
Angiosperms 127
Annona
  glabra 19, 138, CP 15
  squamosa 20, 138, CP 16
Annonaceae 18, 138
Apocynaceae 109, 110, 140
Aquifoliaceae 25, 140
Aralia spinosa 111, 146, CP 24
Araliaceae 111, 146
Ardisia escallonioides 38, 235, 236, CP 99
Arecaceae 13
Aristida stricta 9
Asimina
  obovata 19, 139
  parviflora 19, 139
  triloba 19, 139, **140**
Asteraceae 102
Ateramnus lucidus 53, 177, **179**, 234
Avicennia germinans 100, 148, 260, CP 25
Avicenniaceae 148
Baccharis halimifolia 102, 168, **169**
Bauhinia
  purpurea 95, 212
  variegata 95, **211**, 212, CP 76
Beaumontia grandiflora 110
Betula
  lutea 83
  nigra 88, 89, 148, **149**, 150
  papyrifera 105
Betulaceae 87, 88, 148
Bignoniaceae 107, 151
Boraginaceae 115, 152
Bougainvillea spp. 80
Bourreria 115
  cassinifolia 115
  ovata 115, 152, CP 29
  radula 115, 152
Brassaia actinophylla 111

Broussonetia papyrifera 51, 230, **232**, 234

Bucida buceras 101, 166, **167**

Bumelia 34, 35, 58, 247
anomala 35, 291
celastrina 35, 291, **292**
var. angustifolia 291
lanuginosa 35, 291, **292**, CP 134
lycioides 35, 293
reclinata 35, 291, 293, CP 135
tenax 35, 291, 293, CP 136

Burscra simaruba 65, 135, **153**, 154, CP 30

Burseraceae 61, 65, 76, 154

Byrsonima lucida 61, 224, **226**, CP 84

Cactaceae 82, 154

Callicarpa americana 116

Callistemon 105
speciosus 105
viminalis 105

Calyptranthes
pallens 105, 237
zuzygium 105, 237, **239**

Canella winterana 24, 155, CP 31

Canellaceae 24, 155

Capparaceae 40, 155

Capparidaceae 40

Capparis 55, 258
cynophallophora 40, 155
flexuosa 40, 155, **156**
spinosa 40

Caprifoliaceae 113, 156

Carica papaya 40, 158, CP 38

Caricaceae 40, 158

Carpinus caroliniana 89, **149**, 150, 306

Carya 73, 250
aquatica 74, 199, **201**, 202, 203
cordiformis 75, 199
floridana 75, 199, 200, **201**, 202
glabra 74, 200, CP 65
illinoensis 74, 199, 200, **201**, 203
pallida 75, 202
tomentosa 74, 202

Casasia clusiifolia 108, 165, 273, CP 124

Castanea
alnifolia 84
ashei 84
dentata 84
floridana 84
pumila 83, 84, 180, **181**

Casuarina 7
cristata 12
cunninghamiana 11, 160
equisetifolia 11, 12, 160, **161**, CP 37
glauca 12, 160
lepidophloia 12

Casuarinaceae 7, 160

Catalpa bignonioides 107, 151, CP 26

Celastraceae 57, 161

Celastrales 76

Celtis 48, 49
laevigata 49, 304, 306, **307**
tenuifolia 50, 306, **307**

Cephalanthus occidentalis 108, 273, 277, CP 125

Cercis canadensis 94, **211**, 212, CP 77

Cereus
gracilis var. simpsonii 82, 154
robinii 82, 154

Chamaecyparis
thyoides 5, 120, CP 1
var. henryae 120

Chiococca alba 109

Chionanthus virginicus 59, **247**, CP 107

Chrysobalanaceae 91, 164

Chrysobalanus icaco 91, 164, **165**

Chrysophyllum
cainito 34, 294
oliviforme 35, **292**, 294, CP 137

Cinnamomum camphora 22, 204, CP 66

Citharexylum fruticosum 116, 311, CP 153

Citrus 63
aurantifolia 63, 278
aurantium 63, 278, **279**
grandis 63

Citrus (*cont'd.*)
  limon 63
  medica 63
  paradisi 63
  reticulata 63
  sinensis 63
Clerodendrum spp. 116
Cliftonia monophylla 28, 172, CP 45
Clusia rosea 39, 164, 273, CP 42
Clusiaceae 38, 164
Coccoloba
  diversifolia 81, 256, CP 109
  uvifera 81, **256**
Coccothrinax argentata 14, 128, 131, 132, CP 12
Cocos nucifera 15, 127, 128, **129**
Colubrina 54
  arborescens 55, 257, CP 110
  cubensis 257
  elliptica 257, **259**, CP 111
Combretaceae 101, 103, 166
Compositae 102, 168
Coniferales 7
Conocarpus
  erectus 100, 166
    var. sericeus 166, CP 43
Cordia 115
  boissieri 115
  sebestena 115, 152, **153**, CP 28
Cornaceae 96, 112, 169
Cornus 114
  alternifolia 112, 169, 170, **171**
  amomum 112
  asperifolia 112, 170
  florida 112, 158, 170, **171**, CP 46
  foemina 112, 170, **171**
Crataegus 90
  aestivalis 260, 262, 264
  crus-galli 261, **263**, CP 114
  flava 262, **263**, 266, CP 115
  marshallii 262, CP 116
  phaenopyrum 261, 263, **265**
  pulcherrima 264, **265**, 266

spathulata 261, 264, **265**, CP 117
uniflora 262, 266
viridis 264, 266
Crossopetalum rhacoma 57, 161, **162**, CP 39
Cupania glabra 78, 288, CP 132
Cupressaceae 120
Cybistax donnell-smithii 107
Cyrilla racemiflora 28, 172, CP 47
Cyrillaceae 28, 172
Delonix regia 95, 213
Diospyros
  ebenum 34
  virginiana 34, 158, 170, 172, 246, CP 48
Dipholis salicifolia 35, 294, CP 138
Dodonaea viscosa 78, 288, CP 133
Drypetes
  diversifolia 53, 177, **179**, CP 53
  lateriflora 53, 177, **179**
Duranta repens 116, 312
Ebenaceae 34, 172
Ebenales 34
Ericaceae 30, 173
Erithalis fruticosa 109, 180, 273, **275**, CP 126
Ervatamia coronaria 110
Erythrina herbacea 96, 213, **215**
Eugenia 104
  axillaris 104, 237, **239**, 240, 246
  confusa 104, 238, **239**
  foetida 104, 238, **239**
  rhombea 104, 238, 240
  simpsonii 104
Euonymus
  americanus 57, 162
  atropurpureus 57, 161
Euphorbiaceae 53, 176
Exostema caribaeum 109, 274, **275**
Exothea paniculata 78, 288, **289**
Fabaceae 93
Fagaceae 83, 89, 180
Fagales 87

Fagus grandifolia 83, 180, **181**
Ficus 20, 50, 51, 138
  aurea 51, 231, 232, CP 92
  carica 51, 231, CP 90
  citrifolia 51, 231, **232**, CP 91
Firmiana simplex 46, 299, CP 144
Forestiera 59, 60, 254
  acuminata 248, **249**
  godfreyi 248
  ligustrina 60, 248, **249**
  segregata 248, **249**, 250
Fraxinus 58, 74, 199
  americana 58, 250
  caroliniana 59, 250, **251**, 252
  pennsylvanica 59, **251**, 252
  profunda 59, **251**, 252
Gleditsia
  aquatica 95, 214, **215**
  triacanthos 95, 214
Gordonia lasianthus 18, 29, 300, 302,
  303, CP 148
Gossypium hirsutum 45, 227, CP 85
Guaiacum sanctum 64, 312, CP 151
Guapira
  discolor 80, 180, 242, CP 100
  longifolia 80
Guettarda
  elliptica 108, 274, **276**
  scabra xii, 108, 274, CP 127
Guttiferae 38, 164
Gyminda latifolia 57, 162, CP 40
Gymnosperms 120
Halesia 36
  carolina 36, 299, 300, **301**, 302
  diptera 36, 299, 300, **301**
  parviflora 36
  tetraptera 36
Hamamelidaceae 87, 196
Hamamelidales 87, 89
Hamamelis virginiana 87, 196, **197**
Hamelia patens 109, 277, CP 128
Heliotropium angiospermum 115
Hibiscus tiliaceus 45, 227, **229**, CP 86

Hippocastanaceae 77, 198
Hippomane mancinella 53, 178, CP 54
Hypelate trifoliata 78, **289**
Hypericum chapmanii 39, 165
Ilex 25
  ambigua 27, 140, 146, CP 19
  amelanchier 27, 141, **142**, 143, 146
  aquifolia 27
  cassine 25, 141, **142**, CP 20
  coriacea 25, 26, 143, CP 22
  decidua 26, 27, 141, 143, **145**, 146,
    157, 158
  glabra 26, 143
  krugiana 25, 27, 143, **145**
  myrtifolia 25, 27, 144, CP 23
  opaca 25, 26, 144, **145**
    var. arenicola 144
  verticillata 27, 141, 143, 144, **147**
  vomitoria 26, 143, 146, **147**, 158,
    CP 21
Illiciaceae 20, 198
Illicium 20
  floridanum 20, 198, 199, CP 67
  parviflorum 20, 199, CP 64
Jacquinia keyensis 39, 304, **305**, CP 149
Juglandaceae 73, 199
Juglans
  nigra 73, 199, 202, **203**
  regia 73
Juniperus virginiana 5, 120, CP 2
Kalmia latifolia 30, 173, CP 49
Krugiodendron ferreum 55, 258, **259**
Lagerstroemia indica 103, 221, CP 79
Laguncularia racemosa 100, 167, 260,
  CP 44
Lamiales 115
Lantana camara 116
Lauraceae 22, 204
Leguminosae 90, 93, 107, 208
Leitneria floridana 71, 221, CP 81
Leitneriaceae 69, 71, 221
Leitneriales 71
Leucaena leucocephala 94, 214, **215**

Leucothoe 31
Licania michauxii 91
Licaria triandra 22, 204
Ligustrum 59
   lucidum 59, 157, 252, **253**, 254, CP 106
   sinense 59, **253**, 254
Lindera benzoin 22, 24, 204, **205**, 206
Liquidambar styraciflua 87, 196, **197**
Liriodendron tulipifera 18, **222**
Lithospermum caroliniense 115
Lycium carolinianum 56
Lyonia 31
   ferruginea 31, 173, CP 50
   fruticosa 31, 173
   lucida 32
Lysiloma latisiliquum 94, **215**, 216
Lythraceae 103, 221
Maclura pomifera 50, 51, 233, CP 93
Magnolia
   acuminata 18, 222
   grandiflora 17, 83, 223, CP 80
   macrophylla
      subsp. ashei 18, 223, 224, CP 82
   pyramidata 18, 223, **225**
   tripetala 18, 224
   virginiana 17, 29, 166, 224, **225**, 303, CP 83
Magnoliaceae 17, 222
Malpighiaceae 61, 224
Malus angustifolia 90, 266, CP 118
Malvaceae 45, 227
Malvales 45
Mandevilla 110
Mangifera indica 70, 135
Manihot grahamii 54, 178, CP 55
Manilkara 35
   bahamensis 35, 294, 295, CP 139
   zapota 34, 35, 295, CP 140
Mastichodendron foetidissimum 36, 295, CP 141
Maytenus phyllanthoides 57, 163, CP 41
Melaleuca quinquenervia 105, 240, **241**

Melastomataceae 103, 109, 228
Melia azedarach 66, 228, CP 88
Meliaceae 61, 65, 76, 228
Metopium toxiferum 70, 135, **137**, CP 11
Mimosoideae 93
Mirabilis jalapa 80
Moraceae 48, 50, 230
Morus 50, 304
   alba 50, 233, CP 95
   rubra 50, 233, CP 94
Mosiera longipes xii, 104, 238, 240, CP 102
Myosotis spp. 115
Myrcianthes fragrans 104, **241**, 242
Myrica
   cerifera 69, 234, CP 96
   heterophylla 69, 234, **235**, CP 97
   inodora 38, 69, 235, CP 98
Myricaceae 69, 234
Myrsinaceae 38, 235
Myrsine floridana 38, **236**
Myrtaceae 104, 237
Myrtales 103
Nectandra coriacea 22
Nerium oleander 110
Nyctaginaceae 80, 242
Nyssa
   aquatica 113, 244, **245**
   biflora 29, 113, 166, 244, CP 101
   ogeche 113, 244, **245**
   sylvatica 113, 172, 246, CP 103
Nyssaceae 113, 244
Ocotea coriacea 22, 177, 205, CP 68
Olacaceae 57, 246
Oleaceae 57, 58, 247
Opuntia spp. 82
Osmanthus 59
   americanus 59, 254, 255, CP 108
      var. megacarpa 59
   megacarpa 59, 255
Ostrya virginiana 89, **149**, 150, 306, 309
Oxydendrum arboreum 31, 174, **175**
Palmae 13, 127

Panax 111
Papilionoideae 96
Persea 22, 254
  americana 22, 23, 205
  borbonia 22, 205, 206, CP 69
  humilis 22, 206, **207**
  palustris 18, 22, 206, 303, CP 70
Phoenix
  canariensis 16
  dactylifera 15, 128
Phyla nodiflora 116
Physalis spp. 55
Picramnia pentandra 67, 288, 297,
  CP 142
Pieris phillyreifolius 5
Pinaceae 120
Pinckneya bracteata 108, 273, 277,
  CP 129
Pinus 7
  clausa 10, 120, 124
  echinata 10, **121**, 122
  elliottii 8, 122, **123**, 124
    var. densa 9, 122
  glabra 10, 122, CP 3
  palustris 8, 122, **123**, 124, 125, CP 4
  serotina 10, **121**, 124, CP 5
  taeda 11, **121**, 124
Piscidia piscipula 95, 216, **217**
Pisonia
  discolor 80
  rotundata 80, **243**
Pithecellobium 93
  guadalupense 96, 97, 216, **217**, 218,
    CP 78
  unguis-cati 97, **217**, 218
Planera aquatica 49, 306, **310**
Platanaceae 87, 255
Platanus occidentalis 88, **255**
Plumeria spp. 110
Polygonaceae 81, 256
Poncirus trifoliata 63, 280
Pongamia pinnata 218, **219**
Populus 42

  deltoides 44, 284, **285**
  heterophylla 44, 284, **285**
Pouteria
  campechiana 34
  mammosa 34
Primulales 38
Prunus 91, 260
  alabamensis 267, **268**, 270
  americana 267, **268**, CP 119
  angustifolia 267, **268**, 270, CP 120
  caroliniana 269, CP 121
  myrtifolia 269, **271**
  persica 91, 269, CP 122
  serotina 174, 267, 270, CP 123
  umbellata 269, 270, **271**
Pseudophoenix sargentii 15, 130
Psidium
  guajava 104, **241**, 242
Psychotria 109
  ligustrifolia 109
  nervosa 109
  sulzneri 109
Ptelea trifoliata 62, 280, **281**, 299
Pyrus
  calleryana **272**
  communis 272
Quercus 84
  alba 182, **183**, 184
  arkansana 182, **183**, 189
  austrina 85, 182, 184
  chapmanii 86, 184, 186, 190, CP 57
  falcata 85, 184, **185**, 187, 189, 192
    var. pagodaefolia 192
  geminata 86, 185, 186, 196, CP 58
  hemisphaerica 85, 186, 192, CP 59
  incana 86, 186, CP 60
  inopina 184, 186, 190, CP 61
  laevis 86, 185, 187, **188**
  laurifolia 84, 85, 186, 187, **188**
  lyrata 85, 187, **188**
  margaretta 86, 187, 189, **191**, 194
  marilandica 182, 189, CP 62
  michauxii 84, 182, 189, 190, **191**

Quercus (*cont'd.*)
  muehlenbergii 85, 189, 190, **191**
  myrtifolia 86, 184, 186, 190, **193**
  nigra 85, 190, **193**
  pagoda 192
  phellos 85, 186, 192
  pumila 86
  shumardii 85, 189, 192, **193**, 194
  stellata 85, 187, 189, 194, **195**
  velutina 85, 194, **195**
  virginiana 84, 85, 196, CP 63
Randia aculeata 109, **276**, 277
Rapanea
  guianensis 38
  punctata 38
Reynosia septentrionalis 55, 258, **259**
Rhamnaceae 54, 257
Rhamnus caroliniana 54, 258, CP 112
Rhexia spp. 103
Rhizophora mangle 100, 260, CP 113
Rhizophoraceae 260
Rhus
  copallina 70, 135, 136, **137**, CP 13
  glabra 70
Robinia pseudoacacia 95, 218, **219**
Rosaceae 90, 91, 260
Rosales 90
Roystonea elata 13, **129**, 130
Rubiaceae 108, 273
Rutaceae 61, 63, 76, 278
Sabal palmetto 13, 14, 130, 132, CP 8
Salicaceae 42, 284
Salix 42, 85, 88
  caroliniana 43, 71, 284, 286, CP 130
  eriocephala 43, 286, **287**
  floridana 43, 286, CP 131
  humilis 42
  nigra 43, 284, 286, **287**
Sambucus canadensis 113, 156, CP 32
Sapindaceae 67, 77, 288
Sapindales 76
Sapindus 77
  marginatus 78, 290

saponaria 78, 136, 288, **290**
Sapium sebiferum 54, 178, CP 56
Sapotaceae 34, 35, 291
Sassafras albidum 22, **207**, 208
Savia bahamensis 53, **179**, 180
Schaefferia frutescens 57, **163**, 164
Schinus terebinthifolius 71, 136, **137**, 157, CP 14
Schoepfia chrysophylloides 58, 246, CP 104
Serenoa repens 9, 14, 131, CP 12
Simarouba glauca 67, 297, **298**, CP 143
Simaroubaceae 61, 65, 66, 67, 76, 295
Solanaceae 55, 297
Solanum 56
  bahamense 55, 298
  erianthum 55, 297, **298**
Sophora tomentosa 67, 96, **219**, 220, 296
Staphylea
  bolanderi 79
  trifolia 79, 280, 299
Staphyleaceae 79, 299
Sterculiaceae 45, 46, 299
Stewartia malacodendron 29, 303, **305**
Stillingia aquatica 72
Styracaceae 36, 299
Styrax 36
  americanum 36, 300, **301**, 302, CP 145
  grandifolia 36, 246, 300, **301**
Suriana maritima 67, 302, CP 146
Surianaceae 65, 67, 302
Swietenia mahagoni 66, **230**
Symplocaceae 37, 302
Symplocos tinctoria 37, 254, 299, 302, CP 147
Tamaricaceae 41, 303
Tamarindus indica 94, 220, **221**
Tamarix gallica 3, 41, 303
Taxaceae 125
Taxodiaceae 4, 125
Taxodium 29, 166
  ascendens 4, 125, **126**, 127
  distichum 4, 125, **126**, 127

Taxus
canadensis 3
floridana 3, 125
Tecoma stans 107, 151, CP 27
Terminalia catappa 102, 167, **168**
Tetrazygia bicolor 103, 109, 228, **229**, CP 89
Theaceae 29, 303
Theophrastaceae 39, 304
Thespesia populnea 45, 227, **229**, CP 87
Thevetia peruviana 110
Thrinax
morrisii 14, 128, 131, 132, CP 10
radiata 14, 131, CP 18
Tilia americana 46, 304, **305**
Tiliaceae 45, 304
Torreya taxifolia 3, 125, CP 6
Torrubia
discolor 80
longifolia 80
rotundata 80
Toxicodendron
radicans 70
toxicarium 70
vernix 70, 138
Trachelospermum jasminoides 110
Trema 48, 49, 50
lamarckiana 50, 307, 308, **311**
micrantha 50, 308, **311**
Ulmaceae 48, 49, 304

Ulmus 48, 151
alata 49, 308, 309, CP 150
americana 48, 308, 309, **310**
crassifolia 49, 309, CP 152
laevis 48
rubra 49, 308, 309, **310**
Vaccinium 32
arboreum 32, 174, **175**, 176
corymbosum 32, 174, **175**, CP 52
elliottii 33
stamineum 32, **175**, 176
Vallesia antillana 110, 140, CP 17
Verbena spp. 116
Verbenaceae 116, 311
Viburnum 169
dentatum 114, 157, **159**, CP 33
nudum 114, 157, 158, CP 34
obovatum 114, 143, 146, 157, 158, 248, CP 35
rufidulum 114, 157, 158, **159**, CP 36
Washingtonia robusta 14, **129**, 132
Ximenia americana 57, 246, CP 105
Zanthoxylum 61, 88
americanum 62, 280, 281
clava-herculis 62, 281, **283**
coriaceum 62, 282
fagara 62, 282, **283**
flavum 62, 282
Zygophyllaceae 61, 64, 312